THE PANZERS OF
PROKHOROVKA

OSPREY
PUBLISHING

THE PANZERS OF
PROKHOROVKA

THE MYTH OF
HITLER'S GREATEST
ARMOURED DEFEAT

BEN WHEATLEY

OSPREY PUBLISHING
Bloomsbury Publishing Plc
Kemp House, Chawley Park, Cumnor Hill, Oxford OX2 9PH, UK
29 Earlsfort Terrace, Dublin 2, Ireland
1385 Broadway, 5th Floor, New York, NY 10018, USA
E-mail: info@ospreypublishing.com
www.ospreypublishing.com

OSPREY is a trademark of Osprey Publishing Ltd

First published in Great Britain in 2023

A catalogue record for this book is available from the British Library.

ISBN: HB 9781472859082; PB 9781472859099; eBook 9781472859075; ePDF 9781472859068;
XML 9781472859105

23 24 25 26 27 10 9 8 7 6 5 4 3 2 1

Captions and credit lines for plate section images are given in full in the List of Illustrations
(pp. 232–41).

Maps by www.bounford.com
Index by Zoe Ross

Typeset by Deanta Global Publishing Services, Chennai, India
Printed and bound in Great Britain by CPI (Group) UK Ltd, Croydon CR0 4YY

Osprey Publishing supports the Woodland Trust, the UK's leading woodland conservation charity.

To find out more about our authors and books visit www.ospreypublishing.com. Here
you will find extracts, author interviews, details of forthcoming events and the option to
sign up for our newsletter.

Contents

Foreword

On 12 July 1993, the 50th anniversary of the battle of Prokhorovka, I gave a lecture at a conference in Moscow. I was the first historian from the West to be invited to such an event. While the Russian speakers claimed that the German armoured forces had suffered a devastating defeat, I explained – based on archive files – that the Germans had only suffered a maximum of three total losses. The Russian audience was shocked and during the discussion some generals attacked me. But the veterans came to my aid. They reported that the battlefield was full of Soviet tank wrecks, while only a few German tanks were destroyed.

In the meantime, Ben Wheatley also confirmed my thesis and even went a few steps further. Amazingly, of all people, a British historian penetrated this difficult subject more deeply than anyone before him. He researched the exact numbers of all operational tanks and also the losses of II SS Panzer Korps during these fierce fights.

Ben Wheatley has previously published a trilogy on this topic. His first article 'A Visual Examination of the Battle of Prokhorovka' was based on a sensational file find. In an American archive he discovered Luftwaffe air reconnaissance images of the battlefield immediately after the battle of Prokhorovka. He was able to identify each single tank wreck in the area. In his second article 'Surviving Prokhorovka: German Armoured Longevity on the Eastern Front 1943/44' he proved that a large proportion of the German tanks, which, according to the Soviet claims, were allegedly destroyed at Prokhorovka, in reality were still in action during the fights in the winter of 1943/44.

In his most recent article 'Citadel, Prokhorovka and Kharkov' he extended the spectrum to include all phases in the 50-day battle of Kursk. It was the greatest battle in military history. Here he relied on recent archival discoveries, including, remarkably, post-Prokhorovka German armoured inventories for

20 July and 1 August 1943. The footnotes overflow with file signatures, resulting in an abundance of evidence. The focus is of course on the German *Citadel* offensive, where the most violent tank battles of the Second World War took place. II SS Panzer Korps lost only 41 of its original 547 armoured fighting vehicles. Therefore, it is impossible that the Germans lost 400 tanks at Prokhorovka on a single day, as claimed by Soviet data.

This book combines this research with further revelations. To put Wheatley's findings in a nutshell: He finally dealt the fatal blow to the Prokhorovka myth.

Dr Karl-Heinz Frieser (b. 1949), Colonel (ret.) in the *Bundeswehr*. From 1985 to 2009, research associate at the *Militärgeschichtliches Forschungsamt* (Military History Research Office; MGFA) of the *Bundeswehr*, between 2002 and 2009 head of Research Department II (World War era).

Preface

It is important to preface this book by stating the author's sincere admiration for the Soviet tank crews and their supporting units' heroism. The scale of the armoured losses experienced by 5th Guards Tank Army on 12 July 1943 should not in any way diminish the immense sacrifice the Red Army's troops made for their Motherland and for victory at Prokhorovka. This book is often based on photographic evidence of the battlefield south-west of Prokhorovka and, as such, the photographs paint a truly horrific picture of destruction. The impact of seeing so many destroyed tanks and the knowledge that the majority of Soviet tanks contained four soldiers is deeply sobering. The author felt it only right to mark this sacrifice.

Equally, when reading this book at no point should it be forgotten that the SS Panzergrenadier Divisions Leibstandarte SS Adolf Hitler, Das Reich and Totenkopf which constituted II SS Panzer Korps at the start of July 1943 were part of a paramilitary organization that fought for, and was an integral part of, an evil and abhorrent ultra-nationalist regime that was based on a racist ideology of intolerance, hatred and aggressive expansionism.

Introduction

In Russia today there are three sacred battlefields. The first is at Kulikovo. At this location Dmitry Donskoy defeated the Mongols in 1380.[1] The second is at Borodino, where in 1812 Russian troops headed by Mikhail Kutuzov slowed Napoleon's *Grande Armée* before Moscow. The third is at Prokhorovka. It is written that it was here on 12 July 1943 that the most critical tank battle of the Second World War took place. The battle is said to have resulted in the annihilation of Hitler's elite panzer force in the largest armoured clash in history. This armoured defeat supposedly left Hitler with no alternative but to halt Germany's offensive against the Kursk salient, Operation *Citadel*, from 5 to 16 July 1943. As a result, victory over Hitler's vaunted SS troops at Prokhorovka has traditionally been described as a turning point in the Second World War. As we reach the 80th anniversary of the battles of Kursk and Prokhorovka in 2023, this book, thanks to numerous visual and textual archival discoveries, will be the first to conclusively correct this narrative. As we shall see, the battle of Prokhorovka was indeed an important Soviet victory but, in reality, this victory looked very different to the one described above.

First, it is important to note that by the summer of 1943 the war on the Eastern Front had long since been lost by Germany. The Red Army's vast superiority in men and materiel meant that ultimate victory was now impossible for Germany. The German Army had been worn down during the years 1941–43 when the Red Army had been the only force capable of fighting the bulk of the Wehrmacht. However, in order to achieve complete victory over the Wehrmacht vast battles still had to be fought. The battle of Kursk was the largest of these battles; indeed the 50-day battle (5 July– 23 August 1943) is regarded as the largest in military history. The battle consisted of the German offensive Operation *Citadel*, a pincer attack on the Kursk salient (this book focuses on the southern arm of this pincer), and two Soviet counteroffensives aimed at Orel, 12 July–18 August 1943, and

Kharkov, 3–23 August 1943. During the fighting the two sides deployed more than four million troops, 69,000 cannon and launchers, 13,000 tanks and self-propelled guns, and almost 12,000 aircraft. The bitterness of the fighting is shown by the fact that the Red Army lost a total of at least 6,064 tanks.[2] It is clear that the Soviet Union contributed the most towards the overall Allied victory over Germany during the Second World War. Yes, economic factors and the Western Allies' air and sea power need to be taken into consideration, but by the time the Western Allies finally landed in Normandy in the summer of 1944 the Wehrmacht was a shadow of its former self. The reason for this was chiefly down to the massive loss of materiel and years of bloodletting the Wehrmacht had suffered on the Eastern Front (Appendices F to I).[3] There is no doubt that the Red Army, despite suffering very high losses in men and materiel, won a convincing victory at Kursk.[4] However, in a battle of the size and scope of the battle of Kursk some setbacks for the Red Army were inevitable. The overall Soviet victory at Kursk, indeed at Prokhorovka, is not in any way diminished by highlighting examples (such as at Prokhorovka) where the Germans inflicted serious losses on the Red Army.

In 2020, on the anniversary of the by now legendary tank battle at Prokhorovka, the Ministry of Foreign Affairs of Russia tweeted the following from its official Twitter account: 'On 12 July 1943 the largest tank battle in history commenced at Prokhorovka, part of the enormous Battle of Kursk. The Red Army withstood Nazi onslaught, pushed them back, destroying 75% of their tanks. That same day Soviets launched counter offensive to crush the enemy.' Similarly, on 12 July 2022 the Russian Foreign Ministry posted on its official Facebook account: 'The Soviet forces that possessed 800 tanks before the battle lost about 500 of them and the Germans who had 400 tanks lost 300.'[5] Although these social media posts quite rightly proclaim with great pride an important Soviet victory at Prokhorovka, as we shall see in terms of German armoured losses, they do not quite reflect the reality of the battle. However, such statements are understandable given that both Soviet and Western historiography for many years claimed that between 300 and 400 German tanks were destroyed during the battle of Prokhorovka. If these German armoured losses had occurred, they would have in fact represented the loss of between 58 per cent (300) and 77 per cent (400) of the total German armoured force in the Prokhorovka area (II SS Panzer Korps). One might ask where these extremely high claims of German armoured losses originated from. The Soviet claim of 300 German tanks destroyed during the battle can be traced back to 17 July 1943. On this date a report by the 5th Guards Tank Army claimed that between 12 and 16 July 1943 its four tank corps involved in the battle had destroyed 298 German tanks, including 55 of the formidable heavy Tiger tanks. Later in 1960 Gen Pavel Rotmistrov, the commander of the 5th Guards Tank Army, claimed in his memoirs (*Tankovoe srazhenie pod Prokhorovki*) that his units had destroyed 400 German tanks, including 70 Tiger tanks, at Prokhorovka.[6]

As Karl-Heinz Frieser has already articulated, the historiography of the battle of Prokhorovka took a dramatic turn on 12 July 1993, the 50th anniversary of the battle of Prokhorovka, with his lecture in Moscow. The audience were shocked to learn that the German records stated a maximum of 33 German SS tanks and assault guns were lost during Operation *Citadel* and of these only three occurred at Prokhorovka.[7] Although Frieser's thesis was dismissed by the generals present, tellingly he was supported by the Soviet veterans of the battle of Prokhorovka, who remembered seeing far more destroyed Soviet tanks than their German equivalents. In the West Frieser's revelation seemed to immediately give credence to German veterans' post-war testimony, which spoke of Soviet tank attacks being defeated in and around an anti-tank ditch.[8] This has become the accepted view of the battle in the West.

Given Frieser's findings, why then has some historiography of the battle continued to speak of the mass destruction of Hitler's armoured forces at Prokhorovka? The reason for this may lie in the fact that Frieser (and subsequent studies by other historians) only presented German armoured total loss reports, many of which gave contradictory numbers. Although clearly in the correct 'ballpark', these German total loss reports were not detailed enough to correct the 'myth of Prokhorovka'. As no historian had presented any post-battle German armoured inventories, it proved possible to dismiss Frieser and other historians' findings.

What was then required was the immediate post-battle German inventories (20 July and 1 August 1943) which could easily allow the true number of German armoured losses at Prokhorovka to be calculated. These inventories were akin to the 'Holy Grail' for historians of the battle. They were considered to be lost or even destroyed by the Germans themselves to hide the scale of their 'defeat'.[9] However, in 2020 the author managed to locate these missing German armoured inventories in the archives.

For the first time this book is able to reveal the true number of armoured fighting vehicle (AFV – tanks, assault guns and tank destroyers) losses II SS Panzer Korps sustained during Operation *Citadel*.[10] As only units from II SS Panzer Korps fought in the armoured battle of Prokhorovka on 12 July this discovery will also greatly impact the historiography of that battle. The book will confirm that in July 1943, instead of being crushed, II SS Panzer Korps emerged relatively unscathed from Operation *Citadel* and, were it not for

Hitler's operational and strategic incompetence, would have played a decisive part, at least initially, in the defence of Kharkov the following month.

As a result of the author's archival discovery of II SS Panzer Korps' first post-Operation *Citadel* armoured inventory (20 July 1943), this book can reveal that in reality a maximum of 3 per cent (16 AFVs – including two AFVs requiring homeland maintenance) of II SS Panzer Korps were destroyed between 11 and 20 July. As stated, this included the battle of Prokhorovka on 12 July. Remarkably, the author can also state for the first time that II SS Panzer Korps lost just 8 per cent (41 AFVs) of its pre-Operation *Citadel* AFV inventory during the entire operation. In addition, it is clear that the battle of Prokhorovka had no long-term impact on German AFV operational readiness. In the early hours of 11 July 1943, the day prior to the battle, II SS Panzer Korps possessed 339 operational AFVs, while on the evening of 18 July the Korps could call on 349 operational AFVs. Therefore, the Korps' operational strength actually increased over this short period by ten AFVs; a maximum of four new AFVs were received by II SS Panzer Korps between 5 and 18 July 1943.[11]

The 20 July and 1 August inventories finally provide us with the required total accuracy regarding German AFV losses at Prokhorovka.[12] The inventories present cold hard evidence of German armoured strength on 20 July 1943, just four days after the end of Operation *Citadel* and eight days after the battle of Prokhorovka, and on 1 August 1943 in the same document. As recently as 2022 there were still claims being made that the Germans lost 75 per cent of their tanks during the battle of Prokhorovka. However, even if the 20 July and 1 August inventories are read in isolation (without including assault guns, tank destroyers and Leibstandarte command tanks), the document proves for the first time that the German divisions involved in the battle of Prokhorovka possessed at least 88 per cent of their pre-Operation *Citadel* complement of tanks following the conclusion of the battle.

One might quite reasonably ask the question why these inventories had not been discovered in the archives before (disregarding the myth that the Germans destroyed their own ten-day status reports/inventories for 20 July 1943 to conceal the scale of their 'defeat' on 12 July). It is to be assumed that the chief reason for this oversight is due to the inventories being located in a separate, once classified, annex to the German 6th Army's records at NARA (National Archives and Records Administration). This is no doubt why historians, even those who have spent their working life researching Kursk/Prokhorovka, had failed to track down this most important of documents.

As Martijn Lak has written, the classic image of the battle of Prokhorovka is that of thousands of Soviet and German tanks and assault guns clashing on the 'tank fields' south-west of Prokhorovka.

The narrative of the battle reads that under an overcast sky the Red Army and the Wehrmacht/Waffen-SS were locked in battle, often only a few feet and barrel's lengths apart, tanks colliding head-on amidst the incredible chaos of the battle. Because the belligerents were so close, the air forces and artillery of both sides could hardly intervene. By nightfall, the battlefield was littered with smouldering wrecks and thousands of dead soldiers. This image has become commonplace in descriptions of the battle, which has obtained an almost mythical status. Exemplified by books with titles like *The Tigers are Burning* (Martin Caidin, New York: Hawthorn Books, 1974), German losses at Prokhorovka were put at hundreds of tanks with Soviet losses being even higher.[13]

In 1993 the BBC's flagship history documentary series *Timewatch* declared that during the battle of Prokhorovka 'in 18 hours more than 600 tanks had been destroyed. The German panzer divisions were terminally damaged'.[14] As Lak points out, along with Frieser:

One of the first western historians to doubt these numbers was Robin Cross in *The Battle of Kursk: Operation Citadel 1943* (London: Penguin Books 1993). Already in the early 1990s, he referred to the clash at Prokhorovka as 'one of the great myths of military history ... , a confused free-for-all in which every tank and its crew fought individually amid a packed mass of armour, like knights on a fifteenth-century battlefield'. According to Cross, German losses were relatively slight: 'If, as the Russians claimed, over 400 tanks were dug up from the fields around Prokhorovka after the war, the great majority of them must have been the T-34s of the Red Army's 29th and 18th Tank Corps [of the Soviet 5th Guards Tank Army – ed.].'[15]

The focus of this book is on the three divisions of II SS Panzer Korps, SS Panzergrenadier Divisions Leibstandarte SS Adolf Hitler (LSSAH), Das Reich (DR) and Totenkopf (SS-T) which fought in (LSSAH and DR) or near (SS-T) the battle of Prokhorovka on 12 July 1943. These three SS panzergrenadier divisions, along with the German Army's Grossdeutschland Panzergrenadier Division, were all considered to be *Sonderverbände* (special units) due to their expanded table of organization and strength. As a result the *Sonderverbände* played a central role in German operations during the battle of Kursk in July and August 1943.[16] In July 1943 the divisions of II SS Panzer Korps were arguably at their peak in terms of troop quality, tactical knowledge, technological advancement of weaponry and AFV operational readiness vis-a-vis the Red Army.[17] Although late August 1943 saw the introduction of the advanced Panther tank into the Waffen-SS, by contrast AFV operational levels began to plummet and supply issues developed. Furthermore, troop quality started to ebb and consequently tactical superiority became diluted.

In the summer of 1943 the Red Army, despite massive superiority in tank numbers, was still reliant on the T-34 tank with its 76mm main gun which had become inferior in firepower to the latest German Panzer IV with its 75mm long-barrelled weapon. Significantly the Panzer IV was present with II SS Panzer Korps in large numbers (168, eight of which were infantry support tanks) at the start of July. The Panzer VI Tiger tank with its 88mm main gun, although only available in small numbers (42), was imperious on the battlefield. The, by now outdated, Panzer III with its 50mm long-barrelled main gun was still present with the Korps (138, primarily with Das Reich and Totenkopf) but it could still prove a threat to Red Army tanks if operated by an experienced crew.[18] Superior German tactics (often flexible), excellent command and control (all German tanks possessed two-way radios, whereas only Red Army company command tanks were so equipped), three-man turrets (as opposed to the Soviet two), high-calibre optics and accurate weapons all added to the difficult task faced by Soviet tankers in the summer of 1943.[19] These factors undoubtedly contributed to the disproportionally low AFV losses suffered by the three SS divisions compared to the Red Army armoured units that they faced in July and August 1943. Ironically it seems that from late August 1943 the Germans' inability to return large numbers of their damaged tanks to action also contributed to a reduction in German AFV total losses (*Totalausfälle*; TF) – their AFVs were simply not on the battlefield to be shot at![20]

The book gives a detailed visual description of the battle of Prokhorovka by presenting both original and freshly analysed Luftwaffe reconnaissance images of the battlefield taken in July, August, September and October 1943. These images visualize such fundamentals as the location of the notorious anti-tank ditch and Hill 252.2 as well as a post-battle site which contained over 150 destroyed/heavily damaged Soviet AFVs; this aspect of the book will explore the immediate impact of the battle.[21] The book will also highlight the fact that the vast majority of the German armour present with the main participants of the battle (Leibstandarte and Das Reich) survived the battle of Prokhorovka and indeed many of these AFVs were still in service well into the winter of 1943/44: 49 per cent of the German AFVs that took part in the battle of Prokhorovka were still in SS inventories at the start of December 1943.[22] This aspect of the book will therefore explore the long-term impact of the battle of

Prokhorovka. In regards to Das Reich this is largely achieved by matching the chassis numbers of its AFVs (including 52 ex-Leibstandarte panzers received on 28 July 1943, 51 of which had been present at Prokhorovka) before and after the battle (from October 1943) in the monthly divisional inventories. After Operation *Citadel* the Leibstandarte did not see action again until November 1943. As a result it has been relatively straightforward to establish in the post-Operation *Citadel* records which of the Leibstandarte's AFVs were of Prokhorovka vintage. In addition, even though Totenkopf did not, to any great extent, participate in the battle of Prokhorovka, the division's post-Operation *Citadel* AFV losses are also chronicled, primarily as on 28 July 1943 Totenkopf received 42 ex-Leibstandarte panzers (38 of which had been present at Prokhorovka).[23]

The photographs in this book were taken by Luftwaffe reconnaissance planes in the days immediately following the battle of Prokhorovka; as such, they are historically significant. The chief protagonists of the battle of Prokhorovka, the Soviet 5th Guards Tank Army's 29th Tank Corps and II SS Panzer Korps' Leibstandarte, fought over a battlefront of little more than 3km between the River Psel and the Storozhevoye Woods. Therefore, the location of one of the most famous battles of the Second World War was able to be photographed by the Luftwaffe in a single shot. Specifically and importantly, photographs are available from 14 and 16 July 1943 when the battlefield was still in German hands (the Germans withdrew from the area on 17 July) and the battlefield remained largely unaltered from 12 July.[24] That day, according to Soviet records, the 29th Tank Corps lost at least 102 tanks and assault guns as total write-offs; the author's research indicates the figure may well have been as high as 132 tanks and assault guns destroyed.[25] There are also important photographs from 7 August which, although three weeks later, highlight the scale of the Soviet armoured losses.

Comparisons made between the NARA July photographs GX-2696-SK-23, GX-2696-SK-24, GX-2696-SK-52, GX-3734-SK-61 and the NARA August photographs GX-3942-SK-69, GX-3942-SD-124 are highly revealing.[26] Destroyed tanks visible in both July and August indicate that they were in all probability lost on 12 July. We know this as, in the main attack sectors from 13 July, the Soviets went onto the defensive as a result of the extremely heavy losses they sustained the previous day.[27] Equally the Leibstandarte, having recaptured their forward positions on 12 July, had to await developments on their flanks before resuming the advance.[28] These factors are of real importance. As a result the front lines of 16 July were virtually identical to those of the 12th which protected the authenticity of the Prokhorovka battlefield in photograph GX-3734-SK-61 taken on 16 July which depicts the majority of the battlefield. As we have seen, German AFV losses were minor by comparison, around 5–10 on 12 July 1943, with a maximum of 16 AFVs lost, including two AFVs sent back to Germany for major overhaul. All other damaged tanks were located in secure firing positions (i.e. behind the line of the anti-tank ditch), recovered before 16 July and later repaired close to the front by the troops.[29]

The Leibstandarte fought much of the battle of Prokhorovka at arm's length, firing from strongly fortified defensive positions. These positions actually formed part of the Soviets' own 3rd (army) line of defence which was part of the wider Kursk defensive system.[30] As the Leibstandarte mostly used superior modern 75mm long-barrelled, high-velocity, long-range weapons such as the Pak 40 L46 anti-tank gun, Panzer IV L43 tank, StuG L48 assault gun and Marder III (or equivalent) L46 tank destroyer, this meant the Germans were able to outrange the Soviets' main tank, the T-34, which had a less powerful 76mm main gun; in addition the Leibstandarte's four Tiger tanks, with their 88mm L56 main gun and thick armour, proved devastating.[31] As a result, the vast number of destroyed tanks forward of the anti-tank ditch and the adjacent Stalinsk state farm visible in photograph GX-3734-SK-61 of 16 July 1943 are almost without exception Soviet.[32]

To further aid the reader the author has included contemporary photographs of the battlefield obtained via Google Earth which are highly useful in establishing the topography of the battlefield. For example, one cannot get a true understanding of the available fields of fire from the Luftwaffe photographs. Therefore, Google Earth has proved to be a vital tool in the formulation of this book. The reader is advised to regularly refer to and compare Map 5 and Plates 32 to 36 when viewing the battlefield photographs for the purposes of battlefield orientation.[33]

The Historical Record

THE PRIMARY SOURCES: DOCUMENTARY EVIDENCE OF THE ULTIMATE FATE OF GERMAN AFVS

It is only possible to establish the individual fate of the 'Panzers of Prokhorovka' if detailed AFV records exist. We are then fortunate that a large proportion of the 4th Panzer Army's Motor Transport Officer (MTO) reports have survived in the archives. It was the MTO's role to document the status of all the AFVs under his jurisdiction. The 4th Panzer Army was the controlling army of II SS Panzer Korps during Operation *Citadel*, while in turn the 4th Panzer Army was under the jurisdiction of Army Group South. Amongst the documents to have survived are monthly AFV chassis number reports from January 1943 through to June 1944.[1] These reports list the individual chassis number for every AFV in the divisional inventories. Importantly, for the three Waffen-SS divisions that constituted II SS Panzer Korps at the launch of Operation *Citadel* on 5 July 1943, there is such a report for 1–2 July 1943.[2] Overall these reports afford us the opportunity to track the AFVs of Leibstandarte and Das Reich that were with the divisions during the battle of Prokhorovka on 12 July 1943 until their ultimate demise on the Eastern Front before the spring of 1944. Another important source of information for AFVs from the 4th Panzer Army's MTO's records are the divisional ten-day status reports from February through to July 1943; these include the participating SS divisions' ten-day status reports for 1–2 and 10 July 1943.[3] These reports provided an early detailed collective assessment of the status of a unit's AFVs over a ten-day period; Figure 1 provides an example of one such document, that of Das Reich on 10 June 1943. The ten-day status reports were also available from January 1943 through to June 1944.[4] The monthly chassis number inventories and ten-day status reports are by far the most important documents available to us as they were written by the divisional engineers. Only divisional engineers and their Korps-level equivalent were permitted to write off tanks from a unit's inventory. Until recently, however, no immediate post-Prokhorovka ten-day armoured status reports were thought to have survived for 20 July 1943. What the historiography of Operation *Citadel*/Prokhorovka always lacked was a single stand-alone post-Prokhorovka (12 July) and post-Operation *Citadel* (5–16 July) II SS Panzer Korps armoured inventory which could simply be compared with the pre-Operation *Citadel* and 10 July II SS Panzer Korps armoured inventories. For corroboration both the SS ten-day armoured status reports for 20 July (four days after the end of Operation *Citadel* and eight days after the battle of Prokhorovka) and 1 August 1943 were required. As already articulated, in 2020 the author discovered these inventories in a secret annex of the NARA 6th Army files.[5] The discovery of these reports (hidden in a separate once-classified file) is a key moment in the evolution of the historiography of the battle of Prokhorovka.

Sadly, after the 20 July and 1 August ten-day status reports there are no surviving ten-day armoured status or monthly chassis number reports for the three SS divisions for the rest of August or September. This is because the three SS divisions left the jurisdiction of the 4th Panzer Army within a week of final termination of the *Citadel* offensive on the south side of the Kursk salient on 16 July 1943 (the Leibstandarte eventually headed to Italy on a political mission to bolster the Axis partner's faltering resolve to fight, while Das Reich and Totenkopf, after a brief stint on the Mius Front between 30 July and 2 August 1943, fought near Kharkov); therefore, any later reports were issued to alternative armies.[6] However, no MTO monthly chassis number or ten-day status reports for this period have yet to materialize in the archives.

In terms of operational AFV numbers the ten-day status reports are by far the most accurate source of information. The divisional and Korps' 1a (operations officer) did issue daily reports that stated the number of operational AFVs per type; however, these daily reports need to be treated with caution. For example, the 1a's daily reports regularly included some AFVs which, although belonging to the division in question, were not actually present on the Eastern Front at the time of the report. It seems this peculiarity occurred as the 1a regularly compiled reports without consulting the divisional engineers or repair troops, who were better placed to know the true location and totals of operational AFVs. Nevertheless, for reporting outside of the ten-day status reports, final coverage date (ten-day status reports covered the periods 1–10, 11–20, 21–28/29/30/31), the author often had little option but to utilize '1a' reports. For this reason in the interests of accuracy throughout this book data is as far as possible presented in ten-day intervals.[7]

The MTO also pooled TF reports (again available February 1943–June 1944) that were written by the divisional and Korps-level engineers. These documents, although produced less frequently, detailed the chassis numbers of AFVs which were written off in the 3b category for losses – these AFVs were believed to be beyond all hope of repair.[8] A 3b AFV would understandably be removed from the divisional inventory. We have TF reports for Leibstandarte, Das Reich and Totenkopf that cover the period 5–10 July 1943, i.e. the first six days of the *Citadel* offensive.[9] This allows us to establish accurately the number of AFVs in the inventories of the Leibstandarte, Das Reich and Totenkopf on 11 July, the day prior to the battle of Prokhorovka. There was also a 3a category for losses; these were AFVs which were often deemed repairable, but the damage was such that the AFV had to be sent to homeland maintenance in Germany for factory repair. As 3a AFVs faced an extended absence from the front (and at this stage there was no guarantee they would return to their former division), this meant they too were to be removed from the divisional AFV inventory; however, as we will see there were exceptions to this rule.

On the whole, monthly AFV chassis number inventory reports can be regarded as the more accurate source of information than ten-day status reports. The former's formulation was more considered due to the fact that as a monthly report they could take into account any AFV reclassifications that had been made since the issue of ten-day status reports. The ten-day status reports should be viewed as rapid assessments conducted when information was sometimes still in short supply as to an AFV's true level of damage or fate. However, both the ten-day and chassis number AFV reports often contained amendments from previous issues. Sometimes significant changes occurred. For example, there were instances of AFVs having first been declared as TF ultimately returning to operational status.

From October/November 1943 through to March 1944, first Das Reich and then the Leibstandarte returned to the 4th Panzer Army's control. As a consequence, chassis number reports (unfortunately no longer for Leibstandarte which are only available until mid-January 1944), sporadic TF reports and ten-day AFV status reports are available in the archives for both divisions over this period.[10] Das Reich chassis number reports are significant as they allow us to see how many of the division's AFVs, including those formally belonging to the Leibstandarte, had survived since the battle of Prokhorovka. Totenkopf, which had also received ex-'Prokhorovka' Leibstandarte panzers, remained on the southern portion of the Eastern Front below 4th Panzer Army throughout this period which meant the ultimate fate of Totenkopf's ex-Leibstandarte 'Prokhorovka' panzers is far harder to decipher. However, good estimates are possible by using other sources. These sources include an AFV status report from 8th Army dating to early October 1943 (in the surviving records it is extremely rare for armies to report overall AFV strength in detail – usually only operational AFV numbers are reported), replacement AFV shipment reports and monthly divisional *Meldung* (reports), the latter containing: the number of operational AFVs, the number of AFVs expected to be repaired within three weeks and Order of Battle charts. When used together with the Operation *Citadel*/July-era reports, we can establish fairly accurately when the ex-Leibstandarte panzers with Totenkopf succumbed. The replacement AFV shipment reports and monthly divisional *Meldung* are also available for the Leibstandarte and Das Reich. This is particularly useful in establishing the AFV strength of these divisions between August and October 1943 when few other reports are available.[11]

Throughout the book (where possible every ten days from February 1943 to April 1944) the reader will be presented with clear unobtrusive tables which will articulate the armoured strength of the German divisions that had once fought at Prokhorovka. The tables give the number of AFVs possessed by the Germans (in their AFV inventory) and the number ready for combat (operational AFVs). The tables will also highlight precisely what proportion of the AFVs were of Prokhorovka vintage. The book's appendix also contains detailed tables which give the exact date when individual 'Prokhorovka' AFVs (listed by chassis number) were destroyed on the Eastern Front.

THE GERMAN PROCEDURE FOR CATEGORIZING
DAMAGED AND LOST AFVS

The procedure for writing off AFVs was not a straightforward one. AFVs could be listed as damaged (in various categories) for many weeks or even months before a final decision to write them off as TF was taken. However, this represented a small percentage of the overall TF. Most TF occurred straight away on the battlefield. As a result, one should not expect initially reported TF loss counts to be drastically amended upwards. Equally the same is true in the reverse; few AFVs were listed as TF only to reappear operational later. Nevertheless, both instances did occur and would create subtle changes to overall TF and damaged AFV counts. However, that this scenario occurred at all should always be borne in mind when one is determining the fate of a specific AFV.

When assessing German armoured losses it is important to fully understand the German procedure for categorizing damaged and lost AFVs. We shall use the first page of Das Reich's AFV ten-day status report for 10 June 1943 as an example (see Figure 1).[12]

Category 1 (*Soll*) indicates the number of AFVs the unit is authorized to possess. Category 2 (*Ist*) indicates the number of AFVs the division possesses.

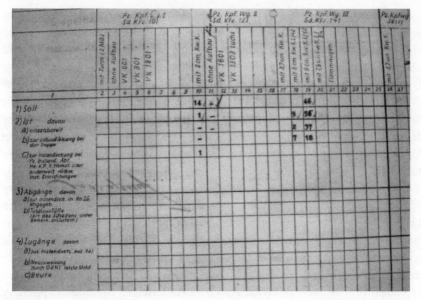

FIGURE I. 4th Panzer Army, O.Qu.V, DR, Gep. Kfz. Bestandsmeldung. 10.6.43. (NARA T313, R387)

Category 2a declares the number of operational AFVs available. Category 2b are tanks that are under repair by the field troops (within the division); AFVs that it was hoped could be repaired quickly or at least relatively quickly in the field would be included in this category.[13]

There were three levels of AFV repair in the field. First, at company level, an attempt would be made to repair the AFV by the driver and co-driver; if this was not possible they would seek assistance from *I-Gruppe* (repair group) personnel. Second, at the battalion level, there was another *I-Gruppe* for HQ vehicles. At the third level where work was permitted to exceed 60 hours was the regimental *Werkstattkompanie* (workshop company); this unit performed the heaviest repairs in the field. AFVs were regularly sent straight to the *Werkstattkompanie* for assessment and repair, though the hope was levels 1 and 2 could repair AFVs if possible.

To quote from the excellent work by Lukas Friedli on AFV maintenance:

If due to overwork or the severity of the damage, the *I-Dienste* (repair service) of a unit could not cope with the accumulating repair work, a panzer was sent outside the panzer regiment to a panzer *Werkstattkompanie* in the area of its superior armies, to a stationary *Panzer-Instandsetzungs-kraftfahr-Werk* (Tank Repair Automotive Plant or *K-Werk*) of the Army Group or even to homeland maintenance.[14]

Category 2c covered those AFVs which required repair at army and army group level repair facilities. These AFVs were in need of heavier, more complex and time-consuming repair. Prior to 1942, AFVs requiring repair above the independent army-level *Werkstattkompanie* would have had to be sent back to Germany. However, the great distances involved in transporting an AFV from the Eastern Front to Germany meant that it was no longer practical to send AFVs this great distance for heavy repair. The solution was the establishment of forward heavy factory level repair facilities (*K-Werk*) in the occupied Soviet Union, one for each of the three army groups on the Eastern Front. The forward heavy repair facilities were civilian-run and the brainchild of Jakob Werlin, a director of Daimler-Benz. Army Group North's facility (staffed by MAN personnel) was established in Riga, Army Group Centre's (staffed by Daimler-Benz personnel) was established in Smolensk, while Army Group South's *K-Werk* (staffed by Krupp personnel) was located in Dnepropetrovsk. AFVs sent to 2c repair facilities officially remained in their parent unit's inventory – once repaired the AFV would return to its parent unit.

Category 3 represents losses; AFVs in this category were to be removed from the division's inventory. Those AFVs in sub-category 3a required the heaviest level of repair and required transport back to Germany for homeland maintenance (*Heimat-Instandsetzung*). These AFVs were first to be sent to an Army ordnance supply depot (*Heereszeugamt* H.Za., located in Magdeburg, Vienna and Konigsberg); from there the AFV would be forwarded to the manufacturer for major repairs. Only AFVs with heavy hull and superstructure damage such as cracks in the armour and full penetrations with simultaneous warping of the faces, full penetrations that resulted in heavily damaged interior equipment, heavier damage caused by fire, and water damage to panzers that were under water for any length of time, had to be sent to a *K-Werk* or homeland maintenance. It is worth stating that AFVs that did not *have* to be sent to the *K-Werk* or homeland maintenance were so treated in times of overwork for the lower level field repair units. This latter consideration can obscure the real level of damage to those AFVs listed as requiring 2c- or 3a-level repair. Despite being listed as 3a and removed from units' *Ist* (actual) totals, some AFVs, against regulations, remained in divisional inventories. This arrangement would later be formalized with AFVs officially returning to homeland maintenance in the 2c category in order keep them within the units' inventory. Thus, once repairs were complete, the AFVs would (despite the distances involved) return to their parent unit. In all probability, this was a formalization of a long-running practice, one that can be traced back to at least early 1943. This reluctance on the part of the divisions to relinquish tanks from their inventory is well articulated by William Auerbach who wrote: 'German commanders were loath to write off panzers and instead carried them on their books ad infinitum, wary of sending them back to the homeland for fear they would never be replaced. As a result deadlined vehicles would be dragged forward during an attack and dragged backward in retreat.'[15] Category 3b was for a total loss (TF); these were AFVs which had been totally destroyed or whose level of damage put them beyond hope of repair.

Finally, Category 4 was for replacement AFVs; these weapons were immediately included in a unit's inventory and *Ist* (actual) total within the ten-day status reports. Category 4a were AFVs which had returned to the front after being repaired by homeland maintenance and 4b indicated that these were newly manufactured AFVs, while 4c was reserved for captured AFVs.

Prelude to Prokhorovka, February–11 July 1943

THE ARRIVAL OF THE SS PANZER REGIMENTS AND THE ORIGINS OF THE BATTLES OF KURSK AND PROKHOROVKA, FEBRUARY–4 JULY 1943

The three SS divisions that constituted the SS Panzer Korps, as II SS Panzer Korps was initially known, first began active operations complete with armoured regiments in early February 1943.[1] The divisions, all having suffered severe losses on the Eastern Front in 1941/1942, had been withdrawn to the West in 1942 in order to be reconstituted as *Sonderverbände* or in other words reinforced panzergrenadier divisions. Each of these special panzergrenadier divisions was to have a reinforced panzer regiment and an organic heavy tank company equipped with the extremely formidable Tiger tank which had thick armour and was armed with an 88mm long-barrelled high-velocity gun. From the beginning, the Leibstandarte Panzer Regiment was further strengthened with its two panzer battalions, each consisting of three medium companies which almost entirely consisted of modern Panzer IVs armed with a long-barrelled L43 75mm main gun (ten per company). The Leibstandarte could also call on a fully equipped assault gun battalion outfitted with StuGs (Plate 1) which was also armed with long-barrelled 75mm weapons and (highly unusual for early 1943) a fully equipped self-propelled (Sf) anti-tank gun (Pak) battalion which was armed with similar 75mm long-barrelled main guns. Das Reich and Totenkopf, although extremely well equipped for the early part of 1943, still relied heavily on Panzer IIIs with long-barrelled 50mm guns to fill their panzer regiments' ranks. Four of their six panzer companies were light, which by 1943 standards meant they were issued with Panzer IIIs, while the other two companies were medium and like Leibstandarte operated long-barrelled 75mm L43 Panzer IVs. As mentioned, both Das Reich and Totenkopf like the Leibstandarte had an organic Tiger tank company and a fully equipped assault gun battalion. However, unlike the Leibstandarte, there was no fully self-propelled anti-tank battalion. In fact, only Das Reich had a company of such guns to supplement its towed anti-tank guns; Totenkopf had to make do with a battalion equipped purely with towed anti-tank guns.

The SS Panzer Korps was sent to the Eastern Front in a desperate attempt to provide Field Marshal Manstein's Army Group South with fresh armour to stem the tide of the hugely successful Soviet winter offensives. The offensives had already resulted on 22 November 1942 in the encirclement and destruction, on 2 February 1943, of the German 6th Army at Stalingrad, and liberated the Caucasus and all the territory east of the Mius. Although the introduction of the SS Panzer Korps could not prevent the initial loss of Kharkov in mid-February, Manstein would utilize the Korps' fresh troops as the main driving force for his famed counteroffensive that resulted in the recapture of Kharkov and Belgorod and more critically helped to save the southern portion of the Eastern Front from the very real threat of total collapse.[2]

Table 1 shows the initial AFV strength of the three component SS divisions of the SS Panzer Korps when they arrived on the Eastern Front in early February 1943.

TABLE 1.[3] Initial SS Panzer Korps AFV strength, February 1943									
	Pz II	Pz III	Pz IV	Pz VI	Bef	StuG	Sf Pak	Wespe	Hummel
LSSAH inventory	12	10	52	9	9	28	28		
DR inventory	10	81	21	10	9	22	9		
SS-T inventory	9	81	22	9	9	22	0		

With the recapture of Kharkov and Belgorod in late March 1943, the southern portion of the Eastern Front was stabilized on the line of the Donets and Mius rivers. This coupled with 2nd Panzer Army's successful defence of its positions formed the Kursk salient and the front lines for the battle of Kursk in July 1943. Further north the German evacuation of the Rzhev salient in March 1943 freed 9th Army for redeployment to the northern flank of the Kursk salient.[4] The SS Panzer Korps did sustain AFV losses during its engagements in February and March. The SS Panzer Korps' AFV strength on 1 April 1943 is shown in Table 2. The SS Panzer Korps had not yet received any additional panzers.

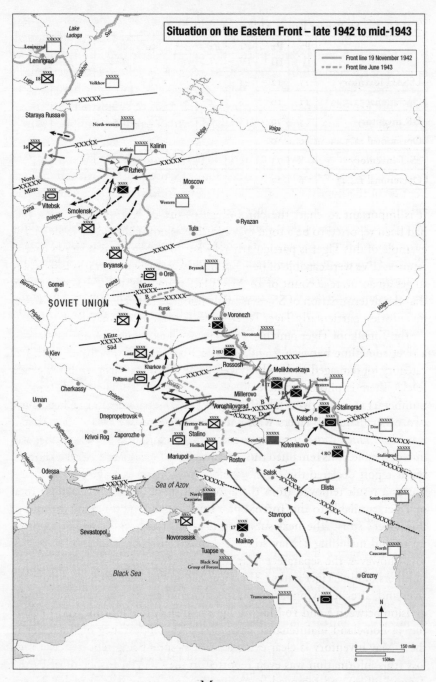

Map 1

TABLE 2.5 SS Panzer Korps AFV strength, 1.4.43

	Pz II	Pz III	Pz IV	Pz VI	Bef	StuG	Sf Pak	Wespe	Hummel
LSSAH inventory	11	12	41	8	10	22	20		
Operational 31.3.43	11	10	28	5	10	18	14		
DR inventory	5	70	13	8	9	20	11		
Operational 28.3.43	0	0	0	0	0	4	0		
SS-T inventory	8	73	19	8	9	21	0		
Operational 1.4.43	6	27	3	2	4	10	0		

It is important to chart the chronology of the Totenkopf Tiger tank that had been reported to be a total loss and thus is not included in Table 2. The example of this Tiger is particularly relevant to our study as it shows that in reports AFVs were capable of being radically reclassified, that it is impossible to get an accurate account of an AFV's fate from a solitary AFV report and that the determination of SS divisional engineers to keep AFVs in divisional inventories, particularly Tiger tanks, cannot be underestimated.

The Totenkopf Tiger tank had fallen through ice while attempting to cross a river sometime between 2 and 10 March 1943 and was placed in the 2c category for damaged tanks which were to be repaired at army or army group level.[6] There is photographic evidence of this stranded Tiger tank (tactical number 411) in the river.[7] The Tiger was placed separately in brackets above two other damaged Tigers within the 2c category due to the fact that it was 'Steht unter Wasser' or submerged and therefore due to the weather was unrecoverable. This remained the case until the 21 March to 1 April armoured status report declared the Tiger was now categorized as a 3b, total loss, and was as a result removed from the armoured status report's Ist (actual) total of Tigers available to the Totenkopf.[8] This though would not be the end of this Tiger's story. The next surviving ten-day status report which reported up to and including 1 May still listed only eight Tigers in Totenkopf's Ist total; however, the separate 1 May divisional inventory reported the chassis numbers of nine Tiger tanks.[9] The Tiger had in fact been recovered from the river and, after receiving factory inspection and repair, was 'returned' to the division between 2 and 10 May via the 4a category (for returning AFVs from the 3a homeland maintenance category).[10] The appearance of the Tiger in the 1 May inventory is clear evidence that despite being reported as a total loss (this information was even reported to the General Inspector of Panzer Troops' office) and removed from the division's Ist total of available Tigers, Totenkopf's engineer had against regulations kept the Tiger in the division's inventory throughout this period.[11] The indications are that this Tiger was simply being reclassified as opposed to any repairs having been completed. The 1 May armoured status report lists eight Tigers in the division's (2) *Ist* total of which six were (2a) operational and two were (2c) under army or army group level repair. While the 10 May armoured status report (issued on 12 May 1943), which reported the return of the formerly semi-submerged Tiger, lists nine Tigers in the division's (2) *Ist* total of which once again six were (2a) operational, now three Tigers were listed as (2c) under army or army group level repair. Clearly, this raises the distinct possibility that the 'returning' Tiger had gone straight back into the division's 2c category and had in fact physically always remained at Army Group South's *K-Werk* in Dnepropetrovsk.[12] There is also a strong probability that the Tiger in question was specifically Tiger 250 101.[13]

Even after the arrival of the SS Panzer Corps and II Battalion of Grossdeutschland's Panzer Regiment (its existing I Battalion was already at the front) by 1 April, on the entire Eastern Front, the Germans were down to only 1,336 tanks and assault guns, of which just 612 were operational. The Germans, by contrast, estimated they were already facing an enemy with over 6,000 tanks and assault guns at its disposal.[14] Consequently, April–June 1943 was one of the quietest periods on the Eastern Front as both sides (exhausted from their monumental efforts over the winter) undertook an extended period of planning, reorganization and reinforcement. The Soviets were settling on a policy of initial strategic defence to be followed by massive simultaneous offensive operations. The Germans recognizing their inability to win the war on the Eastern Front in 1943 instead sought to conduct a major pre-emptive attack (Operation *Citadel*) as part of an overall policy of strategic defence.[15]

On 1 May 1943, the panzer regiments of the Leibstandarte, Das Reich and Totenkopf were ordered to reorganize in preparation for Operation *Citadel*, the planned German pincer attack on the Kursk salient.[16] Personnel from one battalion of both SS Panzer Regiment 1 and SS Panzer Regiment 2 were to be sent back to Germany to create a Panther tank battalion for each panzer regiment. The remaining elements of the panzer regiments were to be reorganized at the front and filled with 75 newly issued Panzer IVs, so that Totenkopf would have a panzer regiment with two battalions each with two medium and one light panzer companies, the Leibstandarte would have a reinforced panzer battalion with four medium panzer companies, and Das Reich would have one panzer battalion with two medium and two light panzer companies and one battalion (its anti-tank battalion) with two T34 companies and one light panzer company. During this time, the SS Panzer Korps was also renamed II SS Panzer Korps effective from 1 June 1943. The ultimate aim of the General Inspector of Panzer Troops (Heinz Guderian) at this time was made clear by an order issued by OKH GenStdH/Org.Ab on 14 June 1943 to reorganize the panzer regiments and panzer battalions on the Eastern Front:

> It is expected that it will be possible to fill every Panzer battalion in all Panzer Divisions in the Eastern Army with 96 Panzers (mostly Pz IV, several Pz III with long barrels) by December 1943. In addition, it is intended that a Panther battalion be created in Germany for the majority of the Panzer Divisions. Therefore, it is necessary to reorganize the Panzer battalions in the Eastern Army.[17]

Guderian hoped to reinstate the organic panzer brigade in each panzer division, something which had not been uniformly seen since 1940. Ideally Guderian hoped the panzer brigades would consist of four or three tank battalions, but he recognized that due to sluggish tank production, two tank battalions, an StuG battalion and a Panzer Jäger (Sf Pak) battalion was a more realistic target. As a minimum Guderian desired a panzer regiment with two battalions for his panzer divisions, one outfitted with modern variants of the Panzer IV and the other with the new Panther tank (the Panther's 75mm L70 main gun was even more powerful than the Tiger's 88mm L56 equivalent).[18]

The heavy Tiger tank companies of the three SS divisions, as with all other Tiger tank units, received the order to convert to purely Tiger operated companies each with 14 Tigers (previously nine). This resulted in the loss of the Tiger companies' supporting Panzer IIIs. In spring 1943, all three SS Tiger companies transferred their Panzer IIIs to their respective regiments for reallocation; however, the Leibstandarte Tiger company did keep four of its 13 Panzer IIIs in a light platoon (Table 3). On 22 April, a further order was issued for the three organic SS Tiger tank companies with the divisions to be combined into a new Korps-level heavy SS panzer Abteilung (Abt; battalion) with an authorized strength of 45 Tigers. A battalion staff company was to be created in Germany which would later take over command of the three existing SS Tiger tank companies already at the front. This order was resisted particularly by the Leibstandarte, and for the time being, each of the SS divisions maintained an organic Tiger tank company. As a result, the 17 new Tigers that were intended to complete the establishment of this new heavy Abteilung were instead sent in May 1943 to the Eastern Front in order to allow the divisional SS Tiger companies to reach their new authorized strength of 14 Tigers per company. As Table 1 indicates, the three SS Tiger companies had originally been issued 28 Tiger tanks; the 17 new additions meant that the SS Panzer Korps had received the equivalent of a heavy Abteilung's full allocation of 45 Tigers. On 1 May orders were then issued to further boost the three divisional

Tiger tank companies to an authorized strength of 15 as each company was to receive a command Tiger. Despite this order, no additional Tigers were shipped to accomplish this expansion prior to the launch of Operation *Citadel* on 5 July 1943. In May, Das Reich and Totenkopf each received their six new Tigers, while the Leibstandarte received just five Tigers (together these Tigers constituted the 17 new Tigers mentioned above).[19] This left the Leibstandarte Tiger tank company with 13 Tigers (it had lost one Tiger as a total write-off between 1 and 10 March during the Kharkov counteroffensive); Totenkopf on the other hand, following the conclusion of the submerged Tiger tank escapade, had lost no Tigers and was now in possession of 15 Tigers – including a command Tiger. Das Reich, which had begun with ten Tigers, had lost two Tigers during the Kharkov counteroffensive; therefore, it now possessed the first updated authorized company strength of 14 Tigers.[20]

The desire to increase AFV strength as embodied within the 14 June 1943 order had already been on display for some months prior to the order's issue. From March, the Leibstandarte was permitted to possess an authorized strength of 84 Panzer IVs, regardless of the official organizational structure.[21] By the launch of Operation *Citadel* on 5 July 1943 the Leibstandarte had in effect achieved this desired strength, having reached a strength of 83 Panzer IVs.

As the last shipment of 16 Leibstandarte Panzer IVs only arrived between 1 and 5 July, it proved impossible to distribute these panzers amongst the proposed 8th company of 1 SS Panzer Regiment (lack of crew availability was also a major factor).[22] Taking into account the new organizational order for 96 panzers per battalion, the Leibstandarte 1 SS Panzer Regiment's II Battalion had already chosen to distribute its 67 existing Panzer IVs amongst its three existing companies. Therefore, the 5th, 6th and 7th panzer companies now had an expanded strength of 22 Panzer IVs per company. The spare Panzer IV was converted into a regimental command tank.[23] Therefore, when the Leibstandarte received its additional 16 Panzer IVs just prior to Operation *Citadel* these tanks helped to populate the division's regimental command and reconnaissance platoons (Table 3), while the remainder created a pool of replacements for damaged tanks. The Leibstandarte command would have expected the number of operational AFVs to plummet following the commencement of any offensive; therefore, a small pool of replacement Panzer IVs for the three existing companies of the Leibstandarte's II Panzer Battalion would have been viewed as being highly advantageous.[24] During Operation *Citadel*, there is no photographic evidence of any panzers operating in an 8th company of the Leibstandarte's II Panzer Battalion. However, there is documentary evidence from 23 July 1943 which confirms that the Leibstandarte's II Panzer Battalion consisted of only three panzer companies during July 1943.[25] The non-standard tanks of SS Panzer Regiment 1 (i.e. other than Panzer IVs or Tigers) were distributed amongst the command units, while as we have noted the Tiger company against regulations had kept a light platoon containing four Panzer IIIs (Table 3).

TABLE 3.[26] Non-typical panzers of the LSSAH		
Unit	**Number**	**Panzer**
Regiment (Stab)		
Nachrichten Zug	055	Panzer IV Ausf G
	054	Befehlspanzer III Ausf J
	053	Befehlspanzer III Ausf J
	052	Panzer II Ausf F
	051	Befehlspanzer III Ausf H
	050	
Aufklärung Zug	067	Panzer II Ausf F
	066	
	065	Panzer IV Ausf G
	064	Panzer IV Ausf G
	063	
	062	Panzer IV Ausf G
	061	
	060	Panzer III Ausf M
2nd Abteilung Stab	559	Panzer III Ausf M
	558	Panzer III Ausf M
	557	Panzer III Ausf M
	556	Panzer III Ausf J
	555	Befehlspanzer III Ausf J
	554	Befehlspanzer III Ausf J
13th Kompanie/le Zug	1344	Panzer III Ausf M
	1343	Panzer III Ausf M
	1342	Panzer III Ausf M
	1341	Panzer III Ausf M

Although designated a panzergrenadier division the Leibstandarte drew on elements of the table of organization for panzer divisions, panzergrenadier divisions and even infantry divisions. For example, the Leibstandarte (alongside the army's Grossdeutschland Division and the other classic SS divisions Das Reich and Totenkopf) possessed six motorized panzergrenadier battalions (three per panzergrenadier regiment) as would be expected in a panzergrenadier division. However, one of its six battalions (III Battalion 2nd SS Panzergrenadier Regiment in the Leibstandarte's case) travelled in semi-tracked armoured personnel carriers (SPWs) rather than trucks. This type of battalion would normally only be the preserve of panzer divisions. The SPW battalion gave the panzers vital infantry support as they advanced, while affording the troops protection against small arms and shrapnel. The Soviets possessed no equivalent throughout the war. A lack of infantry support was one of the key reasons why Soviet armoured spearheads were regularly decimated. By contrast a conventional panzer division only possessed four panzergrenadier battalions in its two panzergrenadier regiments (typically a panzer division had a ration strength of around 15,000 men). In actual fact the Leibstandarte was even substantially stronger than the army's Grossdeutschland Division and its sister SS divisions Das Reich and Totenkopf. The Leibstandarte possessed more powerfully equipped specialist organic units and although still awaiting its Panther battalion (as were all panzer divisions) it was the strongest German division in terms of manpower. On 10 July 1943 the division had a ration strength of 24,240 men. In comparison, on the same date, the ration strength of the army's Grossdeutschland Division stood at 21,475. The ration strength of the other 'classic' SS divisions was as follows: Das Reich 20,110 (4 July combat strength: 7,350) and Totenkopf 20,830. By way of further comparison, the 3rd Panzer Division's ration strength on 10 July was 14,126 (4 July combat strength: 5,170) while the 11th Panzer Division's ration strength was 16,520. During Operation *Citadel* all of these units fought as part of Manstein's Army Group South.[27]

In terms of the Leibstandarte's anti-tank capability the 1st and 2nd SS Panzergrenadier Regiments each had a designated towed (heavy) anti-tank company equipped with six 75mm Pak 40 anti-tank guns, which had a similar long-barrelled high-velocity gun to the modern variants of the Panzer IVs which equipped the vast majority of the Leibstandarte's panzer battalion. In addition, six more Pak 40s could be found within the Leibstandarte's reconnaissance battalion, which could boast its own heavy anti-tank company. Together these three companies added 18 heavy 75mm Pak 40 anti-tank guns (Plate 7) to the already formidable defensive capability of the Leibstandarte.[28]

In regards to medium anti-tank guns, the Leibstandarte divisional headquarters possessed an armoured heavy company which contained a platoon equipped with three (medium) 50mm Pak 38 anti-tank guns. This gun (the same weapon mounted on the division's 13 Panzer IIIs) could only penetrate the frontal armour of the T-34 at very close range and only then when using AP40 ammunition (which contained a cemented tungsten-carbide core); such shells were expensive to produce and in short supply. At

Prokhorovka, however, flanking targets were not in short supply and, therefore, standard armour piercing shells were often effective against T-34s. Each of the division's six panzer grenadier battalions were also equipped with a further platoon of three Pak 38s, while the division's two Nebelwerfer batteries would each have a single Pak 38 for close protection. Overall then the division was authorized to possess 23 medium anti-tank guns.[29] In comparison Das Reich was authorized to possess 30 medium anti-tank guns and 27 heavy anti-tank guns, the latter number being higher than the Leibstandarte's equivalent in order to compensate for Das Reich's smaller complement of Marder tank destroyers. Totenkopf was authorized 33 medium anti-tank guns and 21 heavy anti-tank guns.[30]

The Leibstandarte could also call upon 12 88mm 36 or 41 Flak guns which could be (and often were) deployed in an anti-tank role to devastating effect. A modified version of the Flak 36 formed the main gun of the Tiger tank. The Leibstandarte also possessed strong divisional indirect fire support. The division had a full allocation of self-propelled artillery consisting of 12 105mm 'Wespe' (light) howitzers and six 150mm 'Hummel' (heavy) howitzers. Together these weapons formed one of the three battalions that constituted the division's artillery regiment. In terms of divisional artillery the Leibstandarte was also authorized to possess a further 12 105mm towed light field howitzers and 12 150mm heavy field howitzers. Taken together the division had 18 heavy howitzers and 24 light howitzers either self-propelled or towed. In addition, the regiment had a battery of four 105mm guns.[31] The division could also call on the support of II SS Panzer Korps HQ which possessed two artillery battalions, two 150mm Nebelwerfer rocket regiments and one 150mm Nebelwerfer battalion. Uniquely the Leibstandarte also possessed two organic 150mm Nebelwerfer batteries, equipped with a total of 12 Nebelwerfers.[32]

Perhaps crucially then at Prokhorovka the 5th Guards Tank Army would face highly concentrated anti-tank fire from at least 53 towed anti-tank and Flak guns which were all very capable of destroying its armour, 30 of which were capable from long-range. This coupled with fact that the Leibstandarte would be entrenched in strong defensive positions and could count on effective artillery and Luftwaffe support made the 5th Guards Tank Army's task of effecting a breakthrough in depth in the Leibstandarte sector an extremely arduous one.

PROKHOROVKA LOOMS: THE SOUTHERN PINCER OF OPERATION *CITADEL*, 5–11 JULY 1943

It is no exaggeration to say that by the summer of 1943 Germany's overall strategic situation on the Eastern Front was hopeless. Following the tremendous losses sustained during the first two years of the war on the Eastern Front, and faced with an enemy with a seemingly endless supply of troops and tanks, the German Army's only realistic course of action for 1943 was one of strategic defence.[33] Indeed, on 18 February 1943 Hitler stated that he was 'unable to undertake any large-scale operations this year' but 'only small forays'; Operation *Citadel*, as the German offensive against the Kursk salient would ultimately be known, was therefore conceived by Gen Kurt Zeitzler, Chief of the Army General Staff, within this overall defensive context.[34] On 13 March Hitler issued Operations Order No. 5 for a pincer attack on the 120km-deep and 200km-wide Kursk Salient. Army Group Centre's (Field Marshal Günther von Kluge) 9th Army was to form the northern arm of the pincer, while the southern arm was to be formed of Army Group South's (Field Marshal Erich von Manstein) 4th Panzer Army under ColGen Hermann Hoth comprising LII Korps, XXXXVIII Panzer Korps and II SS Panzer Korps, and Army Detachment Kempf led by Gen Werner Kempf with III Panzer Korps and Korps Raus.[35] It was assumed the offensive would commence in the second half of April with the operation expected to last no more than 18 days.[36] Operation *Citadel* had two key objectives. First, the operation was to straighten the front. By cutting off the protruding Kursk salient, a more favourable defensive line would be achieved, enabling troops to be withdrawn from the Eastern Front for the anticipated two-front war with the Western powers. The second objective was to weaken the massive Soviet forces concentrated in the Kursk area before they could launch an avalanche-like summer offensive in a concerted action with the western powers. Unlike in 1941 and 1942 no German plans existed for a strategic offensive to follow. Operation *Citadel* constituted only a preventive attack with limited aims within an overall defensive strategy.[37]

Following numerous delays to its launch chiefly caused by slow panzer production (particularly the new Panther tank) and the concerns of ColGen Walter Model, commander of 9th Army, (over the weakness of his forces and the prospect of a counteroffensive in his rear) Operation *Citadel* would be finally launched on 5 July 1943.[38] For their part the Soviets had decided on a strategic defence to absorb the coming German offensive at Kursk to be followed by strong counteroffensives against the fatally weakened German forces.[39] To help ensure the success of these counteroffensives a large strategic reserve had been formed: Steppe Front under the command of Gen Ivan Stepanovich Konev comprising 449,133 troops and 1,632 operational tanks and assault guns. For Operation *Citadel*, in the north 9th Army with 223,000 troops and 1,072 operational tanks, assault guns and tank destroyers was opposed by Central Front under Gen Konstantin Konstantinovich Rokossovsky with 510,983 troops and 1,607 operational

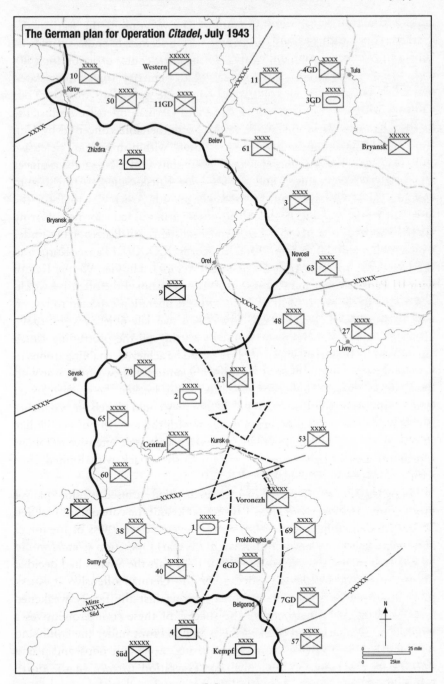

MAP 2

tanks and assault guns, while to Model's rear Bryansk Front led by Gen Markian Popov with 335,068 troops and 1,525 operational tanks and assault guns and Western Front under the command of Gen Vasily Sokolovsky with 226,043 troops and 1,737 operational tanks and assault guns stood ominously poised to strike against 2nd Panzer Army led by Erich-Heinrich Clössner with 107,000 troops and 234 operational tanks and assault guns in the Orel salient. In the south Army Group South's 4th Panzer Army and Army Detachment Kempf with a combined strength of 215,271 troops and 1,451 operational tanks, assault guns and tank destroyers were opposed by Voronezh Front under Gen Nikolai Fedorovich Vatutin comprising 466,236 troops and 1,699 operational tanks and assault guns. The German 2nd Army led by Gen Walter-Otto Weiss with 80,000 troops and 100 operational assault guns, which saw no significant fighting in July, held the western edge of the Kursk salient.[40]

Overall, on 5 July 1943 625,271 German combat troops were located in the Kursk-Orel area, of which 518,271 were earmarked for Operation *Citadel*. The Germans could also call on 2,523 operational tanks, assault guns and tank destroyers for the offensive: 9th Army, 4th Panzer Army and Army Detachment Kempf. On the Soviet side 1,426,352 Red Army combat troops awaited the German onslaught; of these, 449,133 formed part of the Strategic Reserve, Steppe Front. The Soviets had 4,938 operational tanks in the area; of these 1,632 belonged to Steppe Front. On 12 July a further 3,262 operational Soviet tanks and assault guns would be launched against 2nd Panzer Army which initially had just 234 operational tanks and assault guns, in a major counteroffensive named Operation *Kutuzov* that threatened 9th Army's rear and the entire Orel salient.[41]

On 5 July Model launched 9th Army's offensive with his infantry divisions in the vanguard. However, Model's divisions quickly became bogged down in the extensive Soviet defences. It soon became evident that no operational breakthrough was likely to occur without the vigorous commitment of all of 9th Army's panzer divisions. This was something Model was loathe to do for he was fully aware that a major Soviet offensive was about to be launched in his rear against 2nd Panzer Army. Model simply could not afford for his precious armoured formations to be worn down in a battle of attrition with Central Front. On 10 July Model called a temporary halt to 9th Army's offensive so that its formations could rest and reorganize. Model intended to resume 9th Army's offensive on 12 July; however, the launch of Operation *Kutuzov* on the same day immediately ensured that 9th Army's offensive would not recommence. In confronting 9th Army's offensive Central Front lost 526 AFVs, while Model's cautious approach meant 9th Army lost just 77 AFVs.[42]

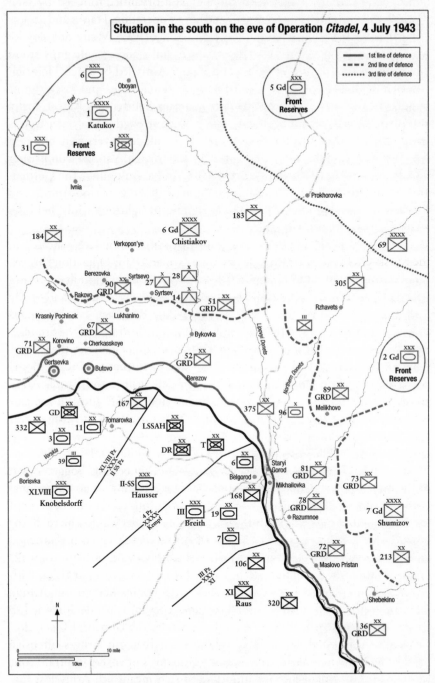

Situation in the south on the eve of Operation *Citadel*, 4 July 1943

MAP 3

In contrast to 9th Army's struggles, by 9 July, the fifth day of Operation *Citadel*, the armoured units of Army Group South, under the command of Field Marshal Erich von Manstein, had already reached the River Psel, the last natural obstacle before Kursk.[43] The original idea was for XXXXVIII Panzer Korps under Gen Otto von Knobelsdorff, deployed on the left flank with 3rd Panzer Division, Grossdeutschland Division, Panzer Rgt. v. Lauchert, 11th Panzer Division and 911th StuG Abt to carry the main thrust of the attack, but this plan had to be abandoned as the Korps had struggled to break through in depth; between 1 and 10 July XXXXVIII Panzer Korps' operational AFVs fell from 575 to 275 (these figures included the Korps' mechanically troublesome new Panther tanks whose numbers fell from 200 to 48 operational Panthers). II SS Panzer Korps under the command of SS *Obergruppenführer* Paul Hausser, in the centre with Leibstandarte, Das Reich and Totenkopf, made faster progress, breaking through the Soviets' second defensive system on the second day of the offensive; this shifted the main thrust of the offensive north-east in the direction of Prokhorovka (between 1 and 10 July II SS Panzer Korps' operational AFV numbers fell more moderately from 468 to 339). The III Panzer Korps under Gen Hermann Breith on the right flank with 6th, 19th and 7th Panzer Divisions, 503rd s.Panzer.Abt and 228th StuG Abt, fared even worse than XXXXVIII Panzer Korps and was for some time stuck close to its start lines (between 1 and 10 July III Panzer Korps' operational AFVs fell from 366 to 163) which exposed the right flank of II SS Panzer Korps. There was a shortage of infantry to man such an unplanned overextension of the front. As a result, after its rapid initial advance II SS Panzer Korps was forced to spend the next few days securing its flanks. It would not be until 10 July that II SS Panzer Korps, with the Leibstandarte in the vanguard, renewed its drive towards Prokhorovka (Plates 8 to 31).[44]

The Soviet leadership were deeply concerned by the rapid progress of II SS Panzer Korps. Nikolai Vatutin, commander of Voronezh Front, had deployed almost all his operational reserves including 1st Tank Army under the command of Gen Mikhail Efimovich Katukov, which had been deployed defensively, by 6 July 1943. The Soviet High Command (Stavka) was forced to call upon the Strategic Reserve which had been earmarked for the strategic summer offensives to follow. 2nd and 10th Tank Corps and 5th Guards Tank Army were put to march on 8 July, and other major formations of Steppe Front were also called upon such as 5th Guards Army, 27th Army, 53rd Army and finally 4th Guards Army.[45]

Despite Vatutin's defensive deployment during Operation *Citadel*, Soviet armour had suffered very heavy losses. The tank units of 6th Guards Army under Gen Ivan Mikhailovich Chistyakov and 7th Guards Army led by Gen Mikhail Stepanovich Shumilov were largely destroyed in the first two days of the offensive. By 10 July, 1st Tank Army had shrunk from an original 646 to 100 tanks and assault guns. Up to and including 13 July, Voronezh Front (together with reserves brought in) lost a total of 1,223 tanks and assault guns. A large proportion of those losses were incurred in the first few days of the battle. By contrast, up to and including 10 July, the attacking units of Army Group South lost only 107 tanks, assault guns and tank destroyers, although they had to fight their way through enemy positions under the most adverse conditions. During this period operational AFVs of the same units, which included, on the extreme right flank, Korps Raus under the command of Gen Erhard Raus, and its 905th StuG Abt and 393rd StuG Battery, fell from 1,451 to 814.[46]

Table 4 lists the AFVs that II SS Panzer Korps reported as being TF (3b) between 5 and 10 July.[47] This together with those losses listed as being sent for homeland repair (3a: one Panzer IV and one Tiger tank both from the Leibstandarte) over the same period gives us the available strength of II SS Panzer Korps on 11 July – the day prior to the battle of Prokhorovka.[48]

TABLE 4.[49] Reported total losses of II SS Panzer Korps during Operation *Citadel*, 5–10.7.43

	Pz I	Pz III	Pz IV	T-34	Pz VI	StuG	Sf Pak
LSSAH	15 014	77 604	84 088			92 150	1 851
			83 291			91 143	1 821
			83 181				
			83 293				
DR		73 102 (514)	84 223 (823)	19 (L14)	250 085 (S24)		
		72 267 (902)	84 231 (832)	15 (932)			
SS-T		77 603	84 245 (323)		250 095	92 247	
		74 996 (302)	84 232 (711)				
			84 227 (713)				
			82 877 (222)				

There are some points of note from Table 4. The Leibstandarte 50mm L60 Panzer III 77 604 which was reported as TF was in fact later transferred to Das Reich on 28 July; the Leibstandarte began Operation *Citadel* with 13 Panzer IIIs of which three had short-barrelled 50mm L42 guns.[50] The 10 July ten-day status report lists one short-barrelled Panzer III as TF – this must have been the case as we know all ten Leibstandarte long-barrelled L60 Panzer III were transferred away from the Leibstandarte before it headed to Italy – none appear in any subsequent Leibstandarte reports while a total of 11

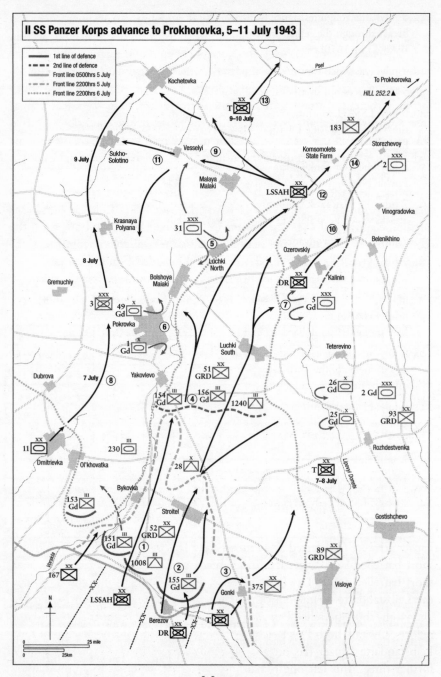

II SS Panzer Korps advance to Prokhorovka, 5–11 July 1943

——	1st line of defence
– – –	2nd line of defence
·····	Front line 0500hrs 5 July
·····	Front line 2200hrs 5 July
·····	Front line 2200hrs 6 July

MAP 4

1. 5 July: after tough resistance from the 1008th Anti-Tank Regiment, LSSAH breaks through the centre of the 52nd Guards Rifle Division and captures Bykovka by 1650hrs.

2. 5 July: Das Reich captures Berezov and defeats a Soviet armoured counter-attack.

3. 5 July: Totenkopf smashes through the 375th Rifle Division.

4. 6 July: LSSAH continues to advance to the north-east, overrunning a regiment of the 51st Guards Rifle Division. Hausser has broken through Chistiakov's second line of defence.

5. 6 July: the 31st Tank Corps fights a meeting engagement with LSSAH near Luchki North, but loses 110 tanks.

6. 7 July: the 31st Tank Corps and 3rd Mechanized Corps mount local counter-attacks which keep LSSAH on the defensive all day.

7. 7 July: Das Reich advances east, pushing 5th Guards Tank Corps aside.

8. 7 July: 11th Panzer Division advances from the west, rolling up the 3rd Mechanized Corps and forcing the Soviets to partly withdraw from the salient between II SS Panzer Korps and XLVIII Panzer Korps.

9. 8 July: LSSAH pivots and attacks west to link up with XLVIII Panzer Korps. LSSAH fights a tank battle with 31st Tank Corps near Vesselyi.

10. 8 July: advancing eastwards on its own, Das Reich runs into the 2nd Tank Corps and elements of the 10th Tank Corps and 5th Guards Tank Corps, which force it onto the defensive with a series of poorly coordinated counter-attacks.

11. 9 July: Hausser continues to attack westwards, mopping up around Pokrovka and Sukho-Solotino, which closes the gap with XLVIII Panzer Korps.

12. 10 July: LSSAH resumes the attack towards Prokhorovka and captures the Komsomolets State Farm.

13. 10 July: Totenkopf shifts to Hausser's left flank and crosses the Psel with infantry.

14. 11 July: LSSAH advances to capture Hill 252.2 on the outskirts of Prokhorovka.

Panzer III were transferred away on 28 July. This figure must have included a short-barrelled L42 Panzer III. This is made certain as only one conventional short-barrelled 50mm L42 Panzer III (i.e. not a command tank) travelled with the Leibstandarte to Italy and then back to the Eastern Front in November 1943 – the short-barrelled Panzer III then appears in subsequent Leibstandarte reports, Overall, both Das Reich and Totenkopf each took ownership of four Leibstandarte Panzer IIIs on 28 July while II SS Panzer Korps HQ took a further three. This left one remaining Panzer III which as mentioned went with the Leibstandarte to Italy. The loss of a Panzer III between 5 and 10 July must then have been (as the ten-day status report indicated) a short-barrelled 50mm Panzer III rather than 77 604. Second, Das Reich's Panzer IV 84 223 is listed as TF between 5 and 10 July in a TF report which was updated with knowledge gained up to 13 July. However, Das Reich's 10 July ten-day status report lists only one Panzer IV as TF (this would be 84 231). Later, on 31 October Das Reich lists 84 223 as being part of its inventory. It is then listed as 3a and sent to Germany for repair between 1 and 10 January 1944. Like the Leibstandarte's Panzer III 77 604 on the evening of 10 July the tank must have been recoverable, not as badly damaged as first feared or simply caught up in a case of mistaken identity. These two examples highlight that it is important not to view specific AFV ten-day status or TF reports as being final. Finally, the Das Reich TF Tiger (250 085 – see Plate 6) is one of the three Tigers listed in the Das Reich 1–10 July ten-day status report as '*noch nicht geborgen*' (not yet recovered). The updated Das Reich TF report allowed for this to be refined to one TF – the other two Tigers once recovered returned to service.

The ten-day status reports were often correct in terms of numbers; however, in the heat of battle, it was difficult to assess the exact condition of damaged or originally declared TF AFVs, particularly if the AFV was close to or even behind enemy lines. A good example of this can be seen in the case of Das Reich Panzer IV 82 712 (an ex-Leibstandarte Prokhorovka-era Panzer) which was reported 3b TF between 11 and 20 January 1944. In fact, it transpired that this panzer was written off as TF (and removed from the division's inventory by the engineer) as it had been abandoned behind enemy lines. However, following a change in the front line, the panzer was recovered on 23 January and returned to the division's inventory. This case highlights how quickly a radical reclassification could be made. Tank 82 712 was eventually handed over by Das Reich to the 19th Panzer Division on 29 February for further service and, along with Das Reich stalwart 84 242 (transferred to the 19th Panzer Division on the same date), these were the only Das Reich Panzer IVs present at the battle of Prokhorovka, with either the Leibstandarte or Das Reich, to survive on the Eastern Front into March 1944.[51] (See Appendix E for full details).

Another example of administrative failure occurred when Das Reich Panzer IV 85 087 was reported 3b TF between 20 and 31 October and removed from the division's inventory. However, the next report on 1–10 November states 85 087 was listed as 3a for homeland maintenance and was *again* removed from the inventory of the division. Das Reich's *Ist* total of on-hand Panzer IVs was not adjusted to compensate for this anomaly; therefore, the same tank in consecutive reports was chalked off twice. The 20–31 October report recorded three Panzer IV total losses (84 904, 83 852 and 85 087) which took the *Ist* total down to 46 Panzer IVs, while the next report, 1–10 November, stated that the division received one new Panzer IV from 4a homeland maintenance

(83 875), lost one Panzer IV 3b as a total loss (83 256) and lost one Panzer to homeland maintenance (85 087) which according to the report brought Das Reich's inventory down to 45 Panzer IVs. Clearly, these numbers do not align and point to an administrative error in the report, either in terms of the correct *Ist* total or in the identification of 85 087 as being the lost/damaged Panzer IV in question in one of the reports.[52]

3

The Battle of Prokhorovka, 12 July 1943: The Statistical Battle

THE IMPORTANCE OF THE 6TH ARMY'S WEEKLY PANZER AND ASSAULT GUN STATUS REPORT OF 1 AUGUST 1943

There has hitherto been a lack of confirmatory evidence regarding the number of total losses (3a and 3b types) that II SS Panzer Korps suffered during Operation *Citadel*, even though one could point to a few total loss reports from July 1943.[1] One of these total loss reports came from a seemingly very creditable and reliable source namely II SS Panzer Korps' engineer (Figure 2). The report covered losses the Korps suffered between 5 and 18 July 1943.[2] The report recorded losses as either total losses (category 3b) or those requiring homeland maintenance in Germany (category 3a but also potentially unofficially in category 2c, i.e. allowed to remain in a divisional inventory). This document first appeared in the historiography of the battle of Kursk in 2007.[3] As only an engineer had the authority to write off an AFV as a total loss the importance of this document is clear.

However, without any (seemingly) surviving SS *Sonderverbände* ten-day status reports or end-of-month chassis number inventories for the period of 11–20 July or 21 July–1 August which covered the latter period of Operation *Citadel* (11–16 July, including the battle of Prokhorovka on 12 July), the subsequent defensive operations of 17–20 July (II SS Panzer Korps HQ, Leibstandarte and Das Reich withdrew from the front on 17 July, while Totenkopf left the front on the evening of 20 July) and the period prior to II SS Panzer Korps' return to combat on 30 July (21–30 July) we had no way of confirming whether II SS Panzer Korps' engineer's loss report was truly accurate, particularly in regards to Totenkopf losses.[4] The engineer's report

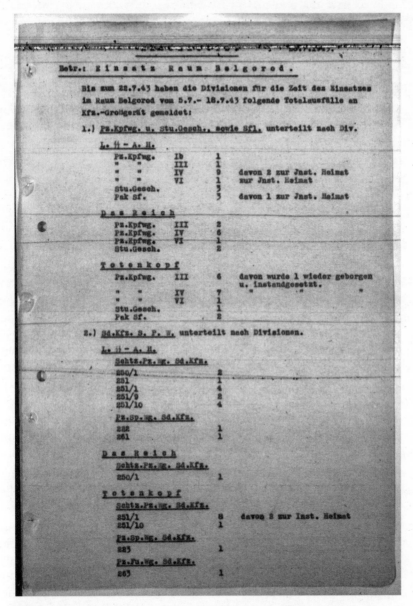

FIGURE 2. II SS Panzer Korps, Ingenieur, Betr.: Kinsatz Raum Belgorod, 5–18.7.43, updated to 22.7.43 (written 28.7.43). (NARA T354, R607, F000629-31)

did look to have the potential to be definitive, but without the necessary confirmatory evidence from the latter half of July this could not be declared to be the case.

Importantly, it proved possible to locate the 6th Army's *Wochenmeldung über Panzer und Sturmgeschülzlage Stand* (weekly panzer and assault gun status report) for 1 August which covered the period 21 July–1 August (Figure 3). This document gives the number of operational, short-term damaged (under 14 days) and long-term damaged (over 14 days) AFVs (per type) that were in the inventories of the armoured units of 6th Army on the Mius Front on 1 August.[5] Crucially, the document includes Das Reich and Totenkopf, which in the previous few days had been transferred to 6th Army's control.[6] The *Wochenmeldung* tells us that Das Reich had 172 panzers in its inventory on 1 August 1943, while Totenkopf had 159 panzers on the same date.[7] If we include the assault guns and tank destroyers that Das Reich and Totenkopf were known to have had on 1 August the numbers for AFVs are: Das Reich 216 and Totenkopf 202.[8]

Remarkably, the *Wochenmeldung* also offers us the first opportunity to view the respective AFV inventories for Das Reich and Totenkopf in the previous ten-day status report of 20 July; these reports covered the period 11–20 July 1943. We can see that on the 20th Das Reich had 130 panzers in its inventory, while Totenkopf had 132 panzers on its books.[9] Again if we include assault guns and tank destroyers we can see Das Reich had 174 AFVs while Totenkopf had between 175 and 177.[10] This 20 July AFV status report is of fundamental importance to our understanding of II SS Panzer Korps' losses during Operation *Citadel* and of course the battle of Prokhorovka which, as we know, was fought on 12 July 1943 solely by units of II SS Panzer Korps, principally the Leibstandarte and Das Reich. By comparing the SS divisional inventories at the launch of Operation *Citadel* on 4 July (the offensive began the following day) with those of 10 and 20 July and 1 August we are finally able to obtain the true number of AFV losses II SS Panzer Korps suffered during Operation *Citadel*.[11] The main importance of the 1 August status report is that it allows us to accurately decipher the makeup of the 20 July status report per tank type. This allows us to explore the short-term impact of Operation *Citadel* and the battle of Prokhorovka on the divisions of II SS Panzer Korps (Tables 5 to 12).

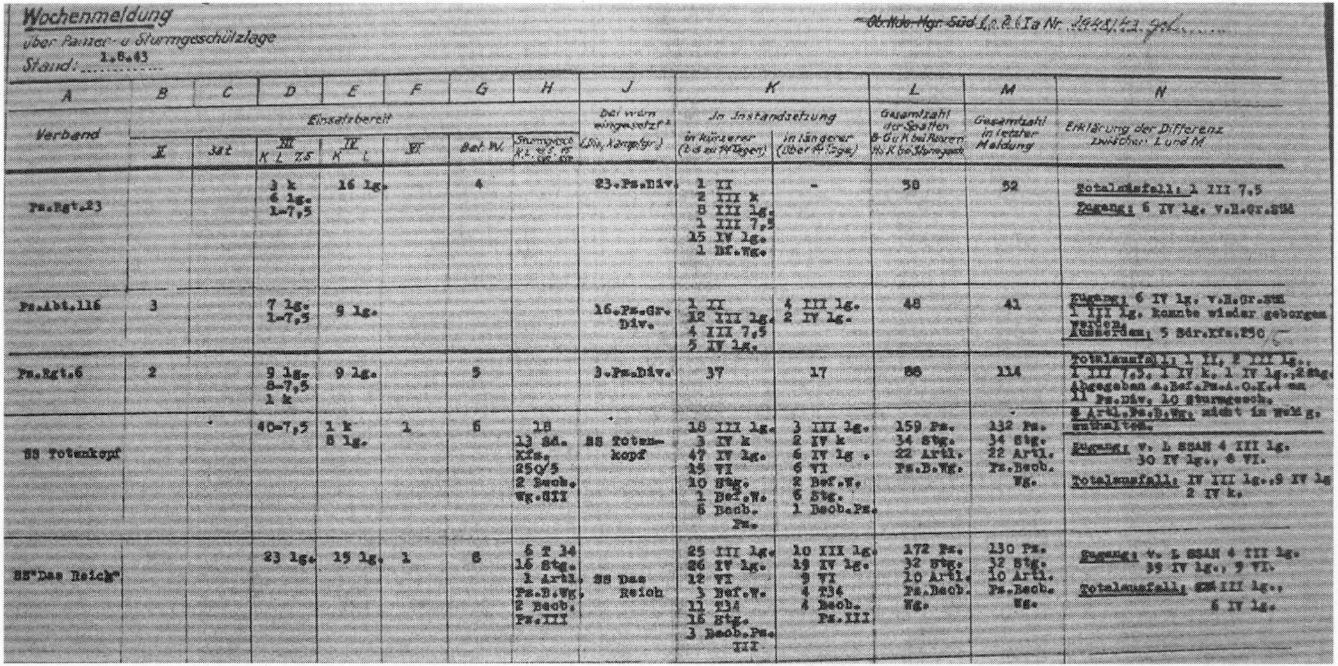

Wochenmeldung
über Panzer- u. Sturmgeschützlage
Stand: 1.8.43

Ob.Kdo. Hgr. Süd I.c. R. I.a Nr. 1944/43 geh.

A	B	C	D	E	F	G	H	J	K		L	M	N
Verband	Einsatzbereit							Bei wem eingesetzt?	In Instandsetzung		Gesamtzahl der Spalten B-G u. K bei Panzern, H u. K bei Sturmgesch.	Gesamtzahl in letzter Meldung	Erklärung der Differenz zwischen L und M
	II	38t	III K L 7.5	IV K L	VI	Bef.W.	Sturmgesch. K L 7,5 15 GK SIG	(Div., Kampfgr.)	in kürzerer (bis zu 14 Tagen)	in längerer (über 14 Tage)			
Pz.Rgt.23			3 k 6 lg. 1-7,5	16 lg.		4		23.Pz.Div.	1 II 2 III k 8 III lg. 1 III 7,5 15 IV lg. 1 Bf.Wg.	-	58	52	Totalausfall: 1 III 7.5 Zugang: 6 IV lg. v.H.Gr.Stl
Pz.Abt.116	3		7 lg. 1-7,5	9 lg.				16.Pz.Gr.Div.	1 II 12 III lg. 4 III 7,5 5 IV lg.	4 III lg. 2 IV lg.	48	41	Zugang: 6 IV lg. v.H.Gr.Stl 1 III lg. konnte wieder geborgen werden. Ausserdem: 5 Sdr.Kfz.250
Pz.Rgt.6	2		9 lg. 8-7,5 1 k	9 lg.		5		3.Pz.Div.	37	17	88	114	Totalausfall: 1 II, 8 III lg., 1 III 7,5, 1 IV k, 1 IV lg., 2 Stg. Abgegeben a.Bef.Pz.A.O.K.4 an 11 Pz.Div. 10 Sturmgesch. 8 Artl.Pz.B.Wg. nicht in Meldg. enthalten.
SS Totenkopf			40-7,5	1 k 8 lg.	1	6	18 13 Sd.Kfz. 250/5 2 Beob.Wg.SIII	SS Totenkopf	18 III lg. 3 IV k 47 IV lg. 15 VI 10 Stg. 1 Bef.W. 6 Beob.Pz.	3 III lg. 2 IV k 6 IV lg. 6 VI 2 Bef.W. 6 Stg. 1 Beob.Pz.	159 Pz. 34 Stg. 22 Artl.Pz.B.Wg.	132 Pz. 34 Stg. 22 Artl.Pz.Beob.Wg.	Zugang: v. L SSAH 4 III lg. 30 IV lg., 6 VI. Totalausfall: IV III lg., 9 IV lg 2 IV k.
SS "Das Reich"			23 lg.	15 lg.	1	6	6 T 34 16 Stg. 1 Artl. Pz.B.Wg. 2 Beob. Pz.III	SS Das Reich	25 III lg. 26 IV lg. 12 VI 3 Bef.W. 11 T34 16 Stg. 3 Beob.Pz.III	10 III lg. 19 IV lg. 9 VI 4 T34 4 Beob.Pz.III	172 Pz. 32 Stg. 10 Artl.Pz.Beob.Wg.	130 Pz. 32 Stg. 10 Artl.Pz.Beob.Wg.	Zugang: v. L SSAH 4 III lg. 39 IV lg., 9 VI. Totalausfall: [illegible] III lg., 6 IV lg.

FIGURE 3. 6th Army, 1a, KTB 9, *Zustandsberichte, Wochenmeldung über Panzer und Sturmgeschülzlage Stand* 1.8.43 (written 6.8.43). (NARA T312, R1483, F000441)

TABLE 5.[12] II SS Panzer Korps – pre-Operation *Citadel* AFV inventory (5.7.43)

	Pz III	Pz IV	T-34	Pz VI	Bef	Total Pz	StuG	Sf Pak	Total AFV
LSSAH inventory 4.7.43	13	83		13	9	118	35	21	174
DR inventory 4.7.43	62	33	24	14	9	142	34	12	188
SS-T inventory 4.7.43	63	52		15	9	139	35	11	185
Total	138	168	24	42	27	399	104	44	547

TABLE 6.[13] II SS Panzer Korps – pre-Operation *Citadel* operational AFV (5.7.43)

	Pz III	Pz IV	T-34	Pz VI	Bef	Total Pz	StuG	Sf Pak	Total AFV
LSSAH operational DR 4.7.43	11	79		12	9	111	34	20	165
DR operational 4.7.43	47	30	18	12	8	115	33	10	158
SS-T operational 4.7.43	59	47		11	8	125	28	11	164
Total	117	156	18	35	25	351	95	41	487

TABLE 7.[14] II SS Panzer Korps – pre-battle of Prokhorovka AFV inventory (12.7.43)

	Pz III	Pz IV	T-34	Pz VI	Bef	Total Pz	StuG	Sf Pak	Total AFV
LSSAH inventory (0100hrs 11.7.43)	12	78		12–13*	9	111–112	33	19	163–164
DR inventory (0100 11.7.43)	60	31	22	13	9	135	34	12	181
SS-T inventory (0100 11.7.43)	61	48		14	9	132	34	11	177
Total	133	157	22	39–40	27	378–379	101	42	521–522

* This depends on which LSSAH Tiger was actually written off.

TABLE 8.[15] II SS Panzer Korps – pre-battle of Prokhorovka operational AFV (12.7.43)

	Pz III	Pz IV	T-34	Pz VI	Bef	Total Pz	StuG	Sf Pak	Total AFV
LSSAH operational 0100hrs 11.7.43	5	41		4	6	56	23	17	96
DR operational 0100 11.7.43	40	16	8	1	5	70	29	11	110
SS-T operational 0100 11.7.43	53	30		11	7	101	21	11	133
Total	98	87	8	16	18	227	73	39	339

TABLE 9.[16] II SS Panzer Korps AFV inventory following Operation *Citadel* and its aftermath (21.7.43)

	Pz III	Pz IV	T-34	Pz VI	Bef	Total Pz	StuG	Sf Pak	Total AFV
LSSAH Inventory 0100hrs 21.7.43 (following *Citadel*)	12	74		12	9	107	32	22	161
DR Inventory 0100 21.7.43 (following *Citadel*)	60	27	21	13	9	130	32	12	174
SS-T Inventory at 0100 21.7.43 (following *Citadel*)	61	48		14	9	132	34	9–11*	175–177
Total	133	149	21	39	27	369	98	43–45	510–512

*2 SS-T Sf Pak lost sometime between 11.7.43 and the end of the Mius operation.

TABLE 10.[17] II SS Panzer Korps operational AFV following Operation *Citadel* and its aftermath (evening 18.7.43)

	Pz III	Pz IV	T-34	Pz VI	Bef	Total Pz	StuG	Sf Pak	Total AFV
LSSAH operational 1925hrs 18.7.43	7	55		9	8	79	28	16	123
DR operational 1925 18.7.43	36	24	17	9	7	93	28	10	131
SS-T operational 1925 18.7.43	30	28		7	7	72	20	3	95
Total	73	107	17	25	22	244	76	29	349

TABLE 11.[18] SS *Sonderverbände* AFV inventory following the capture of Hill 213.9 (1.8.43)

	Pz III	Pz IV	T-34	Pz VI	Bef	Total Pz	StuG	Sf Pak	Total AFV
DR inventory 0100hrs 2.8.43	58*	60	21	22	11*	172	32	12	216
SS-T inventory 0100 2.8.43	61	67		22	9	159	34	9	202
Total	119	127	21	44	20	331	66	21	418

* 2 Pz III lg listed under Bef.

TABLE 12.[19] SS *Sonderverbände* operational AFV following the capture of Hill 213.9 (1.8.43)

	Pz III	Pz IV	T-34	Pz VI	Bef	Total Pz	StuG	Sf Pak	Total AFV
DR operational 0100hrs 2.8.43	23	15	6	1	8	53	16	10	79
SS-T operational 0100 2.8.43	40	9		1	6	56	18	6	80
Total	63	24	6	2	14	109	34	16	159

It is unlikely that any record dealing with large numbers of AFVs is going to be 100 per cent accurate as the odd AFV may well have been reclassified at some point. But there is little doubt the 6th Army *Wochenmeldung* brings us as close as is realistically possible to obtaining a definitive account of II SS Panzer Korps' AFV losses during Operation *Citadel*, and with it the maximum number of German AFV losses that could have occurred during the battle of Prokhorovka.

On the day of the *Wochenmeldung* (1 August) Das Reich and Totenkopf were in the midst of a counteroffensive, launched on 30 July, which aimed to crush the Soviet Mius bridgehead which in turn was centred on Dmitrijewka.[20] The bridgehead had been created following the Red Army's diversionary offensive that had begun on 17 July. The Soviet offensive had been designed to lure the strongest German armoured formations away from the Kharkov area prior to the major Soviet summer offensive in that sector (Operation *Rumyantsev*) which was to be launched on 3 August. This tactic proved entirely successful when II SS Panzer Korps (now including the 3rd Panzer Division as a replacement for the departing Leibstandarte) arrived on the Mius Front.[21]

The *Wochenmeldung* alone provides us with the opportunity to establish the exact number of fully tracked AFVs (bar Panzer I, self-propelled tank destroyers, artillery and heavy infantry guns) in the inventories of Das Reich and Totenkopf directly after their participation in Operation *Citadel* (5–16 July) and its immediate aftermath (17–20 July).[22] From other sources we know the number of new deliveries of AFVs the units of II SS Panzer Korps received at the front between the launch of Operation *Citadel* on 5 July and the end of July. Therefore we can adjust the *Wochenmeldung* inventories accordingly to reflect the actual inventories of the SS divisions at the conclusion of Operation *Citadel*. The only new AFVs dispatched to II SS Panzer Korps were five Panzer VI Tiger tanks which were received by the Leibstandarte on 25 July (on 28 July one of these new Leibstandarte Tigers was transferred to Das Reich, while the other four were transferred to Totenkopf) and four Sf Pak which reached the Leibstandarte front line sometime after 10 July 1943. Having only departed Germany on 6 July it is highly debatable whether these four new Sf Pak reached the Leibstandarte front-line troops prior to the battle of Prokhorovka on 12 July (Tables 13 to 15).[23]

TABLE 13.[24] LSSAH new AFV deliveries, July 1943–March 1944					
Estimated arrival date	Pz IV	Pz V	Pz VI	StuG/StuH	Sf Pak
July	16 (pre-*Citadel*)	71 (joined LS-SAH in Italy)	5 for LSSAH (post-*Citadel*) and 27 for 1 SS Pz Korps (joined LSSAH in Italy)		4 (mid-July)

August	53			9 StuH	6
September					
October	29	96 (Full exchange for unreliable 71 above)			
November	11			24 StuG (14 exchanged for newer models)	
December					
January	20	30 mid-Jan and 14 late Jan		5 StuG	
February			5 late Feb		
March		3 (probably sent to the West)	6 (used with XXXXVIII Pz Korps)		

TABLE 14.[25] DR new AFV deliveries, July 1943–March 1944

Estimated arrival date	Pz IV	Pz V	Pz VI	StuG/ StuH	Sf Pak
July		71 (entered combat with DR 22 Aug)			
August	10 (mid-Aug)				
September		3 (recovery Panthers)	5 (did not arrive)		
October	10 (early October did not reach front by 5.10.43)				
November	10				
December					
January					
February	17	10	5		3 (75mm 38 t)
March					

TABLE 15.[26] SS-T new AFV deliveries, July 1943–March 1944

Estimated arrival date	Pz IV	Pz V	Pz VI	StuG/ StuH	Sf Pak
July					
August					
September					
October	5 (early October did not reach front by 5.10.43) and 5 (mid-late Oct)		5 (either the re-routed DR shipment or 5 assigned to AGS) reached front by 5.10.43		
November	5				11 (75mm 38 t)
December					
January					
February					
March					

As the 1 August *Wochenmeldung* is in reality a 'ten-day' status report for the armoured units of 6th Army, the report also includes the origin and number of new AFV deliveries that had been received by each unit between 21 July and 1 August (in a similar way to the divisional 'ten-day' status reports). The *Wochenmeldung* therefore once again confirms that on 28 July the Leibstandarte transferred the majority of its panzers to Das Reich (4 Panzer III, 39 Panzer IV, 9 Panzer VI) and Totenkopf (4 Panzer III, 30 Panzer IV, 8 Panzer VI).[27] We also have alternative documentary evidence that states the Leibstandarte passed a further three Panzer III to II SS Panzer Korps HQ and retained two Panzer Is, four Panzer IIs, one Panzer III and five Panzer IVs as well as all its StuG assault guns and Sf Pak tank destroyers when it began its transfer to Italy on 29 July.[28] Neither Das Reich nor Totenkopf received any other new AFVs in July 1943.[29] The result of the Leibstandarte additions to Das Reich and Totenkopf inventories are as follows: on 29 July Das Reich had 182 panzers and Totenkopf had 174 panzers.[30] If we include assault guns and tank destroyers Das Reich had 226 AFVs while Totenkopf had between 217 and 219.[31]

PANZER, ASSAULT GUN AND TANK DESTROYER LOSSES

As the *Wochenmeldung* lists the number of AFVs declared to be total losses between 21 July and 1 August per unit, per type, it indicates the intensity of the fighting during the first few days of the Mius counteroffensive and in particular the battle for possession of the key Hill 213.9, which was finally captured on 1 August after a three-day battle.[32] The inclusion of the TF allows us to retrospectively add these losses back to the 1 August Das Reich and Totenkopf inventories in order to further establish both divisions' inventory on 29 July, the day prior to the 30 July launch of the Mius counteroffensive. If we then subtract the recent Leibstandarte additions to Das Reich and Totenkopf we are presented with the final inventories of Das Reich and Totenkopf following their deployment in the Belgorod/Prokhorovka area in Operation *Citadel* and its aftermath – Das Reich 5–17 July and Totenkopf 5–20 July. Most significantly these figures match the number of panzers shown by *Wochenmeldung* as being in Das Reich and Totenkopf inventories on 20 July which is 130 and 132 AFVs respectively. Clearly this further validates the 20 July Das Reich and Totenkopf inventory figures. When we compare the information in the *Wochenmeldung* with the 1–2 July pre-Operation *Citadel* inventories of the three SS divisions and II SS Panzer Korps' engineer's report which covered losses of the Korps in the Belgorod area between 5 and 18 July (updated with information received to 22 July) then we can see that in relation to Totenkopf the results are particularly illuminating.[33]

If we subtract from the 4 July pre-Operation *Citadel* Leibstandarte inventory (118 panzers – not including light panzers) II SS Panzer Korps' engineer's reported panzer losses of 1 Panzer III, 9 Panzer IVs (2 of which were homeland maintenance), 1 Panzer VI (homeland maintenance), therefore 118 - 11 = 107, the panzers passed to II SS Panzer Korps HQ were 3 Panzer IIIs, therefore 107 - 3 = 104, and the small number of panzers that we know were retained by the Leibstandarte being 1 Panzer III, 5 Panzer IVs, 9 Befs, so 104 - 15 = 89, then we are presented with the same number of panzers the *Wochenmeldung* declares the Leibstandarte handed over to Das Reich and Totenkopf being 8 Panzer IIIs, 69 Panzer IVs and 12 Panzer VIs = 89, not including the 5 new Panzer VIs the Leibstandarte received on 25 July.[34] This therefore proves that II SS Panzer Korps' engineer's report gave the correct number of Leibstandarte losses for the period 5–18 July. However, some specific panzer 'losses' were ultimately replaced in the records, like for like, by a panzer of the same type. In practice this meant an additional tank being written off (either 3a or 3b) while another which was at first considered a write-off either physically or administratively returned to service. The author's research has shown that AFV reclassifications were a fairly regular occurrence. For example, during Operation *Citadel* this occurred with Leibstandarte Panzer III 77 604, and potentially with a Leibstandarte Panzer VI – the 'replacement' loss for the latter stemming from the battle of Prokhorovka.[35]

It was planned that once in Italy the Leibstandarte would link up with its I Panzer Battalion (newly equipped with 71 Panthers) and receive a new complement of Panzer IVs for its II Panzer Battalion. The handover of the Leibstandarte's existing 'Prokhorovka' panzers to Das Reich and Totenkopf was scheduled to take place on 28 July. The decision to initiate the transfer of the Leibstandarte tanks involved Hitler who on 26 July ordered that the division leave behind all its tanks in order to boost the strength of Das Reich and Totenkopf. The Chief of the Army General Staff Kurt Zeitzler expressed his concern that the Leibstandarte would not voluntarily hand over all their tanks – Zeitzler's concerns were not without foundation. The next day, the Leibstandarte reported that it would transfer 11 Panzer IIIs, 69 Panzer IVs and 17 Tigers the following day. Taking into account the losses sustained during Operation *Citadel*, we can see this meant that the Leibstandarte was refraining from transferring one Panzer III and five Panzer IVs from its panzer regiment's inventory. Table 16 lists those tanks that the Leibstandarte transferred to its sister SS units on 28 July and to what extent this bolstered Das Reich's and Totenkopf's inventories.

TABLE 16.[36] LSSAH transfer of panzers to DR and SS-T, 28.7.43									
	Pz III	Pz IV	T-34	Pz VI	Bef	Total Pz	StuG	Sf Pak	Total AFV
LSSAH Inventory 0100hrs 19.7.43 (following *Citadel*)	12	74		12	9	107	32	22	161
LSSAH Inventory 25.7.43	12	74		17	9	112	32	22	166
Transferred to DR on 28.7.43	4	39		9	0	52	0	0	52
Transferred to SS-T on 28.7.43	4	30		8	0	42	0	0	42
Transferred to II SS Pz Korps HQ on 28.7.43	3	0		0	0	3	0	0	3
LSSAH Inventory 29.7.43 (following transfer to DR, SS-T and II SS Pz Korps HQ)	1	5		0	9	15	32	22	69
DR Inventory 0100 21.7.43 (following *Citadel*)	60	27	21	13	9	130	32	12	174
DR Inventory 29.7.43 (following LSSAH transfer)	64	66	21	22	9	182	32	12	226

SS-T Inventory at 0100 21.7.43 (following *Citadel*)	61	48		14	9	132	34	9–11*	175–177
SS-T Inventory 29.7.43 (following LSSAH transfer)	65	78		22	9	174	34	9–11*	217–219

*2 SS-T Sf Paks were lost sometime between 11.7.43 and the end of the Mius operation.

There are a number of ways we can substantiate that the Leibstandarte kept one Panzer III and five Panzer IV 'Prokhorovka'-era tanks in its inventory apart from the simple mathematical calculation of panzers transferred added to panzers recorded as having been lost (either TF or sent for homeland repair) during Operation *Citadel*. We can establish with confidence that four of the five retained Panzer IVs were significantly damaged and that they required extensive repairs that were assessed would take over three weeks to complete. Sadly the Leibstandarte produced no further chassis number inventory reports, so it is not possible to identify exactly which specific tanks remained with the Leibstandarte.

On 20 August, the Leibstandarte, by now in northern Italy, reported that it had four Panzer IIs, one Panzer III, 58 Panzer IVs, 71 Panzer Vs (Panthers), nine Panzer Befs (command tanks) and 27 Tigers in its inventory.[37] This included its returning I Battalion with its mechanically troublesome Panthers and two companies of Tigers from the still forming Heavy SS Panzer Abteilung of the equally new I SS Panzer Korps 'Leibstandarte' (the Tigers would be used by the Leibstandarte division in a single standard, but greatly expanded, heavy company).[38] As Table 13 indicated, the Leibstandarte received 53 new Panzer IV in August for its II Battalion.[39] On Hitler's orders, the Leibstandarte was not initially re-equipped with a full-strength Panzer IV battalion. Hitler felt this was unnecessary as the division would be amply equipped with Tigers and Panthers.[40] As a result of Hitler's micromanagement no more Panzer IVs were issued to the Leibstandarte until October 1943, by which time the Leibstandarte was preparing for transfer back to the Eastern Front.[41] As no further Panzer IVs were sent to the Leibstandarte in Italy it is clear the division must have retained five of its 'Prokhorovka' Panzer IVs.

Another indicator that the Leibstandarte retained some 'Prokhorovka'-era Panzer IVs can be found in the Leibstandarte monthly *Meldung* for 1 September and 1 October. These reports respectively, list 50 Panzer IVs and 53 Panzer IVs as being operational with the division while also listing four Panzer IVs and one Panzer IV respectively being repairable within three weeks.[42] To the uninformed the 1 October *Meldung* gives the impression that just one Panzer IV was brought from the Eastern Front to Italy. The

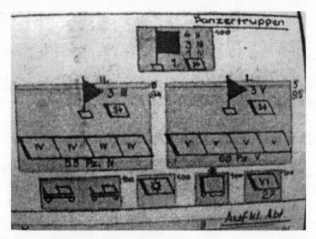

FIGURE 4. GenInsp.d.Pz.Truppen, Waffen-SS monthly divisional *Meldung* and OB charts, LSSAH, 1.10.43. (NARA T78, R719)

accompanying Order of Battle for SS Panzer Regiment 1 for 1 October (see Figure 4) also lists (alongside the new shipment of 53 Panzer IVs) one Panzer IV as belonging to the Panzer Regiment's staff together with Panzer Bef (listed as Panzer III) and the four Panzer IIs which were also retained by the Leibstandarte.[43]

In fact, we know the Panzer IV in question had been converted into a command tank (Bef – tactical number 055) and belonged to the commander of the Leibstandarte's Panzer Regiment. Visual evidence exists of the Leibstandarte command Stab (staff) travelling by rail with its 'Prokhorovka' panzers through the unique surroundings of the Semmering Pass, conducting repairs and parading in northern Italy.[44] It seems clear, however, that the Order of Battle chart like the *Meldung* for 1 October only included tanks which were operational or expected to return to action within three weeks.[45] Following 10 July 1943 (during Operation *Citadel*), the next surviving divisional Leibstandarte ten-day armoured status report dates from 1 November as the Leibstandarte prepared to re-enter combat on the Eastern Front.[46] It reports the arrival of the next shipment of 29 Panzer IVs for a collective *Ist* total of 87 Panzer IVs, including six Panzer IVs which were under long-term repair (these latter tanks would not all have appeared in the previous *Meldung* reports). Clearly, the Leibstandarte had 58 Panzer IVs prior to these latest 29 additions; it is also clear that the Leibstandarte had the same 58 Panzer IVs in its inventory on 20 August prior to the *Meldung* for September and October.[47] Given our knowledge of the dates new tanks were received by the Leibstandarte during this period, it is clear that the August shipment of 53 Panzer IVs were additions to the original five 'Prokhorovka' Panzer IVs which had not been transferred to Das Reich and Totenkopf along with the other 69 'Prokhorovka' Panzer IVs on 28 July.[48] As four of the five 'Prokhorovka'-era Panzer IVs were not listed in the *Meldung*, there is little doubt they were undergoing long-term repair.[49] The visual evidence of 055 alone highlights that the precedent had been set for the Leibstandarte to retain small numbers of ex-'Prokhorovka' Panzer IVs – clearly this was in defiance of Hitler's 26 July command and confirmed Zeitzler's suspicions regarding the Leibstandarte.[50] The Leibstandarte ten-day status report from the start of November also lists the last remaining short-barrelled Panzer III and the presence of the division's existing complement of StuG and Sf tank destroyers.[51] As Table 13 indicates it was also during this period that the Leibstandarte received 24 new StuGs and returned 14 of its original ex-'Prokhorovka' complement of StuGs. This further reduced the number of AFVs which had been with the Leibstandarte during the battle of Prokhorovka. The Leibstandarte did not re-enter combat on the Eastern Front until mid-November 1943.[52]

With regards to the transfer of 17 Leibstandarte Tiger tanks to Das Reich (9) and Totenkopf (8), it is interesting to note that eight of the nine Tigers received by Das Reich were pre-Operation *Citadel* originals.[53] Therefore on 28 July, Das Reich only took possession of one of the new batch of five Tigers that the Leibstandarte had received on 25 July (250 197 – which was most likely a command Tiger). Conversely, Totenkopf as a result received an even split of new (4) and original Leibstandarte Tigers (4). From a chronological perspective, we are fortunate that all nine of Das Reich's ex-Leibstandarte Tigers survived until the Das Reich 31 October inventory. This was the first Das Reich inventory or ten-day armoured status report (they were subsequently coupled together) to have survived since the division had returned to 4th Panzer Army control. The 31 October report has enabled the identification of these Das Reich Tigers (see Appendix E) and as a consequence the makeup of Totenkopf's contingent of Tigers. Das Reich received no other new (factory new) Tigers between the 28 July Leibstandarte transfer and the late October inventory (a scheduled October delivery of five Tigers did not arrive); so it is possible to identify Das Reich's sole 'new' ex-Leibstandarte Tiger as 250 197 (received by Leibstandarte on 25 July) – Das Reich tended to list its AFVs in its inventory by the chronological order it received them.[54] For example, Das Reich lists first its own Tigers received at the turn of 1942/43; then those Das Reich received in May 1943; and only then the ex-Leibstandarte Tigers. The eight pre-*Citadel* ex-Leibstandarte Tigers are listed first followed by 250 197. The Leibstandarte cluster of Tiger tanks is not listed in order of age; Das Reich did not know – or perhaps care – which tanks the Leibstandarte had received first in 1942/43; however, it would have been obvious to Das Reich that 250 197 had not yet seen combat. This therefore accounts for its position in the inventory. The 31 October Das Reich report also lists one other Tiger (250 147) which was received that month; the report states the Tiger was commandeered in October from an unspecified unit or source (we are fortunate that the report lists this detailed clarifying information).

In regard to the Leibstandarte assault guns the 1 September divisional *Meldung* states that the Leibstandarte still had 32 StuGs on hand which correctly matches the three total losses reported by II SS Panzer Korps' engineer. The Leibstandarte began Operation *Citadel* with 35 StuGs. The *Meldung* also states the division was issued with nine new StuH in Italy.[55] In terms of tank destroyers we know from the daily operational strength report of 24 July that the Leibstandarte had all of its 22 Sf Pak operational, including the four new Sf Pak additions. This therefore confirms that II SS Panzer Korps' engineer correctly listed three Sf Pak as losses, two as a total loss and one in need of homeland maintenance repair (3a). The Leibstandarte began Operation *Citadel* with 21 Sf Paks in its inventory.[56] The 1 September *Meldung* also states that the Leibstandarte received a further six new Sf Paks in addition to the four Sf Paks it had received in July after the battle of Prokhorovka.[57]

The total number of panzers that the 6th Army's *Wochenmeldung* stated Das Reich held in its inventory on 20 July was 130, while on 1 August the report declared that 182 panzers were with Das Reich (the latter after retrospective addition of the ten losses that appear in *Wochenmeldung*; these losses occurred between 30 July and 1 August 1943 during the Mius offensive, 172 + 10 = 182). These figures match per tank type the 20 July *Wochenmeldung* panzer inventory for Das Reich (130, which was also Das Reich's final inventory following Operation *Citadel*) after we remove from the updated 1 August figure the recent 28 July Leibstandarte additions (182 - 52 = 130, 2 Panzer III lg had been included, either in error or by design, alongside the division's Bef Panzer III).[58] While if we remove II SS Panzer Korps' engineer's reported losses and the 3 T-34 losses (together 12 total losses) from Das Reich's pre-Operation *Citadel* 142-strong panzer inventory (142 - 12 = 130) this also gives us the *Wochenmeldung* 20 July panzer inventory of 130.[59] These calculations mutually corroborate in respect to Das Reich's panzer inventory (per tank type) all elements of the 6th Army *Wochenmeldung* and II SS Panzer Korps engineer's reported losses.

By following the same formula we can see that the *Wochenmeldung* and II SS Panzer Korps engineer report are also in alignment in respect to Das Reich's assault gun strength on 20 July and 1 August (both 32). Das Reich began Operation *Citadel* with 34 StuGs while II SS Panzer Korps' engineer reported two StuG losses.[60] Although the *Wochenmeldung* did not record tank destroyer strengths we know that II SS Panzer Korps' engineer's report was also correct to declare that Das Reich suffered no Sf Pak losses during

Operation *Citadel*. We know this as on 11 August the division reported that all 12 of its Sf Paks were operational – no new Sf Paks were issued prior to this date.[61]

Therefore, we can say with confidence that II SS Panzer Korps' engineer's losses report is accurate in terms of the number of declared AFV losses for both the Leibstandarte and Das Reich (bar T-34s) for the period 5–18 July. The Leibstandarte and Das Reich along with II SS Panzer Korps HQ withdrew from the front on 17 July. Given that II SS Panzer Korps' engineer's report covered AFV reclassifications up to 22 July, this must have given adequate time for an accurate report to be filed in regard to these two divisions (though of course as already mentioned like-for-like reclassifications in the report still occurred).

The *Wochenmeldung* provided the first accurate account of the number of T-34 losses Das Reich sustained during Operation *Citadel*. Das Reich began Operation *Citadel* with 24 T-34s in its inventory (Plate 5). The use of T-34s by Das Reich (reportedly obtained from the tank factory in Kharkov) was a stop-gap measure prior to the arrival of Das Reich's Panther battalion (Das Reich's Panthers would first enter combat west of Kharkov on 22 August 1943). The T-34s were also used extensively in the Mius counter-attack. We know that Das Reich lost two T-34s prior to 11 July 1943 as they appear in the 5–10 July 1943 Das Reich and Totenkopf total loss report (Figure 5). II SS Panzer Korps' engineer's loss report did not record Das Reich's T-34 losses. However, the fact that the 1 August *Wochenmeldung* states Das Reich had an inventory of 21 T-34s, indicates that one further T-34 was lost between 11 and 20 July.[62] Each of Das Reich's T-34s had undergone fairly extensive reconditioning prior to Operation *Citadel*. For example, they were converted to carry a two-way radio. Therefore it is extremely doubtful that Das Reich had the time or will to adapt any further T-34s as replacements during this period as the repair troops would have had other priorities.[63]

What is perhaps most interesting about the 6th Army *Wochenmeldung* is that unlike the Leibstandarte and Das Reich elements of the report those regarding Totenkopf for 20 July and 1 August (again including the 30 July–1 August Mius offensive losses) do not align with II SS Panzer Korps' engineer's report after the latter's reported losses have been subtracted from Totenkopf's pre-Operation *Citadel* inventory. The Totenkopf *Wochenmeldung* status for 20 July and 1 August tells us that, after comparison with the Totenkopf pre-Operation *Citadel* inventory and the 5–10 July Totenkopf total loss report, Totenkopf in fact lost no panzers (TF or 3a) between 11 and 20 July – a quite remarkable revelation.[64]

The total number of panzers the 6th Army *Wochenmeldung* declared Totenkopf possessed on 1 August was 174 (after the retrospective addition

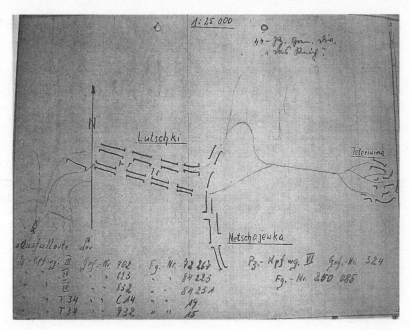

FIGURE 5. Extract showing majority of DR panzer 5–10.7.43 losses. DR's other AFV loss during this period (Pz III 73 102) can be found on a separate page: 4th Panzer Army, O.Qu.V. V, DR and SS-T, Betr.: Totalausfälle an Pz. Kpfwg. und gep. Kfz. 1-10.7.43, Lageskizzen written 23.7.43. (NARA T313, R390)

of the 15 Mius offensive losses of 30 July–1 August, 159 + 15 = 174). After the removal of the recent 42 Leibstandarte additions from this figure (174 - 42 = 132) we are given the number of panzers shown as being in the *Wochenmeldung* Totenkopf inventory on 20 July which was 132. II SS Panzer Korps' engineer reported a total of 12 Totenkopf panzers as being lost between 5 and 18 July, while the Totenkopf pre-Operation *Citadel* panzer inventory stood at 139. However, when we subtract 12 tanks from the pre-Operation *Citadel* inventory of 139 (139 - 12 = 127) we can see that there is a five-tank deficit between the 132 panzer inventory total reported in the 20 July *Wochenmeldung*. The 5–10 July Das Reich and Totenkopf loss report and the 1–10 July Totenkopf ten-day status report both confirm that Totenkopf lost seven panzers in the early part of Operation *Citadel*, which meant Totenkopf closed 10 July with a panzer inventory of 132, which is of course the same total reported by the 20 July *Wochenmeldung* status report (see Table 4 and Figure 6).[65]

The *Wochenmeldung* Totenkopf status of 20 July cannot in fact be a delayed (or duplicated) reporting of Totenkopf's earlier 10 July status report as quite obviously the distribution of panzers in the 1 August status would also be in

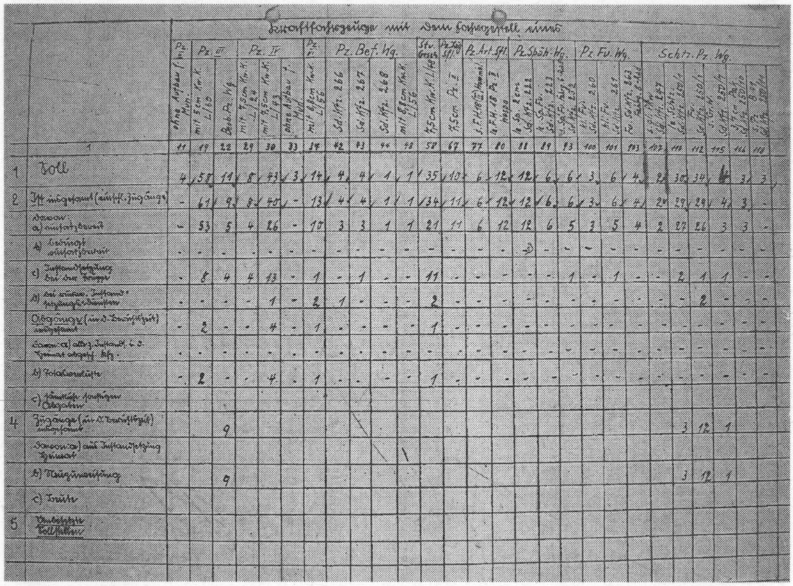

	Pz. I/II	Pz. III		Pz. IV			Pz. VI	Pz. Bef. Wg.				Stu. Gesch.	Pz. Jäg. Sfl.	Pz. Art. Sfl.		Pz. Späh-Wg.			Pz. Fu. Wg.			Schtz. Pz. Wg.					
1	11	19	22	29	30	33	34	42	43	44	48	58	67	77	80	81	89	93	100	101	103	107	111	112	115	116	118
1 Soll	4	58	11	8	43	3	14	4	4	1	1	35	10	6	12	12	6	6	3	6	4	22	30	34	[illegible]	3	3
2 Ist insgesamt (einschl. Zugänge)	-	61	9	8	40	-	13	4	4	1	1	34	11	6	12	12	6	6	3	6	4	24	29	29	4	3	-
davon: a) einsatzbereit	-	53	5	4	26	-	10	3	3	1	1	21	11	6	12	12	6	5	3	5	4	2	27	26	3	3	-
b) bedingt einsatzbereit	-	-	-	-	-	-	-	-	-	-	-	-	-	-	-	1)	-	-	-	-	-	-	-	-	-	-	-
c) Instandsetzung bei der Truppe	-	8	4	4	13	-	1	-	1	-	-	11	-	-	-	-	-	1	-	1	-	-	2	1	1	-	-
d) bei außer. Instandsetzungsdiensten	-	-	-	-	1	-	2	1	-	-	-	2	-	-	-	-	-	-	-	-	-	-	-	2	-	-	-
Abgänge (in d. Berichtszeit) insgesamt	-	2	-	-	4	-	1	-	-	-	-	1	-	-	-	-	-	-	-	-	-	-	-	-	-	-	-
davon: a) [illegible]	-	-	-	-	-	-	-	-	-	-	-	-	-	-	-	-	-	-	-	-	-	-	-	-	-	-	-
b) Totalverluste	-	2	-	-	4	-	1	-	-	-	-	1	-	-	-	-	-	-	-	-	-	-	-	-	-	-	-
c) sämtliche sonstigen Abgaben																											
4 Zugänge (in d. Berichtszeit) insgesamt			9																			3	12	1			
davon: a) aus Instandsetzung Heimat																											
b) Neuzuweisung			9																			3	12	1			
c) Beute																											
5 Unbesetzte Sollstellen																											

FIGURE 6. 4th Panzer Army, O.Qu.V. V, SS-T, Gep. Kfz. Bestandsmeldung, 1–10.7.43. (NARA T313, R390)

error. The distribution of panzers on 1 August into categories of operational, short-term damaged, long-term damaged, new and lost panzers has clearly been undertaken in great detail. This information could only have been offered on or after 1 August. The fact that the 1 August Totenkopf panzer status can then be traced back accurately to 20 July by removing the various losses and new additions between those dates proves that the 20 July *Wochenmeldung* figure for Totenkopf is indeed factual.[66]

The fact that the Leibstandarte and Das Reich elements of the *Wochenmeldung* and II SS Panzer Korps' engineer report are in alignment gives us confidence that the *Wochenmeldung* is overall an accurate document. The *Wochenmeldung* status report for 1 August reported that total losses in the first three days, by far the most intense period, of the four-day battle on the Mius were as follows. For Das Reich four Panzer IIIs and six Panzer IVs. The Das Reich Panzer III figure is unclear in the original document – but this has been substantiated by removing the clearly stated six Panzer IV losses from the 29 July Das Reich panzer inventory total of 182 (182 - 6 = 176) which means four Panzer IIIs must have also been lost in order for the confirmed 1 August panzer inventory total of 172 to be met. Totenkopf lost four Panzer III lg, nine Panzer IV lg and two Panzer IV kz. Clearly the short Mius offensive was proving very costly for both of the SS divisions.[67] The intensity of the fighting on the first day of the battle for Hill 213.9 is highlighted by a 2330hrs 30 July

1. The assault gun (StuG) had a powerful 75mm main gun which was similar to that used in the upgraded Panzer IV medium tank. (NARA)

2. The Marder tank destroyer also had a powerful 75mm main gun; however, weak armour meant it was vulnerable to attack. (NARA)

3. The Soviet SU-76 assault gun mounted the 76mm main gun on the T-70 light tank's chassis; typically this gun was seen on the medium T-34 tank. (Dreamstime.com)

4. The Soviet SU-122 assault gun mounted a 122mm howitzer on the T-34's chassis. (Dreamstime.com)

5. In March 1943, Das Reich captured 24 new Soviet T-34s in Kharkov; the tanks were absorbed into the division's inventory. (NARA)

6. Das Reich's sole Tiger tank (chassis number 250 085) loss during Operation *Citadel* occurred during the period 5–10 July. Note the Tiger's 88mm main gun. (Author's collection)

7. Leibstandarte troops training with the powerful 75mm Pak 40 in May 1943. (Bundesarchiv).

8. At 1000hrs on 10 July, the Leibstandarte renewed its drive on Prokhorovka. All subsequent Waffen-SS Photographer plates appear in chronological order. (NARA)

9. The attack outflanked the strong Soviet defensive positions around Hill 258.2 on the Teterevino–Prokhorovka road, 10 July. (NARA)

10. At Teterevino we see Panzer IVs of the Leibstandarte's 7th Panzer Company awaiting their turn to advance, 10 July. (NARA)

11. The village of Teterevino no longer exists. (Google Earth)

12. At 1000hrs, Das Reich first engaged Soviet armour to the east and advanced the short distance to the Prokhorovka–Belgorod railway line, 10 July. (NARA)

13. At 1345hrs, Das Reich drove north, parallel with the Prokhorovka–Belgorod railway line. Das Reich's 1943 two bar divisional insignia is clearly visible on its Panzer III and IV, 10 July. (Getty Images)

14. By 1500hrs, Das Reich's armour (including the Panzer IIIs shown here) had pivoted and crossed the Prokhorovka–Belgorod railway line, 10 July. (NARA)

15. At Teterevino the II SS Panzer Korps' Nebelwerfer troops attempted to further suppress the Soviet defenders, 10 July. (NARA)

16. The Leibstandarte panzers soon discovered that the Teterevino–Prokhorovka road had been mined, 10 July. (NARA)

17. The relaxed nature of the Leibstandarte panzer troops clearly indicates that combat was not expected, 10 July. (NARA)

18. The order is soon given to leave the Teterevino–Prokhorovka road. The Leibstandarte Panzer Regiment's Aufklärung Zug leads the way, 10 July. (NARA)

19. The Leibstandarte's 'Wespe' 105mm self-propelled artillery supported the advance, 10 July. (NARA)

20. Officers of Leibstandarte's Panzer Regiment taking cover behind one of the division's Bef (Command) tanks, 10 July. (NARA)

21. At 1300hrs the Leibstandarte Panzer Regiment resumed the advance, this time under combat conditions, 10 July. (NARA)

22. Once again Panzer IVs of the Leibstandarte's Panzer Regiment's Aufklärung Zug were in the vanguard of the advance, 10 July. (NARA)

23. By 1420hrs the Leibstandarte had occupied Komsomolets State Farm and the heights of Hill 241.6, 10 July. (NARA)

24. At Komsomolets state farm the Leibstandarte's 'Hummel' 150mm self-propelled artillery were aimed across the river Psel, 10 July. (NARA)

25. The farm at Komsomolets. (Google Earth)

26. On the evening of 10 July the Leibstandarte began to prepare for the following day's assault on Prokhorovka. (NARA)

27. The majority of the Leibstandarte's SPW were also repositioned for the coming drive on Prokhorovka, 10 July. (NARA)

28. At 0450hrs on 11 July the final drive on Prokhorovka began. The Leibstandarte defeated numerous armoured counter-attacks. (NARA)

29. The right flank of the assault advanced along the Teterevino–Prokhorovka road and the Prokhorovka–Belgorod railway embankment, 11 July. (NARA)

30. The Prokhorovka–Belgorod railway line's embankment offered the Leibstandarte troops excellent flank protection, 11 July. (NARA)

31. In this image we see an anti-tank gun being brought forward past resting troops of the 2nd SS Panzergrenadier Regiment, 11 July. (NARA)

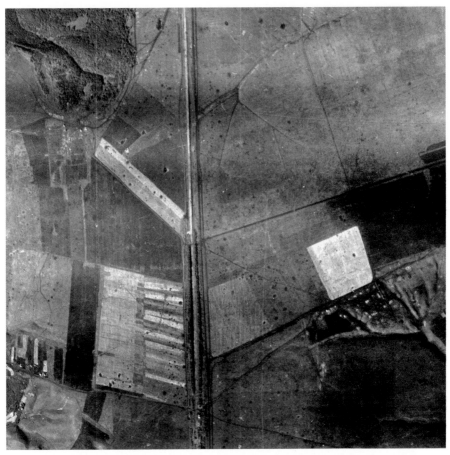

32. The battlefield of 29th Tank Corps. The main Teterevino/Belgorod (top) – Prokhorovka (bottom) road/rail route splits the picture, 16 July. (NARA)

33. A contemporary perspective of the 29th Tank Corps battlefield. (Google Earth)

34. The battlefield of 18th Tank Corps (the location of the tank corps' morning breakthrough), 16 July. (NARA)

35. The battlefield of 18th Tank Corps (the late morning battlefield of 181st Tank Brigade vs. Leibstandarte Tiger Company), 14 July. (NARA)

36. A contemporary perspective of the 18th Tank Corps battlefield (for orientation note the anti-tank ditch crossing point, bottom left of image, and compare this with Plate 33). (Google Earth)

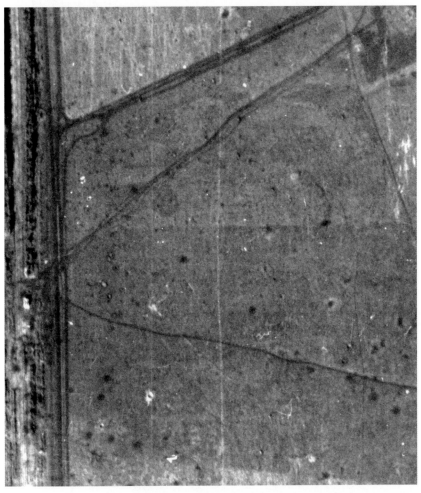

37. The battlefield beyond Hill 252.2, 16 July. (NARA)

38. The second field from the anti-tank ditch includes the crest of Hill 252.2, 16 July. (NARA)

39. The second field from the anti-tank ditch includes the crest of Hill 252.2, 7 August. (NARA)

40. The second field from the anti-tank ditch includes the crest of Hill 252.2. (Google Earth)

41. Looking up to the crest of Hill 252.2 from the parallel road. (Google Earth)

42. Looking down the slope of Hill 252.2 to the anti-tank ditch from the parallel road (the gap through the trees, centre, gives an excellent impression of the view in 1943). (Google Earth)

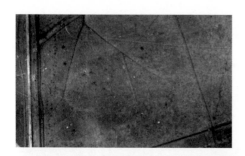

43. The first field in front of the anti-tank ditch, 16 July. (NARA)

44. The first field in front of the anti-tank ditch, 7 August. (NARA)

45. The first field in front of the anti-tank ditch. (Google Earth)

46. The anti-tank ditch three weeks before the battle, 22 June. (NARA)

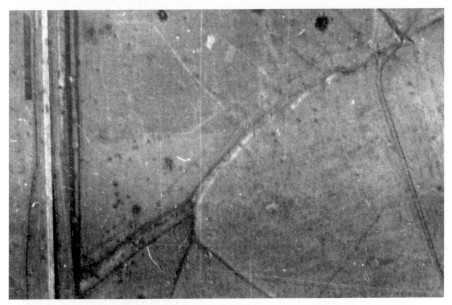

47. The anti-tank ditch, 16 July. (NARA)

48. The anti-tank ditch today is packed with trees. (Google Earth)

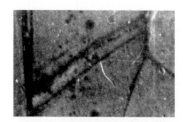

49. The left half of the anti-tank ditch, 16 July. (NARA)

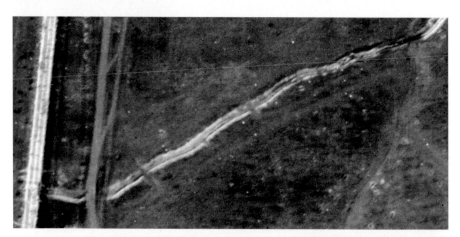

50. The left half of the anti-tank ditch, 7 August. (NARA)

51. The left half of the anti-tank ditch. (Google Earth)

II SS Panzer Korps loss report that stated that Das Reich suffered 25 panzers lost or damaged, while the same report declared Totenkopf had suffered as many as 48 panzers (including eight Tigers) and 12 StuGs lost or damaged (Figures 7 to 10).[68]

Given the high number of AFV causalities Totenkopf had suffered between 30 July and 1 August and the knowledge that Totenkopf had not engaged in any serious fighting between 19 and 29 July one has to conclude that all of

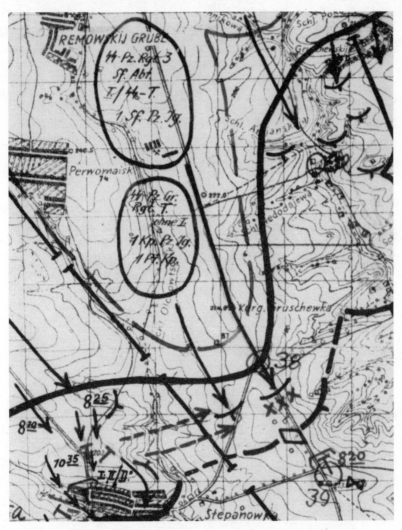

FIGURE 7. SS-T assault on Hill 213.9, 30.7.43. II SS Panzer Korps, Bereitstellung des II SS Panzer Korps am 29.7.3 und Verlauf des 30.7.43. (NARA T354, R606, F000050-51)

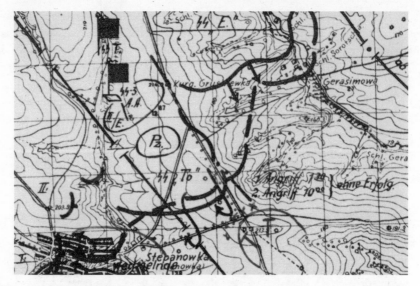

FIGURE 8. SS-T assault on Hill 213.9, 31.7.43. II SS Panzer Korps, Verlauf des 31.7.43. (NARA T354, R606, F000052-53)

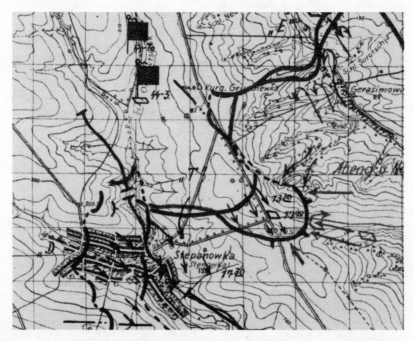

FIGURE 9. SS-T capture of Hill 213.9, 1.8.43. II SS Panzer Korps, Verlauf des 1.8.43. (NARA T354, R606, F000055-56)

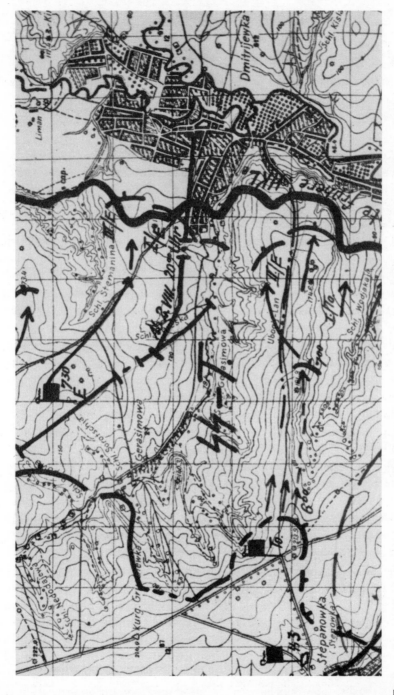

FIGURE 10. SS-T advance to the Mius, 2.8.43. II SS Panzer Korps, Verlauf des 2.8.43. (NARA T354, R606, F000059)

Totenkopf's 21 July–1 August reported losses must have occurred following the commencement of the Mius offensive on 30 July and were not late additions from the *Citadel* era. Totenkopf losses during the Mius offensive were greater than Das Reich because Totenkopf conducted a costly frontal assault on the extremely well-fortified and defended Hill 213.9; Das Reich was attempting to outflank the hill from the south and as a result avoided the worst fighting.[69]

SUPPORTING EVIDENCE

There are a number of factors that help us understand why there is a discrepancy between II SS Panzer Korps' engineer's reported panzer losses for 5–18 July for Totenkopf and those indicated by the post-*Citadel* inventories for 20 July and 1 August for the same division that can be found in the 6th Army's *Wochenmeldung*.[70]

On 17 July, II SS Panzer Korps HQ (along with the Korps' engineer), the Leibstandarte and Das Reich disengaged from the front. On 18 July these units then began travelling south to 1st Panzer Army's sector in order to prepare to face the forming Soviet bridgehead on the Donets (Figures 11 and 12). As a result, Totenkopf was from 18 July no longer under II SS Panzer Korps' control. Instead, Totenkopf fought further defensive battles until 20 July under the command of XXXXVIII Panzer Korps on which date it also disengaged and began to be transported south to 6th Army's sector – where it would re-join II SS Panzer Korps prior to the Mius attack. As a result, from 18 July there was a physical separation between II SS Panzer Korps' engineer and Totenkopf that simply did not exist between II SS Panzer Korps' engineer and the Leibstandarte and Das Reich. This may have had a bearing on the ability of II SS Panzer Korps' engineer to source up-to-date and accurate information regarding Totenkopf AFV losses. Although II SS Panzer Korps' engineer made amendments to his report until 22 July this is unlikely to have clarified matters in regards to Totenkopf AFV losses as by this stage all three divisions and II SS Panzer Korps HQ were in the midst of a transport either to 1st Panzer Army on the Donets (HQ, Leibstandarte and Das Reich) or 6th Army on the Mius (Totenkopf).[71]

The final day that Totenkopf's panzer regiment was engaged in major defensive operations was 18 July 1943. On 19 July it may have been called upon to repel a minor attack by 15 Soviet tanks (apparently eight Soviet tanks were destroyed), while on the 20th Totenkopf's panzer regiment did not engage in any action prior to its departure from 4th Panzer Army control at 2100hrs that night. Therefore Totenkopf AFV losses between 19 and 20 July are extremely unlikely to have occurred. As Totenkopf compiled its own status reports, the division would have had plenty of time to source and report correct

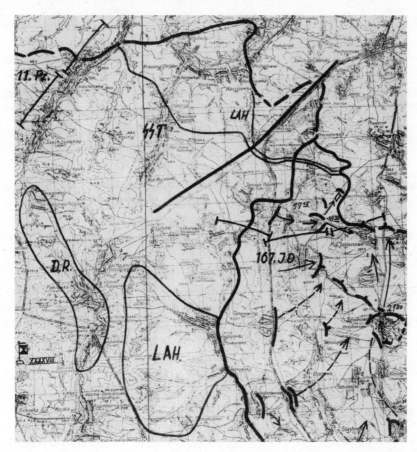

FIGURE 11. II SS Panzer Korps, Map of Korps actions, new and proposed front lines 14–18.7.43. (NARA T354, R606, F000035)

AFV information to its controlling XXXXVIII Panzer Korps and 4th Panzer Army prior to the 20 July status report being issued. However, at this stage we cannot say for sure which controlling staff actually issued the original 20 July status report. As already mentioned, Totenkopf left XXXXVIII Panzer Korps and 4th Panzer Army control on the evening of the 20th to begin its transfer south to the Mius. Therefore, we are extremely fortunate that the 20 July status report for Totenkopf is included in the 1 August 6th Army *Wochenmeldung*.[72]

In the event, on 24 July Hitler cancelled the 1st Panzer Army's Donets operation at the last moment with the Leibstandarte and Das Reich already in their assembly areas for the offensive (Figure 13 – the Soviet bridgehead had been contained prior to the Leibstandarte and Das Reich arrival). Both divisions then continued south to 6th Army's sector arriving on 25–26 July. Totenkopf due to transportation delays did not arrive with 6th Army until

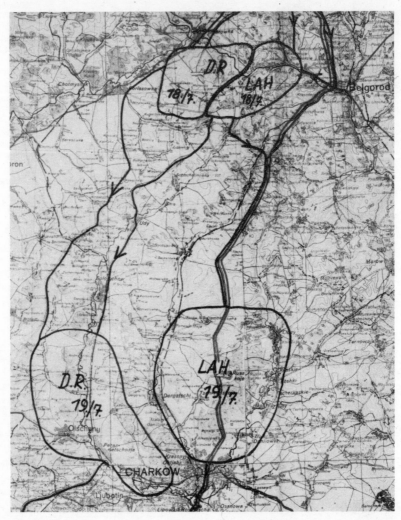

FIGURE 12. II SS Panzer Korps, Ablauf der Marschbewegungen II SS Panzer Korps, 18–22.7.43. (NARA T354, R606, F000038)

26–27 July (Figure 14). Therefore the physical separation between Totenkopf and II SS Panzer Korps' engineer stretched between 18 and 26 July. The various transports which took place over this period would have hardly aided II SS Panzer Korps HQ's effective evaluation of the Totenkopf AFV status. It seems a real possibility that II SS Panzer Korps' engineer, due to his remoteness from Totenkopf, was out of touch with the real situation on the ground in regards to Totenkopf AFV losses in the latter stages of Operation *Citadel* and the offensive's immediate aftermath.[73]

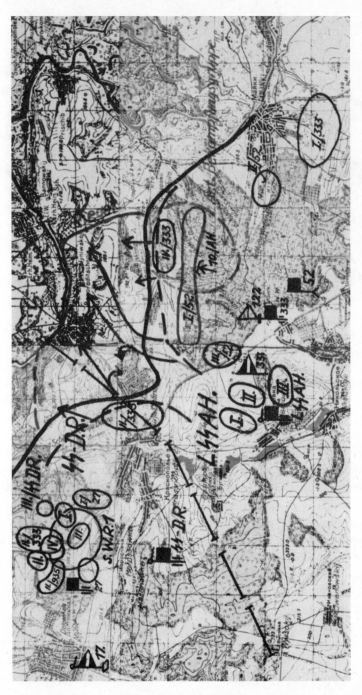

FIGURE 13. Leibstandarte and Das Reich plan of attack with 1st Panzer Army, 24.7.43. II SS Panzer Korps, Bereitstellungs u. Angriffsplan für den Angriff am 24.7.43. (NARA T354, R606, F000040)

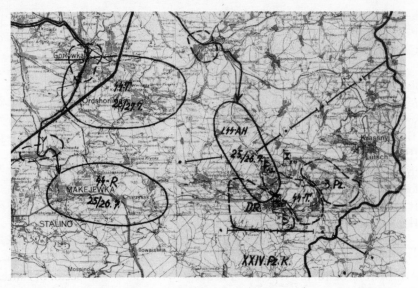

FIGURE 14. II SS Panzer Korps, Ablauf der Marschbewegungen II SS Panzer Korps, 24–29.7.43. (NARA T354, R606, F000043)

II SS Panzer Korps' engineer's report makes clear that two of Totenkopf's tanks (one Panzer III and one Panzer IV) which were initially recorded as total losses had in fact already been recovered and repaired. This obviously sets a precedent for errors in the reporting of Totenkopf AFV losses in the report; perhaps pertinently no such errors were reported by the engineer in regards to the Leibstandarte or Das Reich losses. As discussed, AFV damage/loss classifications were in a constant state of flux. There were many examples of panzers initially being reported as total losses (3b) only to be later reclassified as needing factory repair (3a) or even rapidly returning to service. There are also instances of tanks, despite being listed as TF or requiring factory repair, remaining in divisional inventories. Therefore no AFV loss report should ever be considered to be 100 per cent accurate. However, it is unlikely that as many as five Totenkopf panzers were reclassified from lost to damaged or operational over this period. Single adjustments were commonplace but relatively large post-battle adjustments are unlikely to have occurred. It is more likely the report was simply incorrect regarding Totenkopf losses. It is also possible that having left the front on 17–18 July II SS Panzer Korps' engineer was lacking a direct report from Totenkopf in regards to Totenkopf AFV losses and was forced to work with outdated or erroneous information.[74]

Another indicator that points to the greater accuracy of the *Wochenmeldung* over II SS Panzer Korps' engineer's loss report (in regards to Totenkopf AFV losses) can be seen when one compares the 5–10 July total loss (chassis numbers) report for Das Reich and Totenkopf (that II SS Panzer Korps supplied to 4th Panzer Army) with the divisional losses reported by Army Group South to the General Inspector of Panzer Troops' office for the same period.[75]

In terms of the *number* (a couple of panzer chassis numbers are incorrectly listed) of AFVs reported in the combined 5–10 July Das Reich and Totenkopf total loss report over this period, the figures for Das Reich match the known sources, meaning it is likely that this document is also correct for Totenkopf. Therefore we can say with relative confidence that Totenkopf lost two Panzer IIIs, four Panzer IVs and one Panzer VI between 5 and 10 July. As we have seen this would mean that according to the 6th Army *Wochenmeldung* Totenkopf lost no further panzers after 10 July during Operation *Citadel*. This is despite II SS Panzer Korps' engineer's report alluding to a further loss of three Panzer IIIs and two Panzer IVs.[76]

There are a few indicators that support the belief that no Totenkopf post-10 July total losses occurred during Operation *Citadel*. First, the 5–17 July Army Group South loss report that was sent to the General Inspector of Panzer Troops' office lists only two Panzer IIIs as being lost by Totenkopf throughout Operation *Citadel*. Second, although the same 5–17 July Army Group South loss report lists eight Panzer IV losses, they are all recorded in Army Group South's 5–10 July edition (Table 17). Therefore, although the number of AFV losses in 5–10 July's Army Group South loss report may not be in alignment with the 5–10 July Das Reich and Totenkopf (chassis number) total loss report, the clear implication is that no Totenkopf losses occurred after 10 July. This perhaps indicates the true chronology of Totenkopf losses, i.e. they all occurred between 5 and 10 July.[77] We also know that Totenkopf withdrew in good order from its bridgehead across the River Psel on the night of 17/18 July (e.g. the division even had time to deconstruct its bridging equipment) so perhaps some of the panzers which II SS Panzer Korps' engineer believed were total losses on the far side of the Psel were in fact recovered and remained in Totenkopf's inventory beyond 20 July.[78]

The confirmed knowledge that II SS Panzer Korps' engineer's report concerning Totenkopf AFV losses in the latter half of Operation *Citadel* (post-10 July) is inaccurate further raises the possibility that II SS Panzer Korps' engineer had not yet recorded a Leibstandarte Tiger tank as a total loss following the battle of Prokhorovka. A Leibstandarte Tiger tank was said to have been immobilized close to Totenkopf troops during the battle of Prokhorovka on 12 July. Any immobilized Leibstandarte Tiger would have remained close to Totenkopf's frontage after 12 July until Totenkopf withdrew from the area on the night of 18/19 July. We know roughly the location of the four operational Leibstandarte Tigers on the 12th as the tanks had to crest a hill in order to bring the known Soviet tank wrecks near Andreyevka into their line of fire – this was the Leibstandarte Tiger tanks' second battle of the day. II SS Panzer Korps' engineer would have been just as susceptible to the same lack of clarity as to the ultimate fate of a Leibstandarte 'Prokhorovka' Tiger tank located in Totenkopf's sector of operations as he would have been with panzers that belonged to Totenkopf. It is also very possible that the Leibstandarte Tiger tank that II SS Panzer Korps' engineer reported as requiring homeland maintenance (see Leibstandarte 1–10 July ten-day status report in Figure 16) remained, against regulations, in the Leibstandarte inventory (we know for example that a Totenkopf Tiger took a similar path in the spring of 1943) and was transferred in its current state of repair to Das Reich or Totenkopf's inventory on 28 July.

TABLE 17.[79] **General Inspector of Panzer Troops – *Totalverluste* – Army Group South – Operation *Citadel*, 5–17.7.43**

	LSSAH			DR			SS-T		
	Pz III	Pz IV	Pz VI	Pz III	Pz IV	Pz VI	Pz III	Pz IV	Pz VI
5–10.7.43	1	5	1		1			8	1
5–13.7.43	1	7	1	1	1		2	8	1
5–14.7.43	1	9	1	1	1		2	8	1
5–15.7.43	1	9	1	1	6	1	2	8	1
5–16.7.43	1	9	1	1	6	1	2	8	1
5–17.7.43	1	9	1	1	6	1	2	8	1
Final total	1	9	1	1	6	1	2	8	1

The issue of units refusing to turn over heavily damaged AFVs (for fear of receiving no replacement) to homeland maintenance became so acute that ultimately an order had to be issued that stipulated that AFVs requiring homeland maintenance would officially be allowed to remain the property of their parent division. On 21 October OKH/GenStdH/GenQu/Abt III stated: 'The armoured vehicles sent to the homeland for maintenance henceforth remain property of the delivering troop outfit and will be returned to it after maintenance has been carried out.'[80] As we have seen with the example of Totenkopf in the spring of 1943 (at least in regards to SS Tigers) this practice was already taking place. On 28 July, Das Reich received eight *Citadel*-era Leibstandarte Tigers (and one new post-*Citadel* Leibstandarte Tiger), while Totenkopf took on four *Citadel*-era Leibstandarte Tigers (and four new post-*Citadel* Leibstandarte Tigers).[81]

II SS Panzer Korps' engineer's report also declared that Totenkopf lost two Sf Paks as total losses. We are still not in a position to confirm whether two Sf Paks were lost during the latter part of operation *Citadel* (11–18 July) or later on the Mius Front. However, a shortage report after the Mius offensive, which declared how far below establishment Totenkopf was, stated that the division was short of one Sf Pak. Given that official establishment (*Soll*) was ten Sf Paks, we can see that Totenkopf must have ended the Mius battle with nine Sf Paks (Totenkopf began Operation *Citadel* with 11 Sf Paks). One of the nine Sf Paks was under long-term repair. We know this as the divisional *Meldung* and OB chart for 1 August declared that eight Sf Paks were available to the division (in this case operational or under three weeks' repair – the OB chart did not list Totenkopf panzer strengths). II SS Panzer Korps' engineer's report does correctly state that Totenkopf lost one StuG during this period (recorded as occurring between 5 and 10 July) which tallies with the inventory of 34 StuGs shown in the 1 August *Wochenmeldung*.[82]

The daily divisional reports during the Mius offensive list Totenkopf as having only a limited number of operational Panzer IIIs. On 1 August this number was as low as five, whereas on the same date the *Wochenmeldung* lists 40 Panzer IIIs as being operational (albeit listed in error as Panzer III 75mm kz – Totenkopf only possessed Panzer IIIs with long-barrelled 50mm weapons). The most likely reason for the large difference in the number of operational Panzer IIIs in the reports is that only a proportion were committed to the battle area. The daily divisional report for 28 July declared that Totenkopf had 52 Panzer III lg operational, while the declared operational numbers of the other panzer types in the *Wochenmeldung* are in broad alignment with the daily divisional reports for 1 August. No new panzer crews accompanied the transfer of Leibstandarte armour to Das Reich and Totenkopf on 28 July; therefore it is probable that a large number of former Totenkopf Panzer III crews were switched to manning the far more potent additional 30 long-barrelled Panzer IVs that had been transferred from the Leibstandarte. Further evidence that Totenkopf did in fact have a larger number of operational Panzer IIIs than were committed to the Mius offensive can be located in a monthly report of the General Inspector of Panzer Troops which was also issued on 1 August. The report declared that Totenkopf had 49 operational Panzer IIIs, including a Bef Panzer. This report, however, did not include AFVs in long-term repair – in this case over three weeks. There are a number of errors in the figures presented in the General Inspector of Panzer Troops' report – for example the report lists Totenkopf as having 49 StuGs operational and 21 StuGs under three weeks' repair, while ten Panzer VIs were reported as operational and 18 under three weeks' repair. However, despite these and other errors the panzer inspector's report does at least provide further evidence that Totenkopf had not committed a good proportion of its operational Panzer IIIs to the Mius battle. Therefore, it seems that the daily Totenkopf reports during the Mius battle were ignoring these additional operational Panzer IIIs in their reports.[83]

REAPPRAISING PROKHOROVKA

It is the author's view that it is only sensible that the historiography of the battle of Prokhorovka, regarding German AFV losses, shifts to offering the maximum number of AFV losses that the Germans *could* have suffered on 12 July. This is achieved by highlighting the AFV losses recorded by the Leibstandarte and Das Reich between 11 and 20 July (Tables 18 and 19). For the first time this figure can be given with certainty. The maximum number of AFV losses that the Germans suffered at Prokhorovka was 14 AFV losses; 12 (TF) and two (homeland maintenance). Even if Totenkopf losses are taken into account (the majority of the division was not directly involved), this only raises the number to 16 AFVs lost.[84]

TABLE 18.[85] **Maximum number of II SS Panzer Korps AFV losses (3a and TF) during the battle of Prokhorovka on 12.7.43 (11–20.7.43)**

	Pz III	Pz IV	T-34	Pz VI	Bef	Total Pz	StuG	Sf Pak	Total AFV
LSSAH (11–18.7.43)		4		1		5	1	1	7
DR (11–18.7.43)		4	1			5	2		7
SS-T (11–20.7.43)								2	2
Total		8	1	1		10	3	3	16

No archival documents can be proved reliable enough to establish correctly, individually or collectively, which of the small number of AFV losses II SS Panzer Korps suffered between 11 and 20 July actually resulted from the battle of Prokhorovka on the 12th. There are simply too many AFV reclassifications and errors in the daily records taking place for this to be possible. We can reach the likely number of losses for 12 July (particularly in the Leibstandarte sector) via combat diaries, testimonies, reconnaissance images and so forth. However, unlike the period 5–10 July 1943 and 21 July–1 August 1943, we cannot yet ascertain the required accuracy from the few documents which have been proven to be accurate. As a result it is simply impossible to make any certain claim as to the exact number of German AFV losses that occurred on 12 July during the battle of Prokhorovka. However, the figure is likely, almost certainly in fact, to be between five and ten German AFVs lost.[86]

Although II SS Panzer Korps recorded no losses at all on 12 July, this was clearly an incorrect early assessment. The General Inspector of Panzer

Troops' 5–17 July AFV loss report (daily from 10 July onwards) for Army Group South has proved to be inaccurate in attributing AFV losses to specific dates. II SS Panzer Korps' engineer's 5–18 July AFV loss report is accurate in terms of the number of AFVs it lists as lost by Leibstandarte and Das Reich (even though reclassifications within these numbers still occurred), the exception being Das Reich's T-34 losses which were not recorded. When II SS Panzer Korps' engineer's report is matched with the reliable 5–10 July total loss reports for the Leibstandarte, Das Reich, Totenkopf, the 6th Army's *Wochenmeldung über Panzer und Sturmgeschülzlage Stand* 1 August 1943 and Leibstandarte documents from the autumn of 1943, then this allows us to gauge accurately the maximum number of Leibstandarte and Das Reich AFV losses that occurred between 11 and 18 July.[87]

However, as stated, there is simply no way to determine precisely what proportion of the 11–18 July 1943 Leibstandarte and Das Reich losses occurred as a result of the fighting on the 12th. There remains the possibility that some of these losses occurred on 11 July when the Leibstandarte first advanced into what would become the Prokhorovka battlefield, on 13 July during the Leibstandarte's last push to reach Prokhorovka itself, or indeed on other less active dates. Without reliable location-determining TF reports that cover the period 11–20 July, complete accuracy will always elude us. It is not even possible to state with total confidence that the Leibstandarte Panzer IVs that are visible close to the crest of Hill 252.2 in the Soviet low-level fly-past and German photo reconnaissance images from 16 July, 7 August and thereafter were actually lost on 12 July. Alongside photo reconnaissance, we are forced to rely on battle reports and German testimony, neither of which can be regarded as watertight sources (for example, an AFV crew would not normally know what had happened to their vehicle after they had abandoned it). Nevertheless, it should be stated that the body of evidence means that it is almost certain that on 12 July itself the Germans lost three Panzer IVs (TF) and one Panzer IV (homeland maintenance) close to Hill 252.2.[88]

The maximum number of AFV losses that the Germans could have suffered during the battle of Prokhorovka are distributed as follows: for the Leibstandarte three Panzer IVs TF and one Panzer IV homeland maintenance, one Panzer VI TF, one StuG TF, and one Sf Pak homeland maintenance. For a Leibstandarte Panzer VI TF to have occurred at Prokhorovka the Leibstandarte '5–10 July 1943 homeland maintenance Panzer VI' would have had to have remained in the Leibstandarte inventory (similar cases are known to have occurred); we know the '5–10 July 1943' Leibstandarte Panzer VI was never considered to be a total loss, see Figure 15. The Leibstandarte 'Prokhorovka Panzer VI TF' would have been located in Totenkopf's sector where errors in II SS Panzer Korps' engineer's reporting are known to have occurred.

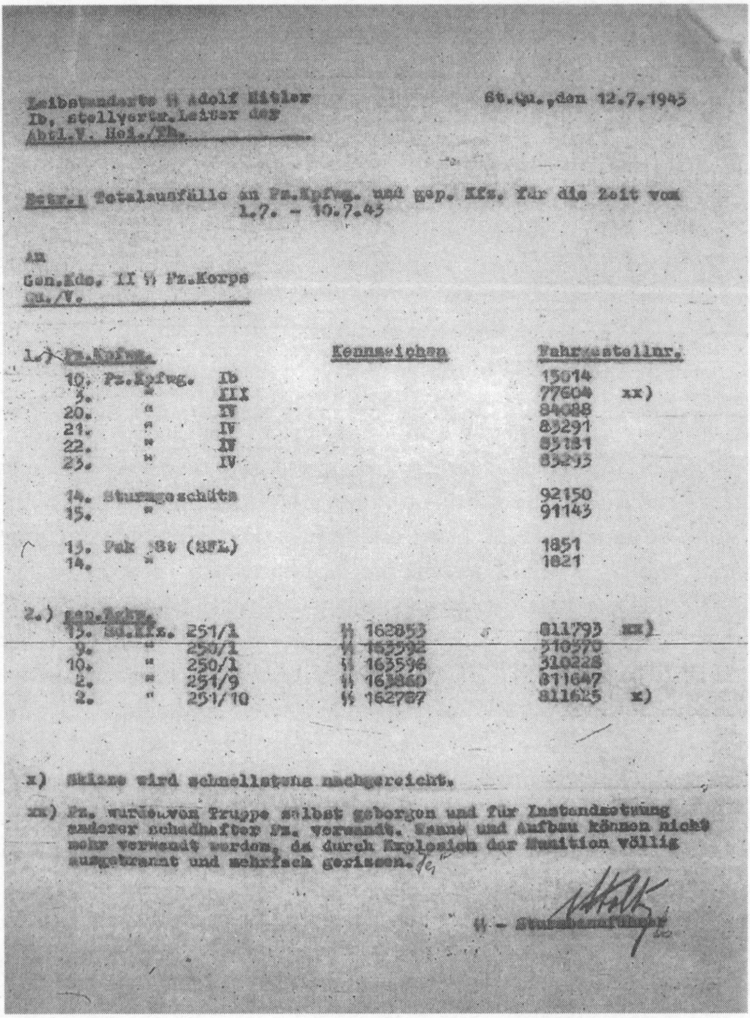

Leibstandarte SS Adolf Hitler
Ib, stellvertr. Leiter der
Abtl. V. Hei./Th.

St.Qu., den 12.7.1943

Betr.: Totalausfälle an Pz.Kpfwg. und gep. Kfz. für die Zeit vom 1.7. – 10.7.43

An
Gen.Kdo. II SS Pz.Korps
Qu./V.

		Kennzeichen	Fahrgestellnr.	
1.) Pz.Kpfwg.				
10. Pz.Kpfwg.	Ib		15014	
3. "	III		77604	xx)
20. "	IV		84088	
21. "	IV		83291	
22. "	IV		83181	
23. "	IV		83293	
14. Sturmgeschütz			92150	
15. "			91143	
13. Pak 38 (SFL)			1851	
14. "			1821	
2.) gep.Kfz.				
13. Sd.Kfz.	251/1	SS 162853	811793	xx)
9. "	250/1	SS 163592	310570	
10. "	250/1	SS 163596	310228	
2. "	251/9	SS 163860	811647	
2. "	251/10	SS 162787	811625	x)

x) Skizze wird schnellstens nachgereicht.

xx) Pz. wurden von Truppe selbst geborgen und für Instandsetzung anderer schadhafter Pz. verwandt. Wanne und Aufbau können nicht mehr verwandt werden, da durch Explosion der Munition völlig ausgebrannt und mehrfach gerissen.

SS – Sturmbannführer

FIGURE 15. 4th Panzer Army, O.Qu.V. V, LSSAH, Betr.: Totalausfälle an Pz. Kpfwg. und gep. Kfz. 1–10.7.43 (written 12.7.43). (NARA T313, R390)

We can also deduce from the same records that the Leibstandarte lost eight of its 13 Operation *Citadel* armoured personnel carrier (SPW) losses and both of its armoured car losses between 11 and 18 July. As we shall see, the losses sustained by the Leibstandarte 2nd SS Panzergrenadier Regiment's III Battalion close to Hill 252.2 on the morning of 12 July contributed significantly to this total.

Another post-Operation *Citadel* summary report is known to exist, one produced for Hitler's SS adjutant Fritz Darges. The report, sent to Darges

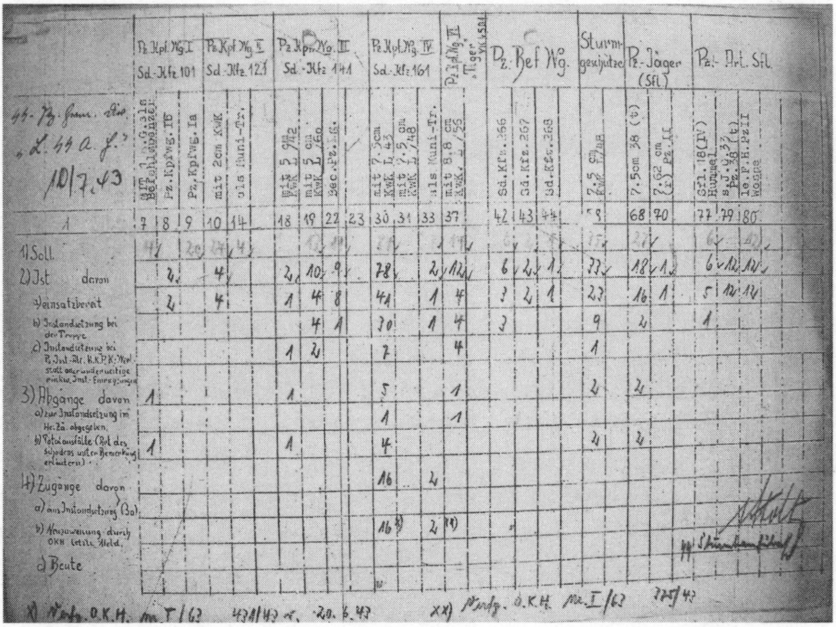

SS-Pz.Gren.Div. „L.SS A.H." 10/7.43

	Pz.Kpf.Wg.I Sd.Kfz.101		Pz.Kpf.Wg.II Sd.Kfz.121			Pz.Kpf.Wg.III Sd.Kfz.141				Pz.Kpf.Wg.IV Sd.Kfz.161			Pz.Kpf.Wg.VI „Tiger" Sd.Kfz.181	Pz.Bef.Wg.			Sturmgeschütze	Pz.-Jäger (Sfl)		Pz.-Art.Sfl.		
	[illegible] Befehlspanzer	Pz.Kpfwg. IB	Pz.Kpfwg. Ia	mit 2cm KwK	als Muni-Tr.	mit 5 cm KwK L/42	mit 5 cm KwK L/60	Bef.Pz.Wg.		mit 7.5cm KwK L/43	mit 7.5 cm KwK L/48	als Muni-Tr.	mit 8.8 cm KwK L/56	Sd.Kfz.266	Sd.Kfz.267	Sd.Kfz.268	7.5 cm KwK L/48	7.5cm 38 (t)	7.62 cm (r) Pz.II	Sfl. 18(IV) Hummel	s.I.G.33 Pz.38(t)	le.F.H. Pz.II Wespe
1	7	8	9	10	14	18	19	22	23	30	31	33	37	42	43	44	58	68	70	77	79	80
1) Soll	[illegible]		[illegible]	[illegible]	[illegible]		[illegible]	[illegible]		[illegible]		[illegible]	[illegible]	[illegible]	[illegible]	[illegible]	[illegible]	[illegible]		[illegible]	[illegible]	
2) Ist davon		2		4		2	10	9		78		2	12	6	2	1	33	18	1	6	12	12
a) einsatzbereit		2		4		1	4	8		41		1	4	3	2	1	23	16	1	5	12	12
b) Instandsetzung bei der Truppe							4	1		30		1	4	3			9	2		1		
c) Instandsetzung bei Pz.Inst.Abt., H.K.P., K.-Werkstatt oder anderweitige einheim. Inst.-Einrichtungen						1	2			7			4				1					
3) Abgänge davon	1					1				5			1				2	2				
a) zur Instandsetzung im Hr.Gebiet abgegeben										1			1									
b) Totalausfälle (Art des Schadens unter Bemerkung erläutern)	1					1				4							2	2				
4) Zugänge davon										16		2										
a) aus Instandsetzung (3a)																						
b) Neuzuweisung durch OKH letzte Meld.										16 x)		2 xx)										
c) Beute																						

x) Verfg. O.K.H. Nr. I/63 431/43 v. 20.6.43 xx) Verfg. O.K.H. Nr. I/63 725/43

SS-Sturmbannführer

FIGURE 16. 4th Panzer Army, O.Qu.V, LSSAH, Gep. Kfz. Bestandsmeldung. 1–10.7.43. (NARA T313, R390)

at Hitler's headquarters, was written by II SS Panzer Korps' 1a and gives his view of the status of II SS Panzer Korps on 21 July. This was another only vaguely accurate 1a report. However, the report is still useful as it offers us a record of II SS Panzer Korps' artillery and anti-tank gun losses during Operation *Citadel*. It is interesting to note that II SS Panzer Korps' 1a reported losing a relatively high number of Pak 40 towed heavy anti-tank guns (16) between 5 and 21 July 1943. Given that the Leibstandarte had 18 of these powerful weapons and that its three towed anti-tank companies faced the majority of the 5th Guards Tank Army's attacking armour on 12 July, it can be assumed a proportion of these weapons would have been lost by the Leibstandarte that day.[89] After all, the firing positions of some of the division's anti-tank guns were overrun at the Oktiabrskiy state farm, while the Leibstandarte reconnaissance battalion's heavy anti-tank company lines were also breached by the 170th and 181st Tank Brigades. Fierce fighting also raged around the gunners of 1st SS Panzergrenadier Regiment's heavy anti-tank company when faced by the 25th Tank Brigade close to Stalinsk state farm and Storozhevoye Woods. The German troops firing across the anti-tank ditch would also have received heavy fire from the floundering Soviet tanks.[90]

As Zetterling and Frankson state, the loss of 16 Pak 40 anti-tank guns is 'testimony to the German practice of pushing anti-tank guns as far forward as possible'. This loss is even more noteworthy when one considers that the whole of 2nd Panzer Army only lost 26 Pak 40s throughout July 1943 despite facing the mammoth Soviet offensive against the Orel salient. In addition, II SS Panzer Korps lost one 105mm field howitzer (towed) which almost certainly belonged to the Leibstandarte, the loss probably occurring when Soviet tanks broke into the artillery regiment's firing positions on 12 July. The loss of two 150mm heavy infantry guns (towed) was also recorded, though it is unclear which division these belonged to. In terms of personnel losses, on 12 July the Leibstandarte lost 39 men KIA, 235 WIA and five MIA.[91]

For Das Reich the maximum number of AFV losses at Prokhorovka was: one T-34 TF, four Panzer IVs TF and two StuGs TF. The majority of Das Reich losses between 11 and 18 July 1943 may well have occurred during the division's short drive to the east to link up with III Panzer Korps that began on 14 July. Das Reich Panzer IV losses were fed into the General Inspector of Panzer Troops' report on 15 July. This would seemingly tie in with the notion that Das Reich losses occurred as a result of its drive east. However, we know that the Das Reich confirmed pre-11 July Panzer VI loss was also only fed into the General Inspector of Panzer Troops' daily records on 15 July (its true loss location was shown in the SS 5–10 July total loss report). Naturally this indicates that some of Das Reich's Panzer IV losses reported by the General Inspector of Panzer Troops may have also occurred on an earlier date than 15 July, perhaps even on the 12th. The General Inspector of Panzer Troops (like II SS Panzer Korps' engineer) did not list Das Reich's T-34 losses. However, we know from the Das Reich total loss report that two T-34s were lost between 5 and 10 July, meaning the one further T-34 loss that the 1 August *Wochenmeldung* highlights occurred during the latter part of Operation *Citadel*, and indeed may have been lost at Prokhorovka. The records also show that remarkably Das Reich only lost one SPW throughout Operation *Citadel* and that this loss occurred between 11 and 18 July; therefore, it is possible the loss occurred during the battle of Prokhorovka. On 12 July Das Reich lost 41 men KIA, 190 WIA and 12 MIA.[92]

It is sometimes mentioned that Totenkopf's assault gun battalion fought south of the River Psel and thus was involved in the battle of Prokhorovka. However, Totenkopf lost no panzers or StuGs between 11 and 20 July, so this does not affect the final number of German AFV losses that occurred during the battle of Prokhorovka. However, Totenkopf did lose two Sf Paks between 11 July and 2 August which leaves open the possibility that these AFVs may have been lost on 12 July at Prokhorovka.[93]

TABLE 19.[94] Surviving AFV from the battle of Prokhorovka, 18.7.43									
	Pz III	Pz IV	T-34	Pz VI	Bef	Total Pz	StuG	Sf Pak	Total AFV
Surviving AFV on 18.7 in LSSAH inventory the day prior to the battle of Prokhorovka (11.7.43 0100hrs)	12	74		12	9	107	32	18	157
Surviving AFV on 18.7 in DR inventory the day prior to the battle of Prokhorovka (11.7.43 0100)	60	27	21	13	9	130	32	12	174
Combined total of surviving German AFV on 18.7.43 which were in LSSAH and DR inventories for the battle of Prokhorovka	72	101	21	25	18	237	64	30	331
Combined German inventory the day prior to the battle of Prokhorovka (11.7.43 0100)	72	109	22	25–26	18	246–247	67	31	344–345

It was only on 17 July, when II SS Panzer Korps withdrew from the front, that the approaching Soviet troops were able to see the extent of their armoured losses on 12 July. Thus, the first seemingly reliable report of Soviet AFV losses also bears that date. A report written by the chief of staff of 5th Guards Tank Army revealed that the army wrote-off 222 T-34s, 89 T-70s, 12 Churchill Tanks and 11 assault guns for a total of 334 AFVs between 12 and 16 July (Table 20). The same report states that the four Soviet tank corps that participated in the battle of Prokhorovka (i.e. not the 5th Guards Mechanized Corps and some attached army units) suffered a total of 235 AFV losses during this period: 29th Tank Corps: 60 T-34s, 31 T-70s, 8 SU-122s, 3 SU-76s (102 AFVs); 18th Tank Corps: 32 T-34s, 12 T-70s, 11 Churchill tanks (55 AFVs); 2nd Guards Tank Corps: 38 T-34s, 24 T-70s (62 AFVs); 2nd Tank Corps: 10 T-34s, 5 T-70s, 1 Churchill tank (16 AFVs). The report also states that the four tank corps ended 16 July with a total of 133 AFVs under repair or in transit to the front.[95]

On 12 July at Prokhorovka according to Valeriy Zamulin's latest research the 5th Guards Tank Army's four participating tank corps lost 192 tanks and assault guns as total write-offs rising to 235 AFVs by 17 July, chiefly as a result of German post-battle destruction of abandoned Soviet tanks. The 235 AFV figure matches Frieser's assessment.[96] In light of Zamulin's findings, it is interesting to note that on 13 July the Leibstandarte reported that on the previous day it had either captured or destroyed 192 Soviet tanks.[97] As the battlefield of the 29th Tank Corps remained in German hands between 12 and 16 July, from 12 July damaged and abandoned Soviet tanks were destroyed by special squads.

TABLE 20.[98] 5th Guards Tank Army reported total AFV losses, 12–16.7.43

	T-34	T-70	Church-ill	122mm Sf gun	76mm Sf gun	Total AFV
29th Tank Corps	60	31		8	3	102
18th Tank Corps	32	12	11			55
2nd Guards Tank Corps	38	24				62
2nd Tank Corps	10	5	1			16
Maximum Soviet AFV lost during the battle of Prokhorovka on 12.7.43 (inc not-involved 26th Guards Tank Brigade)	140	72	12	8	3	235
5th Guards Mechanized Corps	59	14				73
Army units	23	3				26
Total	222	89	12	8	3	334

There is, however, an alternative way to attempt to determine the total AFV losses sustained by the 5th Guards Tank Army between 12 and 16 July. In a similar fashion to II SS Panzer Korps it is possible to compare the 5th Guards Tank Army's pre-battle 11 July inventory (Table 21) with its 17 July post-battle inventory (Table 22).[99] It is striking that the tank corps' inventories of 11 July after the removal of the AFV losses that the 5th Guards Tank Army reported on 17 July do not match (with the exception of the 18th Tank Corps) the tank corps' inventories for 17 July that can be deduced from the same report. On 11 July the four 'Prokhorovka' Soviet tank corps reported an inventory of 663 AFVs (375 T-34s, 233 T-70s, 33 Churchill tanks, 1 KV-1, 11 122mm SUs, 10 76mm SUs) while the 17 July report from the 5th Guards Tank Army indicates an inventory of 451 AFVs (244 T-34s, 183 T-70s, 14 Churchills, 4 122mm SUs, 6 76mm SUs). This latter figure is reached be adding together the four corps' operational, damaged and in-transit AFVs and represents a decrease of 212 AFVs by 17 July. If we recall that the 5th Guards Tank Army reported the loss of 235 AFVs on 17 July then we can see there is a discrepancy of 23 AFVs (Table 23).

TABLE 21.[100] 5th Guards Tank Army AFV inventory (of which in transit) 1700hrs 11.7.43						
	T-34	T-70	Churchill	122mm Sf gun	76mm Sf gun	Total AFV
29th Tank Corps (inc 3 T-34 of 363 Sep Signals Bn and 7 T-70 of 38 Sep AC Bn)	139 (8)	89 (4)	1 KV-1	11	10	250 (12)
18th Tank Corps (inc 2 T-34 of 419 Sep Signals Bn)	103 (26)	63 (5)	20 (2)			186 (33)
2nd Guards Tank Corps	86	52	3			141
2nd Tank Corps (inc 4 T-34 of 894 Sep Signals Bn)	47	29	10			86
Inventory of units involved in battle of Prokhorovka on 12.7.43 (inc not-involved 26th Guards Tank Brigade 30 T-34, 14 T-70)	375 (34)	233 (9)	33 (2) and 1 KV-1	11	10	663 (45)
5th Guards Mechanized Corps	157 (43)	48 (4)		11	10	226 (47)
Sep Army Units	52	12				64
Total	584 (77)	293 (13)	33 (2) and 1 KV-1	22	20	953 (92)

TABLE 22.[101] 5th Guards Tank Army AFV inventory (operational, under repair and in transit) 0100hrs 17.7.43

	T-34	T-70	Church-ill	122mm Sf gun	76mm Sf gun	Total AFV
29th Tank Corps	56	52		4	6	118
18th Tank Corps	71	51	9			131
2nd Guards Tank Corps	63	35				98
2nd Tank Corps	54	45	5			104
Inventory of units involved in battle of Prokhorovka on 12.7.43 (inc not-involved 26th Guards Tank Brigade)	244	183	14	4	6	451
5th Guards Mechanized Corps	103	46	6	12	9	176
Sep Army Units	21	7				28
Total	368	236	20	16	15	655

TABLE 23.[102] 5th Guards Tank Army (GTA) total AFV losses, 12–16.7.43

	T-34	T-70	Church-ill	122mm Sf gun	76mm Sf gun	Total AFV
29th Tank Corps reported losses by 5GTA	60	31		8	3	102
29th Tank Corps variation between 11.7.43 and 17.7.43 inventories	83	37	1 KV-1	7	4	132
18th Tank Corps reported losses by 5GTA	32	12	11			55
18th Tank Corps variation between 11.7.43 and 17.7.43 inventories	32	12	11			55
2nd Guards Tank Corps reported losses by 5GTA	38	24				62
2nd Guards Tank Corps variation between 11.7.43 and 17.7.43 inventories	23	17	3			43
2nd Tank Corps reported losses by 5GTA	10	5	1			16
2nd Tank Corps variation between 11.7.43 and 17.7.43 inventories	Gain of 7	Gain of 16	5			Gain of 18

Maximum Soviet AFV lost during the battle of Prokhorovka on 12.7.43 as reported by 5GTA (inc not-involved 26th Guards Tank Brigade)	140	72	12	8	3	235
Total variation (aka losses) between 11.7.43 and 17.7.43 inventories for the 4 'Prokhorovka' Tank Corps (inc not-involved 26th Guards Tank Brigade)	131	50	19 and 1 KV-1	7	4	212
5th Guards Mechanized Corps reported losses by 5GTA	59	14				73
5th Guards Mechanized Corps variation between 11.7.43 and 17.7.43 inventories	54	2	Gain of 6	Gain 1	1	50
Army units reported losses by 5GTA	23	3				26
Army units variation between 11.7.43 and 17.7.43 inventories	31	5				36
Total reported losses by 5GTA	222	89	12	8	3	334
Total variation between 11.7.43 and 17.7.43 inventories	216	57	13 and 1 KV-1	6	5	298

As Table 23 indicates between the inventories of 11 July and 17 July, with the exception of the 29th Tank Corps, every major tank formation of the 5th Guards Tank Army seemingly either suffered the same number of AFV losses (18th Tank Corps) or fewer AFV losses (2nd Guards Tank Corps, 5th Mechanized Corps, Army Units) than was reported by the 5th Guards Tank Amy in its 17 July status report. In the case of the 2nd Tank Corps its number of AFVs actually increased between the two inventories.[103]

The results of this calculation perhaps indicate that the author of the 5th Guards Tank Army's status report of 17 July had not yet correctly established the number of AFV losses suffered by the 29th Tank Corps between 12 and 16 July. This is hardly surprising given that the 5th Guards Tank Army only reclaimed the majority of the Prokhorovka 'tank field' on the day the report was written. As we have seen, the German reporting of AFV losses during Operation *Citadel* was often erroneous; it seems highly plausible that similar errors occurred on the Soviet side as well.

Looking at the 29th Tank Corps AFV losses, how can we account for this discrepancy in the figures? The 29th Tank Corps had 250 AFVs in its inventory of 11 July. This figure included 12 tanks (8 T-34s and 4 T-70s) which were in transit to the corps on the evening of 11 July. The corps had the support of 10 tanks (3 T-34s and 7 T-70s) from independent army units which were also included in the corps' 11 July inventory. If we collectively remove these 22 AFVs we can say the 29th Tank Corps launched its attack on 12 July against the Leibstandarte with no fewer than 228 AFVs in its 12 July inventory. The difference between the 29th Tank Corps' 11 July inventory and that of 17 July would then be reduced from 132 to 110 AFVs, which is closer to the 102 AFV losses that the 5th Guards Tank Army reported the corps suffered in its 17 July status report. However, it is more likely that the 5th Guards Tank Army's 17 July status report did include the '11 July 1943' supporting units and in-transit tanks in its assessments of 29th Tank Corps AFV losses. The AFV losses of the 18th Tank Corps that were reported by the 5th Guards Tank Army in its 17 July status report clearly took into account the 33 tanks that were listed by the 11 July inventory as being in transit to the corps as well and two tanks that belonged to the supporting 419th Separate Signals Battalion. We know this as the decrease between the 18th Tank Corps inventories of 11 July and 17 July (55 AFVs) when including these 35 AFVs matches the number of 18th Tank Corps AFV losses reported by the 5th Guards Tank Army on 17 July (also 55 AFVs). From this we can deduce the 5th Guards Tank Army was including supporting units' AFVs in their recording of AFV losses in its 17 July status report. As the 18th Tank Corps AFV loss figures (55 AFVs) match by either method of deduction, it is clear that the corps had not yet received any further new AFVs. As the 29th Tank Corps has a lower inventory on 17 July than would be expected if the AFV loss figures provided by the 5th Guards Tank Army's status report were accurate, then it is highly unlikely that the 29th Tank Corps had received any new AFVs since 12 July either. This obviously increases the likelihood that the 29th Tank Corps did indeed lose 132 AFVs between 12 and 16 July. For these reasons, in the case of 29th Tank Corps, one is inclined to lean towards the inventory variations formula (132 AFV losses) for determining the corps losses between 12 and 16 July rather than the losses reported by the 5th Guards Tank Army on 17 July (102 AFVs). The 5th Guards Tank Army's three organic corps (29th and 18th Tank Corps and 5th Guards Mechanized Corps) reached the front on 11 July with full or near full inventories; it is extremely unlikely, therefore, that additional new AFVs (other than those listed as being in transit in the 11 July inventory) would have been ready to be dispatched (by 17 July) to these three corps so rapidly after their first battle. As a result, for the 5th Guards Tank Army's three organic corps the use of the inventory variation method is likely to be the most accurate way of establishing AFV losses between 12 and 16 July.[104]

The increase in inventory strength of the (already weakened) 2nd Tank Corps between 11 and 17 July was obviously due to new AFV arrivals being received. As a result we have little choice but to take the AFV losses reported by 5th Guards Tank Army on 17 July at face value. These reported losses were extremely light (16 AFVs); there is no reason to doubt them given the largely supportive nature of the 2nd Tank Corps operations on 12 July. 2nd Tank Corps had already been in fierce and costly combat in the days prior to the 5th Guards Tank Army's attack on 12 July; therefore, new AFVs would have been requested prior to 12 July.

The 2nd Guards Tank Corps had also previously been in combat opposing Operation *Citadel*; however, on 11 July it still had considerable AFV strength (141 AFVs). The higher AFV losses reported on 17 July by 5th Guards Tank Army for the 2nd Guards Tank Corps compared to the variation in the 11 July and 17 July inventories is also likely to be due to new AFV arrivals offsetting losses. The majority of the 2nd Guards Tank Corps fought on the flank of the battle of Prokhorovka primarily against Das Reich. The 2nd Guards Tank Corps' 26th Guards Tank Brigade (44 AFVs), however, did not participate in the battle of Prokhorovka on 12 July. On the morning of 12 July the brigade was sent to block any attempted advance by the III Panzer Korps on Prokhorovka from the south (in the event the III Panzer Korps made no attempt to reach Prokhorovka after daybreak on 12 July).

It is difficult to assess which of the barometers of AFV losses is more accurate in reference to the 2nd Guards Tank Corps. For example, the 5th Guards Tank Army 17 July report does not list any Churchill tanks as being destroyed, operational or under repair with the 2nd Guards Tank Corps, whereas the inventory for 11 July does list three Churchill tanks as being with the Corps. Of course these tanks may have been transferred away; the 5th Guards Mechanized Corps contained six Churchill tanks in its 17 July inventory which are not found in the corps' 11 July inventory. The author has decided to use the AFV losses for the 2nd Guards Tank Corps which are indicated by the comparison of the two inventories (43 AFVs).[105]

Overall, we can see that the four Soviet tank corps that participated in the battle of Prokhorovka suffered AFV losses in the range of 212 (inventories comparison formula for all four of the 'Prokhorovka' tank corps) to 265 AFVs (17 July 5th Guards Tank Army status report losses for three of the

'Prokhorovka' tank corps plus the additional 30 AFV losses of the 29th Tank Corps that are revealed by the inventories comparison formula) between 12 and 16 July. It is the author's personal belief that the 246 AFV total loss figure for the four 'Prokhorovka' tank corps is the most accurate number (the inventory variations formula for three of the 'Prokhorovka' tank corps, plus the reported losses by the 5th Guards Tank Army for the 2nd Tank Corps). Regardless, the four 'Prokhorovka' tank corps lost a minimum of 212 AFVs between 12 and 16 July which can be directly compared to the confirmed maximum of 16 AFVs lost by II SS Panzer Korps between 11 and 20 July.[106]

In addition to its own AFV losses the 5th Guards Tank Army's 17 July status report declared that the four Soviet 'Prokhorovka' tank corps had destroyed 298 German tanks (of which 55 were Tiger tanks) between 12 and 16 July (Table 24). The report was one of the first documents to chronicle in statistical terms the 'myth of Prokhorovka'. As we have seen, in fact the four 'Prokhorovka' tank corps (bar the 26th Guards Tank Brigade) destroyed a maximum of 16 German AFVs (of which a maximum of one was a Tiger tank) at Prokhorovka during this period. This knowledge inevitably means that the wider claims made by the 17 July 5th Guards Tank Army status report have to be viewed with caution.[107]

TABLE 24.[108] **5th Guards Tank Army German AFV and personnel kill claims, 12–16.7.43**

	Tanks	of which Tigers	Men
29th Tank Corps	85	14	3,780
18th Tank Corps	92	21	1,190
2nd Guards Tank Corps	73	11	2,755
2nd Tank Corps	48	9	1,373
Maximum Soviet claims for the battle of Prokhorovka on 12.7.43	298	55	9,098
5th Guards Mechanized Corps	213	22	5,432
Army units	41	16	390
Total	552	93	14,920

As soon as Stalin heard of the extremely high AFV losses the 5th Guards Tank Army had suffered at Prokhorovka he demanded answers. Stalin is alleged to have asked Rotmistrov directly, 'What have you done to your magnificent armoured army?' Stalin, so Zamulin has written, wanted Rotmistrov sacked and even court marshalled. Rotmistrov, well aware of the likely fate of failing

Stalin, instead declared that German AFV losses at Prokhorovka were even higher than that of his own formations. The birth of this 'myth of Prokhorovka' can clearly be seen in the reporting of German AFV losses in the 5th Guards Tank Army status report of 17 July.[109]

The casualty figures for 5th Guards Tank Army's four participating tank corps as of 16 July (including late reports) were as follows: total casualties were 5,276 (1,665 KIA, 1,088 MIA, 2,523 WIA); the figure of 2,753 for dead and missing was higher than that for the wounded.[110]

4

The Battle of Prokhorovka, 12 July 1943:
A True Narrative

THE OPPOSING FORCES

The Stavka (the Soviet high command) envisaged 12 July as the decisive day in the battle of Kursk. To the north of the Kursk salient, Bryansk Front and large parts of West Front launched an offensive against Germany's thinned-out 2nd Panzer Army. When the front collapsed, Walter Model's 9th Army would have to halt its advance on Kursk. A destructive strike on the attacking formations of Army Group South was also planned for the same day. The strongest weapon was the fresh 5th Guards Tank Army under the command of Pavel Rotmistrov, whose total of 911 tanks and 42 assault guns were intended to smash the 'battle-worn' II SS Panzer Korps, under the command of SS *Obergruppenführer* Paul Hausser, at Prokhorovka.[1] In the early hours of 11 July II SS Panzer Korps still had an inventory of 521–522 AFVs (378–379 tanks, 101 assault guns and 42 tank destroyers).[2] The Korps had begun Operation *Citadel* with an inventory of 547 AFVs (399 tanks, 104 assault guns and 44 tank destroyers).[3]

On the morning of 12 July, the whole of II SS Panzer Korps had at its disposal a total of 329 operational AFVs (including 232 battle tanks, 58 assault guns and 39 tank destroyers, see Table 25). However, since Totenkopf led by SS *Oberführer* Hermann Priess was attacking northwards that day on the far side of the River Psel, there remained only the Leibstandarte (SS *Brigadeführer* Theodor Wisch) and Das Reich (SS *Gruppenführer* Walter Krüger), with a total of 131 battle tanks, 37 assault guns and 28 tank destroyers, that is, 196 AFVs in total, which could be deployed against 5th Guards Tank Army (the Leibstandarte did receive flanking supporting from Totenkopf – see below).[4]

TABLE 25.[5] **II SS Panzer Korps (Korps and Divisional 1a reported) pre-battle of Prokhorovka operational AFV 1925hrs 11.7.43**

	Pz III	Pz IV	T-34	Pz VI	Bef	Total Pz	StuG	Sf Pak	Total AFV
LSSAH operational 1925hrs 11.7.43	5	47		4	7	63	10	16*	89
DR operational 1925 11.7.43	34	18	8	1	7	68	27	12	107
Operational AFV of units involved in battle of Prokhorovka on 12.7.43	**39**	**65**	**8**	**5**	**14**	**131**	**37**	**28**	**196**
SS-T operational 1925 11.7.43	54	30		10	7	101	21	11#	133
Total	93	95	8	15	21	232	58	39	329

* Excludes 4 Sf Pak en route from Germany.

No data available – Previous day's figure given.

On the morning of 12 July, Rotmistrov possessed 805 operational AFVs (Table 26). Of his five corps, he kept 5th Guards Mechanized Corps (MajGen B. M. Skvortsov with 169 AFVs) and a number of supporting units (57 AFVs) in reserve. Early in the morning of the 12th, Rotmistrov also removed the 2nd Guards Tank Corps' (Col Alexei Burdeinei), 26th Guards Tank Brigade (44 AFVs) from his striking units and ordered the brigade to support elements of 5th Guards Mechanized Corps in securing his left flank against the III Panzer Korps. The III Panzer Korps had finally begun to threaten from the south. Thus, during the battle of Prokhorovka on 12 July, 535 Soviet AFVs were effectively engaged in action against 196 AFVs of the Leibstandarte and Das Reich. Rotmistrov's operational plan involved thrusts in two directions:

- The main thrust was directed from the north-east frontally against the Leibstandarte through the Prokhorovka corridor between the railway embankment and the River Psel. The riverbank was boggy and there were several ribbon villages along it, leaving a strip only about 3km wide in which to manoeuvre. In this section of the main thrust, 18th Tank Corps (MajGen B. S. Bacharev) with 151 tanks (75 T-34s, 58 T-70s and 18 Churchill tanks) was to attack on the right along the River Psel, and 29th Tank Corps

(MajGen I. F. Kirichenko) with 207 tanks (126 T-34s and 81 T-70s) and 21 assault guns (11 SU-122s and 10 SU-76s; Plates 3 and 4) on the left along the railway embankment. This meant that, in the very first phase of the battle, 379 AFVs advanced on the Leibstandarte, which had only 63 battle tanks (5 Panzer IIIs, 47 Panzer IVs, 4 Panzer VIs and 7 Befs), 10 assault guns and 16 tank destroyers at its disposal (89 AFVs). Although Totenkopf's panzer regiment was totally committed north of the Psel (with 54 Panzer IIIs, 30 Panzer IVs, 10 Panzer VIs and 7 Befs), elements of the division's assault guns (21) and tank destroyers (11) may have assisted the Leibstandarte's left flank to resist the 18th Tank Corps on the south side of the river.[6]

- Another thrust was to be directed simultaneously from the east at the German flank, against Das Reich, which was deployed on the right alongside the Leibstandarte. Here the attack was to be carried out by 2nd Guards Tank Corps (56 T-34s, 38 T-70s, 3 Churchill tanks) minus its 26th Guards Tank Brigade (meaning a further 30 T-34s and 14 T-70s did not take part), supported by 2nd Tank Corps (MajGen A. F. Popov with 34 T-34s, 22 T-70s, 3 Churchill tanks). Altogether 156 Soviet tanks stood ready, against which Das Reich could deploy 68 battle tanks (34 Panzer IIIs, 18 Panzer IVs, 8 T-34s, 1 Panzer VI and 7 Befs), 27 assault guns and 12 tank destroyers (107 AFVs).[7]

TABLE 26.[8] 5th Guards Tank Army operational AFV 1700hrs (not including in transit) 11.7.43

	T-34	T-70	Church-ill	122mm Sf gun	76mm Sf gun	Total AFV
29th Tank Corps (inc 3 T-34 of 363 Sep Signals Bn and 7 T-70 of 38 Sep AC Bn)	126	81		11	10	228
18th Tank Corps (inc 2 T-34 of 419 Sep Signals Bn)	75	58	18			151
2nd Guards Tank Corps	86	52	3			141
2nd Tank Corps (inc 4 T-34 of 894 Sep Signals Bn)	34	22	3			59

Operational AFV of units involved in battle of Prokhorovka on 12.7.43 (inc not-involved 26th Guards Tank Brigade 30 T-34, 14 T-70)	321	213	24	11	10	579
5th Guards Mechanized Corps	114	44		7	4	169
Army Units	45	12				57
Total	480	269	24	18	14	805

Account must also be taken of Voronezh Front's formations, especially 69th Army (Gen Vasily Dmitrievich Kriuchenkin), which were fighting in this sector anyway. In addition, units of 5th Guards Army (Gen Aleksey Semenovich Zhadov), which was also part of the strategic reserve, were deployed in the zone of action of 5th Guards Tank Army, for example, 9th Guards Paratroop Division. German intelligence was expecting a counter-attack but by no means one of such dimensions.

THE BATTLE OF PROKHOROVKA – 12 JULY 1943

At 0850hrs on 11 July the Leibstandarte overcame an anti-tank ditch which was to play an important role in the following day's fighting; SS War Correspondent Johan King's photographs confirm that the road bridge over this obstacle was captured intact, see Plates 52 to 63. Beyond the anti-tank ditch stretched Hill 252.2, 'like an enormous wave' – the Leibstandarte was now just 2.5km from Prokhorovka. The 9th Guards Paratroop Division put up a fierce defence of the heights, which delayed the German advance and forced the Leibstandarte to deploy its SPW battalion (2nd SS Panzergrenadier Regiment III Battalion), panzer battalion and Sf Grille to complete the capture of Hill 252.2 and the hilltop Oktiabrskiy state farm. The heights were finally captured by the Leibstandarte at 1410hrs. The Leibstandarte's SPW battalion and Sf Grille would later embark on a probing attack in the direction of Prokhorovka. However, beyond Hill 252.2 the Germans came under intense Soviet bombardment, as a result of which the SPW battalion only managed to advance a short distance before having to retreat to its start lines (Johan King's photographs captured some of the fighting for Hill 252.2, see Plates 68 to 85). By the close of 11 July, the Leibstandarte had manoeuvred itself into a very exposed position with open flanks. Only a loose connection remained to its right-hand neighbour Das Reich. An even more dangerous situation had developed on the left wing, which was hanging in the air. Since Totenkopf had attacked northwards across the River Psel rather than eastwards, the two thrust wedges had drifted apart, leaving a gap which the Leibstandarte's Reconnaissance Battalion could only monitor but by no means secure. As a result, II SS Panzer Korps ordered the Leibstandarte (and Das Reich) to halt its assault on Prokhorovka for the time being, and instead directed the attack by Totenkopf on the dominating Hill 226.6 in the Psel bridgehead to be pressed forward the next day (12 July) with 'all the artillery available' to the Korps.[9]

On 12 July the Leibstandarte's units remained widely dispersed. On the right wing, south of the railway embankment, stood 1st SS Panzergrenadier Regiment, and on the left, far forward in the wake of Hill 252.2, 2nd SS Panzergrenadier Regiment. The division's panzer regiment, on the other hand, was recovering from its exertions of the previous day behind Hill 252.2 and the anti-tank ditch. As we have seen, at this time the LSSAH's panzer regiment consisted of just one panzer battalion (its II) with three companies (47 operational Panzer IVs – it began Operation *Citadel* with 79 operational Pz IVs), to which a heavy panzer company had been attached (four operational Panzer VIs – Tiger tanks – the company began Operation *Citadel* with 12 operational Tigers). The panzer regiment's other battalion (its I) was back in Germany undergoing conversion to the Panther tank. Therefore, on 12 July between the railway embankment and the River Psel two full-strength tank brigades of the 5th Guards Tank Army would face a single reinforced panzer battalion.

When Rotmistrov launched the attack on the morning of 12 July from the brick factory 1km north-west of Prokhorovka, many of the Leibstandarte's exhausted troops were still fast asleep; this was made possible as the Soviets chose to launch their attack without a preparatory artillery barrage. The foremost German unit at that moment was once again the 2nd SS Panzergrenadier Regiment's III (SPW) Battalion. At 0915hrs on the morning of 12 July the following scene took place on Hill 252.2: 'We were all fast asleep when they were suddenly all over us with aircraft and an endless mass of tanks with infantry riding on them. It was hell. They were around us, over us, among us. We fought man to man.'[10]

The first German panzer officer to see this Soviet tank avalanche was SS *Obersturmführer* Rudolf von Ribbentrop, the commander of the Leibstandarte panzer battalion's 6th company. Looking up at Hill 252.2 that morning he saw violet signal flares, meaning 'tank alarm' (Plates 41 and 68). The signals were 'seen all along the crest of the slope' and also appeared 'farther to the right at the railway embankment'. While the other two panzer companies remained behind the anti-tank ditch, Ribbentrop,

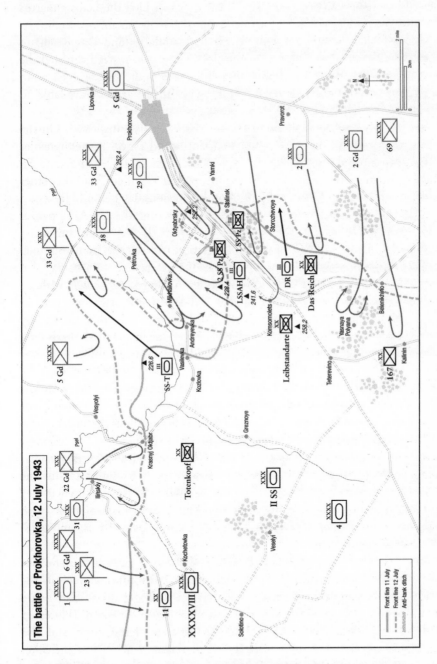

MAP 5

in Panzer IV '605', set off up the hill along with his company's other six operational Panzer IVs.

> On reaching the crest of the slope we saw another low rise about 200 metres away on the other side of a small valley, on which our infantry positions were obviously located... The small valley extended to our left, and as we drove down the forward slope we spotted the first T-34s which were apparently attempting to outflank us from the left. We halted on the slope [for exact location see Plates 86 to 91] and opened fire, hitting several of the enemy. A number of Russian tanks were left burning. For a good gunner 800 metres was the ideal range.

Ribbentrop then saw a huge column of tanks approaching:

> As we waited to see if further enemy tanks were going to appear, I looked around... about 150 to 200 metres in front of us there emerged from a slight dip in the terrain 15, 20, 30, 40 Russian T-34s, and then too many to count. The wall of tanks rolled towards us. Tank by tank, wave upon wave, an unimaginable mass of armour approaching at top speed.

The seven German tanks stood no chance against such overwhelming odds. Two of the leading Panzer IVs were destroyed immediately (unknown tactical numbers), another Panzer IV (most likely '615'), positioned further back on the crest of Hill 252.2, met the same fate soon afterwards, a fourth Panzer IV was severely damaged and immobilized (probably '616'). The other three Panzer IVs ('605', '618' and '625') managed to survive the encounter.[11]

The attacking formation which appeared so suddenly was the mass of 29th Tank Corps, led by MajGen Kirichenko, consisting of 228 operational AFVs.[12] The attack at this location was carried out by 31st and 32nd Tank Brigades and 53rd Motorized Rifle Brigade, supported by a self-propelled gun regiment and 26th Guards Paratroop Regiment. Once the Soviet tanks had passed the crest of Hill 252.2, they raced down the incline towards the two German panzer companies, which opened fire on them from behind the anti-tank ditch. Mistaking the German Panzer IVs for Tiger tanks, the Soviet tankers wanted to eliminate their range superiority as quickly as possible. If the armada of Soviet tanks broke through in depth, as must have initially seemed likely, it could only result in the collapse of the German front. Then, in a few minutes, everything changed. Due to an incredible oversight the Soviets had overlooked the anti-tank ditch. The obstacle had been dug by Soviet infantry and stretched across the base of Hill 252.2 at right angles to the German – now Soviet – direction of attack. According to German testimony 'more and more T-34s came over the crest, raced down the slope, and overturned in the anti-tank ditch behind which we were positioned'. German testimony even spoke of tanks attempting to hurdle the anti-tank ditch. How many Soviet tanks actually crashed into the anti-tank ditch is a moot point, but there is no doubt the presence of the obstacle was either directly or indirectly the chief cause of the 29th Tank Corps' armoured difficulties. Ribbentrop's Panzer IV '605' and '618' had managed to get away by moving alongside the Soviet tanks in a thick cloud of dust. Ribbentrop's other remaining operational Panzer IV '625' is said to have stayed on the battlefield (close to the railway embankment) with a lowered and temporarily jammed main gun. Ribbentrop continued:

> Now the T-34s recognized the ditch and tried to veer left to the road, in order to get across the ditch via the bridge, which had been repaired [author's note – Johan King's photographic evidence from 11 July 1943 clearly shows that the bridge had been captured intact]. What happened then is indescribable [...] as they converged on the bridge; the Russians were exposed on the flanks and made easier targets. Burning T-34s ran into and over each other. An inferno of fire, smoke, burning tanks, dead and wounded!

On the other side of the anti-tank ditch the two companies of Panzer IVs would normally have stood no chance of stopping the Soviet avalanche of steel. However, now it was simply 'target practice at moving targets'.[13]

By noon the Leibstandarte's 2nd SS Panzergrenadier Regiment had recaptured Hill 252.2 and the Oktiabrskiy state farm. By this time the slope of the hill looked like a tank graveyard, covered with the still-burning wrecks of some 100 Soviet tanks and a handful of SPWs from the 2nd SS Panzergrenadier Regiment's III Battalion. The figures reported seemed so incredible that SS *Obergruppenführer* Paul Hausser, the commanding general of II SS Panzer Korps, drove to the front in person to see for himself. Once again, according to Zamulin's most recent estimate, on 12 July the Soviet 29th Tank Corps alone lost 102 tanks and assault guns as write-offs (60 T-34s, 31 T-70s, 8 SU-122s, 3 SU-76s). After reviewing the available Soviet records it is the author's calculation that between 12 and 16 July the 29th Tank Corps lost 132 of its 250 tanks and assault guns as write-offs (83 T-34s, 37 T-70s, 1 KV-1, 8 SU-122s, 3 SU-76s). The Soviet records also show that the 29th Tank Corps casualties over the same period totalled 2,020, including 1,003 dead and missing. The vast majority of these equipment and personnel losses unquestionably would have occurred on 12 July.[14]

The photographs which encompass the fighting in the 29th Tank Corps area of operations are as follows: the photographs from 16 July GX-3734-SK-61 (incorrectly dated as 15 July 1943 by NARA); 7 August GX-3942-SK-69, GX-3942-SD-123, GX-3942-SD-124; 15 August GX-3958-SD-10 and 6 October GX-3977-SD-45 most strongly relate to the fighting on the line of advance of 32nd and 31st Tank Brigades in the central area of the battlefield.[15] The 32nd and 31st Tank Brigades advanced with the railway embankment on their left flank and the Oktiabrskiy state farm (and the surrounding area) on their right flank. This route traversed Hill 252.2 and ultimately the notorious anti-tank ditch at its foot (Plates 37 to 46).

As the Germans recaptured their forward positions by the end of the day, the front lines of 16 July were virtually identical to that of the 12th; therefore, photograph GX-3734-SK-61 is truly remarkable as it is the only known photograph in existence that shows the mass destruction of the 29th Tank Corps across a still-German-controlled battlefield. There are vast numbers of destroyed Soviet tanks and equipment visible in the area of the anti-tank ditch and the fields around the obstacle. It is possible that we can see a mangled mass of Soviet tanks in the left-hand half of the anti-tank ditch (the half nearest the main road) and many individually destroyed tanks in the right-hand half of the anti-tank ditch (Plates 42 to 67).[16] As the crest of Hill 252.2 and the Oktiabrskiy state farm were back in German hands by the end of 12 July, we know that any disabled German tanks in this area were able to be recovered from the battlefield. We also know that the destroyed tanks that can be seen on the field of battle in these photographs in the area between the Oktiabrskiy state farm and the anti-tank ditch will almost exclusively be Soviet.[17]

Three of the four likely permanent Leibstandarte tank losses of 12 July were located close to or forward of the German front line (i.e. on or just beyond the crest of Hill 252.2). The tanks in questions were Panzer IVs belonging to Ribbentrop's 6th Panzer Company.[18] Given the detailed information available to us the author can confirm the likely location of all three lost German tanks amongst the mass of Soviet tank losses in the battlefield photographs.[19] From German testimony we know four of the seven operational Panzer IVs of 6th Panzer Company were disabled on, or just over the summit of, Hill 252.2 after being faced with the mass tanks of 31st and 32nd Tank Brigades. As we have seen three of the seven Panzer IVs rapidly went up in flames, two of which were immediately written off, the other soon afterwards.[20] Another Panzer IV was immobilized and left heavily damaged; this tank, however, was later recovered and sent back to Germany for major repair.[21]

Ribbentrop stated that his lead tanks advanced beyond the summit of Hill 252.2 and onto the slope of a small valley. They then opened fire on tanks advancing to their left about 800m away; it was on this small slope that his tanks were ambushed frontally. Looking at the photographs beyond Hill 252.2, the author has located two tanks that are likely to be destroyed Leibstandarte Panzer IVs (Plates 86 to 91). The German tanks in question are sited on undulating ground beyond the crest of Hill 252.2 (slightly beyond the German front line) between the railway line and Oktiabrskiy state farm. The slightly different size and shape of the tanks (compared to the Soviet wrecks visible elsewhere), the centrally placed turret (the T-34's turret was sited further forward), the direction the hulls face (towards the Soviet front lines), the length of their gun barrels (Soviet tanks had shorter barrels), all indicate that the two tanks are destroyed Leibstandarte Panzer IVs.[22] It has also proved possible to pinpoint the exact location on today's battlefield of these potential Leibstandarte Panzer IVs (Plate 88).

In addition to the Luftwaffe pictures of the battlefield we are extremely fortunate to have two remarkable post-battle pictures taken from a Soviet aircraft flying low over the Prokhorovka battlefield (Plates 92 to 95). These pictures were kindly passed to the author by Valeriy Zamulin and can be found in his excellent book *The Battle of Kursk 1943: The View through the Camera Lens* (Solihull: Helion 2015).[23]

In the foreground of the first image (Plate 92) we can clearly see a destroyed Leibstandarte Panzer IV. The tank was lost just behind the diagonal running dirt track that stretches from the Belgorod–Prokhorovka road/railway crossing to the Oktiabrskiy state farm. Close by a destroyed Soviet T-34 is seen behind an infantry trench. This site is just on the crest of Hill 252.2 and can easily be found in the Luftwaffe pictures of 16 July and 7 August. Given that the Panzer IV is located close to Hill 252.2's crest (from the Germans' point of view) it is likely that this Panzer IV saw combat slightly later than Ribbentrop's leading panzers and as a result it was probably the third and final Leibstandarte Panzer IV lost on the morning of 12 July.[24] It is also likely that the destroyed Panzer IV was '615' commanded by *Obersturmführer* Malchow. According to the testimony of '615's loader, Walter Kettle, the tank was hit, caught fire and after being abandoned exploded. Kettle implies that his tank (unlike the lead Panzer IVs) did not open fire on the first group of Soviet tanks that had attempted to outflank Ribbentrop's leading tanks. Kettle stated that Malchow instead merely counted the flanking Soviet tanks through his binoculars. Clearly, Malchow's tank was not among the lead Panzer IVs that day; if '615' had been at the forefront of the action on 12 July then it would have also engaged the flanking Soviet tanks. This raises the probability that the destroyed Panzer IV captured on camera by the low-flying Soviet aircraft was indeed Panzer IV '615'; its location away from the undulating terrain (the first point of engagement) mentioned by

Ribbentrop supports this view. The second photograph from the Soviet flight (Plate 95) was taken slightly closer to the parallel road that separates the two fields in front of the anti-tank ditch; a destroyed Leibstandarte SPW is particularly prominent on the right of the picture. The destruction caused to the 29th Tank Corps armour in the fields in front of the anti-tank ditch is clearly visible in these two photographs.[25]

The Luftwaffe photographs from 7 August are highly significant. Looking at GX-3942-SD-123 and GX-3942-SD-124 the destruction in and around the trenches close to Hill 252.2 remains largely untouched – the closer focus of the photograph is useful in identifying the handful of German SPWs belonging to III Battalion 2nd SS Panzergrenadier Regiment which were destroyed in the first moments of the attack.[26]

By closely comparing the photographs of 16 July and 7 August we can see destroyed Soviet tanks in the anti-tank ditch. It seems by 7 August there may well have already been some Soviet attempt to remove the tank wrecks that were located in the left side of the anti-tank ditch. To facilitate this, following the Germans' departure, new access/extraction points appear to have been dug or blown in the anti-tank ditch. The track in front of the anti-tank ditch is less worn on 7 August compared to its clear marking on 16 July, which goes to highlight how many tanks on 12 July must have traversed the route while looking for a crossing.[27]

In a remarkable discovery the researcher Eugene Matyukhin found (and kindly shared with the author) further evidence of a large-scale Prokhorovka battlefield AFV clean-up operation taking place. In Luftwaffe photographs from 7 and 15 August, 7 September and 6 October a railway spur on the outskirts of Prokhorovka can be seen (2km behind the 29th Tank Corps battlefield, see Plates 96 to 103). Beside the spur's railhead, large numbers of severely damaged and destroyed Soviet AFVs were accumulated. There is a modest increase of Soviet AFVs visible between 7 and 15 August, followed by a large increase between 15 August and 7 September; this increase continues in the 6 October photograph. According to Zamulin a special unit was deployed at the site to recover usable equipment and dispose of the AFV wrecks. It is interesting to note that as late as November 1943 there still seems to have been little attempt to remove the Soviet AFV wrecks from the site; instead over the months we see a steady accumulation of extracted equipment beside the railhead. It is important to note that by 7 August a fully re-equipped 5th Guards Tank Army had already re-entered combat near Belgorod. Our statistical knowledge of the protagonists' relative AFV losses in the Prokhorovka area between 11 and 20 July means that these photographs can only contain a maximum of 14 destroyed German AFVs (two other severely damaged German AFVs were recovered and transported back to Germany).

In some of the photographs of the battlefield itself we can clearly see marks in the terrain where heavily damaged/destroyed AFVs (those with tracks no longer functioning) have been dragged off the battlefield in the direction of the Prokhorovka railway spur.[28]

The aerial photographs are remarkable in that they enable a further evolution of the historiography of the battle of Prokhorovka.[29] The aerial photographs allow us to pinpoint for the first time some of the small number of German AFV losses (around Hill 252.2) and the majority of the Soviet 29th Tank Corps AFV losses (on the battlefield in July and August and at the Prokhorovka railway spur thereafter).[30]

At the same time as Hill 252.2 was being defended against frontal attack, the situation was becoming critical on the Leibstandarte's left flank. There MajGen Bacharev's 18th Tank Corps attacked along the Psel with 170th, 181st and 110th Armoured Brigades (the latter held in reserve), supported by 32nd Motorized Rifle Brigade and several unattached units such as 36th Guards Tank Regiment (the latter equipped with British-built 'Churchill' tanks). This sudden thrust occurred at the most unfavourable moment for the Germans and in the most unfavourable place, that is, in the gap between the Leibstandarte and Totenkopf. The Soviet 18th Tank Corps penetrated deep into the gap with almost no opposition. In the left-hand section of 2nd SS Panzergrenadier Regiment's zone of action, tactical coordination dissolved into chaos. There was no longer any stable front. On both sides the leadership lost control, and the combat disintegrated into a multitude of individual clashes in which it was difficult to see 'which side was attacking and which side was defending'.[31] The Leibstandarte heavy panzer company's four Tiger tanks were sent to prevent the 170th and 181st Tank Brigades from breaking into the rear of the Leibstandarte. After a three-hour battle this was successfully achieved. Technically, the Germans lost none of their Tigers on 12 July. However, one of the four Tigers was supposedly left heavily damaged by shell shot. It could not be hauled away the following day because of strong enemy fire, and later had to be written off. The push by 18th Tank Corps failed with considerable losses, including 55 of 190 tanks ultimately being written off (32 T-34s, 12 T-70s, 11 Churchill tanks). After all the attacks had been repelled, the corps was withdrawn in the early afternoon and thereafter essentially deployed only defensively.[32]

Photographs relating to the 18th Tank Corps offensive are as compelling as those relating to the 29th Tank Corps. The major tank duel between the four Tiger tanks (recently placed under the command of Michael Wittmann) and Soviet armour that occurred following the mass breakthrough of 170th Tank Brigade into the Leibstandarte's weakly defended left flank (west of the anti-tank ditch) is covered in the following photographs: GX-3734-SK-61 of

16 July and GX-3942-SK-69 of 7 August, but also partially in photographs: GX-2696-SK-23, GX-2696-SK-24, GX-2696-SK-52 of 14 July; while the results of the Tiger tanks' subsequent action in the late morning/early afternoon against the 181st Tank Brigade which was advancing uphill from the River Psel towards the Tigers' original firing positions on the summit of Hill 241.6 (on the most detailed maps this precise point is labelled as 228.4; this point is located on the same plateau as the governing Hill 241.6) is clearly visible in photographs GX-2696-SK-23, GX-2696-SK-24 and GX-2696-SK-52 of 14 July.[33]

The 170th Tank Brigade attacked in the first echelon and succeeded in penetrating the German line en masse – according to Soviet reports with 50 tanks (Plates 104 to 110).[34] We can see the evidence of this breakthrough south-west of the anti-tank ditch in photographs GX-3734-SK-61 of 16 July and GX-3942-SK-69 of 7 August.[35] The 181st Tank Brigade also launched attacks early on 12 July with the same initial objective as the 170th Tank Brigade of reaching the Komsomolets state farm in the Leibstandarte's rear.[36] The Tigers engaged the units of the 170th Tank Brigade first. Given the fluid nature of the battlefield in this sector a number of T-34s did not engage the German tanks and pushed on towards the Leibstandarte artillery regiment's firing positions close to Komsomolets state farm (Plates 23 to 25).[37] These Soviet tanks were ultimately tracked down and destroyed either by the artillerymen themselves firing across open sights or by elements of the Leibstandarte's Panzer Regiment.[38]

The four Tiger tanks were faced with a mass of Soviet tanks approaching from at least two lines of advance. As Glantz described:

> on the 1st SS Panzer Regiment's left flank north of Oktiabrskiy state farm [sic], its 13th (Tiger) Company ran into a force of 60 Soviet tanks, which it engaged at ranges 600 to 1000m. As the ranges rapidly closed, another Russian force of like strength descended on the 13th Company. A swirling, deadly, three-hour battle ensued, during which the Soviet tanks suffered appalling losses.[39]

Testimony of this conflict is provided by Georg Lötzsch, who was one of the four Tiger tank commanders that day: 'In the morning, the company was on the left wing of II Panzer Battalion when about 50 enemy tanks, from the cover of copses and hedges, came storming towards us in a broad wedge formation.'[40] As the extracts taken from GX-3734-SK-61 (16 July) and GX-3942-SK-69 (7 August) show, Lötzsch's testimony matches the events portrayed in the photographs from this location. We can see destroyed tanks from the 170th Tank Brigade which, after making a frontal advance largely unopposed, have begun to deploy in a wedge formation upon seeing the Tiger tanks – it is possible to follow the 170th Tank Brigade's tracks in the field. We can establish these tanks are Soviet via a number of methods. First, the wrecks appear in both the 16 July photograph and 7 August photograph. Given our knowledge of the small losses incurred by the Leibstandarte throughout its deployment in the Prokhorovka area (maximum of seven AFVs 11–20 July) a large number of knocked-out tanks in a single location must be Soviet. We can also see the route of advance of other tanks which have advanced out of the eastern gullies into the area. These tanks (as described by Glantz) formed part of the second group of Soviet tanks which descended on the Leibstandarte Tigers. The Tiger tanks' position on the high ground of Hill 241.6's Point 228.4 gave them an excellent field of fire along the Soviet tankers' chosen lines of advance.[41] The four Tiger tanks took full advantage of their vastly superior armour (a T-34 with its 76mm main gun could not penetrate a Tiger tank frontally even at point-blank range) and the lethal penetrating power of their 88mm main gun, which could penetrate the frontal armour of a T-34 from ranges of over 2,000m.[42] The battlefield photographs testify to this success.

Early in the afternoon a further thrust by the 181st Tank Brigade directly uphill towards the summit of Hill 241.6 (Point 228.4) from the direction of the River Psel and the ribbon village of Andreyevka encouraged the Tiger tanks to move forward to the downward slope of the hill in order to engage this new threat.[43] The Tigers then fought the Soviet tanks from various positions on the declivity. We can make this assumption with confidence as to engage the Soviet tanks the Tiger tanks would have had to move from their original firing positions (on Point 228.4) in order to bring the Soviet tanks into their line of fire. The topography of the battlefield forced the Tigers of the heavy company forward (Plates 110 to 113).

It was during this engagement that the heavy company supposedly lost its only Tiger tank during Operation *Citadel*. Reportedly, the Tiger, having been immobilized by shell shot, was ultimately deemed unrecoverable due to enemy fire.[44] We can establish that any lost Tiger tank would have been lost forward of Hill 241.6's Point 228.4 (in the direction of Andreyevka) because to be under consistent enemy fire the tank must have been forward of the Leibstandarte's front line.[45] This was the only location on 12 July that the Tigers fought close to enemy lines. In all probability the Tiger was lost in the middle of this battlefield, in range of Soviet fire from Andreyevka at the base of the hill.[46] Had the Tiger been immobilized in the earlier fighting with the first echelon of the 170th Tank Brigade on the summit of Hill 241.6 at Point 228.4 then the damaged Tiger would have been recovered by the Germans. Any immobilized and then lost Tiger would have resulted from the later engagement with the 181st Tank Brigade. Soviet and German testimonies both indicate that the Soviet tanks managed to get in close proximity to the firing positions of the Tigers.[47] Overall one wonders if the loss of a Leibstandarte Tiger tank is evidence of the cavalier tactics used by the heavy company's commander Michael Wittmann. The use of similar tactics would ultimately cost Wittmann his life the following year in Normandy when on 8 August 1944 (as commander of 2nd Company, 101st SS s.Panzer.Abt) his no longer invulnerable Tiger tank was destroyed while charging across open terrain.[48]

We are once again fortunate to have this section of the Prokhorovka battlefield entirely covered by Luftwaffe photographs. Soviet wrecks and sheltering or abandoned Soviet tanks are particularly concentrated on the western edge of the battlefield close to the ribbon village of Andreyevka. In this area there seems to be at least two columns of Soviet tanks on the periphery of the battlefield. It is clear from the photographs GX-2696-SK-23, GX-2696-SK-24 and GX-2696-SK-52 (which were taken on 14 July) that the four Tiger tanks halted a much larger opposing force in the 181st Tank Brigade.[49]

The Soviet attacks on the Leibstandarte's right wing, south-east of the Prokhorovka–Belgorod railway embankment, were even less successful. The 1st SS Panzergrenadier Regiment held the front near the Stalinsk state farm, where it had to manage without the support of tanks and was initially only reinforced with Marder tank destroyers. The attacking forces consisted of 25th Tank Brigade of 29th Tank Corps, supported by 1446th Self-Propelled Gun Artillery Regiment and 28th Guards Paratroop Regiment, as well as parts of 169th Tank Brigade of 2nd Tank Corps.[50]

The battlefield of the 29th Tank Corps' 25th Tank Brigade (Plates 114 to 118) is depicted in photographs GX-3734-SK-61 (16 July), GX-3942-SK-69, GX-3942-SD-124 (7 August) and GX-3977-SD-45 (6 October).[51] The 25th Tank Brigade advanced along the line of Prokhorovka–Iamki towards the Stalinsk state farm in the direction of the gap between Storozhevoye Woods and the railway embankment. The photographs capture the drama that unfolded when the advancing 25th Tank Brigade was ambushed and savaged by flanking fire from the Leibstandarte's Marder tank destroyers (which were located in the confines of Stalinsk state farm, see Plates 2 and 118) and withering frontal fire from 75mm Pak 40 anti-tank guns from 1st SS Panzergrenadier Regiment's anti-tank company (located on the edge of the Storozhevoye Woods).[52] Finally, the rapidly depleting 25th Tank Brigade had to face a proportion of the Leibstandarte's assault gun battalion which had hitherto been held in reserve.[53]

The 25th Tank Brigade's demise is made visible by the trail of explosions on its route of advance from Prokhorovka and Iamki towards the Stalinsk state farm, Storozhevoye Woods and the gap between the woods and the railway embankment.[54] It is also possible to identify tanks that in all probability belonged to 1st Battalion, 32nd Tank Brigade, which after crossing over the railway line near Hill 252.2 followed the railway embankment and ultimately managed to reach Komsomolets state farm.[55]

The right flank of II SS Panzer Korps, which curved back far to the south, was defended by Das Reich. In that sector the attacking forces were 2nd Guards Tank Corps and 2nd Tank Corps. Their attacks, in the direction of Yasnaya Polyana and Kalinin, were repelled following heavy fighting, after which Das Reich counter-attacked and captured the village of Storozhevoye on its left wing.[56] The most significant territorial gains on 12 July were achieved on the left flank by Totenkopf. All of Totenkopf's panzers were in the bridgehead on the far side of the River Psel and attacked in a northerly direction. The only significant fighting unit of the division to remain south of the river and therefore in the Prokhorovka corridor was the 6th SS Panzergrenadier Regiment, possibly supported by some of Totenkopf's assault guns and Sf Pak, which was protecting the engineer's bridge over the Psel. North of the Psel Totenkopf attacked 5th Guards Army, as well as 31st Tank Corps and parts of 6th Guards Army. After beating off heavy Soviet attacks in the morning, Totenkopf's panzers succeeded in pushing forward as far as the Prokhorovka–Kartashevka road (this was the northernmost thrust of Operation *Citadel*); the 5th Guards Tank Army's attacking units were now threatened in the rear, while the army's HQ, in Prokhorovka, was threatened in the flank.[57]

A key reason for the high number of Soviet armoured losses on 12 July can be traced back to the events of the previous day when the Stavka representative, Marshal Aleksandr Mikhailovich Vasilevsky, overreacted after learning that the proposed marshalling areas for the 5th Guards Tank Army's offensive had fallen into German hands. Vasilevsky rashly ordered the offensive be launched as soon as possible and, as a result, the 5th Guards Tank Army was forced to attack on 12 July without sufficient intelligence and reconnaissance. Not even the anti-tank ditch at the base of Hill 252.2 was taken into account. Instead of the properly prepared attack that had been planned, the attack was carried out hastily, in a hectic rush, and it was impossible to coordinate the actions of the various forces. A report by 29th Tank Corps stated: 'The attack began without artillery fire [...] and with no aerial support.' The Military History Institute in Moscow made the following statement concerning the battle: 'Despite its [...] numerical superiority, 5th Guards Tank Army did not manage to give the battle a decisive turn. Towards evening, after losing 500 tanks and assault guns, its units went over to the defensive.'[58] However, it is important to remember that even though the Soviets had indeed taken heavy losses on 12 July they had also achieved their central aim of halting II SS Panzer Korps' drive on Prokhorovka. As a result, the Red Army won the battle of Prokhorovka.

TABLE 27.[59] **II SS Panzer Korps (Korps and Divisional 1a reported) post-battle of Prokhorovka operational AFV, 1835hrs 16.7.43**

	Pz III	Pz IV	T-34	Pz VI	Bef	Total Pz	StuG	Sf Pak	Total AFV
LSSAH operational 1835hrs 16.7.43	5	42		9	6	62	30	19*	111
DR operational 1835 16.7.43	37	18	11	5	7	78	25	12	115
Operational AFV of units involved in battle of Prokhorovka on 12.7.43	**42**	**60**	**11**	**14**	**13**	**140**	**55**	**31**	**226**
SS-T operational 1835 16.7.43	30	27		9	7	73	20	3	96
Total	72	87	11	23	20	213	75	34	322

* Possibly 15 depending on when 4 new Sf Paks arrived at the front.

TABLE 28.[60] **5th Guards Tank Army operational AFV, end of 16.7.43**

	T-34	T-70	Church-ill	122mm Sf gun	76mm Sf gun	Total AFV
29th Tank Corps	42	47		4	6	99
18th Tank Corps	45	44	9			98
2nd Guards Tank Corps	35	18				53
2nd Tank Corps	31	32	5			68
Operational AFV of units involved in battle of Prokhorovka on 12.7.43 (inc not-involved 26th Guards Tank Brigade)	153	141	14	4	6	318
5th Guards Mechanized Corps	57	33		9	6	105
Army units	15	6				21
Total	225	180	14	13	12	444

The seeds of Soviet victory were sown prior to the battle when a formidable artillery capability (on Hill 252.4 in particular) and an almost impenetrable anti-tank screen was installed close to Prokhorovka. By the evening of 11 July the Leibstandarte had already recognized the unfeasibility of a frontal assault on Prokhorovka (confirmed by the Leibstandarte SPW battalion's probing attack on the 11th). That day the Leibstandarte stated, 'The frontal attack on Prokhorovka, because of the strong anti-tank and artillery fire from the southeast outskirts [of the town] and the commanding elevation 252.4, is possible only with great losses. Proposal, after the capture of Hill 252.4 by the left-hand neighbour [Totenkopf], conduct an artillery preparation and bombing of Prokhorovka.'[61] However, Hill 252.4 was destined never to be captured. On 13 July Totenkopf, under heavy pressure, was forced to retreat from the Prokhorovka–Kartashevka road to its 12 July start lines around Hill 226.6 (close to the Psel crossings). As a result, Totenkopf was never able to launch the flanking assault on Hill 252.4 that the Leibstandarte deemed was a prerequisite to its own assault on Prokhorovka. Totenkopf's inability to suppress Hill 252.4's devastating artillery fire meant that any prospect of a serious Leibstandarte assault on Prokhorovka evaporated. On 13 July the Leibstandarte again probed the Soviet defences in front of Prokhorovka, this time north of Oktiabrskiy state farm, but as on 11 July no weak spots could be found. Furthermore, by 17 July, despite its recent high number of armoured losses, the 5th Guards Tank Army was still capable of bringing together 444 operational AFVs for the defence of Prokhorovka (for a comparison between German and Soviet operational AFV strength on the evening of 16 July see Tables 27 and 28). In addition, a further 211 Soviet AFVs were under repair or in transit to the front. It was the combination of these complicating factors that forced the Germans to shift their intended axis of advance (away from Prokhorovka) towards the north-west and Oboyan. (For details of the planned renewed offensive, Operation *Roland*, see Chapter 5.)[62]

Meanwhile, on the same day that the battle of Prokhorovka took place, the Soviets launched Operation *Kutuzov*, a massive offensive against 2nd Panzer Army in the Orel salient. Under the onslaught the panzer army's front collapsed in several places. However, as a result of 9th Army's reserved use of armour during Operation *Citadel*, 2nd Panzer Army, which had also been placed under Model's command, was able to conduct a flexible armoured defence and safely evacuate its forces from the Orel salient; the city itself was abandoned on 5 August. During July, Army Group Centre was able to call on eight panzer divisions from within its own pool of armour, six from 9th Army alone, for a strength of 464 tanks and 161 assault guns and tank destroyers.[63] Soviet armoured losses during Operation *Kutuzov* (the Soviets having deployed 2nd, 3rd and 4th Tank Armies) were extremely high, with 2,586 tanks and assault guns being written off during the battle which lasted from 12 July to 18 August 1943. German armoured losses for Army Group Centre in July are estimated at 343 tanks, assault guns and tank destroyers (including 77 AFV losses during Operation *Citadel*). The number of German armoured losses fell in August during the phased withdrawal to the Hagen Line from 1 to 16 August.[64]

TIGER TANK LOSSES AT PROKHOROVKA:
MYTH VERSUS REALITY

The Tiger tank holds an important symbolic role in the collective memory of the battle of Prokhorovka. This symbolism is best highlighted by the sculpture of two Tiger tanks being rammed and destroyed by two Soviet T-34s that stands outside the entrance to the 'Third Battlefield of Russia' museum in Prokhorovka (Plate 119). The sculpture fits perfectly into the Soviet narrative of the battle which describes a mass armoured meeting engagement (Plate 120). As we have seen, the 5th Guards Tank Army claimed that its four participating tank corps destroyed 55 Tiger tanks between 12 and 16 July 1943, while Rotmistrov claimed his units had in fact destroyed as many as 70 Tiger tanks during the battle of Prokhorovka. However, the records show that a maximum of one Tiger tank was written off as a result of the battle of Prokhorovka. To recap, according to German testimony during the battle of Prokhorovka on 12 July, a Leibstandarte Tiger tank was immobilized by shell shot close to Totenkopf positions; the tank was ultimately deemed unrecoverable due to enemy fire.[65]

After the termination of Operation *Citadel* in the south on 16 July and the abandonment of Operation *Roland* (the planned renewed offensive towards Oboyan – see Chapter 5 for details), II SS Panzer Korps was sent to the Mius Front. The Leibstandarte and Das Reich began leaving the front on 17 July.[66] Totenkopf, however, remained at the front longer, having been transferred to XXXXVIII Panzer Korps jurisdiction on 18 July. On its final day at the front, the Leibstandarte withdrew its exposed front line a few kilometres south along the Prokhorovka–Belgorod road, away from the notorious anti-tank ditch, Storozhevoye Woods and beyond Komsomolets farm. This new position formed part of the Attila line, which was the first of three designated lines which would form defensive fall-back positions to allow the front to withdraw to its pre-Operation *Citadel* positions near Belgorod in a controlled manner. The first line (Attila) was in effect a readjustment of the final *Citadel* front line. The Leibstandarte's final positions in the Attila line were centred on Hill 258.2, 1km north of Teterevino, on the Prokhorovka road. Totenkopf's frontage was then extended to this road to cover the Leibstandarte withdrawal. The 167th Infantry Division took over the positions of Das Reich and linked with Totenkopf's right flank. Totenkopf, whose front at this stage still overlooked the immobilized Leibstandarte Tiger, finally completed a controlled evacuation of its Psel bridgehead in the early hours of 18 July; the division was even able to dismantle its bridging equipment as it withdrew. Totenkopf did not, however, immediately withdraw from the south bank of the river and remained on the Kozlovka to Andreyevka line into 18 July. As a result, Totenkopf's troops also continued to overlook the base of Hill 241.6 well into the 18th. This latter consideration is particularly important when one considers the potential fate of the Leibstandarte Tiger tank which was disabled during the battle of Prokhorovka in the late morning/early afternoon when advancing down the slope of Hill 241.6 (from Point 228.4) towards the ribbon village of Andreyevka.

The Leibstandarte Tiger tank could not have been immobilized earlier in the fighting against the first echelon of the 170th Tank Brigade close to Point 228.4 (on the summit of Hill 241.6) as the damaged Tiger would have been recovered by the Germans. The Leibstandarte Tiger tank could only have been lost on the declivity of Hill 241.6 (in range of Soviet fire from Andreyevka at the base of the hill) during the later engagement with the 181st Tank Brigade.[67]

The Leibstandarte Tiger remained close to friendly Totenkopf troops until 19 July. Totenkopf's continued proximity to Hill 241.6 on 18 July can be judged by the fact that its troops were able to report on the build-up of enemy armour on the hill. Totenkopf faced enemy attacks on its positions throughout 18 July from the direction of Vasilevka (next to Andreyevka) and Hill 241.6. The Soviet attack from Vasilevka did not begin until 1230hrs; it ran parallel and past the location of the Leibstandarte Tiger (the Tiger was in no-man's-land up until this time). The attack which consisted of infantry and reportedly 60 tanks was aimed in the direction of Totenkopf's new front line which ran from Hill 258.2 then north to Hill/Point 231.5 and then west to Greznoye. The Soviet attack in this sector was broken up by Totenkopf anti-tank guns which had been sited on the northernmost extension of the new German front line on point 231.5; this position (which looked down on the ribbon villages and potentially the Leibstandarte Tiger tank) straddled the exit of the area's two dominating gullies which stretched up from Vasilevka. From 1430hrs Totenkopf counter-attacked and only withdrew from the area on the night of 18/19 July. The archival record simply does not allow for a more specific assessment of Totenkopf's operations to the north of Hill 258.2 on 18 July.

As we have seen, initial classifications of AFVs in battlefield reports were often subject to amendments over time before they finally reached an accurate account; so it is extremely problematic to attribute complete accuracy to individual ten-day status and total loss reports. It is important to compare these types of reports over a period of time in order to get an accurate picture. The examples of reclassifications and inconsistencies that have already been raised highlight the need for caution in this regard. As no subsequent Leibstandarte, Das Reich or Totenkopf divisional TF reports have survived for the period 11–20 July (if indeed they were ever produced) it is the author's belief that it cannot be definitively determined whether or not a Tiger tank was lost as a result of damaged sustained during the battle of Prokhorovka on 12 July. As the Leibstandarte Tiger tank would have remained close to Totenkopf's frontage until the 19th, a date outside the chronological range of II SS Panzer Korps' engineer's report, it should not be seen as a surprise that such a precious AFV had not yet been recorded as TF in this report.

As a result of Totenkopf's continued proximity to Hill 241.6, it seems plausible that the immobilized Leibstandarte Tiger tank would not have been classified as total loss until the 19th at the earliest. Between 12 and 18 July the Leibstandarte Tiger tank would not have been written off in case the situation at the front changed to allow a battlefield recovery to take place. However, over this period, neither Totenkopf nor the Soviets advanced to any great extent in this sector, until Totenkopf withdrew from the Attila line during the night of 18/19 July, meaning a battlefield recovery from no-man's-land of the Leibstandarte Tiger tank would have been as impossible as it was on 12 July. In addition, even though 19 July is the first realistic date that a Leibstandarte Tiger tank on the slope of Hill 241.6 could have been declared as a 3b TF, there is no guarantee this administrative procedure would have been enacted immediately, particularly due to the complicating factor that the Leibstandarte and II SS Panzer Korps HQ had already departed the area. As we know that II SS Panzer Korps' engineer's report is inaccurate regarding Totenkopf AFV losses between 11 and 20 July it is fair to assume that a Leibstandarte Tiger tank in Totenkopf's sector may have also been subject to the same administrative errors.

The case of the Totenkopf Tiger tank from the previous spring shows that it was possible for an AFV to be removed from 'Ist' (actual) totals yet remain in divisional inventories.[68] A Tiger tank's removal from the Ist total in a ten-day status report was one thing, but it did not always follow that the engineer would be willing to remove the Tiger from the inventory. At this point in time (spring/summer 1943), this may have been a unique policy for heavily damaged Tigers in the so-called Sonderverbände (the three divisions of II SS Panzer Korps and the Army's Grossdeutschland division) which would have been only too aware of a Tiger's expense, scarcity and battlefield supremacy in the first half of 1943.[69] According to the 4th Panzer Army's MTO, the Sonderverbände had exclusive privileges, such as, for example, having their own evacuation channel; perhaps this policy is another example of such privileges. What is known is that from the autumn of 1943 SS divisions such as Das Reich were officially permitted to send AFVs (not just Tigers) to homeland maintenance via the 2c category, which meant an AFV could now officially remain part of a division's inventory despite requiring homeland maintenance.[70] For example, in November 1943, a Das Reich Tiger tank (250 219) was sent for homeland maintenance via the 2c category.[71] This may well have been *de jure* recognition of a long-running *de facto* operation. It is interesting to note II SS Panzer Korps' engineer's report from July 1943 only states that a Leibstandarte Tiger was '*Inst. Heimat*' (homeland maintenance) and not whether this was homeland maintenance via the category 3a or 2c.[72]

The fact that 17 Tiger tanks (the Leibstandarte began Operation *Citadel* with 13 Tigers and received 5 new Tigers on 25 July) were ultimately transferred from the Leibstandarte to Das Reich (9) and Totenkopf (8) on 28 July has previously been cited as a reason why no Leibstandarte Tiger could have been lost during or as a result of the battle of Prokhorovka.[73] The argument is that as one Tiger was already listed in the Leibstandarte 1–10 July ten-day status report as 3a (i.e. to be sent to Germany for homeland maintenance) and that one Leibstandarte Tiger loss appears throughout the Army Group South (AGS) 5–17 July *Totalverluste* reports (the *Totalverluste* reports did not distinguish between 3a or 3b losses), there is no possibility that another Leibstandarte Tiger was ultimately written off from damage sustained during the battle of Prokhorovka.[74] However, as the reader will now be aware, without viewing subsequent Leibstandarte divisional ten-day status and/or specific AFV TF reports through to 30 July, it is impossible to rule out the possibility that a Leibstandarte Tiger that was recorded as 3a (for homeland maintenance) in the 1–10 July ten-day status report and AGS *Totalverluste* reports (A), against regulations, covertly remained in the Leibstandarte inventory (B), was later reclassified as 2c (homeland maintenance) and remained in the division's inventory (C), was eventually deemed repairable in the *K-Werk* in category 2c and as a result returned to the Leibstandarte inventory. As we have seen Totenkopf's semi-submerged Tiger tank from early 1943 seems to at some stage have experienced all three such eventualities. In addition, as the Totenkopf Tiger 'returned' to the division's *Ist* total via the 4a category (3a AFVs that had been repaired by homeland maintenance) the Tiger must have at some stage also been reclassified from 3b to 3a.[75]

The 3a Leibstandarte Tiger from the 1–10 July ten-day status report was said to have been ordered to be cannibalized for spare parts between 5 and 10 July (6 July typically being the reported date), but there is no documentary evidence that this was actually the case.[76] It is worth noting that prior to the start of Operation *Citadel* the SS spare parts situation was said to 'not look bad'; while if spare parts were not available orders could be placed directly at the Army level. There was also a regular spare parts channel for rail and air transport (on 17 July Totenkopf received Tiger tank spare parts via air transport). Troops even went, against regulations, straight to the Army Group level for spare parts (the Leibstandarte Tiger Company obtained two transmissions during Operation *Citadel* via this route).[77] The Panzer Officer of the Chief of the General Staff reported on 7 July that six Tiger tank transmissions were sent by air to AGS (without the Army Group requesting such a move) and that the six planes carrying the transmissions stopped over in Magdeburg and were 'filled with spare parts'. The Panzer Officer also stated that a special mechanic was sent along to AGS 'who supposedly can repair a part of the damaged transmissions with single parts on site'. The fact that after the battle of Prokhorovka on the night of 12/13 July II SS Panzer Korps informed the 4th Panzer Army's MTO that it could repair 13 of its 39 Tiger tanks within four to six days clearly indicates that the SS spare parts situation was still by this date, at the very least, 'not too bad'.[78]

There is no mention of a Leibstandarte Tiger tank total loss in the Leibstandarte 5–10 July TF report; though one would not expect this Tiger to be mentioned, it does confirm that the Tiger was not thought to be beyond repair.[79] It is worth restating that AFV that did not *have* to be sent to the *K-Werk* or homeland maintenance (as their damage did not warrant such a classification) were so treated in times of overwork for the lower level field repair units.[80] This latter consideration would make reclassifications even more likely, particularly if repairs were not considered as heavy as for a typical 3a case. The Leibstandarte would have also transferred both operational and non-operational tanks (including Tigers) to Das Reich and Totenkopf. There is a possibility the transferred Panzer III 77 604 was an example of the latter (the tank was at first considered to be a total loss during Operation *Citadel*).[81] Finally, it must be remembered that the Leibstandarte engineer would have been loath to remove any Tiger tank from the Leibstandarte's inventory; he would have given every opportunity to the possibility of further utilizing these extremely expensive weapons.[82] Related to this point is the consideration that (after much vacillating on Hitler's part) it was not until 26 July that the Leibstandarte received the order that it was to depart for Italy. Up to this point the Leibstandarte's engineer would have had every incentive to keep as many Tiger tanks with the division as possible.[83] Even after the arrival of five new Leibstandarte Tiger tanks on 25 July, a pool of 17 Tiger tanks was by no means excessive, being only two tanks above the heavy company's official establishment at this time.[84]

Having reviewed the body of evidence as a whole, it seems clear that the possibility remains open that an irretrievable Leibstandarte Tiger tank on the Prokhorovka battlefield was subsequently declared a 3b (total loss) before 28 July. This would have meant the 'cannibalized' Leibstandarte Tiger returning (if it had left) to the Leibstandarte inventory and an eventual 'Prokhorovka 3b' Leibstandarte Tiger being declared between 19 July (after the tank was left behind enemy lines when Totenkopf withdrew from the vicinity of Hill 241.6) and the 28th, the day the Leibstandarte handed over 17 Tigers to Das Reich (9) and Totenkopf (8).[85] This would certainly explain why German testimony, despite some records seemingly discounting the possibility, strongly indicated that a Leibstandarte Tiger tank was indeed lost as a result of damage sustained during the battle of Prokhorovka.[86]

From Attack to Defence: The Battle of Kursk Following Operation *Citadel*, mid-July–31 August 1943

WASTING FIREMEN: HITLER'S INFLUENCE ON POST-PROKHOROVKA ARMOURED STRENGTH PRIOR TO THE DEFENCE OF KHARKOV

Field Marshal Erich von Manstein had been prepared both during and after Operation *Citadel* to allow the Red Army a free hand in the southern sectors of his army group in return for a concentrated effort during the battle of Kursk. In May 1943 Manstein declared:

> in the case of *Citadel* the decisive factor is the battle for Kursk, and that battle must be fought out even at the risk of a serious crisis in the Donets area. It must therefore be assumed at the outset that the enemy will succeed in making deep breaches in the Army Group's widely stretched front in the sectors of 6th Army and 1st Panzer Army.[1]

As Karl-Heinz Frieser has succinctly written:

> Manstein developed the brilliant idea that the battle on the Mius had to be fought at Kursk. There, by tying down and destroying the largest possible amount of enemy forces, the risk of offensives on other sections of the front could be averted. His idea was to force the Red Army to throw so many tanks into the Kursk caldron that it would be unable to launch its planned summer offensive or would be able to do so only with insufficient forces. That this was by no means absurd is shown by the strikingly high number of Soviet losses. The Soviet colossus was dangerous only if it was able to throw

its numerical superiority into the balance – especially its strongest weapon, the artillery – in a properly prepared attack. At Kursk, however, there was a chance of entangling the Soviet armoured units in meeting engagements in which the German tank commanders would be able to exploit their tactical superiority.[2]

To a great extent this is indeed what occurred, as during Operation *Citadel* Soviet armour suffered very heavy losses. Up to and including 22 July, Voronezh Front (together with reserves brought in) lost a total of 1,430 tanks and assault guns (1,223 tanks and assault guns up to 13 July). By contrast, up to and including 20 July the attacking units of Army Group South lost only 219 tanks, assault guns and tank destroyers (112 of these AFV losses occurred between 11 and 20 July). The same German units would go on to record a further 85 tank, assault gun and tank destroyer losses between 21 and 31 July; however, 34 of these AFV losses occurred after units had been transferred to other sectors of the Eastern Front. In terms of operational AFVs, between 11 and 21 July XXXXVIII Panzer Korps' AFV strength rose from 275 to 306 AFVs, II SS Panzer Korps' AFV numbers rose from 339 to 349 AFVs, while the III Panzer Korps increased from 163 to 169 AFVs. In total (including Korps Raus) between 11 and 20 July the operational numbers of the attacking units of Army Group South rose from 814 to 861 AFVs.[3]

Following the battle of Prokhorovka Manstein hoped to put his Kursk concept further into practice by launching Operation *Roland*. The operation was intended to shift the main effort of the attack to the north-west, away from Prokhorovka (Soviet artillery and anti-tank strength prohibited further attempts to reach Prokhorovka), in the direction of Oboyan. In this way Manstein hoped to inflict even greater losses on the Soviet armoured reserves.

In the hours following the battle of Prokhorovka the 4th Panzer Army Motor Transport Officer received an urgent request from Major Neu of Army Group South, who was a fellow member of the Motor Transport Department. At 0130hrs on 13 July Neu demanded to know how many of the army's tanks and assault guns currently under short-term repair had the necessary spare parts available to be made ready for action in four days. Neu insisted that the information supplied to him be listed by division and panzer type. The 4th Panzer Army MTO informed Neu that such a report was technically impossible for the desired timeframe. The 4th Panzer Army MTO was no doubt recalling that on 11 July he had agreed with the XXXXVIII and II SS Panzer Korps that 'short-term maintenance for panzers means six days'. After consulting with his colleagues, XXXVIII Panzer Korps and II SS Panzer Korps the 4th Panzer Army's MTO concluded that 'the values could only be given according to the documents available to us', which may well mean that the report the MTO supplied to Neu actually listed AFVs which could be made operational within six days rather than the requested four.[4] The request for this information probably originated from Manstein. The Field Marshal was due to meet Hitler at *Führer* Headquarters (FHQ) later that day (13 July) where he intended to propose Operation *Roland*, anticipated to begin around 18/19 July, to Hitler. Manstein would have wanted a detailed estimate of the number of operational AFVs that he could expect to have available for the launch of this offensive.[5]

At 0300hrs on 13 July the 4th Panzer Army MTO began his report to Army Group South with the following message: 'these are the panzers which can be expected to be operational again in four days according to previous experience' (see Table 29).[6]

TABLE 29.[7] 4th Panzer Army MTO predicted number of 4-day (possibly 6-day) AFV repairs at 0300hrs 13.7.43

	Pz III/Bef	Pz IV	Pz VI	StuG	Total AFV
LSSAH	6	31	7	9	53
DR	15	17	4	3	39
SS-T	11	11	2	6	30
II SS Panzer Korps	32	59	13	18	122

It is interesting to note that in total the 4th Panzer Army reported that II SS Panzer Korps had enough spare parts available to return 122 AFVs to combat within four to six days (Leibstandarte 53, Das Reich 39, Totenkopf 30). It is also interesting that this figure included as many as 13 of II SS Panzer Korps' remaining 39 mechanically complex Tiger tanks. That 122 AFVs were thought possible to be repaired in this timeframe, eight days into Operation *Citadel*, clearly indicates that II SS Panzer Korps was not yet suffering from any real shortage of AFV spare parts.[8]

TABLE 30.[9] II SS Panzer Korps post-Prokhorovka AFV repairs

	Pz III/Bef	Pz IV	Pz VI	StuG	Total AFV
4th Pz Army MTO predicted repairs 0300hrs 13.7.43	32	59	13	18	122
Known to be repaired 13–16.7.43	7	29	21	17	74
Known to be repaired 13–18.7.43	13	50	25	20	108
Known to be repaired 13–18.7.43 including estimated LSSAH 13.7.43 gain	13	57	26	21	117

Table 30 reveals that the 4th Panzer Army MTO's estimate of 122 AFVs to be repaired by 16 July, or more likely 18 July, was not overly optimistic. By 18 July 1943 II SS Panzer Korps had managed to repair at least 108 AFVs (13 Panzer III/Befs, 50 Panzer IVs, 25 Panzer VIs and 20 StuGs) in the six days since the request was made. Understandably, II SS Panzer Korps repair services concentrated their efforts on repairing the Korps' most potent armour; the long-barrelled Panzer IV and Tiger tanks.[10]

As Das Reich and Totenkopf were regularly in combat between 12 and 18 July, the known 63 AFVs that were repaired by these divisions during this period is the minimum number of AFVs that were actually repaired (Tables 31 and 32). In combat Das Reich and Totenkopf would have incurred additional numbers of damaged AFVs which would naturally disguise the true number of repaired armour that can be detected in the daily operational totals. Therefore, in reality Das Reich and Totenkopf would have repaired more than 63 AFVs during this period. Despite this, 63 AFVs repaired was just six less than the 69 AFVs that the 4th Panzer Army's MTO thought was possible to be repaired.[11]

TABLE 31.[12] DR post-Prokhorovka AFV repairs									
	Pz III/ Bef	Gain	Pz IV	Gain	Pz VI	Gain	StuG	Gain	Total
11.7.43 1925hrs operational AFV	34/7		18		1		27		
12.7.43 1800 operational AFV	42/6		18		2		27		
4th Pz Army MTO predicted repairs 13.7.43 0300	15		17		4		3		39
13.7.43 1935 operational AFV	43/8	1/2	20	2	1		24		
14.7.43 1800 operational AFV	41/8		25	5	4	3	25	1	
15.7.43 1840 operational AFV	37/7		17		2		23		
16.7.43 1835 operational AFV	37/7		18	1	5	3	25	2	
Known to be re-paired 13–16.7.43		1/2=3		8		6		3	20
17.7.43 1915 operational AFV	36/6		24	6	9	4	25		

	Pz III/Bef	Gain	Pz IV	Gain	Pz VI	Gain	StuG	Gain	Total
18.7.43 1710 operational AFV	36/7	0/1	24		9		28	3	
Known to be repaired 13–18.7.43		1/3=4		14		10		6	34

TABLE 32.[13] SS-T post-Prokhorovka AFV repairs

	Pz III/Bef	Gain	Pz IV	Gain	Pz VI	Gain	StuG	Gain	Total
11.7.43 1925hrs Operational AFV	54/7		30		10		21		
12.7.43 1800 operational AFV	53/7		30		10		21		
4th Pz Army MTO predicted repairs 0300 13.7.43	11		11		2		6		30
13.7.43 1935 operational AFV	32/5	.	17		0		20		
14.7.43 1800 operational AFV	28/7	0/2	17		5	5	16		
15.7.43 1840 operational AFV	28/6		20	3	7	2	16		
16.7.43 1835 operational AFV	30/7	0/1	27	7	9	2	20	4	
Known to be repaired 13–16.7.43		0/3=3		10		9		4	26
17.7.43 1915 operational AFV	31/7	1/0	29	2	7		20		
18.7.43 1710 operational AFV	30/7		28		7		20		
Known to be repaired 13–18.7.43		1/3=4		12		9		4	29

TABLE 33.[14] LSSAH post-Prokhorovka AFV repairs

	Pz III/ Bef	Gain	Pz IV	Gain	Pz VI	Gain	StuG	Gain	Total
11.7.43 1925hrs operational AFV	5/7		47		4		10		
Official 12.7.43 operational AFV	?		?		?		?		
Estimated operation-al AFVs 12.7.43 2000	5/7		*24 (55–31)*		*2 (9–7)*		*19 (28–9)*		
4th Pz Army MTO predicted repairs 0300 13.7.43	6		31		7		9		53
13.7.43 1935 oper-ational AFV and *estimat-ed gain*	5/7	*0*	31	7	3	*1*	20	*1*	
14.7.43 1800 opera-tional AFV	6/7	1/0	32	1	8	5	21	1	
15.7.43 1840 opera-tional AFV	6/7		32		8		28	7	
16.7.43 1835	5/6		42	10	9	1	30	2	
Known to be repaired 13–16.7.43		1/0=1			11		6	10	28
17.7.43 1915 opera-tional AFV	6/8	1/2	46	4	9		28		

18.7.43 1700 operational AFV	7/8	1/0	55	9	9		28		
Known to be repaired 13–18.7.43		3/2=5		24		6		10	45

By contrast the Leibstandarte, bar a brief attack on 13 July 1943, undertook no further armoured combat over this timeframe. As a result, the repair services for the Leibstandarte would not have received many additional AFVs to repair between 13 and 18 July (Table 33). This, together with the accuracy of the MTO's quote in regards to Das Reich and Totenkopf, means we can with a fair degree of confidence retrospectively remove the reported number of AFVs that the Leibstandarte declared (at 0300hrs on 13 July) was possible to be repaired (53 AFVs) within four (or six) days from those AFVs that were reported operational in the 16 July or 18 July daily operational AFV reports. This calculation then gives us the likely number of operational AFVs that the Leibstandarte possessed on the evening of 12 July after the battle of Prokhorovka. The calculation is important as the Leibstandarte did not issue a daily operational AFV report for 12 July (Table 34).[15]

TABLE 34.[16] **Korps and LSSAH 1a operational AFV, July 1943**

	Pz III	Pz IV	T-34	Pz VI	Bef	StuG	Sf Pak
1.7.43 1840hrs	12	62		11	15*	31	?
2.7.43 1830	12	72		11	15*	31	22#
3.7.43	?	?		?	?	?	?
4.7.43 1845	11	79		12	9	34	21
5.7.43 1858	12	77		7	9	23	22#
6.7.43 1700	?	?		?	?	16	23#
7.7.43	?	?		?	?	?	?
8.7.43 1745	10	40		1	6	20	21
9.7.43 1735	4	32		4	5	21	21
10.7.43 1925	4	41		4	6	20	21#
11.7.43 1925	5	47		4	7	10	20#
12.7.43	?	?		?	?	?	?
13.7.43 1935	5	31		3	7	20	20#
14.7.43 1800	6	32		8	7	21	20#
15.7.43 1840	6	32		8	7	28	18

	Pz III	Pz IV	T-34	Pz VI	Bef	StuG	Sf Pak
16.7.43 1835	5	42		9	6	30	19
17.7.43 1915	6	46		9	8	28	18
18.7.43 1700	7	55		9	8	28	16
19.7.43	?	?		?	?	?	?
20.7.43	?	?		?	?	?	?
21.7.43	?	?		?	?	?	?
22.7.43	?	?		?	?	30	18
23.7.43 2045	9	46		10	6	30	?
24.7.43 2120	7	55		10	6	30	22

* Includes Lt Bef panzers.
# Includes new Sf Paks.

TABLE 35.[17] Korps and DR 1a operational AFV, July 1943

	Pz III	Pz IV	T-34	Pz VI	Bef	StuG	Sf Pak
1.7.43 1840hrs	53*	32	16	12	8	32	10
2.7.43 1830	48*	29	19	12	8	33	9
3.7.43	?	?	?	?	?	?	?
4.7.43 1845	48*	30	18	12	8	33	10
5.7.43	53*	27	16	11	8	21	?
6.7.43	?	?	?	?	?	?	?
7.7.43 0230	48*	16	15	7	6	14	10
8.7.43	43	25	14	6	7	7	?
9.7.43 1800	31	13	7	1	7	26	11
10.7.43 1925	33	15	7	1	7	26	12
11.7.43 1925	34	18	8	1	7	27	12
12.7.43 1800	42	18	8	2	6	27	12
13.7.43 1935	43	20	11	1	8	24	12
14.7.43 1800	41	25	12	4	8	25	12
15.7.43 1840	37	17	13	2	7	23	12
16.7.43 1835	37	18	11	5	7	25	12
17.7.43 1915	36	24	17	9	6	25	11
18.7.43 1710	36	24	17	9	7	28	10
19.7.43	?	?	?	?	?	?	?
20.7.43	?	?	?	?	?	?	?
21.7.43	?	?	?	?	?	?	?
22.7.43 1855	36	24	17	9	7	28	10

23.7.43 1900	14	14	?	8	5	32	11
24.7.43	?	?	?	?	?	32	11
25.7.43	?	?	?	?	?	?	?
26.7.43	?	?	?	?	?	?	?
27.7.43	46	20	1	3	2	?	11
28.7.43 2030	33	17	2	6	3	28	?
29.7.43 2045	18	25	?	6	5	32	11
30.7.43	?	?	?	?	?	?	?
31.7.43 1800	10	12	?	1	5	20	11
1.8.43 1715	11	13	?	?	5	15	10
2.8.43 1720	10	8	?	?	4	?	?

* Includes 1 Pz III L/42 which was reported as operational by the Korps 1a; however, this Panzer III L/42 was one of two (65831 and 65726) which were training with DR's Panther battalion at Mailly le Camp in France, PzAOK 4, O.Qu.V, DR Fahrgestell-Nr. Pz.kpf.Wg. 1.7.43, T313, R390.

TABLE 36.[18] Korps and SS-T 1a operational AFV, July 1943

	Pz III	Pz IV	T-34	Pz VI	Bef	StuG	Sf Pak
1.7.43 1840hrs	52	40		10	7	28	11
2.7.43 1830	52	44		11	7	28	11
3.7.43	?	?		?	?	?	?
4.7.43 1845	59	47		11	8	28	11
5.7.43 1858	57	47		10	7	?	?
6.7.43 1700	52	43		6	7	?	11
7.7.43 1900	53	43		6	8	13	?
8.7.43 1915	52	35		5	7	13	?
9.7.43 1745	47	27		2	5	12	11
10.7.43 1925	48	28		2	5	21	11
11.7.43 1925	54	30		10	7	21	?
12.7.43 1800	53	30		10	7	21	?
13.7.43 1935	32	17		0	5	20	2
14.7.43 1935	28	17		5	7	16	?
15.7.43 1840	28	20		7	6	16	?
16.7.43 1835	30	27		9	7	20	3
17.7.43 1915	31	29		7	7	20	?
18.7.43 1925	30	28		7	7	20	3
19.7.43 1930	30	24		4	?	25	3

20.7.43 1830	29	26		5	?	?	?
21.7.43	?	?		?	?	?	?
22.7.43	?	?		?	?	?	?
23.7.43	?	?		?	?	?	?
24.7.43	?	?		?	?	?	?
25.7.43	?	?		?	?	?	?
26.7.43	?	?		?	?	?	?
27.7.43	?	?		?	?	?	?
28.7.43 1700	52	32		5	5	26	?
29.7.43	?	?		?	?	?	?
30.7.43 1745	13	20		4	5	14	3
31.7.43 1730	5	9		1	5	14	6
1.8.43 1730	5	11		3	6	14	6
2.8.43 1720	3	11		3	6	13	6

For Operation *Roland*, Manstein planned to reposition II SS Panzer Korps further to the west so that the Korps could lead the strike towards Oboyan. Manstein proposed to encircle all the Soviet troops positioned in the south-western section of the Kursk salient, potentially destroying parts of the 38th and 40th Armies, and his old adversaries the 1st Tank Army and 6th Guards Army. Furthermore, Steppe Front was sending 27th, 53rd and parts of 47th Army into the threatened area in preparation for the forthcoming summer offensive against Kharkov. Manstein intended to use his uncommitted Army Group reserve, XXIV Panzer Korps under the command of Gen Walther Nehring with SS Panzergrenadier Division Wiking (SS-W), 17th and 23rd Panzer Divisions (collectively 188 operational AFVs) and III Panzer Korps as eastward flank protection for the westward drive of Operation *Roland*.[19]

If we look at the recovering operational armoured strength of the Leibstandarte and Das Reich on the evening of 18 July (roughly the intended start date of the offensive) then we can see that the German attack would have carried significant force (Table 34 to 36 and 38). However, on 13 July to Manstein's dismay Hitler decided to abandon Operation *Citadel* (the massive Soviet offensive against the Orel salient having begun on the 12th), withdraw II SS Panzer Korps and dismiss Manstein's proposal for Operation *Roland*. Hitler wanted to send II SS Panzer Korps to Italy on a political mission to bolster his Axis partner's faltering resolve to fight. From 17 July Hitler would also be distracted by the economic arguments for using II SS Panzer Korps to protect the industry of the Donets Basin (Table 37 to 41).[20]

TABLE 37.[21] II SS Panzer Korps – pre-Operation *Roland* AFV inventory (*c.*18–19.7.43)

	Pz III	Pz IV	T-34	Pz VI	Bef	Total Pz	StuG	Sf Pak	Total AFV
LSSAH inventory 0100hrs 19.7.43 (following *Citadel*)	12	74		12	9	107	32	22*	161
DR inventory 0100 19.7.43 (following *Citadel*)	60	27	21	13	9	130	32	12	174
SS-T Inventory 0100 21.7.43 (following *Citadel*)	61	48		14	9	132	34	9–11#	175–177
Total	133	149	21	39	27	369	98	43–45	510–512

* Includes 4 new LSSAH Sf Pak.
# 2 Sf Pak lost sometime between 11.7.43 and the end of the Mius operation.

TABLE 38.[22] II SS Panzer Korps – pre-Operation *Roland* operational AFV (*c.*18–19.7.43)

	Pz III	Pz IV	T-34	Pz VI	Bef	Total Pz	StuG	Sf Pak	Total AFV
LSSAH operational 1925hrs 18.7.43	7	55		9	8	79	28	16	123
DR operational 1925 18.7.43	36	24	17	9	7	93	28	10	131
SS-T operational 1925 18.7.43	30	28		7	7	72	20	3	95
Total	73	107	17	25	22	244	76	29	349

TABLE 39.[23] II SS Panzer Korps – peak operational AFV numbers following Operation *Citadel*

	Pz III	Pz IV	T-34	Pz VI	Bef	Total Pz	StuG	Sf Pak	Total AFV
LSSAH operational 24.7.43	7	55		10	6	78	30	22	130
DR operational 18.7.43	36	24	17	9	7	93	28	10	131
SS-T operational 28.7.43	52	32		5	5	94	26	6*	126*
Total	95	111	17	24	18	265	84	38	387

* Unlikely to be less than 6 as this number of SS-T Sf Pak was operational on 31.7.43.

TABLE 40.[24] II SS Panzer Korps AFV inventory prior to LSSAH transfer and Mius offensive (30.7.43)

	Pz III	Pz IV	T-34	Pz VI	Bef	Total Pz	StuG	Sf Pak	Total AFV
LSSAH inventory 27.7.43 (did not participate)	12	74		17	9	112	32	22	166
DR inventory 27.7.43	60	27	21	13	9	130	32	12	174
SS-T inventory 27.7.43	61	48		14	9	132	34	9–11*	175–177
Total	133	149	21	44	27	374	98	43–45	515–517

*2 Sf Pak lost sometime between 11.7.43 and the end of the Mius operation.

TABLE 41.[25] II SS Panzer Korps operational AFV prior to LSSAH transfer and Mius offensive (30.7.43)

	Pz III	Pz IV	T-34	Pz VI	Bef	Total Pz	StuG	Sf Pak	Total AFV
LSSAH operational 24.7.43	7	55		10	6	78	30	22	130
DR operational 28.7.43 (not including LSSAH Pz)	33	17	2	6	3	61	28	11*	100
SS-T operational 28.7.43 (not including LSSAH Pz)	52	32		5	5	94	26	6#	126#
Total	92	104	2	21	14	233	84	39	356

* Previous day.
# Unlikely to be less than 6 as this number of SS-T Sf Pak was operational on 31.7.43.

During the battle of Kursk it would have been to Germany's advantage for Army Group South to retain as many of its panzer units in the Kharkov area throughout the battle, which of course included the defence of Kharkov itself. If loss of territory away from the centre of gravity on the Eastern Front (Kursk/Kharkov) was the inevitable consequence of this decision, then that should have been a price worth paying.[26] Despite the cancellation of Operations Citadel and Roland, Hitler should have been able to recognize the absolute necessity of keeping an intact II SS Panzer Korps in the region, in order that it could be immediately deployed in the defence of Kharkov. Instead of sending its divisions to 1st Panzer Army and 6th Army, the German High Command would have been better served allowing II SS Panzer Korps to rest its troops, repair the majority of its damaged AFVs and then become the main armoured reserve of Army Group South in the Kharkov area. By mid-July 1943 it was obvious that Kharkov was going to be the target of the next major Soviet offensive. Had Hitler allowed Manstein to deploy a near full strength and concentrated II SS Panzer Korps in a major counter-attack into the flank of the advancing Soviet armoured formations, then this would have caused untold damage to the Soviets' plans to rapidly retake Kharkov.

The subsequent deployment of Army Group South's reserve (XXIV Panzer Korps) to the south meant that the 17 July Soviet offensives in 1st Panzer Army (SS-W and 17th Panzer Division – Donets) and 6th Army's (23rd Panzer Division – Mius) sectors could be contained. Given the dire strategic situation on the Eastern Front, the fact that without further reinforcement by II SS Panzer Korps neither of the resulting Soviet bridgeheads could be crushed seems of little relevance. As a result, Manstein's overall strategy of concentration at Kursk, which included II SS Panzer Korps, need not have been impeded.[27]

Although II SS Panzer Korps (minus the Leibstandarte) did eventually manage to crush the Soviet bridgehead on the Mius, in reality the operation, along with Hitler's insistence of sending the Leibstandarte and II SS Panzer Korps HQ to Italy, had a 'disastrous' effect on the Germans' ability to resist the major Soviet offensive against Kharkov, Operation *Rumyantsev*, which began on 3 August. The decision to relocate II SS Panzer Korps removed the most powerful panzer korps at Germany's disposal away from the centre of gravity on the Eastern Front and reduced the number of AFV repairs that could realistically be expected to be completed. The SS divisions near-constant transportations in the latter half of July and the accompanying departure away from the main concentration of spare parts on the Eastern Front impeded the repair services work (particularly regarding Das Reich). Furthermore, the resulting Mius counteroffensive severely reduced Das Reich and Totenkopf AFV operational readiness for the battle of Kharkov as both divisions suffered a large number of damaged tanks, while over 25 AFVs were lost.[28]

In addition, even though the vast majority of Leibstandarte panzers were left on the Eastern Front to boost the inventories of Das Reich and Totenkopf, in real terms there was a loss of panzer strength. As already mentioned, Das Reich and Totenkopf clearly did not have enough crews to man all of the additional panzers prior to the start of the Mius counter-attack. The loss of the experienced Leibstandarte tank crews would prove particularly damaging throughout the rest of the battle of Kursk. In addition, the Eastern Front was also shorn of the Leibstandarte assault gun battalion, its 22-strong tank destroyer battalion and the division's returning I Panzer Battalion which was on the cusp of becoming operational with 71 (granted mechanically

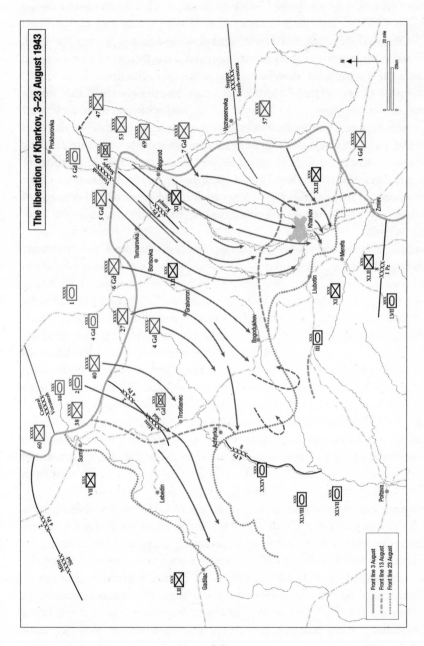

MAP 6

unreliable) Panther tanks. The Leibstandarte's I Panzer Battalion would have been ready for action in the Kharkov area around 19 August. Its preparation for combat was reported to be three days ahead of Das Reich's own Panther battalion which entered combat on 22 August 1943 (Plate 121).[29]

As a result of these negative developments, when Das Reich and Totenkopf, now under the command of III Panzer Korps, did finally launch a coordinated counter-attack (alongside SS-W) west of Kharkov on 12 August, they could only contribute 155 operational AFVs.[30] By contrast, just prior to the Leibstandarte departure on 28 July, II SS Panzer Korps had 356 operational AFVs.[31] Therefore the combination of Hitler's decision to send the Leibstandarte to Italy and the undertaking of the unnecessary Mius offensive meant that the SS counter-attack at Kharkov on 12 August was reduced in strength by at least 200 operational AFVs.[32] To put these figures into context, as a direct consequence of the German high command's decision to strip away many of Army Group South's armoured formations (3rd Panzer, Grossdeutschland, Leibstandarte, Das Reich and Totenkopf) following the termination of Operation *Citadel*, the entire German defence (4th Panzer Army and Army Detachment Kempf) against the 3 August Soviet Kharkov offensive possessed only 344 operational AFVs. This represented a wholly unnecessary decline of 517 operational AFVs since 21 July, down from 861 operational AFVs. By 10 August five armoured divisions (3rd Panzer, Grossdeutschland, Das Reich, Totenkopf and SS-W) had been rushed back to the Kharkov area; however, by this time the damage had been done to the centre of gravity on the Eastern Front.[33] Had II SS Panzer Korps remained in the Kharkov area (the same could be said of the 3rd Panzer and Grossdeutschland Divisions – the latter was briefly sent to the Orel salient) between 20 July and 3 August in order to conduct AFV repairs, then it is beyond doubt that an even greater number of the Korps' AFVs (greater than 356 AFVs) would have been available to oppose the Red Army's Kharkov offensive. The German repair services would have had around two weeks to conduct further AFV repairs in the same high quality repair facilities II SS Panzer Korps had been using since the spring. The Korps would have also been able to tap into the stocks of spare parts that had been located in the area as part of the preparations for Operation *Citadel*. This clearly had already been occurring given the rapid rise in the Leibstandarte and Das Reich AFV operational status (following the battle of Prokhorovka) between 13 and 18 July 1943.[34] There was certainly good scope for further repairs as II SS Panzer Korps, including the Leibstandarte, still had an inventory of 515 AFVs (an additional 142 Panthers for the Leibstandarte and Das Reich were expected to arrive at the front in late August).[35] Even following the Leibstandarte's withdrawal, Das Reich and Totenkopf (after the Leibstandarte panzer transfers) still had a collective inventory in excess of 400

AFVs, which again gives us a clear sense of how costly the Mius offensive had been for Das Reich and Totenkopf AFV operational status, which to recap stood at just 155 AFVs on 11 August (Table 42).[36]

TABLE 42.[37] SS *Sonderverbände* operational AFV pre-Kharkov counter-attack (12.8.43)

	Pz III	Pz IV	T-34	Pz VI	Bef	Total Pz	StuG	Sf Pak	Total AFV
DR operational 11.8.43	17	26	6*	8	4*	61	20	12	93
SS-T operational 11.8.43	9	22		7	1	39	16	7	62
Total	26	48	6	15	5	100	36	19	155

* Closest recorded operational number. 2.8.43 for T-34 and 13.8.43 for Bef.

A fully operational and complete II SS Panzer Korps (including the Leibstandarte) in the hands of Manstein would have been a fearsome prospect. Had II SS Panzer Korps been held in reserve (close to Kharkov) following Operation *Citadel*, then the Korps would have been quite capable of launching a coordinated counter-attack with over 400 operational AFVs, crucially, at a much earlier date than 12 August. However, even if a major counteroffensive at Kharkov by an undiluted II SS Panzer Korps had been successful, the Korps divisions would soon have been worn down by constant combat with the inevitable result that AFV operational numbers would have plummeted.[38]

Even if Manstein could have initially pulled off another masterstroke at Kharkov, as he had in February/March 1943, there is absolutely no doubt, given the Red Army's massive overall superiority in men and materiel, that the fall of Kharkov would have only been delayed for a short period. The Red Army was by now capable of conducting multiple simultaneous offensives on the Eastern Front; as a result by the summer of 1943 one localized German success, however great, would have made little impact on the course of the war on the Eastern Front.[39]

By comparing the 1 August 6th Army *Wochenmeldung* AFV inventory for Das Reich with the division's inventory for 1 September (that is located in the order of battle chart which accompanied the 1 September divisional *Meldung*) we can see that in reality during the defence of Kharkov and its surrounding area Das Reich lost: 18 Panzer IIIs or Befs (at least 13 of which were conventional Panzer III), 12 Panzer IVs (Das Reich had received ten new Panzer IVs in mid-August), five Panzer Vs (as mentioned Das Reich's 71-strong Panther battalion entered combat on 22 August) and three Panzer VIs. Das Reich also lost four StuGs and four Sf Paks over this period. As a result, in total Das Reich lost 46 AFVs in the unsuccessful defence of Kharkov. Of course, there is a possibility that a few of these losses occurred on 2 August, on the last day of the Mius offensive. However, in stark contrast to the previous days' fighting, that of 2 August consisted of a rapid advance to the Mius. As a result, few AFV losses can be expected on this day (Tables 43 to 48).[40]

TABLE 43.[41] **DR operational AFV, Kharkov, August 1943**

	Pz III	Pz IV	Pz V	Pz VI	Bef	StuG	Sf Pak
9.8.43	?	?		?	?	20	?
10.8.43	9	19		5	?	22	?
11.8.43	17	26		8	?	20	12
12.8.43	7	13		2	?	23	?
13.8.43	4	10		4	4	19	?
14.8.43	5	15		6	4	19	9
15.8.43	4	22		6	4	16	9
16.8.43	6	25		5	5	20	9
17.8.43	6	25		7	4	21	9
18.8.43	10	15		3	6	21	9
19.8.43	4	20		4	5	19	9
20.8.43	9	20		5	5	20	9
21.8.43	8	25		5	4	19	9

TABLE 44.[42] **SS-T operational AFV, Kharkov, August 1943**

	Pz III	Pz IV	Pz V	Pz VI	Bef	StuG	Sf Pak
9.8.43	14	27		?	?	21	?
10.8.43	14	13		?	4	16	?
11.8.43	9	22		7	1	16	7
12.8.43	15	22		5	8	17	?
13.8.43	15	22		1	8	16	?
14.8.43	11	17		1	7	?	?
15.8.43	10	17		3	7	16	6
16.8.43	?	?		?	?	15	?
17.8.43	6	18		2	8	16	?
18.8.43	14	25		3	8	16	7
19.8.43	17	27		4	?	?	?
20.8.43	15	26		5	8	?	7
21.8.43	18	24		5	8	16	7
22.8.43	15	21		5	8	20	?

TABLE 45.[43] Wiking operational AFV, Kharkov, August 1943

	Pz III	Pz IV	Pz V	Pz VI	Bef	StuG	Sf Pak
11.8.43	20	10			1	5	6
12–14.8.43?	?	?			?	?	?
15.8.43	11	7			1	4	4
16.8.43	11	5			1	?	4
17.8.43	13	9			1	?	5
18–19.8.43 ?	?	?			?	?	?
20.8.43	10	6			1	3	3
21.8.43	12	7			1	3	5
22.8.43	12	7			1	3	3
23.8.43	16	7			1	2	2
24.8.43	17	7			1	2	4

TABLE 46.[44] SS *Sonderverbände* AFV inventory, 1.9.43

	Pz III	Pz IV	Pz V	Pz VI	Bef	Total Pz	StuG	Sf Pak	Total AFV
DR inventory 1.9.43	51	58	66	19	4–9	?	28	8	?
SS-T inventory 1.9.43	50–61	32–67		18–22	8–9	?	30	7	?

TABLE 47.[45] SS *Sonderverbände* operational AFV, 1.9.43

	Pz III	Pz IV	Pz V	Pz VI	Bef	Total Pz	StuG	Sf Pak	Total AFV
DR operational 1.9.43	3	10	21	2	?	?	23	7	?
SS-T operational 1.9.43	23	9		1	?	?	15	4	?

TABLE 48.[46] SS-T operational AFV, September 1943

	Pz III	Pz IV	Pz V	Pz VI	Bef	StuG	Sf Pak
15.9.43	14	12		3	7	14	4
16.9.43	14	12		3	7	12	4
17.9.43	14	12		3	7	10	5
18.9.43	12	10		3	7	10	5
19.9.43	12	9		0	7	10	5
20.9.43	13	11		0	7	10	5
21.9.43	13	9		0	7	8	5

22–27.9.43?	?	?		?	?	?	?
28.9.43	7	3		0	6	?	?
29.9.43	5	3		0	5	1	3
30.9.43	5	3		0	6	0	?

It is far harder to accurately assess the AFV losses Totenkopf sustained in the defence of Kharkov. Following the 1 August 6th Army *Wochenmeldung* the next surviving complete panzer inventory (including panzers under long-term repair) for Totenkopf is contained in an 8th Army report from 5 October (Figure 17). The report states that Totenkopf still had 50 Panzer IIIs; however, only 26 Panzer IVs are recorded (3 operational, 15 short-term repair, 8 long-term repair). The divisional *Meldung* from 1 September stated Totenkopf had 32 Panzer IVs operational or under short/medium term repair (three weeks); the rest of the panzer types had greater values in the 5 October 8th Army report. Therefore on 1 September Totenkopf must have had in excess of 50 Panzer IIIs and 32 Panzer IVs in its inventory; the divisional *Meldung* for this date did not include AFVs under long-term repair. The 5 October 8th Army report also states that Totenkopf possessed eight Befs and 23 Tiger tanks (the division had just received five new Tiger tanks – these were Totenkopf's first new AFVs of any type received since July). Although the order of battle chart which accompanied the 1 September divisional *Meldung* does not include a panzer inventory, it does state that Totenkopf possessed 30 StuGs and seven Sf Paks.[47]

Therefore, the maximum number of panzer losses that Totenkopf could have sustained between 1 August and 1 September is: 11 Panzer IIIs, 35 Panzer IVs, four Panzer VIs and one Bef. Of course, a proportion of these losses would have occurred in September. Totenkopf also suffered the loss of four StuGs and two Sf Paks in the August fighting around Kharkov. Given that Totenkopf Panzer IV operational numbers did not rise above the mid-20s throughout August 1943, it seems likely that many of the 47 Panzer IVs that the 1 August *Wochenmeldung* stated required 'short-term repair' in fact never saw combat again. These panzers would have been either abandoned during September's retreat to the Dnieper or evacuated to homeland maintenance. The lasting detrimental impact of the Mius offensive should not be underestimated.[48]

Overall, during Operation *Rumyantsev* the 5th Guard Tank Army (which had been reconstituted following the battle of Prokhorovka) and the 1st Tank Army once again suffered very heavy losses. In 20 days, the 5th Guard Tank Army's strength fell from 543 tanks to only 50, while 1st Tank Army and attached units lost 1,042 AFVs, the tank army having been continuously

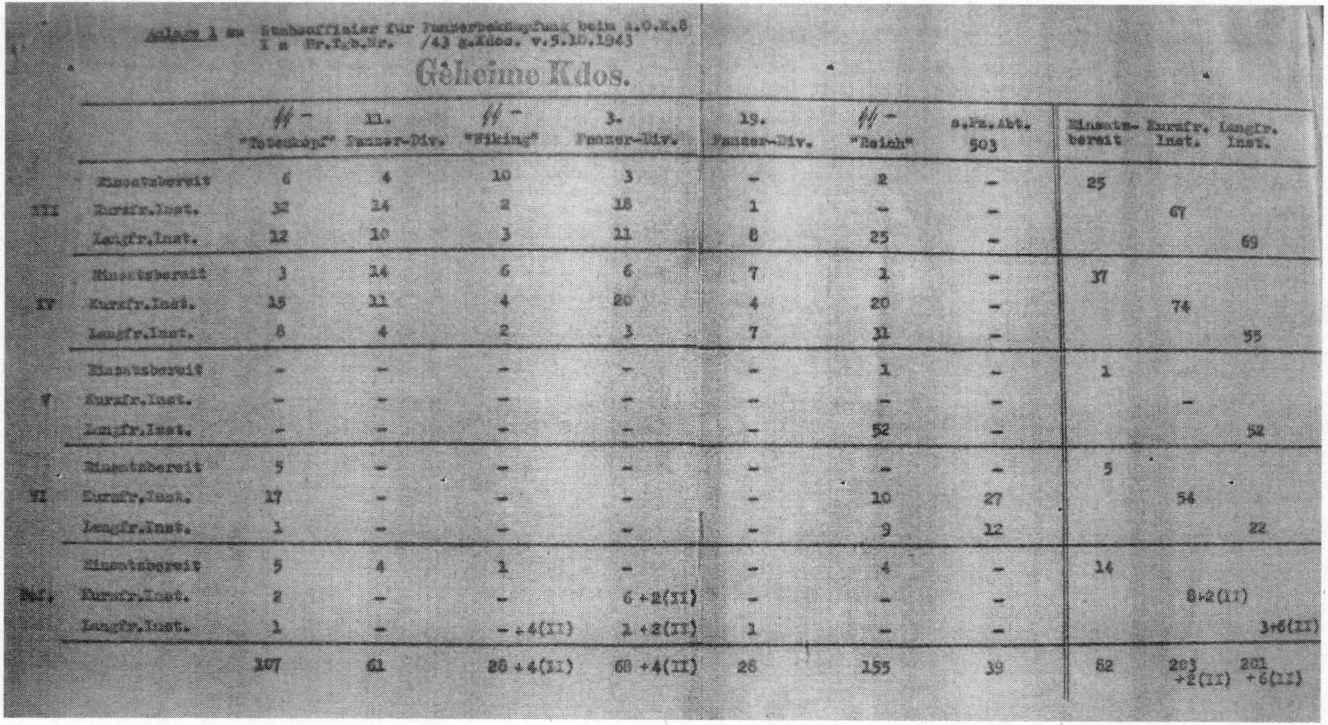

Anlage 1 zu Stabsoffizier für Panzerbekämpfung beim A.O.K.8
I a Br.Tgb.Nr. /43 g.Kdos. v.5.10.1943

Geheime Kdos.

		SS-"Totenkopf"	11. Panzer-Div.	SS-"Wiking"	3. Panzer-Div.	19. Panzer-Div.	SS-"Reich"	s.Pz.Abt. 503	Einsatz-bereit	Kurzfr. Inst.	Langfr. Inst.
	Einsatzbereit	6	4	10	3	–	2	–	25		
III	Kurzfr.Inst.	32	14	2	18	1	–	–		67	
	Langfr.Inst.	12	10	3	11	8	25	–			69
	Einsatzbereit	3	14	6	6	7	1	–	37		
IV	Kurzfr.Inst.	15	11	4	20	4	20	–		74	
	Langfr.Inst.	8	4	2	3	7	31	–			55
	Einsatzbereit	–	–	–	–	–	1	–	1		
V	Kurzfr.Inst.	–	–	–	–	–	–	–		–	
	Langfr.Inst.	–	–	–	–	–	52	–			52
	Einsatzbereit	5	–	–	–	–	–	–	5		
VI	Kurzfr.Inst.	17	–	–	–	–	10	27		54	
	Langfr.Inst.	1	–	–	–	–	9	12			22
	Einsatzbereit	5	4	1	–	–	4	–	14		
Bef.	Kurzfr.Inst.	2	–	–	6 +2(II)	–	–	–		8+2(II)	
	Langfr.Inst.	1	–	– +4(II)	1 +2(II)	1	–	–			3+6(II)
		107	61	26 +4(II)	68 +4(II)	26	155	39	82	203 +2(II)	201 +6(II)

FIGURE 17. GenInsp.d.Pz.Truppen, Stabsoffizier für AOK 8, 5.10.43. (NARA T78, R619, F000836)

resupplied with new tanks during the battle. The vital transport, supply and communications hub of Kharkov was finally captured by the Soviets on 23 August; it had come at great cost, the Soviets having lost 1,864 tanks and assault guns during the offensive. With the fall of Kharkov, a German withdrawal to the Dnieper became inevitable. The Soviet successes on the entire Eastern Front in July and August 1943 came at a staggering cost, with the Red Army losing as many as 9,294 tanks and assault guns. During the same period the Wehrmacht lost 'only' 1,331 tanks and assault guns.[49]

6

The 'Death' of the 'Panzers of Prokhorovka', September 1943–April 1944

THE RETREAT TO THE DNIEPER, SEPTEMBER–NOVEMBER 1943

Das Reich and Totenkopf, like all of the German armoured forces engaged in the battle for Kharkov, had suffered a very significant number of damaged tanks. Consequently, the repair services began to suffer from a chronic lack of spare parts (to reiterate, it is a misconception that this issue began for the *Sonderverbände* during July 1943 – during Operation *Citadel* the repair troops reported good stocks of AFV spare parts).[1] From September, German AFV operational numbers began to reach pitiful levels (Table 49). This largely remained the case for German AFVs on the Eastern Front until the spring of 1944.

TABLE 49.[2] **Former '*Citadel*' SS divisions' AFV strength, 1.9.43**

	Pz II	Pz III	Pz IV	Pz V	Pz VI	Bef	StuG/ StuH	Sf Pak	Wespe	Hum- mel
LSSAH Inventory	4	1	58	71	27	9	32/9	28	11	6
In LSSAH inventory the day prior to the battle of Prokhorov-ka (11.7.43)	4	1	5	0	0	9	32/0	18	11	6
LSSAH operational	?	?	50	65	20	?	28/9	28	?	?
DR inventory	1	51	58	66	19	4–9	28	8	12	4
DR operational	?	3	10	21	2	?	23	7	?	?
SS-T inventory	?	50–61	32–67	0	18–22	8–9	30	7	12	6
SS-T operational	?	23	9	0	1	?	15	4	?	?

The number of operational tanks available to Das Reich and Totenkopf on 1 September compared to those during Operation *Citadel* and its aftermath clearly shows that Das Reich and Totenkopf were now under severe pressure, with their repair services struggling to bring damaged AFVs back to operational status.[3] From now on this would be the rule on the Eastern Front rather than the exception. Although the three 'classic' SS divisions were known to be treated as *Sonderverbände*, in reality after the summer of 1943 this seemed to make little difference to the Germans' ability to return AFVs to the front line. During August and September, with the exception of Das Reich's Panther battalion, the only AFV reinforcements either Das Reich or Totenkopf received were ten new Panzer IVs (for Das Reich) which arrived in August.[4]

On 15 September Hitler finally gave Manstein permission to withdraw to the Dnieper. Although logistically the Germans achieved the difficult task of withdrawing their forces intact behind the Dnieper and then creating a continuous front line, they were not successful in stopping the Soviets from forming numerous bridgeheads across the river.[5]

Although the whole of the Eastern Front was by now under Soviet attack, Stavka's main focus was still against Army Group South's four armies. Stavka concentrated an enormous mass of five army fronts against Army Group South, namely Central Front, Voronezh Front, Steppe Front, South-West Front and South Front. This concentration of forces comprised 27 general armies, three tank armies, five air armies, 22 tank or mechanized corps and two cavalry corps. A total of 2,633,000 troops with over 51,200 cannon and grenade launchers, more than 2,400 tanks and self-propelled guns, and 2,850 combat aircraft were deployed in the main thrust towards the Dnieper. Of the Red Army's forces on the Eastern Front, this grouping comprised almost 50 per cent of the soldiers, 40 per cent of the artillery, 70 per cent of the armour and over 50 per cent of the aircraft. Additionally, according to Soviet figures, around 500,000 partisans were deployed in the hinterland in the battle of the Dnieper which followed.[6]

In the south between 13 August and 22 September, South and South-West Front attacked 6th Army and 1st Panzer Army. In pushing the Germans back to the Dnieper, the Soviets officially lost 273,522 men, of whom 66,166 were dead or missing; they also lost 886 tanks and assault guns. Following the loss of Kharkov, 8th Army (formerly Army Detachment Kempf) was attacked by Steppe Front from 26 August to 30 September, while 4th Panzer Army was attacked by Voronezh Front and elements of Central Front. According to Soviet official figures, the attackers lost 427,952 men of whom 102,957 were dead or missing together with 1,140 tanks.[7]

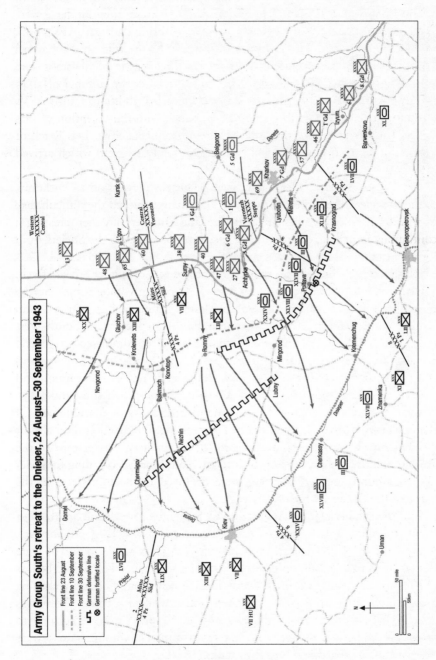

Army Group South's retreat to the Dnieper, 24 August–30 September 1943

Front line 23 August
Front line 10 September
Front line 30 September
German defensive line
German fortified locale

MAP 7

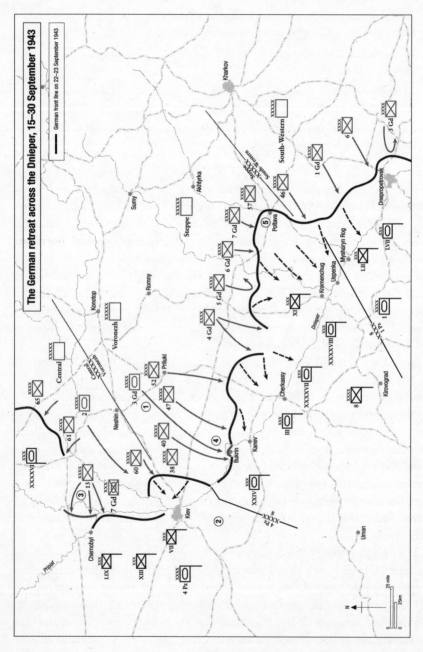

MAP 8

1. 19 September: the Soviet 3rd Guards Tank Army begins advancing towards the Dnieper.

2. 20 September: 19th Panzer Division crosses to the west bank of the Dnieper at Kiev and sends a *Kampfgruppe* to the Bukrin sector.

3. 20 September: the Soviet 13th Army establishes the first crossings over the Dnieper near Chernobyl.

4. 22 September: the 3rd Guards Tank Army and 40th Army establish two bridgeheads over the Dnieper in the Bukrin sector.

5. 23 September: the German XXXXVIII Panzer Korps abandons Poltava and falls back rapidly to Kremenchug.

By the end of September 1943 the retreat to the Dnieper had been completed. However, of the 1,953 available panzers on the Eastern Front, only 605 were now operational.[8] Das Reich and Totenkopf both withdrew across the Dnieper at Kremenchug. Das Reich then moved north of Kremenchug while Totenkopf headed south, under the control of 8th Army and 1st Panzer Army, respectively.[9] As a consequence of the German retreat on 26 September the *K-Werk* at Dnepropetrovsk was forced to relocate to Berdichev and ultimately, the following month, to Zhitomir. The army-level Panzer Inst Abteilung 545 was moved to Uman and Panzer Inst Abteilung 525 was moved to Krivoy Rog.[10]

As we have noted, it is unfortunate that no relevant MTO files have survived for 8th Army and 1st Panzer Army during this period. Nevertheless, it is still possible to utilize SS divisional monthly *Meldung* to give operational AFV numbers (and those expected to return from repair within three weeks) for the SS divisions within these armies.[11] Although these figures do not give us the exact numbers of ex-Prokhorovka AFVs that remained in the inventories of the SS divisions at this time (the AFVs undergoing the very longest repairs were not recorded), they are still very useful. The *Meldung* for Das Reich even gives the monthly total of tanks in its inventory by type in its attached OB charts. Sadly, the Totenkopf equivalents do not list the number of tanks in their inventory.

The only surviving official document that gives the total number of tanks per type in Totenkopf's post-Mius inventory (Das Reich is also included) is a report by 8th Army dated 5 October (Table 50).[12] The document tells us that the new AFV delivery reports for both Das Reich and Totenkopf up to this date are accurate.[13] The shipment reports confirm that Totenkopf did not receive any armoured reinforcements until this date, its first replacements being five Tiger tanks received between 1 and 5 October. The report also confirms that Totenkopf had suffered heavily in terms of Panzer IV total losses.

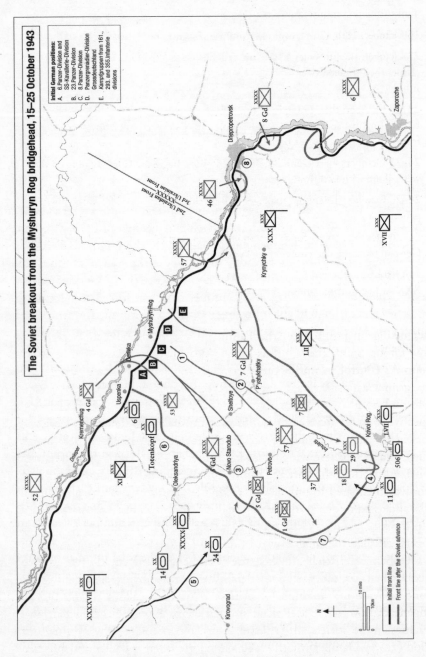

The Soviet breakout from the Myshuryn Rog bridgehead, 15–25 October 1943

Initial German positions:
A. 6.Panzer-Division and SS-Kavallerie-Division
B. 23.Panzer-Division
C. 8.Panzer-Division
D. Panzergrenadier-Division Grossdeutschland
E. Kampfgruppen from 161., 293. and 355.Infanterie divisions

MAP 9

1. 15 October: the 37th Army and 7th Guards Army achieve a major breakout from the Myshuryn Rog bridgehead. Once a breakthrough is achieved, the 5th Guards Tank Army is committed into the breach.

2. 18 October: 18th Tank Corps overruns the German supply base at P'yatykhatky.

3. 22 October: the 5th Guards Mechanized Corps reaches Novo Starodub and crosses the Inhulets River. Initially, there are almost no German units behind the Inhulets.

4. 23–24 October: the 5th Guards Tank Army's spearheads are defeated just outside Krivoy Rog in a series of tank battles with 11th Panzer Division and seven Tigers from 506th Heavy Panzer Battalion.

5. 24–25 October: the 14. and 24.Panzer Divisions begin arriving by rail from the west, along with two fresh infantry divisions.

6. 24–26 October: Totenkopf manages to hold the western shoulder of the Soviet penetration.

7. 24–26 October: Soviet forces continue to push west across the Inhulets River, but German blocking detachments are racing to this sector.

8. 25 October: as the 3rd Ukrainian Front launches attacks across the Dnieper River, XXX Armee Korps abandons Dnepropetrovsk.

After taking up position on the Panther (Dnieper) line on 29 September, Army Group South (now minus 6th Army which was transferred to Army Group A's control in mid-September) had to defend 700km of front with three armies against several Soviet fronts. These were Voronezh Front, Steppe Front and South-West Front, renamed 1st, 2nd and 3rd Ukrainian Front, respectively, on 20 October. In addition, the army group's northern wing was attacked by parts of Central Front (from 20 October renamed Belorussian Front), and its southern wing by several armies of South Front (4th Ukrainian Front). Altogether, the battered Army Group South had a total of 719,000 men, which equated to only about 1,000 men per km, and 271 operational tanks and assault guns available to face this Soviet colossus.[14]

In the first few days of October, Das Reich (with virtually no operational panzers) crushed the small Soviet bridgehead at Gerbeni. Following this, on 10 October, Das Reich attacked the Rzhishchev bridgehead with limited success. Then, on the 21st, Das Reich was heavily involved in halting the second of Vatutin's attempts to achieve a major breakout of the Bukrin bridgehead; however, Das Reich's strong defensive positions inflicted large casualties on the Soviets, on 3rd Tank Army in particular.[15] It was during this period (20–31 October) that Das Reich reported that it had commandeered an additional Tiger tank (250 147) from an unspecified unit or source.[16]

Meanwhile, Totenkopf between 15 and 25 October attempted to hold together the northern flank of the huge salient that had been created by the Soviet offensive out of the Myshuŕyn Rog bridgehead. This offensive (with the, once again, re-equipped 5th Guards Tank Army in the vanguard) successfully attacked the seam between 1st Panzer Army and 8th Army and effected a breakout.

TABLE 50.[17] Former '*Citadel*' SS divisions' AFV strength, 5.10.43

	Pz II	Pz III	Pz IV	Pz V	Pz VI	Bef	StuG/ StuH	Sf Pak	Wespe	Hum-mel
LSSAH inventory (1.10.43)	4	1	58	71	27	9	32/9	28	11	6
In LSSAH inventory the day prior to the battle of Prokhorovka (11.7.43)	4	1	5	0	0	9	32/0	18	11	6
LSSAH operational (1.10.43)	?	1	53	60	21	?	30/9	28	?	?
DR inventory (5.10.43)	1	27	52	53	19	4	24–27	?	?	?
DR operational (5.10.43)	?	2	1	1	0	4	13	7	?	?
SS-T inventory (5.10.43)		50	26	0	23	8	25–32	?	?	?
SS-T operational (5.10.43)		6	3	0	5*	5	0	3	?	?

* Totenkopf's five operational Tigers were all from a recently arrived new delivery.

On 28 October, Totenkopf along with Grossdeutschland participated in a short counteroffensive that blunted any immediate hope of the (by now overextended) 5th Guard's Tank Army reaching Krivoy Rog.[18] These operations were part of the Soviets' overall Lower Dnieper Offensive Operation (26 September–20 December) in which 1,500,000 men, 1,160 tanks and assault guns were deployed. The Soviets after regular resupply lost 2,639 tanks and assault guns during the overall offensive which for much of its course focused on 1st Panzer Army.[19] On 22 October all three of the SS *Sonderverbände* were redesignated panzer divisions.[20]

KIEV'S LIBERATION AND SUBSEQUENT GERMAN COUNTER-ATTACKS, NOVEMBER–DECEMBER 1943

On 3 November (Tables 51 and 52), having secretly shifted the 3rd Tank Army from Bukrin to the Lyutezh bridgehead north of Kiev (which had been expanded at great cost to 15km wide and 5–10km deep the previous month), Vatutin launched a major offensive to take Kiev (Map 10).

TABLE 51.[21] **Former '*Citadel*' SS divisions' AFV strength, 1.11.43**

	Pz II	Pz III	Pz IV	Pz V	Pz VI	Bef	StuG/ StuH	Sf Pak	Wespe	Hummel
LSSAH inventory (1.11.43)	4	1	87	85	27	9	41/9	26	11	6
In LSSAH inventory the day prior to the battle of Prokhorovka (11.7.43)	4	1	5	0	0	9	17/0	16	11	6
LSSAH operational AFV 1.11.43	2	1	75	22	17	9	33/9	13	9	4
DR inventory (31.10.43)	0	28	46	52	19	6	23	1	12	6
Known to be in DR or *LSSAH* inventory the day prior to the battle of Prokhorovka (11.7.43)	0	28 (24 and 4)	39 (15 and 24)	0	17 (9 and 8)	6	23	1 (7 under major repair)	12	6
DR operational AFV (31.10.43)	0	3	8	0	3	3	8	0	10	1
SS-T inventory (1.11.43)	?	16–50	33–36	0	11–23	?	25–32	5–9	?	?
SS-T Operational (1.11.43)	?	9	19	0	4	?	5	5	?	?

TABLE 52.[22] **Surviving AFV from the battle of Prokhorovka, 1.11.43**

	Pz III	Pz IV	T-34	Pz VI	Bef	Total Pz	StuG	Sf Pak	Total AFV
In LSSAH inventory the day prior to the battle of Prokhorovka (11.7.43 0100hrs)	1	5	0	0	9	15	17	16	48
DR AFV known to be in DR or *LSSAH* inventory the day prior to the battle of Prokhorovka (11.7.43 0100)	28 (24 and 4)	39 (15 and 24)	0	17 (9 and 8)	6	90	23	8 (7 under major repair)	121
SS-T AFV known to be in LSSAH inventory the day prior to the battle of Prokhorovka (11.7.43 0100)	Max of 4	Max of 26	0	Max of 4	0	Max of 34	0	0	Max of 34
Nordland AFV known to be in LSSAH inventory the day prior to the battle of Prokhorovka (11.7.43 0100)						0	14		14
II SS Panzer Korps HQ AFV known to be in LSSAH inventory the day prior to the battle of Prokhorovka (11.7.43 0100)	3					3			3
Combined total of surviving German AFV on 1.11.43 which were in LSSAH and DR inventories for the battle of Prokhorovka	32–36 (this will be c.34)	44–70 (this will be c.55)	0	17–21 (this will be c.19–20)	15	c.123	54	24	c.201
Combined German inventory the day prior to the battle of Prokhorovka (11.7.43 0100)	72	109	22	25–26	18	246–247	67	31	344–345

In the Kiev Strategic Offensive Operation (3–13 November) 1st Ukrainian Front deployed 671,000 men and 675 tanks and self-propelled guns; it would lose according to official figures 30,569 men, of whom 6,491 were dead or missing, and 271 tanks.[23] The offensive quickly overcame the weak German defence on the south side of the bridgehead and Soviet forces were able to charge headlong for Kiev. On 6 November, Kiev fell to the Soviets; the Germans' full attention was focused on trying to save 4th Panzer Army from annihilation. The Soviet offensive was now in full flow; by 7 November the important railhead at Fastov was captured greatly disrupting German plans to introduce major armoured reinforcements from the West; these included the Leibstandarte, the re-equipped 1st Panzer Division and the inexperienced 25th Panzer Division. Most of these reinforcements (like the Leibstandarte) had originally been scheduled for deployment with 8th Army around Kirovograd (the Leibstandarte had already detrained); however, they were now re-routed north to 4th Panzer Army with orders to detrain at Belaya Tserkov and Berdichev. For this reason, 4th Panzer Army could not afford for these railheads to also fall into Soviet hands. As a result, Das Reich was sent to Belaya Tserkov to protect this vital railhead – primarily so that the 25th Panzer Division and the 509th s.Panzer.Abt could join the battle as quickly as possible.

TABLE 53.[24] LSSAH and DR strength, 10.11.43

	Pz II	Pz III	Pz IV	Pz V	Pz VI	Bef	StuG/ StuH	Sf Pak	Wespe	Hum- mel
LSSAH inventory	4	1	87–95	85	27	9	41/9	26	11	6
In LSSAH inventory the day prior to the battle of Prokhorovka (11.7.43)	4	1	5	0	0	9	17/0	16	11	6
LSSAH operational	?	?	?	?	?	?	?	?	?	?
DR inventory	0	22	45	50	19	6	23	1	12	6
Known to be in DR or *LSSAH* inventory the day prior to the battle of Prokhorovka (11.7.43)	0	22 (18 and 4)	35 (13 and 22)	0	17 (9 and 8)	6	23	1 (7 under major repair)	12	6
DR operational	0	2	15	0	5	4	11	0	9	2

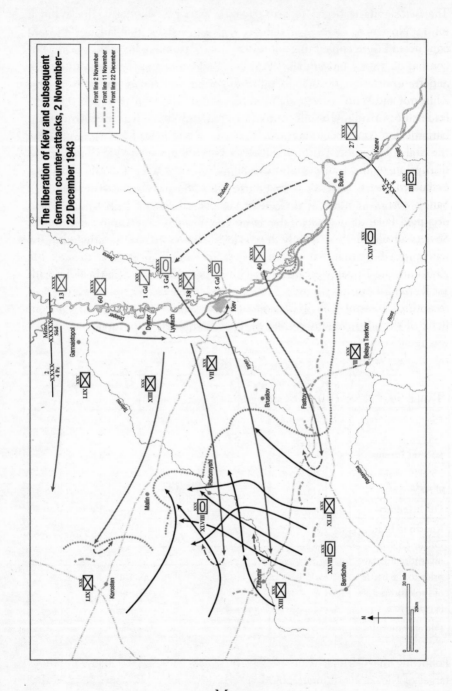

MAP 10

The Leibstandarte began to arrive in 4th Panzer Army's area of command on 11 November (Table 53) having (along with the 1st Panzer Division) conducted a time-consuming additional transport north. It would finally enter combat on 14–15 November.[25] However, other vital supply, communication and transportation hubs soon came under threat. The towns of Korosten, Zhitomir and Vinnitsa were all politically and militarily important to the Nazi leadership; Göring, Himmler and Hitler, respectively, all had expensively (and barbarically) constructed command centres close to these towns. Regardless, the vital rail junction Zhitomir fell on 12 November which caused a disastrous disruption to the transportation of supplies. The *K-Werk* in the town was evacuated and ultimately re-established in ideal conditions at a facility in Sanok west of Lemberg (Lvov) in the General Government (truncated Nazi-occupied Poland). Korosten also fell on 17 November; in some sectors, the Soviets advanced 150km west in ten days. The result was that this took the hard-pressed Germans' attention away from Fastov, northwards towards the Zhitomir and Brusilov area. On 15 November, the Leibstandarte along with 1st Panzer Division were ordered to use their considerable offensive power to recapture Zhitomir. Das Reich and 25th Panzer Division protected the right flank of the advance and despite mud proving a severe hindrance Zhitomir was retaken by German forces on 19 November (Table 54). Further to the north, the Germans also recaptured Korosten on 27 November.

TABLE 54.[26] LSSAH and DR strength, 20.11.43

	Pz II	Pz III	Pz IV	Pz V	Pz VI	Bef	StuG/ StuH	Sf Pak	Wespe	Hum-mel
LSSAH inventory	4	1	87	85	25	9	41/9	24	11	6
LSSAH operational AFV	2	1	18	10	12	9	29/6	12	9	4
DR inventory	0	17	50	45	16	6	23	9	12	6
Known to be in DR or *LSSAH* inventory the day prior to the battle of Prokhorovka (11.7.43)	0	17 (13 and 4)	31 (12 and 19)	0	15 (8 and 7)	6	23	8	12	6
DR operational	0	3	19	6	7	4	8	0	8	2

Following the German counteroffensive which had the extremely ambitious target of Kiev as its ultimate objective, a Leibstandarte TF report declared that between the start of the offensive and 28 November when the main effort of the offensive ended the following AFV losses occurred: 12 Panzer IVs, eight Panzer

Vs, two Panzer VIs, one StuG and three Sf Paks.[27] This gives a total of 26 AFVs TF in 14 days of offensive combat. This loss figure is eight more AFVs lost than the Leibstandarte suffered during Operation *Citadel* which was fought over a nearly identical timeframe of 13 days in the Leibstandarte case.[28] Nevertheless, the numbers of losses are still similar for an offensive. What is also noticeable is that the number of operational Panzer IVs fielded by the Leibstandarte following the battle of Prokhorovka on the evening of 13 July, which was the effective end date of Leibstandarte operations during Operation *Citadel*, was 31.[29] While on 2 December, following the conclusion of the Germans' 'Kiev' counteroffensive 30 Panzer IVs were operational (Table 55 and 56).[30] The Leibstandarte started each offensive with a similar number of Panzer IVs, 83 for commencement of Operation *Citadel* and 87–95 for the commencement of the 'Kiev' counteroffensive.[31] The major difference was that after the latter offensive there was no quiet period to conduct repairs (if the parts were indeed available) and as a result operational levels only continued to reduce. This was something the other panzer units of Army Group South had been experiencing since mid-August. In its supporting role during this period, Das Reich lost a maximum of five Panzer IIIs (2 – 3a), six Panzer IVs (2 – 3a), six Panzer Vs, three Panzer VIs and one StuG.[32] It is clear that even in late 1943, for the Germans, substantial offensive operations were far less costly in terms of TF than major defensive operations. In the course of the wider operations in the area from 9 to 28 November 4th Panzer Army claimed to have destroyed 603 Soviet tanks.[33]

During this period, the Germans were often forced to conduct armoured battles in highly unsuitable wooded terrain or adverse weather conditions which negated their AFV technical superiority. Consequently, German AFV losses began to mount, once again particularly in terms of damaged tanks.[34] The Soviets at this time still relied heavily on the T-34/76 (76mm main gun) which, as we have seen, was inferior to most German AFVs in terms of protective armour and weaponry, the exception being the Panzer III (which was no longer in production and being phased out). The next generation of Soviet tanks, such as the IS II (122mm main gun) and more importantly the T-34/85 (85mm main gun), would start to be introduced in sizeable numbers the following spring. After 30 November, the German counter-attack was paused to allow troops to rest and the ground to harden.

TABLE 55.[35] **Former '*Citadel*' SS divisions' AFV strength, 1.12.43**										
	Pz II	Pz III	Pz IV	Pz V	Pz VI	Bef	StuG/ StuH	Sf Pak	Wespe	Hum- mel
LSSAH inventory	4	1	76	80	25	9	37/9	22	10	6
LSSAH operational AFV	2	0	30	27	2	9	11/1	14	5	3

DR inventory	0	17	49	44	16	6	23	9	12	6
Known to be in DR or *LSSAH* inventory the day prior to the battle of Prokhorovka (11.7.43)	0	17 (13 and 4)	31 (12 and 19)	0	15 (8 and 7)	6	23	8	12	6
DR operational	0	5	6	16	3	3	8	0	4	1
SS-T operational and repair expected within 3 weeks (StuG inventory)		10	24	0	12	?	25–32	?	?	?
Totenkopf operational		3	3	0	1	?	7	2	?	?

TABLE 56.[36] **Surviving AFV from the battle of Prokhorovka, 1.12.43**

	Pz III	Pz IV	T-34	Pz VI	Bef	Total Pz	StuG	Sf Pak	Total AFV
In LSSAH inventory the day prior to the battle of Prokhorovka (11.7.43 0100hrs)	1	Max of 5	0	0	9	Max of 15	13–17	12–16	Max of 48
DR AFV known to be in DR or LSSAH inventory the day prior to the battle of Prokhorovka (11.7.43 0100)	17 (13 and 4)	31 (12 and 19)	0	15 (8 and 7)	6	69	23	8	100
Totenkopf AFV known to be in LSSAH inventory the day prior to the battle of Prokhorovka (11.7.43 0100)	Max of 4	Max of 26	0	Max of 4	0	Max of 34	0	0	Max of 34
Nordland AFV known to be in LSSAH inventory the day prior to the battle of Prokhorovka (11.7.43 0100)						0	14		14
II SS Panzer Korps HQ AFV known to be in LSSAH inventory the day prior to the battle of Prokhorovka (11.7.43 0100)	3					3			3

Combined total of surviving German AFV on 1.12.43 which were in LSSAH and DR inventories for the battle of Prokhorovka	21–25 (this will be c.23)	31–62 (this will be c.42)	0	15–19 (this will be c.17–18)	15	c.97	50–54 (this will be c.52)	20–24 (this will be c.22)	c.171
Combined German inventory the day prior to the battle of Prokhorovka (11.7.43 0100)	72	109	22	25–26	18	246–247	67	31	344–345

On 6 December, after the ground had frozen, the Germans launched Operation *Advent* (Plate 122). By 13 December, Radomyshl was retaken and attacks followed close to Korosten and Malin. The Leibstandarte and Das Reich were both involved in this offensive (Table 57).[37]

TABLE 57.[38] LSSAH and DR strength, 10.12.43

	Pz II	Pz III	Pz IV	Pz V	Pz VI	Bef	StuG/StuH	Sf Pak	Wespe	Hummel
LSSAH inventory	4	1	69	76	24	9	37/9	20	10	6
LSSAH operational AFV	1	0	12	5	4	3	10/4	7	4	3
DR inventory	0	14	50	44	16	6	23	9	12	6
Known to be in DR or *LSSAH* inventory the day prior to the battle of Prokhorovka (11.7.43)	0	14 (11 and 3)	31 (12 and 19)	0	15 (8 and 7)	6	23	9	12	6
DR operational	0	0	3	3	3	2	13	0	4	1

On 18 December, the Leibstandarte along with 1st Panzer Division and 7th Panzer Division broke through the Soviet front line in depth between Meleni and Amlin. However, it soon became clear that pursuing an encirclement operation in this sector was unfeasible due to the fact that the attacking units were about to potentially encircle a massive Soviet grouping which reportedly consisted of three tank corps and four rifle corps. The Germans had no hope of containing such a large force. This episode highlights that the Germans no longer possessed the armoured reserves necessary to exploit successes at the operational level. As a result of this discovery, on 22 December, the German counter-attacks were rapidly brought to a close. When one looks at the number

of operational AFVs available to the Leibstandarte for offensive operations in Tables 57 and 58, it is hardly surprising the operation was not pursued further.[39]

TABLE 58.[40] LSSAH and DR strength, 20.12.43

	Pz II	Pz III	Pz IV	Pz V	Pz VI	Bef	StuG/ StuH	Sf Pak	Wespe	Hum- mel
LSSAH inventory	3	1	66	74	23	8	35/9	19	10	6
LSSAH operational AFV	1	0	9	7	3	2	17/6	4	0	1
KG DR inventory	0	0	22	20	8	2	12	?	?	?
Known to be in DR or *LSSAH* inventory the day prior to the battle of Prokhorov- ka (11.7.43)	0	0	9 (4 and 5)	0	7 (2 and 5)	2	12	?	?	?
KG DR operational	0	0	15	10	4	2	10	?	?	?

RENEWED SOVIET OFFENSIVES: THE CRUSHING OF THE 'PROKHOROVKA PANZERS', DECEMBER 1943–APRIL 1944

By 23 December, the Red Army had lost 1,687,164 men in the battle of the Dnieper, of whom 417,323 were dead or missing. Yet its human and materiel reserves seemed inexhaustible. The same could hardly be said of the German forces. As a result of the lack of replacement personnel, Army Group South had only 328,397 men available at the end of December 1943, plus 109,816 men serving in allied and foreign units. Although Manstein's army group numbered as many 14 panzer divisions, it had only 199 operational tanks ready for action.[41]

As we have seen, in October 1943 the Germans had attempted to increase the number of AFVs which were evacuated to homeland maintenance by officially allowing the dispatching unit to keep the AFV as part of its property; this was coupled with the promise that any AFV received by homeland maintenance would be returned to its parent unit at the front. It was hoped this policy would increase the number of operational AFVs by relieving the pressure on the Army Group (*K-Werk*), Army and divisional-level repair services at the front. In December 1943 another order stated that if the *K-Werk* of Army Group South lacked spares then any tank requiring over eight days' work to repair should also be sent to homeland maintenance.[42] This was clearly an important order, as in the same month Guderian declared after a visit to Army Group South that 'two-thirds of the army group's panzers were

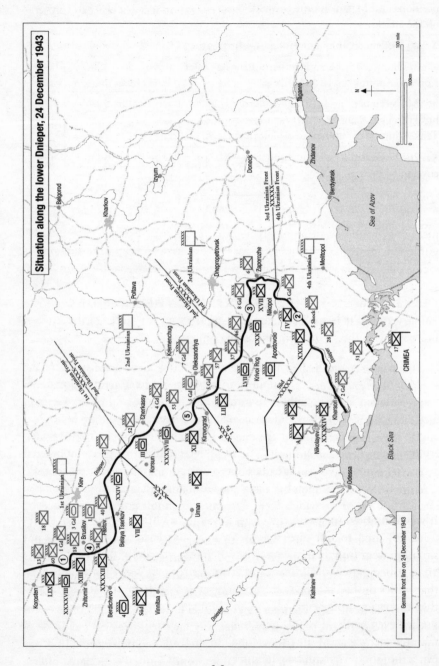

Map 11

1. 18–20 December: the LSAAH and 1st Panzer Division attack 60th Army positions near Malyn, but the Soviet defences are too strong and von Manstein calls off the attacks.

2. 20 December: Tolbukhin's offensive against the Nikopol bridgehead fails.

3. Malinovsky's 3rd Ukrainian Front fails repeatedly to break through XXX Panzer Korps to Apostolovo.

4. 24 December: the 1st Ukrainian Front launches a massive offensive that achieves a breakthrough against XXXXII Armee Korps. Both the 1st Tank Army and 3rd Guards Tank Army are committed to exploit the breach.

5. 26–27 December: a counter-attack by XI Armee Korps defeats Konev's effort to envelop Kirovograd.

---

just lying around awaiting repair due to a lack of spare parts'. After his visit, Guderian immediately requested an increase in spare parts production.[43] It seems that in desperation the panzer troops, having seen that the maintenance services in the East were, to put it mildly, faltering, viewed the October and December orders as a potential solution to their woes. However, as early as January 1944 the homeland maintenance organization declared that it could not cope with the subsequent influx of damaged panzers:

> The panzer maintenance in the homeland is ending in disaster. The *Heimatinstandsetzung* cannot process the evacuated panzers. Despite all preparations the companies are not capable of accepting further panzers. Among the panzers delivered are also vehicles with relatively little damage... The homeland has totally insufficient capacity for maintaining panzers. There is a particular shortage of cranes for heavy panzers. At the moment, a maximum of 250 panzers can be repaired. An improved performance is entirely dependent upon the allocation of labourers.[44]

It was also noted that with the current system the Army Group level *K-Werk* were not used to full capacity. As a result, the Eastern Front AFV repair situation went from bad to worse. It is therefore staggering that on 27 January 1944 Albert Speer, the Minister of Armaments and War Production, noted that Hitler pushed for the policy to be extended further: 'The *Führer* requests that the evacuation of panzers to the homeland and their maintenance be pushed even harder. Even if the number of evacuated panzers will surpass the maintenance capacity, the panzers shall be evacuated because only in this way can a thorough overhaul be guaranteed.'[45]

In addition to this nonsensical order the *K-Werk* were still reporting underused capacity in April 1944; therefore, it is hardly surprising that the

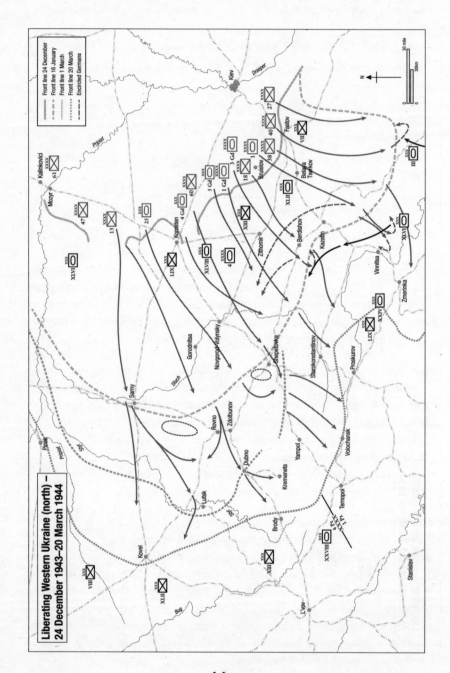

Liberating Western Ukraine (north) –
24 December 1943–20 March 1944

MAP 12

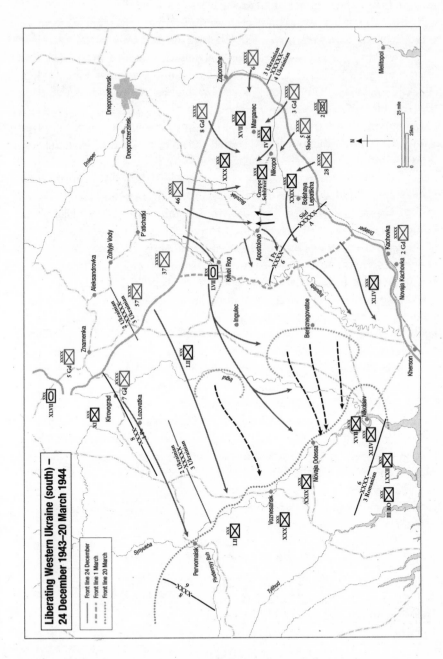

Map 13

number of operational AFVs on the Eastern Front failed to significantly improve before the summer of 1944.[46]

By mid-December 1943 it was clear to the Germans that they were about to face a major Soviet offensive. The offensive erupted on 24 December and lasted, depending on how the endpoint is defined, until 17 April or 6 May 1944; under its weight the front collapsed almost straight away (Maps 11–14.). That day Army Group South was subjected to one of the most powerful offensives of the war. Four Soviet Fronts – 1st, 2nd, 3rd and 4th Ukrainian Fronts – were ranged against it. Not counting the troops deployed against the Crimea, the four fronts started the offensive with 2,230,000 men, 28,654 cannon and grenade launchers, 2,015 tanks and assault guns, and 2,600 combat aircraft. In the course of the operation, the following units were brought in and added to the forces deployed: 2nd Belorussian Front HQ; the operations staff of 47th, 61st and 70th Armies, and of 2nd, 4th and 6th Tank Armies; six tank corps, two mechanized corps, and 33 divisions, as well as 6th Air Army. The enormous scale of the reinforcements is shown by the fact that while 2,015 tanks and assault guns were available at the start of the offensive, the number lost in the course of the operation was 4,666. In this phase of the war, the Red Army's point of concentration lay unambiguously in the sector of Army Group South, against which all six of its tank armies were temporarily deployed. Also important was the deployment of some 50,000 partisans, who caused great damage in the hinterland and tied down large numbers of German troops. The ensuing offensive to liberate Western Ukraine was designated the 'Dnieper-Carpathian Strategic Offensive Operation'.[47]

Once the breakthrough was effected on the Kiev axis, the 1st and 3rd Tank Armies were sent in to exploit the German rear. In response, the Leibstandarte and 1st Panzer Division were sent south in an attempt to provide a blocking force in front of Zhitomir. Nevertheless, the Germans were soon under the threat of encirclement and Zhitomir was abandoned on 30 December (further north Korosten was also abandoned on the same date). The 4th Panzer Army was being mauled, with Berdichev and Belaya Tserkov being captured by 5 January 1944 (Tables 59 and 60).[48]

TABLE 59.[49] **Former 'Citadel' SS divisions' AFV strength, 1.1.44**

	Pz II	Pz III	Pz IV	Pz V	Pz VI	Bef	StuG/ StuH	Sf Pak	Wespe	Hum- mel
LSSAH inventory	4	1	58	53	21	8	35/8	15	8	6
LSSAH operational AFV	0	0	14	7	2	2	6/3	5	5	5
*KG DR inventory	0	0	22	20	8	2	12	?	?	?

Known to be in DR or *LSSAH* inventory the day prior to the battle of Prokhorovka (11.7.43)	0	0	9 (4 and 5)	0	7 (2 and 5)	2	12	?	?	?
SS-T operational and expected repair within 3 weeks	0	22	27	0	10	?	17	11	?	?
SS-T operational	0	7	8	0	2	?	7	4	?	?

* Due to a lack of reporting, DR figures for 1.1.44 will almost certainly be closer to those of 10.1.44.

TABLE 60.[50] **Surviving AFV from the battle of Prokhorovka, 1.1.44**

	Pz III	Pz IV	T-34	Pz VI	Bef	Total Pz	StuG	Sf Pak	Total AFV
In LSSAH inventory the day prior to the battle of Prokhorovka (11.7.43)	1	Max of 5	0	0	8	Max of 14	11–17	4–15	46
*DR AFV known to be in DR or *LSSAH* inventory the day prior to the battle of Prokhorovka (11.7.43)	0	9 (4 and 5)	0	7 (2 and 5)	2	18	12	?	c.30
Totenkopf AFV known to be in *LSSAH* inventory the day prior to the battle of Prokhorovka (11.7.43)	Max of 4	Max of 26	0	Max of 4	0	Max of 34	0	0	Max of 34
Nordland AFV known to be in *LSSAH* inventory the day prior to the battle of Prokhorovka (11.7.43 0100hrs)						0	14		14
II SS Panzer Korps HQ AFV known to be in LSSAH inventory the day prior to the battle of Prokhorovka (11.7.43 0100)	3					3			3

Combined total of surviving German AFV on 1.1.44 which were in LSSAH and DR inventories for the battle of Prokhorovka	4–8 (this will be c.6)	9–40 (this will be c.20)	0	7–11 (this will be c.9)	10	c.45	37–43 (this will be c.39)	4–15 (this will be c.8)	c.92
Combined German inventory the day prior to the battle of Prokhorovka (11.7.43)	72	109	22	25–26	18	246–247	67	31	344–345

* Due to a lack of reporting, DR figures for 1.1.44 will almost certainly be closer to those of 10.1.44.

During the first week of January, the Soviet offensive continued to push the Leibstandarte ever further to the south-west away from the Zhitomir area in the direction of Shepetovka and Starokonstantinov.[51] The overall Leibstandarte losses for 21 December 1943–15 January 1944 in the TF reports highlight that the retreat cost the Leibstandarte dearly in terms of AFVs – a clear sign of the desperate nature of the fighting against greatly superior enemy numbers (Tables 61 and 62).[52]

Between 21 and 30 December, the Leibstandarte TF reports declared the following TF AFVs: seven Panzer IVs, 14 Panzer Vs, one Panzer VI,[53] while between 1 and 10 January 1944, the Leibstandarte reported the following TF AFVs: 30 Panzer IVs, 13 Panzer VIs, 14 StuGs and three Sf Paks.[54] On 15 January, the Leibstandarte reported the further loss of three Panzer IVs and one StuG.[55] We have the chassis numbers for all the TF in these reports. Therefore, during the main thrust of the Soviet offensive, the Leibstandarte reported a total of 40 Panzer IVs, 14 Panzer Vs, 14 Panzer VIs, 15 StuGs and 3 Sf Paks written off as total losses. Added to this, the Leibstandarte ten-day status reports indicate that 1 Panzer IV, 27 Panzer Vs, 1 StuH and 1 Sf Pak were sent for homeland maintenance in Germany during this time.[56] Therefore, overall losses between 21 December 1943 and 15 January 1944 were 41 Panzer IVs, 41 Panzer Vs, 14 Panzer VIs, 15 StuGs, 1 StuH and 4 Sf Paks for a total of 116 AFVs lost, all of which were of modern specification with high-velocity long-range guns. By comparison during the Leibstandarte involvement in Operation *Citadel* (5–16 July plus 17 July, the Leibstandarte's final day at the front) the division lost only 1 Panzer I, 1 Panzer III, 9 Panzer IVs, 1 Panzer VI, 3 StuGs and 3 Sf Paks for a total of 18 AFV losses (16 of which were of modern specification).[57]

Most of the Leibstandarte AFV losses occurred between the start of the Soviet offensive and the conclusion of its main thrust, i.e. between 24 December 1943 and 10 January 1944.[58] Within these 18 days, the Leibstandarte suffered around 112 AFV losses 3b or 3a (all of modern type).[59] As we have seen in the relatively comparable timeframe of Operation *Citadel* 5–16/17 July 1943 (12–13 days) the Leibstandarte in fact lost no more than 18 AFV losses 3b or 3a (two of which were of outdated type: one Panzer I and one Panzer III).[60] It is remarkable to note that in ten days between 1 and 10 January 1944 the Leibstandarte lost 13 Tigers TF.[61] Such losses would have seemed unthinkable to Tiger tank crews in the summer of 1943. For example, the Leibstandarte lost just three fewer Tiger tanks in ten days in January 1944 (west of the Dnieper) than the Germans lost in the whole of July 1943 on the entire Eastern Front! This was a period that included Operation *Citadel* and the most intense fighting in the defence of the Orel salient.[62]

Due to losses (and an overworked AFV repair service), between 10 and 20 December 1943 Das Reich was renamed and reduced to a brigade-sized *Kampfgruppe*.[63] With this change, all the former division's AFVs which were undergoing or in need of long-term repair were removed from *Kampfgruppe* Das Reich's inventory and evacuated to Germany for homeland maintenance.[64] As with the Leibstandarte, *Kampfgruppe* Das Reich lost many AFVs during the Soviet offensive; these losses were all recorded between 1 and 10 January 1944 in a ten-day status report. The losses were one Bef Panzer III, 18 Panzer IVs (13 – 3a), 16 Panzer Vs (12 – 3a), nine Panzer VIs (2 – 3a) and four StuGs.[65] However, it seems Das Reich was committed from the start of the offensive on 24 December 1944; so there must have been an administrative delay in reporting these losses due to the fact that *Kampfgruppe* Das Reich was in the heat of battle.[66] There were no ten-day status, inventory or *Meldung* reports issued by Das Reich for the period 20 December 1943–1 January 1944. Perhaps then the losses were spread between 24 December 1943 and 10 January 1944. Regardless, the high losses, relative to the *Kampfgruppe* size, can be attributed to the fact that Das Reich was fully committed in the face of the vast Soviet armoured attack. It was also during this period that Das Reich lost (bar a few exceptions) the majority of its remaining ex-'Prokhorovka' panzers (Table 62). It was reported that by 10 January 1944 Das Reich had lost all of its nine surviving Tiger tanks (eight of which had been at Prokhorovka) either 3a or TF.[67] It is also worth noting that this total is greater than the entire Tiger tank losses sustained by Army Group South during Operation *Citadel* (7).[68]

To the south, 8th Army was also facing another major Soviet offensive that was launched on 5 January 1944. On the 8th, Kirovograd was taken but a determined counter-attack led by Grossdeutschland and Totenkopf brought the Soviet offensive to an abrupt halt on the 16th.[69]

TABLE 61.[70] LSSAH and DR strength, 10.1.44										
	Pz II	Pz III	Pz IV	Pz V	Pz VI	Bef	StuG/ StuH	Sf Pak	Wespe	Hum- mel
LSSAH **inventory**	4	1	25	30	10	7	28/7	13	8	6
LSSAH oper- ational AFV	0	0	13	8	5	0	14/2	5	5	3
KG DR **inventory**	0	0	8	4	0	1	8	0	4	0
Known to be in DR or *LS- SAH* inventory the day prior to the battle of Prokhorovka (11.7.43)	0	0	3 (2 and 1)	0	0	1	8	0	4	0
KG DR operational	0	0	1	0	0	1	6	0	0	0

Following its humbling experience in early January, the Leibstandarte transferred to the control of 1st Panzer Army (which had just arrived on 4th Panzer Army's right flank) and deployed north of Vinnitsa at Khmelnik. From there it participated from 24 January in a powerful counter-attack on Lipovets at the base of the salient created by the Soviet armoured spearhead towards Vinnitsa. By the 28th, the attack had cut off and mauled seven Soviet divisions. Regardless, despite the many minor German tactical successes since the beginning of the Soviet offensive on 24 December, the Red Army had pushed the Germans back over 100km in places. Even while the Leibstandarte was engaged in its counter-attack, the Red Army had again broken through the German front line further to the east and encircled XI and XXXXII Korps close to Korsun. On 1 February 1944, the Leibstandarte transferred east to aid the relief column (Table 63).[71]

The Leibstandarte played only a supporting role in the relief attempt of the roughly 58,000 German troops trapped in the Korsun pocket, protecting the relief attack's right flank. Following a desperate breakout on the night of 16/17 February 36,262 men managed to escape the pocket, while a further 4,161 were flown out before the pocket collapsed. The two trapped German Korps, however, lost all their heavy equipment during the breakout.[72]

52. At 0850hrs on 11 July the Leibstandarte occupied the anti-tank ditch. (NARA)

53. The location of the road bridge over the anti-ditch. (Google Earth)

54. To consolidate its gains the Leibstandarte rapidly sent its armour across the anti-tank ditch and onto the slope of Hill 252.2, 11 July. (NARA)

55. The Leibstandarte's 2nd SS Panzergrenadier Regiment urgently improved the anti-tank ditch defences. Here we look left, 11 July. (NARA)

56. The view to the left of the bridge over the anti-tank ditch, 11 July. (NARA)

57. The view to the left from the location of the bridge over the anti-tank ditch. (Google Earth)

58. The view to the left of the bridge; the photographer is now looking along the length of the anti-tank ditch, 11 July. (NARA)

59. The view to the left at the location of the bridge over the anti-tank ditch, looking along the length of the former anti-tank ditch. (Google Earth)

60. The view to the right of the bridge over the anti-tank ditch, looking towards the railway embankment, 11 July. (NARA)

61. The view to the right at the location of the bridge over the anti-tank ditch, looking towards the railway embankment. (Google Earth)

62. The view to the right at the location of the bridge over the anti-tank ditch, looking towards the railway embankment. (Google Earth)

63. The view of the anti-tank ditch from the base of Hill 252.2. (Google Earth)

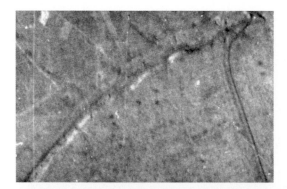

64. The right half of the anti-tank ditch, 16 July. (NARA)

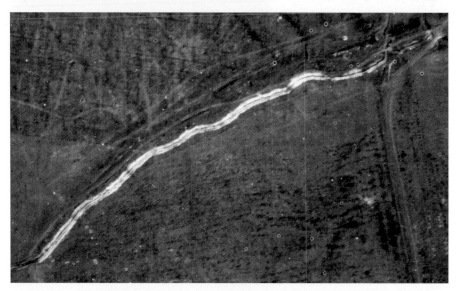

65. The right half of the anti-tank ditch, 7 August. (NARA)

66. The right half of the anti-tank ditch. (Google Earth)

67. German field of fire towards Hill 252.2 from behind the anti-tank ditch.
(Google Earth)

68. The subsequent Johan King
pictures were all taken on Hill
252.2 and once again follow in
chronological order, 11 July.
(NARA)

69. Prior to their attack at 1030hrs, infantry of the 2nd SS Panzergrenadier Regiment occupy part of the hill's trench system, 11 July. (NARA)

70. The Leibstandarte's Sf 150mm heavy infantry guns (Grille), shown here, also participated in the assault on Hill 252.2, 11 July. (NARA)

71. A SPW of III Battalion, 2nd SS Panzergrenadier Regiment on Hill 252.2, 11 July. (NARA)

72. On 12 July the Leibstandarte's 6th Panzer Company lost three of its seven Panzer IVs in battle with the 29th Tank Corps, 11 July. (NARA)

73. This picture captures the start of one of the numerous Soviet armoured counter attacks on Hill 252.2, 11 July. (NARA)

74. The Soviet tanks on Hill 252.2 are destroyed by the Leibstandarte Panzer IVs, 11 July. (NARA)

75. Smoke billows from the destroyed Soviet tanks on Hill 252.2, 11 July. (NARA)

76. The Leibstandarte SPW also opposed the Soviet counter attacks on Hill 252.2, 11 July. (NARA)

77. A member of the 2nd SS Panzergrenadier Regiment operates a MG 42 in the infantry trench system on Hill 252.2, 11 July. (NARA)

78. A Leibstandarte Panzer IV scans the landscape for further Soviet armour, 11 July. (NARA)

79. The Leibstandarte calls for Luftwaffe support in the form of a Stuka attack. A soldier unfolds a Swastika recognition flag, 11 July. (NARA)

80. The Stuka attack on Hill 252.2 commences, 11 July. (NARA)

81. The Stuka attack is not a success and despite German precautions bombs fall on Leibstandarte positions, 11 July. (NARA)

82. A soldier of the 2nd SS Panzergrenadier Regiment liaises with a crew member from the 5th Panzer Company, 11 July. (NARA)

83. By 14:10 the final Soviet positions on Hill 252.2 had been overcome, 11 July. (NARA)

84. Soviet anti-tank and artillery strength meant the Germans only managed to advance a short distance beyond Hill 252.2, 11 July. (NARA)

85. The Leibstandarte was forced to seek cover in the undulating terrain. By 2015hrs the Germans had withdrawn back to Hill 252.2, 11 July. (NARA)

86. Two destroyed Panzer IVs can be identified beyond the crest of Hill 252.2 (bottom left quarter of picture). A third destroyed Panzer IV is located further back close to Hill 252.2's summit (top left quarter of picture), 16 July. (NARA)

87. Two destroyed Panzer IVs can be identified beyond the crest of Hill 252.2 (bottom left quarter of picture). A third destroyed Panzer IV is located further back close to Hill 252.2's summit (top left quarter of picture), 7 August. (NARA)

88. The site of the initial armoured combat on 12 July. The location of three destroyed Panzer IVs has been highlighted. (Google Earth)

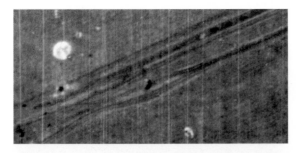

89. Enhanced view of the knocked-out Panzer IV (centre of picture) which is closest to the Prokhorovka–Belgorod railway, 15 August. (NARA)

90. Enhanced view of the knocked-out Panzer IV (left of picture) which was furthest forward of Hill 252.2, 7 August. (NARA)

91. The undulating ground beyond the crest of Hill 252.2 where two Panzer IV were knocked out when the battle of Prokhorovka began on 12 July. (Google Earth)

92. A post-battle picture taken from a Soviet aircraft flying low over the battlefield. A destroyed Panzer IV and T-34 can be seen close to Hill 252.2's summit. (Valeriy Zamulin)

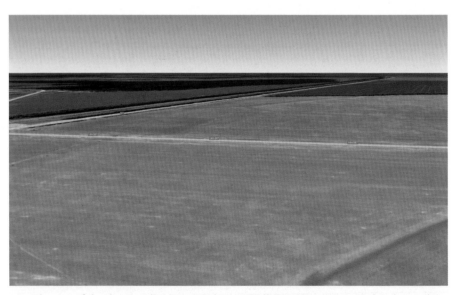

93. The site of the destroyed Panzer IV close to Hill 252.2's summit. Today the track in front of the Panzer IV takes a slightly different route, as does the road on the other side of the railway embankment. (Google Earth)

TABLE 62.[73] Surviving AFV from the battle of Prokhorovka, 10.1.44

	Pz III	Pz IV	T-34	Pz VI	Bef	Total Pz	StuG	Sf Pak	Total AFV
In LSSAH inventory the day prior to the battle of Prokhorovka (11.7.43)	1	Max of 5	0	0	7	Max of 13	0–17	0–13	Max of 43
DR AFV known to be in DR or *LSSAH* inventory the day prior to the battle of Prokhorovka (11.7.43)	0	3 (2 and 1)	0	0	1	4	8	0	12
SS-T AFV known to be in *LSSAH* inventory the day prior to the battle of Prokhorovka (11.7.43)	Max of 4	Max of 26	0	Max of 4	0	Max of 34	0	0	Max of 34
Nordland AFV known to be in *LSSAH* inventory the day prior to the battle of Prokhorovka (11.7.43 0100)						0	14		14
II SS Panzer Korps HQ AFV known to be in LSSAH inventory the day prior to the battle of Prokhorovka (11.7.43 0100)	3					3			3
Combined total of surviving German AFV on 10.1.44 which were in LSSAH and DR inventories for the battle of Prokhorovka	4–8 (this will be c.6)	3–34 (this will be c.10–12)	0	0–4 (this will be c.2)	8	c.26	22–39 (this will be c.30)	0–13 (this will be c.7)	c.63
Combined German inventory the day prior to the battle of Prokhorovka (11.7.43)	72	109	22	25–26	18	246–247	67	31	344–345

TABLE 63.[74] **Former 'Citadel' SS divisions' AFV strength, 1.2.44**

	Pz II	Pz III	Pz IV	Pz V	Pz VI	Bef	StuG	Sf Pak	Wespe	Hummel
LSSAH operational and repair expected within 3 weeks (31.1.44)	?	1	34	49	6	0	32 (at least 3 were StuH)	10	?	?
LSSAH operational AFV (31.1.44)	?	0	15	22	2	0	29	4	?	?
KG DR inventory	0	0	6	4	0	1	8	0	4	0
Known to be in DR or LSSAH inventory the day prior to the battle of Prokhorovka (11.7.43)	0	0	2 (1 and 1)	0	0	1	8	0	4	0
KG DR operational	0	0	3	2	0	0	7	0	0	0
SS-T operational and repair expected within 3 weeks		11	13	0	7	?	16	9	?	?
SS-T operational		3	6	0	4	?	7	4	?	?

Following the conclusion of the Korsun operation, in early March 1944, the majority of the Leibstandarte was transported to Belgium in order to be reconstituted in time to face the expected Allied invasion of North-west Europe. Only a regimental-sized *Kampfgruppe* remained on the Eastern Front with the small remaining number of operational Leibstandarte AFVs. *Kampfgruppe* Leibstandarte was also ordered back to the West in mid-April 1944.[75] As a consequence only a small element of the Leibstandarte was still at the front to face the mighty Soviet offensive launched by 1st Ukrainian Front on 4 March 1944. The offensive pushed the Germans back into eastern Poland.[76] The meagre forces of *Kampfgruppe* Das Reich had remained with 4th Panzer Army throughout February and into March, at which point the *Kampfgruppe* was thrown back by the 1st Ukrainian Front's offensive. After this, in early March the majority of *Kampfgruppe* Das Reich, bar a regimental-sized grouping, was transported to the West to re-join the rest of the reconstituting division, which like the Leibstandarte was preparing to face the Western Allies' invasion of North-west Europe. Mirroring the Leibstandarte, Das Reich's regimental-sized grouping also returned to the West in mid-April 1944.[77]

TABLE 64.[78] Former '*Citadel*' SS divisions' AFV strength, 1.3.44

	Pz II	Pz III	Pz IV	Pz V	Pz VI	Bef	StuG/ StuH	Sf Pak	Wespe	Hummel
LSSAH operational and repair expected within 3 weeks	?	4	30	58	1–5	0	18	9	?	?
LSSAH operational AFV	?	1	0	12	1	0	3	0	?	?
KG DR inventory (29.2.44)	0	0	17	14	5	1	8	0	4	1
In DR inventory the day prior to the battle of Prokhorovka (11.7.43)	0	0	0	0	0	1	8	0	4	1
KG DR operational (29.2.44)	0	0	11	9	5	0	6	0	1	?
SS-T operational and repair expected within 3 weeks		8	15	0	9	?	13	10	?	?
SS-T operational		5	8	0	4	?	7	3	?	?

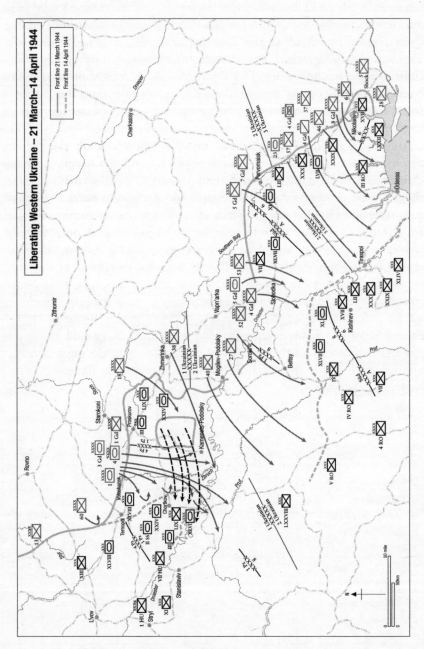

Map 14

Totenkopf's next major involvement was opposing the massive Soviet offensive launched by the 2nd Ukrainian Front on 3 March. The offensive would push the Germans out of southern Ukraine and into Romanian territory.[79] Once again it is clear from Table 64 that Totenkopf's contingent of ex-Leibstandarte 'Prokhorovka' AFVs would have virtually all been written off by this date.[80] Unlike the Leibstandarte and Das Reich, Totenkopf fought on the Eastern Front for the duration of the conflict with the Soviet Union. By mid-April 1944, Totenkopf had lost all of its AFVs and required its panzer regiment to be rebuilt.[81]

The losses sustained by the five Soviet fronts that took part in the 24 December 1943 to 6 May 1944 'Dnieper-Carpathian Strategic Offensive Operation' were extremely heavy. The Red Army lost 1,192,900 men, of whom 288,600 were dead or missing while, as mentioned 4,666 tanks and assault guns were also lost. For the Germans (1st and 4th Panzer Armies, 6th and 8th Armies) their losses from January to April 1944 totalled 'only' 250,956 men (of whom 41,907 were dead and 51,161 missing). However, as a result of the German build-up in the West and the general shortage of new recruits for the Wehrmacht, the Germans were now seldom allocating replacement personnel to the Eastern Front; therefore, the impact of the respective losses was far greater for the Germans than it was for the Soviets. By early May, the Eastern Front had finally entered a period of stability. This would remain the case until the entire Eastern Front was steamrollered by the gigantic Soviet summer offensives of 1944. These offensives brought the Eastern Front to Germany's eastern border.[82]

Conclusion

As a result of the discovery of the 6th Army's *Wochenmeldung über Panzer und Sturmgeschülzlage Stand* for 1 August 1943 we are in a position to adjust the total number of AFV losses that II SS Panzer Korps sustained during Operation *Citadel* and its immediate aftermath (5–20 July 1943, see Table 65). The final number of AFVs lost during the operation is extremely low at just 41 AFVs (42 if we include 1 Leibstandarte Panzer I Bef). This means that of the original 547 AFVs (not including Panzer Is or Panzer IIs) which embarked on the offensive on 5 July with II SS Panzer Korps, 506 AFVs (93 per cent) were still in II SS Panzer Korps divisional inventories on 20 July (four new Sf Paks were received after 10 July).[1]

TABLE 65.[2] **II SS Panzer Korps AFV losses (3a and TF) during Operation *Citadel* and its aftermath, 5–20.7.43**

	Pz III	Pz IV	T-34	Pz VI	Bef	Total Pz	StuG	Sf Pak	Total AFV
LSSAH (5–18.7.43)	1	9		1	1*	12	3	3	18
DR (5–18.7.43)	2	6	3	1	0	12	2	0	14
SS-T (5–20.7.43)	2	4		1	0	7	1	2	10
Total	5	19	3	3	1	31	6	5	42

* Pz I Bef.

In the early hours of 11 July II SS Panzer Korps possessed 521–522 AFVs in its inventory (95 per cent of its pre-Operation *Citadel* inventory). Therefore, II SS Panzer Korps lost just 15–16 AFVs between 11 and 20 July, which of course included the battle of Prokhorovka on 12 July. As II SS Panzer Korps began the battle of Prokhorovka with no more than 522 AFVs in its inventory and concluded the battle with no fewer than 506 of these AFVs, then at least 97 per cent of II SS Panzer Korps' AFVs survived the battle, or to put it another way, II SS Panzer Korps lost no more than 3 per cent of its pre-battle (11 July) AFV inventory on 12 July (Table 66).[3] At this point we need to remind ourselves that for many years post-war Soviet and Western historiography claimed that II SS Panzer Korps lost 300 AFVs during the battle of Prokhorovka (58 per cent of its pre-battle inventory), while the commander of the 5th Guards Tank Army General Rotmistrov declared that II SS Panzer Korps lost 400 AFVs during the battle (77 per cent of its pre-battle inventory).[4]

TABLE 66.[5] II SS Panzer Korps AFV inventory, July–mid-August 1943

	Pz III	Pz IV	T-34	Pz VI	Bef	Total Pz	StuG	Sf Pak	Total AFV
4.7.43 total	138	168	24	42	27	399	104	44	547
0100hrs 11.7.43 total	133	157	22	39–40*	27	378–379	101	42	521–522
0100hrs 21.7.43 total	133	149	21	39	27	369	98	43–45	510–512
26.7.43 total	133	149	21	44	27	374	98	43–45	515–517
29.7.43 total	129#	144	21	44	18	356	66	21–23	443–445
0100hrs 2.8.43 total	119~	127	21	44	20~	331	66	21	418
9.8.43 estimated total (III Pz Korps)	?	?	?	?	?	c.325	?	?	c.412

* This depends which LSSAH Tiger was actually written off.
# Not including 3 ex-LSSAH Pz IIIs with II SS Panzer Korps HQ.
~ 2 Pz III lg listed under Bef.

Clearly during Operation *Citadel* the period 5–10 July was more damaging for II SS Panzer Korps in terms of AFV losses than the period 11–20 July. What is perhaps even more remarkable is that on the evening of 18 July 349 of II SS Panzer Korps' AFVs were operational, an increase of ten AFVs from 11 July (the day prior to the battle of Prokhorovka). This was, however, 138 AFVs less than the 487 AFVs which were operational on 4 July, the day prior to the launch of Operation *Citadel* (Table 67).[6]

TABLE 67.[7] **II SS Panzer Korps operational AFV, July–mid-August 1943**								
	Pz III	Pz IV	T-34	Pz VI	Bef	Total Pz	StuG	Sf Pak	Total AFV
4.7.43 operational total	117	156	18	35	25	351	95	41	487
0100hrs 11.7.43 operational total	98	87	8	16	18	227	73	39	339
2300hrs 18.7.43 operational total	73	107	17	25	22	244	76	29	349
28.7.43 (including LSSAH 24.7.43) operational total	92	104	2	21	14	233	84	39	356
0100hrs 2.8.43 operational total	63	24	6	2	14	109	34	16	159
2300hrs 11.8.43 operational total (III Pz Korps)	26	48	6	15	5	100	36	19	155

What the historiography of Operation *Citadel* always lacked, even after the true course of events became more widely known, was a single stand-alone post-Prokhorovka and post-Operation *Citadel* II SS Panzer Korps AFV inventory which could simply be compared with the well-known pre-Operation *Citadel* II SS Panzer Korps AFV inventory. This therefore is what makes the 6th Army's *Wochenmeldung über Panzer und Sturmgeschülzlage Stand* for 1 August 1943 such a remarkable and historically important document. Even if the *Wochenmeldung* is read in isolation, the document proves that on 20 July, just four days after the conclusion of Operation *Citadel*, II SS Panzer Korps possessed at least 351 (88 per cent) of its original 399 pre-Operation *Citadel* complement of panzers (none of these figures include Panzer Is and Panzer IIs). According to the *Wochenmeldung* on 20 July the panzers were distributed between the three SS divisions in the following way: Leibstandarte 89 (shown as transfers to Das Reich and Totenkopf – not including the five new Panzer VIs received on 25 July), Das Reich 130 and Totenkopf 132.[8] Of course, we also know that after Operation *Citadel* the Leibstandarte passed on three Panzer IIIs to II SS Panzer Korps HQ and retained one Panzer III, five Panzer IVs and nine Befs (again not including Panzer Is and Panzer IIs) which adds a further 18 Panzers to the actual number of Operation *Citadel* survivors. Therefore, in reality the total number of surviving panzers stood at 369 (93 per cent).[9] The importance of the 6th Army *Wochenmeldung* therefore cannot be underestimated as by itself the document tells us that in actual fact at least

88 per cent of II SS Panzer Korps' pre-Operation *Citadel* complement of panzers survived the operation and by default also the battle of Prokhorovka.[10]

A direct comparison of AFV losses sustained by the main protagonists of the battle of Prokhorovka is also possible. The Leibstandarte and Das Reich lost a maximum of 14 AFVs on 12 July (11–20 July) or 4 per cent of their 11 July (morning) inventory of 345 AFVs. The four participating Soviet tank corps of the 5th Guards Tank Army (29th, 18th, 2nd Tank Corps and 2nd Guards Tank Corps) that faced the Leibstandarte and Das Reich in combat lost between 212 (32 per cent) and 268 (40 per cent) of their 11 July (evening) inventory of 663 AFVs between 12 and 16 July (44 of these AFVs were engaged elsewhere). Typically, the figure of 235 (35 per cent) Soviet AFVs lost is reported; however, as described, it is the author's belief that the figure of 246 Soviet AFVs lost (37 per cent) is the more likely figure. As previously stated, the vast majority of these Soviet AFV losses would have occurred on 12 July. Regardless, the disparity between the number of German and Soviet AFVs lost during the battle of Prokhorovka is stark.[11]

If we focus on the fighting between the Leibstandarte and the 18th and 29th Tank Corps which encompassed most of the iconic locations of the battlefield (Hill 252.2, Oktiabrskiy state farm, the anti-tank ditch, Stalinsk state farm and the sites of the tank duels involving the Leibstandarte four Tiger tanks), then the disparity in respective AFV losses is even greater. The Leibstandarte lost a maximum of seven AFVs on the 12th (11–20 July) or 4 per cent of its 11 July (morning) inventory of 164 AFVs. While the Leibstandarte's direct opponents the 18th and 29th Tank Corps (the 5th Guards Tank Army's two organic tank corps) lost between 157 (36 per cent) and 187 (43 per cent) of their 11 July (evening) inventory of 436 AFVs between 12 and 16 July. Individually, the 18th Tank Corps lost 55 (30 per cent) of its 11 July (evening) inventory of 186 AFVs between 12 and 16 July, while the 29th Tank Corps lost between 102 (41 per cent) and 132 (53 per cent) of its 11 July (evening) inventory of 250 AFVs between 12 and 16 July. For the reasons already discussed, tragically it seems that the greater figure of over 50 per cent AFV losses for the 29th Tank Corps is the most logical and likely. Once again almost all of the 29th Tank Corps AFV losses would have occurred on 12 July.[12]

As we have seen, Operation *Citadel* was far from a disaster for II SS Panzer Korps. Thanks to good stocks of spare parts (built up for Operation *Citadel*), in July 1943 a high number of damaged panzers were quickly brought back to operational readiness. By the morning of the 19th (roughly the scheduled date for Operation *Roland*) 349 AFVs were operational with II SS Panzer Korps. To place this figure into context the III Panzer Korps (6th, 7th, 19th Panzer Divisions, 503rd s.Panzer.Abt and 228th Assault Gun Battalion) began Operation *Citadel* with 391 AFVs (366 operational) in its entire inventory.

However, Hitler's frankly suicidal decision to send II SS Panzer Korps south to the Mius and Italy (influenced by economic and political considerations) greatly hampered any further increase in AFV operational numbers. As a result on 12 August when Das Reich and Totenkopf did finally launch a counter-attack west of Kharkov (alongside SS-W's 42 operational AFVs and 503rd s.Panzer.Abt's 13 operational Panzer VIs), they did so with only 155 operational AFVs. If an undiluted II SS Panzer Korps (i.e. including the Leibstandarte) had remained in the Kharkov area, it would have recovered to an operational strength of over 400 AFVs (over 450 AFVs if one assumes SS-W and 503rd s.Panzer.Abt joined the Korps) by early August 1943. Hitler had therefore squandered the opportunity of launching a powerful coordinated counter-offensive in the Kharkov area. Nevertheless, such a counteroffensive would have undoubtedly been the swan song of II SS Panzer Korps (in its original form) on the Eastern Front. Even if a counteroffensive had been successful, by late August with the *Sonderverbände* stocks of AFV spare parts exhausted and the time required to conduct major repairs having evaporated, II SS Panzer Korps' operational AFV strength would have been rapidly eroded. In addition, further major Soviet offensives on its flanks would have ultimately forced II SS Panzer Korps away from Kharkov.[13]

In reality, in three weeks of defensive combat around Kharkov, Das Reich suffered a further 46 AFV losses (not an insufficient number) on top of the ten AFV losses sustained in three to four days' combat on the Mius Front. If we add to this total the 14 AFVs Das Reich lost during Operation *Citadel* we can see that during the two-month-long battle of Kursk (and Mius offensive) Das Reich lost in total 70 AFVs. Most damaging, however, was the number of non-operational AFVs that Das Reich had accumulated by the end of July. Nevertheless, it was not damage to AFVs sustained during Operation *Citadel* that hindered subsequent operations around Kharkov. These had largely been made good by 18 July (as they had with the Leibstandarte); rather it was the lengthy transports and the four-day Mius operation at the end of the month that had a lasting effect on AFV availability.[14]

Although we are unable to establish the exact number of AFV losses Totenkopf sustained during the German defence of Kharkov, similar AFV losses to Das Reich can be expected, given that both divisions re-entered combat around the same time. Prior to its commitment to the Mius counter-attack, Totenkopf had followed a slightly different path to Das Reich, as the division had remained in combat north of Belgorod longer and undertook a more direct (if delayed) transport to 6th Army. This had the effect of slowing the recovery of Totenkopf's AFV numbers following Operation *Citadel*. Totenkopf's operational AFV numbers only recovered in time for the launch of the Mius offensive; however, when the offensive began Totenkopf operational numbers rapidly fell away as a result of the division's difficulties in taking Hill 213.9.[15]

Following Operation *Citadel*, Hitler's misuse of the Leibstandarte and his Donets/Mius dalliance (together with its associated transports) had left the remaining SS *Sonderverbände* of Das Reich and Totenkopf ill prepared to conduct a counter-attack at Kharkov on 12 August. These blunders would have far-reaching consequences for the German defence of the city and the Wehrmacht's ability to fight east of the Dnieper.

Between 1 October 1943 and 31 January 1944, the German Army's tank maintenance companies on all fronts (i.e. including those AFVs in Italy) repaired 8,702 tanks while another 453 were repaired in the rear areas. However, given the consistently appalling level of AFV operational readiness that we have witnessed in the post-Operation *Citadel* period, this number must have been a drop in the ocean of those AFVs that actually needed repair. During the same period, 2,945 tanks were permanently lost.[16]

Zetterling and Frankson correctly stated that as the Germans were on the offensive throughout Operation *Citadel*, they were able to maintain control of the battlefield and therefore able to recover the majority of their disabled AFVs. During the autumn/winter of 1943 and beginning of 1944, the Germans were firmly on the defensive. Consequently, the opportunity to recover disabled AFVs was far less regular. As a result, otherwise serviceable AFVs often had to be blown up by their crews to prevent capture, simply because they had a mechanical failure, a lack of fuel or had become mired. There were also other factors which contributed to the large-scale losses seen by German AFVs towards the end of 1943 and early 1944. On the west side of the Dnieper, unfavourable terrain with large wooded areas and poor visibility in the winter months led inevitably to close proximity fighting which in turn negated the advantage of the Germans' long-range high-velocity guns. There was also a noticeable drop in quality of trained panzer troops and conversely a rise in quality in the Red Army's own armoured training and tactics. The repair services had a lack of spare parts and recovery vehicles (by now these issues also applied to the *Sonderverbände*) while, due to the Soviet advance, they were also faced with a collapsing transportation system. This affected the Germans' ability to evacuate damaged AFVs and contributed to the disastrous situation the German armoured forces found themselves in. These factors added to the large number of panzer losses that devastated the 1st, 2nd and 3rd SS Panzer Regiments following the commencement of the massive Soviet offensives to liberate central Ukraine, Kiev and western Ukraine.[17]

Niklas Zetterling and Anders Frankson's outstanding work on the subject highlights perfectly the main reasons for the low level of operational German

AFVs and the spike in German AFV total losses on the Eastern Front in the autumn and winter of 1943/44. Zetterling and Frankson observed:

> Since the [German – ed.] forces employed in *Citadel* had enjoyed a long lull before the offensive began, they had had ample time to ensure that their vehicles were in good mechanical condition. Also, they had received deliveries of brand new tanks. The German forces in the autumn and winter of 1943/44 on the other hand had to operate with already worn equipment and had less time to carry out repairs and overhauls. Therefore, it seems likely that the *Citadel* forces were less prone to being plagued by mechanical breakdowns. Consequently, it would be expected that the percentage of repairable vehicles would be smaller during *Citadel*.[18]

Perhaps the most prominent example of the contrasting impact of offensive and defensive operations on AFV longevity can be seen by comparing the Leibstandarte's role in Operation *Citadel* with its defence against the Soviet offensive of late 1943. During the 18 days of the Soviet offensive between 24 December 1943 and 10 January 1944 the Leibstandarte suffered around 112 AFV losses 3b or 3a (all of modern type) to a variety of causes relating to enemy action and the impending loss of the battlefield (lack of fuel, lack of rapid recovery units, etc.).[19] While in the relatively comparable timeframe of the *Citadel* offensive between 5 and 16/17 July (12–13 days), the Leibstandarte in fact lost no more than 18 AFV losses 3b or 3a.[20]

As far as ex-Prokhorovka AFVs are concerned, the same Soviet offensive largely brought about their extinction. Having transferred the vast majority of their panzers to Das Reich and Totenkopf in late July 1943, the Leibstandarte's remaining 15 Panzers (one Panzer III, five Panzer IVs, nine Panzer Befs) would have succumbed in the winter of 1943/44. The same can be said for the Leibstandarte's ex-Prokhorovka StuGs and Sf Paks, 17 and 16 of which, respectively, made it back to the Eastern Front with the Leibstandarte in November 1943.[21]

Das Reich, after participating in the battle of Prokhorovka, received a large number of ex-Leibstandarte Panzers.[22] As a result, by 1 November Das Reich still had 121 ex-Prokhorovka AFVs in its inventory (28 Panzer IIIs, 39 Panzer IVs, 17 Panzer VIs, 6 Bef Panzers, 23 StuGs and 8 Sf Paks).[23] By 1 December, this number had dropped to 100 (17 Panzer IIIs, 31 Panzer IVs, 15 Panzer VIs, 6 Bef Panzers, 23 StuGs and 8 Sf Paks).[24] When Das Reich transitioned into *Kampfgruppe* Das Reich between 10 and 20 December, the unit shed many of its long-term damaged AFVs. It was (like the Leibstandarte) then decimated by the 24 December 1943–10 January 1944 Soviet Offensive.[25] By 10 January, Das Reich only had 12 former 'Prokhorovka' AFVs in its inventory (3 Panzer IVs, 1 Bef Panzer and 8 StuGs).[26] The records indicate that it was extremely unlikely (though not impossible) that any Leibstandarte or Das Reich ex-Prokhorovka AFV survived long enough to follow their parent *Kampfgruppe* back to the West in April 1944.[27]

Totenkopf's 30 ex-Leibstandarte 'Prokhorovka' Panzer IVs would have suffered severely from the catastrophic loss of 52 Panzer IVs prior to 5 October (41 between 2 August and 5 October). It is likely that by 1 November there were only around ten ex-Prokhorovka Panzer IVs still in service with Totenkopf. Some of Totenkopf's four ex-Leibstandarte Prokhorovka-era Tiger tanks (i.e. not including those received by the Leibstandarte after the battle on 25 July) may well have survived into 1944; however, their number clearly was not high. Regardless, by mid-April 1944 they were all lost.[28]

The 14 ex-Leibstandarte Prokhorovka StuGs which had been transferred to the Nordland Division in October 1943 incurred serious losses in the retreat from Oranienbaum. This followed the commencement of the major Soviet offensive to completely relieve Leningrad. This offensive, which began on 14 January 1944, resulted in the loss of 20 Nordland StuGs in the final two weeks of January 1944.[29]

While the three ex-Leibstandarte Prokhorovka Panzer IIIs which II SS Panzer Korps HQ had taken ownership of on 28 July only returned to action on the Eastern Front in early April 1944, II SS Panzer Korps (by now comprising 9th SS Panzer Division Hohenstaufen and 10th SS Panzer Division Frundsberg), which had been part of the operational reserve in France, helped 4th Panzer Army successfully free 1st Panzer Army from encirclement. However, the Korps was sorely missed when the Western Allies landed in Normandy on 6 June 1944. The exact fate of the three ex-Leibstandarte Prokhorovka Panzer IIIs is unknown; however, it is possible that they followed II SS Panzer Korps back to France later in June 1944.[30]

Overall, of the 344–345 AFVs (not including light panzer or support AFVs) that were in the inventories of the Leibstandarte and Das Reich on 11 July (the day prior to the battle of Prokhorovka) by 1 November between 186 and 220 former 'Prokhorovka' AFVs (likely to be around 200 or 58 per cent of the 11 July pre-Prokhorovka AFV inventory) were still in service with the Leibstandarte, Das Reich, Totenkopf, Nordland and II SS Panzer Korps HQ.[31] By 1 December, this number had fallen to between 152 and 199 (likely to be around 170 or 49 per cent of the 11 July pre-Prokhorovka AFV inventory); however, this still meant that around half of the original Prokhorovka AFVs were still with SS units on the Eastern Front four and a half months after the battle.[32] Some of these figures may sound fairly impressive in terms of longevity; however, taken in isolation they present a wholly distorted picture of events. When one looks at the extremely low number of operational AFVs that the SS divisions possessed from August 1943 onwards (which was in no way untypical for AFVs on the Eastern Front), it is easy to see one of the chief reasons why the German Army was on its knees.[33] Only new or reconstituted divisions (such as the Leibstandarte in November) had any number of operational AFVs worth mentioning. However, even these divisions' operational numbers soon dropped to that of their sister divisions. Following the conclusion of the main effort of the Soviet offensive on 10 January, the number of former 'Prokhorovka' AFVs shrank to between 37 and 106, likely to be around 60 (of which just around 12 were Panzer IVs or Panzer VIs) or 17 per cent of the 11 July pre-Prokhorovka AFV inventory.[34] The overall armoured losses incurred at the turn of 1943/1944 would have seemed incomprehensible to the SS panzer troops in the summer of 1943.

Given our detailed knowledge of the losses incurred by both sides during the battle of Prokhorovka it is clear that the aerial photographic evidence contained in this book further supports Frieser's overall description of the battle. The photographs allow us to pinpoint for the first time a proportion of the small number of German AFV losses (around Hill 252.2) and the majority of the Soviet 29th Tank Corps AFV losses (on the battlefield in July and August and at the railway spur thereafter) that occurred during the battle of Prokhorovka.[35]

Despite taking extremely heavy armoured losses on 12 July the Soviets won the battle of Prokhorovka. What proved to be decisive was the pre-battle installation of an extremely powerful artillery capability and an almost impenetrable anti-tank defence around Hill 252.4 and the town of Prokhorovka. On two occasions (11 July 1943; Plates 83 to 85; and 13 July) the Germans simply had no answer to these defences. In addition, even after the battle the 5th Guards Tank Army was still capable of fielding over 400 operational AFVs to defend Prokhorovka. As a result of these realities the Germans, having failed to obtain flanking support, had no hope of continuing their advance on the Prokhorovka axis.[36]

On 12 July the tankers of the 5th Guards Tank Army were poorly served by their commanders at Army, Front and Stavka level. Despite the well-equipped nature of their opponent, the tankers of the 5th Guards Tank Army deserved to achieve far more for their high sacrifice. The 29th Tank Corps was the 5th Guards Tank Army's most well-equipped and potent weapon; once it had suffered its fate either side of the railway line on the morning of the 12th, the wider offensive had no chance of achieving its original aims. Following the German capture of the 5th Guards Tank Army's intended jumping off points on 11 July Vatutin and Rotmistrov, despite being under intense pressure to launch the offensive as quickly as possible, should have altered their plans significantly to avoid the anti-tank ditch. At the very least the 29th Tank Corps troops should have been warned of the presence of the anti-tank ditch in their direct line of advance.[37] The Stavka and Soviet Front commanders have been accused of committing their armoured reserves too quickly during Operation *Citadel*. It is therefore ironic that had the Stavka released the 5th Guards Tank Army from the Strategic Reserve (Steppe Front) a day or so earlier, then the tank army would have been in a position to launch its armoured offensive from its intended jumping off points, thereby avoiding combat in the vicinity of Hill 252.2 and the anti-tank ditch. The majority of difficulties faced by the army's tankers on 12 July would then have been avoided.[38]

At Prokhorovka on 12 July, given the clear presence of the anti-tank ditch, it is obvious that a frontal assault on the Leibstandarte's positions should not have been attempted. Instead, the 29th Tank Corps should have been the spearhead in 2nd Tank Corps' sector (specifically the sector allocated to 26th Tank Brigade). Here the 29th Tank Corps would have had a realistic possibility of achieving a breakthrough in Das Reich's front (south of the Storozhevoye Woods), sweeping into the Leibstandarte's rear and effecting a linkup with the 18th Tank Corps. This scenario would have torn Das Reich's northern front to pieces and encircled the Leibstandarte (the latter would have faced multiple threats to its front, flanks and rear). Had this plan been attempted a battle more akin to the Soviet-era 'myth of Prokhorovka' may well have ensued with the bulk of the Leibstandarte's panzer regiment fighting for survival while pinned against the railway embankment and the anti-tank ditch. It is extremely doubtful whether Das Reich and the Leibstandarte would have been able to defend their overextended and isolated positions from the 5th Guards Tank Army's avalanche of armour without the man-made and geographic features that came to their aid on the 12th.[39]

Overall, it is remarkable that the historiography of the battle of Prokhorovka has evolved so radically over the last 30 years, arguably more so than any other battle during the Second World War. In 1993 it was still believed that the Germans had suffered a war-changing armoured disaster at Prokhorovka with the loss of as many as 400 tanks. Now in 2023, this book has verified for the first time, through statistical and imagery analysis, that there was no German armoured disaster at Prokhorovka; the reality of the battle being recognized with the greatest respect to the Soviet loss of life. The post-war testimony of Soviet war photographer Anatoly Yegorov is perhaps telling. His nephew Mikhail Yegorov recalled what Anatoly told him about his work: 'Most of those photos were not published. "Do you know why no panoramic photos of the Prokhorovka battlefield were ever shown in our country?" my uncle asked me. "Because for every burning Tiger there were ten of our smashed-up T-34s! How could you publish such photos in the papers?"'[40]

CONCLUSION

The disproportionally high number of Soviet armoured losses did not, however, equate to a Soviet defeat at Prokhorovka. As we have seen, the Soviets instead gained victory at Prokhorovka by virtue of possessing a formidable artillery capability, establishing an impenetrable anti-tank defence and by maintaining a high number of operational tanks. Even though this victory may not be the one of legend, the Soviet soldiers who fought so courageously against Nazism at Prokhorovka still deserve our deepest respect and gratitude for their victory.

Bibliography

A NOTE ON THE STATISTICAL AND PHOTOGRAPHIC HISTORIOGRAPHY OF THE BATTLE OF PROKHOROVKA

For an excellent account of the Soviet/Russian historiography and a compelling narrative of the battle of Prokhorovka by the leading Russian historian on the subject see Valeriy Zamulin, *Demolishing the Myth: The Tank Battle at Prokhorovka. July 1943: An Operational Narrative* (Solihull: Helion 2011).

Frieser's research from the early 1990s was later included in *Das Deutsche Reich und der Zweite Weltkrieg, VIII. Die Ostfront 1943/44* (München: Deutsche Verlags-Anstalt 2007). This volume was translated into English in 2017 as *Germany and the Second World War Volume VIII – The Eastern Front 1943–1944* (Oxford: Clarendon Press 2017). The volume was part of a 12,000-page, 13-volume semi-official project that has taken the academics at the MGFA 30 years to complete. Frieser's narrative of the battles on the Eastern Front in *Die Ostfront 1943/44* is superbly accurate and concise. These descriptions (one can hardly say interpretations due to the high level of accuracy) often provided this book with its context and battlefield commentary; this is particularly the case in relation to the fighting in the 29th Tank Corps' sector at Prokhorovka on 12 July 1943. In *Die Ostfront 1943/44* Frieser quoted the 5th Guards Tank Army report from 17 July which declared between 12 and 16 July the Soviet units involved lost 235 tanks and assault guns at Prokhorovka (the author estimated that 246 Soviet tanks and assault guns were lost).[1] Although in some respects the Soviet report is not particularly accurate it did at least end any debate regarding the true scale of the tank losses that the Soviets had sustained at Prokhorovka.

The figures Frieser used in *Die Ostfront 1943/44* for German armoured losses during Operation *Citadel* (252 tanks and assault guns) and the battle of Prokhorovka came from the same Army Group Centre (77 tanks and assault guns) and Army Group South (175 tanks and assault guns) daily loss reports that he cited in Moscow in 1993. These figures although flawed subsequently became the basis for all serious research on the subject for the battles of Kursk and Prokhorovka. There has since been a relatively successful attempt to refine Frieser's Operation *Citadel* figures by Alexander Tomzov in *Tankovy udar. Sovetskie tanki v boyakh. 1942–1943* (Moscow:

Eksmo 2007). Tomzov correctly pushed the figure towards 300 German AFVs lost during Operation *Citadel* as he took into account heavily damaged tanks which had to be written off later. It was Tomzov who first brought attention to II SS Panzer Korps' engineer's armoured loss report which declared the SS lost 44 tanks, assault guns and tank destroyers during the course of Operation *Citadel*. The other known SS armoured loss report (a less accurate report sent by II SS Panzer Korps at the front to Hitler's SS adjutant) was first mentioned by Sylvester Stadler in *Die Offensive gegen Kursk, II SS-Panzerkorps als Stosskeil im Grosskampf* (Osnabrück: Munin Verlag 1980).[2]

In terms of refinement of the German 12 July armoured loss figures at Prokhorovka, Roman Töppel has been most prolific. In his article, 'Kursk – Mythen und Wirklichkeit einer Schlacht', in *Vierteljahrshefte für Zeitgeschichte*, 57 (2009) Töppel, while still referring to the flawed Army Group South loss report, adjusted Frieser's figures slightly upwards to four tanks as total losses during the battle (all Leibstandarte Panzer IVs – the author has shown this to be an incorrect assessment).[3] This interpretation was carried over into his book, *Die größte Schlacht des Zweiten Weltkriegs* (Paderborn: Verlag Ferdinand Schöning 2017) published in English as *Kursk 1943: The Greatest Battle of the Second World War* (Solihull: Helion 2018). Minor adjustments were then made in Töppel's next work on the subject, 'Die Panzerschlacht bei Prochorowka, Fakten gegen Fabeln', *Arbeitskreis Militärgeschichte e.V.* (2020) which was reprinted in English as 'The Battle of Prokhorovka: Facts Against Fables', *Journal of Slavic Military Studies*, 34:2 (2021). Töppel's figures in these articles for II SS Panzer Korps' AFV losses during Operation *Citadel* (44) are incorrect as he utilizes the faulty elements of II SS Panzer Korps' engineer's 5–18 July 1943 loss report (in this document Totenkopf losses are incorrect, while the report does not list Das Reich T-34 losses at all – in reality there were three such losses). Töppel also persists with his overall AFV loss assessment for the Germans during the battle of Prokhorovka. It is worth offering a cautionary note against any author who claims to provide a definitive AFV loss total for the 12th.[4]

Other than two unexamined Luftwaffe reconnaissance images of a section of the Prokhorovka battlefield that can be found at the rear of Christopher Lawrence's *Kursk: The Battle of Prokhorovka* (Sheridan: Aberdeen Books 2015) the Luftwaffe reconnaissance images contained in this book are original. An abridged version of Lawrence's book was published in 2019 under the title *The Battle of Prokhorovka: The Tank Battle at Kursk, the Largest Clash of Armor in History* (Mechanicsburg: Stackpole Books 2019). The two images Lawrence selected from the period of the battle sadly missed much of the battlefield. The images are presented verbatim; therefore, they only offer the reader fields seen from thousands of feet in the air.

The Luftwaffe reconnaissance images used by the author are complemented by two remarkable images of the post-battle landscape that were taken from a low-flying Soviet aircraft. The images, which both appear in Valeriy Zamulin's *The Battle of Kursk 1943: The View through the Camera Lens* (Solihull: Helion 2015), clearly highlight the level of destruction that occurred at Prokhorovka on 12 July. The author also made use of SS War Correspondent (*SS Kriegsberichter*) photographic evidence of the

Prokhorovka area. On 11 July Johan King recorded the arrival of the Leibstandarte in the area, the taking of the anti-tank ditch (including the undamaged road bridge over the obstacle) and the subsequent conquest of Hill 252.2. Some of King's images appeared in Volumes 4, 5 and 6 of Remy Spezzano's pictorial series *Waffen-SS Kursk 1943* (Stamford: RZM Publishing 2004–05), Walter Schüle and Martin Månsson's *Pansarslaget vid Prochorovka* (Stockholm: Svenskt Militärhistoriskt Bibliotek 2009) and George Nipe's, *Blood, Steel and Myth: II SS Panzer Korps and the Road to Prochorowka, July 1943* (Stamford: RZM Publishing 2011). It remains a mystery why none of these publications included any of the images Johan King had taken of the notorious Prokhorovka anti-tank ditch.[5]

I. ARCHIVAL SOURCES

I. Bundesarchiv/Militärarchiv
GenInsp.d.Pz.Truppen RH 10

II. US National Archives Records Administration (NARA)
Luftwaffe Aerial Photography, RG 373 DT-TM5-11587, GX-2696-SK-23, GX-2696-SK-24, GX-2696-SK-52, GX-3734-SK-61, GX-3942-SK-69, GX-3942-SD-122, GX-3942-SD-123, GX-3942-SD-124, GX-3958-SD-10, GX-3958-SD-11, GX-3977-SD-45, GX-3977-SD-48, GX-4255-SD-16, GX-4517-SK-65
Photographs taken by Waffen-SS Photographers, RG 242
III Panzer Korps T314 R198, R201
XI Korps T314 R493
XXXXVIII Panzer Korps T314 R1171
II SS Panzer Korps T354 R605, R606, R607
6th Army T312 R1483
8th Army T312 R55
4th Panzer Army T313 R364, R387, R390, R391, R408
GenInsp.d.Pz.Truppen T78 R616, R619, R620, R719

2. PRINTED SOURCES

Heiber, Helmut, and Glantz, David, *Hitler and his Generals: Military Conferences 1942–1945* (New York: Enigma Books 2004)

3. SECONDARY LITERATURE

Archer, Lee, Kraska, Robert, and Lippert, Mario, *Panzers in Berlin 1945* (Old Heathfield: Panzerwrecks Publishing 2019)
Beevor, Antony, *The Second World War* (London: Weidenfeld and Nicolson 2012)
Bergström, Christopher, *Kursk: The Air Battle, July 1943* (Hersham: Ian Allan Publishing 2007)

Caidin, Martin, *The Tigers are Burning* (New York: Hawthorn Books 1974)

Chamberlain, Peter, and Doyle, Hilary, *Encyclopaedia of German Tanks of World War Two* (London: Arms and Armour 2001)

Citino, Robert, *The Wehrmacht Retreats: The Campaigns of 1943* (Kansas: University Press of Kansas 2012)

Clark, Lloyd, *Kursk: The Greatest Battle* (London: Headline Review 2012)

Cross, Robin, *The Battle of Kursk: Operation Citadel 1943* (London: Penguin Books 1993)

Evans, Richard, *The Third Reich at War: How the Nazis led Germany from Conquest to Disaster* (London: Allen Lane 2008)

Forczyk, Robert, *Kursk 1943: The Northern Front* (Oxford: Osprey 2014)

Forczyk, Robert, *Kursk 1943: The Southern Front* (Oxford: Osprey 2017)

Forczyk, Robert, *Panther vs. T-34: Ukraine 1943* (Oxford: Osprey 2007)

Forczyk, Robert, *The Dnepr 1943: Hitler's Eastern Rampart Crumbles* (Oxford: Osprey 2016)

Friedli, Lukas, *Repairing the Panzers: German Tank Maintenance in World War 2 Vol 1.* (Monroe: Panzerwrecks Publishing 2010)

Friedli, Lukas, *Repairing the Panzers: German Tank Maintenance in World War 2, Vol 2.* (Monroe: Panzerwrecks Publishing 2011)

Frieser, Karl-Heinz, *The Battle of the Kursk Salient* in The Research Institute for Military History, Potsdam, Germany, *Germany and the Second World War Volume VIII – The Eastern Front 1943–1944* (Oxford: Clarendon Press 2017)

Frieser, Karl-Heinz, *The Swing of the Pendulum: The Withdrawal of the Eastern Front from Summer 1943 to Summer 1944* in The Research Institute for Military History, Potsdam, *Germany, Germany and the Second World War Volume VIII – The Eastern Front 1943–1944* (Oxford: Clarendon Press 2017)

Glantz, David, *From the Don to the Dnepr* (London: Frank Cass 1991)

Glantz, David, *Soviet Military Intelligence in War* (Oxon: Frank Cass 1990)

Glantz, David, and House, Jonathan, *The Battle of Kursk* (Shepperton: Ian Allan 1999)

Guderian, Heinz, *Panzer Leader* (London: Penguin 2009)

Healy, Mark, *Kursk 1943: The Tide Turns in the East* (Oxford: Osprey 1999)

Hill, Alexander, *The Red Army and the Second World War* (Cambridge: Cambridge University Press 2017)

Jentz, Thomas (ed.), *Panzer Truppen II* (Atglen: Schiffer 1996)

Kroener, Bernhard R., *Management of Human Resources, Deployment of the Population, and Manning the Armed Forces in the Second Half of the War (1942–1944)* in The Research Institute for Military History, Potsdam, Germany, *Germany and the Second World War Volume VIII – Organization and Mobilization in the German Sphere of Power: Wartime Administration, Economy, and Manpower Resources 1942–1944/5* (Oxford: Clarendon Press 2003)

Lak, Martijn, 'The Death Ride of the Panzers? Recent Historiography on the Battle of Kursk', *Journal of Military History,* 82:3 (2018)

Lawrence, Christopher, *Kursk: The Battle of Prokhorovka* (Sheridan: Aberdeen Books 2015)

Lawrence, Christopher, *The Battle of Prokhorovka: The Tank Battle at Kursk, the Largest Clash of Armor in History* (Mechanicsburg: Stackpole Books 2019)

Lower, Wendy, *Nazi Empire-Building and the Holocaust in Ukraine* (Chapel Hill: The University of North Carolina Press 2005)

MacDougall, Roddy, and Neely, Darren, *Nürnberg's Panzer Factory, A Photographic Study* (Monroe: Panzerwrecks Publishing 2013)

Månsson, Martin, *Prokhorovka – Verdens største panserslag in Ostfronten* (2017)

Manstein, Erich von, *Lost Victories* (Munich: Bernard and Graefe Verlag 1982)

Melvin, Mungo, *Manstein, Hitler's Greatest General* (London: Weidenfeld and Nicolson 2010)

Merridale, Catherine, *Ivan's War: Life and Death in the Red Army* (New York: Picador 2006)

Nevshemal, Martin, *Objective Ponyri! The Defeat of XXXXI PanzerKorps at Ponyri Train Station* (Sydney: Leaping Horseman Books 2015)

Niehorster, Leo, *German World War II Organization Series, Volume V/I* (Milton Keynes: The Military Press 2004)

Niehorster, Leo, *German World War II Organization Series, Volume V/III* (Milton Keynes: The Military Press 2005)

Nipe, George, *Blood, Steel and Myth: II SS Panzer Korps and the Road to Prochorowka, July 1943* (Stamford: RZM Publishing 2011)

O'Brien, Phillips, *How the War was Won* (Cambridge: Cambridge University Press 2015)

Overy, Richard, *A History of War in 100 Battles* (London: William Collins 2014)

Overy, Richard, *Russia's War: Blood upon the Snow* (London: Penguin 1997)

Overy, Richard, *The Bombing War: Europe 1939–1945* (London: Penguin 2013)

Overy, Richard, *Why the Allies Won* (New York and London: W.W. Norton and Company 1995)

Rebentisch, Ernst, *The Combat History of the 23rd Panzer Division* (Mechanicsburg: Stackpole Books 2012)

Restayn, Jean, *Operation Citadel, Volume 1: The South* (Wininpeg: J.J. Fedorowicz Publishing 2021)

Roberts, Andrew, *The Storm of War: A New History of the Second World War* (London: Penguin 2009)

Schneider, Wolfgang, *Das Reich Tigers* (Winnipeg: J.J. Fedorowicz 2006)

Schneider, Wolfgang, *Tigers in Combat II* (Winnipeg: J.J. Fedorowicz 1998)

Schneider, Wolfgang, *Tigers in Combat I* (Winnipeg: J.J. Fedorowicz 2000)

Schüle, Walter, and Månsson, Martin, *Pansarslaget vid Prochorovka* (Stockholm: Svenskt Militärhistoriskt Bibliotek 2009)

Shepherd, Ben, *Hitler's Soldiers: The German Army in the Third Reich* (New Haven: Yale University Press 2016)

Showalter, Dennis, *Armor and Blood: The Battle of Kursk: The Turning Point of World War II* (New York: Random House 2013)

Sokolov, Boris V., 'The Battle for Kursk, Orel and Charkov: Strategic Intentions and Results. A Critical View of Soviet Historiography', in *Gezeitenwechsel*, 69–88.

Spezzano, Remy, *Waffen-SS Kursk 1943, Volume 4* (Stamford: RZM Publishing 2004)

Spezzano, Remy, *Waffen-SS Kursk 1943, Volume 5* (Stamford: RZM Publishing 2004)

Spezzano, Remy, *Waffen-SS Kursk 1943, Volume 6* (Stamford: RZM Publishing 2005)

Spielberger, Walter, Doyle, Hilary, and Jentz, Tomas, *Heavy Jagdpanzer: Development, Production, Operations* (Atglen: Schiffer 2007)

Stadler, Sylvester, *Die Offensive gegen Kursk, II SS-Panzerkorps als Stosskeil im Grosskampf* (Osnabrück: Munin Verlag 1980)

Stanley, Roy, *Intelligence Images from the Eastern Front* (Barnsley: Pen and Sword 2016)

Tomzov, Alexander, *Tankovy udar. Sovetskie tanki v boyakh. 1942–1943* (Moscow: Eksmo 2007)

Tooze, Adam, *The Wages of Destruction: The Making and Breaking of the Nazi War Economy* (London: Allen Lane 2006)

Töppel, Roman, 'The Battle of Prokhorovka: Facts Against Fables', *Journal of Slavic Military Studies*, 34:2 (2021)

Töppel, Roman, 'Die Panzerschlacht bei Prochorowka, Fakten gegen Fabeln', *Arbeitskreis Militärgeschichte e.V.* (2020)

Töppel, Roman, *Die größte Schlacht des Zweiten Weltkriegs* (Paderborn: Verlag Ferdinand Schöning 2017)

Töppel, Roman, 'Kursk – Mythen und Wirklichkeit einer Schlacht', in *Vierteljahrshefte für Zeitgeschichte*, 57 (2009)

Töppel, Roman, *Kursk 1943: The Greatest Battle of the Second World War* (Solihull: Helion 2018)

Wegner, Bernd, *From Stalingrad to Kursk* in The Research Institute for Military History, Potsdam, Germany, *Germany and the Second World War Volume VIII – The Eastern Front 1943–1944* (Oxford: Clarendon Press 2017)

Wegner, Bernd, *The War against the Soviet Union 1942–1943* in The Research Institute for Military History, Potsdam, Germany, *Germany and the Second World War Volume VI – The Global War* (Oxford: Clarendon Press 2001)

Wheatley, Ben, '*Citadel*, Prokhorovka and Kharkov: The armoured losses of II SS Panzer Korps *Sonderverbände* during the Battle of Kursk, July–August 1943', *Journal of Intelligence History*, 1–50 (Published online March 2021)

Wheatley, Ben, 'Surviving Prokhorovka: German Armoured Longevity on the Eastern Front in 1943–1944', *Journal of Intelligence History*, 1–87 (published online June 2020)

Wheatley, Ben, 'A Visual Examination of the Battle of Prokhorovka', *Journal of Intelligence History*, 1–48, Vol. 18, No. 2 (2019)

Zaloga, Steven, *Armoured Champion: The Top Tanks of World War II* (Mechanicsburg: Stackpole Books 2015)

Zamulin, Valeriy, 'Soviet Troop Losses in the Battle of Prokhorovka, 10–16 July 1943', *Journal of Slavic Military Studies*, 32:1 (2019)

Zamulin, Valeriy, *The Battle of Kursk: Controversial and Neglected Aspects* (Solihull: Helion 2017)

Zamulin, Valeriy, *The Battle of Kursk 1943: The View through the Camera Lens* (Solihull: Helion 2015)

Zamulin, Valeriy, *Demolishing the Myth: The Tank Battle at Prokhorovka. July 1943: An Operational Narrative* (Solihull: Helion 2011)

Zetterling, Niklas, and Frankson, Anders, *Kursk 1943: A Statistical Analysis* (London: Frank Cass 2000)

Appendices

APPENDIX A.¹ LSSAH AFV strength during July 1943

	Pz III	Pz IV	T-34	Pz VI	Bef	Total Pz	StuG	Sf Pak	Total AFV
Inventory 4.7.43	13	83		13	9	118	35	21	174
In inventory the day prior to the battle of Prokhorovka (0100hrs 11.7.43)	12	78		12–13*	9	111–112	33	19	163–164
Inventory 0100 19.7.43 (following *Citadel*)	12	74		12	9	107	32	22#	161
Inventory 25.7.43	12	74		17~	9	112	32	22	166
Inventory 29.7.43 (following transfer to DR and SS-T)	1	5			9	15	32	22	69
Operational 4.7.43	11	79		12	9	111	34	20	165
Operational 0100 11.7.43	5	41		4	6	56	23	17	96
Operational 18.7.43	7	55		9	8	79	28	16	123
Operational 24.7.43	7	55		10	6	78	30	22	130

* This depends on which LSSAH Tiger was actually written off.

Includes 4 new Sf Pak.

~ Includes 5 new Tigers.

Appendix B.[2] DR AFV strength during July 1943

	Pz III	Pz IV	T-34	Pz VI	Bef	Total Pz	StuG	Sf Pak	Total AFV
Inventory 4.7.43	62	33	24	14	9	142	34	12	188
Inventory the day prior to the battle of Prokhorovka (0100hrs 11.7.43)	60	31	22	13	9	135	34	12	181
Inventory 0100 21.7.43 (following *Citadel*)	60	27	21	13	9	130	32	12	174
Inventory 29.7.43 (following LSSAH transfer)	64	66	21	22	9	182	32	12	226
Inventory 0100 2.8.43	58*	60	21	22	11*	172	32	12	216
Operational 4.7.43	47	30	18	12	8	115	33	10	158
Operational 0100 11.7.43	40	16	8	1	5	70	29	11	110
Operational 18.7.43	36	24	17	9	7	93	28	10	131
Operational 22.7.43	36	24	17	9	7	93	28	10	131
Operational 27.7.43	46	20	1	3	2	72	28#	11	111
Operational 28.7.43 (not including LSSAH Pz)	33	17	2	6	3	61	28	11~	100
Operational 0100 2.8.43	23	15	6	1	8	53	16	10	79

* 2 Pz III lg listed under Bef.
# Following day.
~ Previous day.

Appendix C.[3] SS-T AFV strength during July 1943

	Pz III	Pz IV	T-34	Pz VI	Bef	Total Pz	StuG	Sf Pak	Total AFV
Inventory 4.7.43	63	52		15	9	139	35	11	185
In inventory the day prior to the battle of Prokhorovka (0100hrs 11.7.43)	61	48		14	9	132	34	11	177

	Pz III	Pz IV	T-34	Pz VI	Bef	Total Pz	StuG	Sf Pak	Total AFV
Inventory at 0100 21.7.43 (following *Citadel*)	61	48		14	9	132	34	9–11*	175–177
Inventory 29.7.43 (following LSSAH transfer)	65	78		22	9	174	34	9–11*	217–219
Inventory 2.8.43 at 0100	61	67		22~	9	159	34	9	202
Operational 4.7.43	59	47		11	8	125	28	11	164
Operational 0100 11.7.43	53	30		11	7	101	21	11	133
Operational 18.7.43	30	28		7	7	72	20	3	95
Operational 1645 20.7.43	39	26		5	6	76	?	?	?
Operational 28.7.43 (not including LSSAH Pz)	52	32		5	5	94	26	6#	126#
Operational 0100 2.8.43	40	9		1	6	56	18	6	80

* 2 Sf Pak lost sometime between 11.7.43 and the end of the Mius operation.

\# Unlikely to be less than 6 as this number of SS-T Sf Pak was operational on 31.7.43.

~ At some point after 2.8.43 two damaged pre-*Citadel*-era SS-T Tigers 250 103 and 250 230 were sent to homeland maintenance and then converted into Sturmmörser 38cm 'Tigers'. In October 1944 250 103 was serving with Sturmmörser Kompanie 1001, while in December 1944 250 230 was serving with Sturmmörser Kompanie 1000. Delivery dates can be found at sturmpanzer.com.

APPENDIX D.[4] II SS Panzer Korps HQ AFV strength during July 1943

	Pz III	Pz IV	T-34	Pz VI	Bef	Total Pz	StuG	Sf Pak	Total AFV
Inventory 29.7.43 (following LSSAH transfer)	3					3			3

APPENDIX E.5 Surviving Prokhorovka: Longevity of AFV present with LSSAH and DR on 1.7.43

Key to Appendix:	xx xxx	Confirmed transfer to DR 28.7.43	xx xxx	Due to embedded location in DR inventory almost certainly transferred to DR on 28.7.43	xx xxx	Confirmed TF loss during Citadel
	TF	*Totalausfälle* – total loss and removed from inventory	3a	Inst. Heimat (homeland maintenance) – sent to Germany for factory repair and removed from inventory	2c	Inst. Heimat (homeland maintenance) – sent to Germany for factory repair and kept in inventory

LSSAH Pz 1b + Bef 15 014 (remained with LSSAH)

Fate	Fate	Fate
15 523	~~14 587~~	~~15 014~~ TF 5–10.7.43 *Citadel*

LSSAH Pz II 20mm cannon (only 4 used by the 1st SS Panzer Regiment which then remained with LSSAH)

Fate	Fate	Fate	Fate
28 315 Ausf F	28 307 Ausf F	28 361 Ausf F	28 320 Ausf F
28 322 Ausf F	28 243 Ausf F	28 359 Ausf F	28 199 Ausf F
28 202 Ausf F	28 360 Ausf F	28 274 Ausf F	

LSSAH Pz III 50mm L42 or L60 main gun – including Pz III Bef Sd.kfz. 266 (1 Pz III kz and all Pz III Bef remained with LSSAH)

	Fate		Fate		Fate		Fate
73 733 Ausf K Bef (kz)	With LSSAH in Italy	70 163 Ausf H Bef Dummy gun	With LSSAH in Italy	73 639 Ausf J (kz)		74 576 Ausf L (lg)	Transferred to II SS Pz Korps or SS-T on 28.7.43
68 978 Ausf J (kz)		73 697 Ausf K Bef (kz)		73 726 Ausf K Bef (kz)	With LSSAH in Italy	73 746 Ausf K Bef (kz)	With LSSAH in Italy
73 707 Ausf K Bef (kz)	With LSSAH in Italy	76 476 Ausf M (lg)	Transferred to II SS Pz Korps or SS-T on 28.7.43	75 054 Ausf L (lg)	Transferred to II SS Pz Korps or SS-T on 28.7.43	75 050 Ausf L (lg)	Transferred to II SS Pz Korps or SS-T on 28.7.43
75 411 Ausf L (lg)	In DR inventory on 1.12.43	75 414 Ausf L (lg)	Transferred to II SS Pz Korps or SS-T on 28.7.43	75 556 Ausf L (lg)	Transferred to II SS Pz Korps or SS-T on 28.7.43	77 604 Ausf M (lg)	Listed as TF 5–10.7.43 *Citadel* in a report written on 12.7.43. Yet is transferred to DR 28.7.43! 10.7.43 ten-day status report lists a kz Pz III as TF which is withdrawn from LSSAH Ist total. Later listed by DR as 3a and sent to Reich for repair 1–10.12.43
75 064 Ausf L (lg)	In DR inventory on 1.12.43	75 394 Ausf L (lg)		72 613 Ausf J (kz)	In DR inventory on 1.12.43		

LSSAH Pz III 50mm L42 main gun Bef Sd.kfz. 267 and 268 (remained with LSSAH)

	Fate		Fate		Fate
73 731 Ausf K Bef (kz) Sd.kfz. 267	With LSSAH in Italy	73 689 Ausf K Bef (kz) Sd.kfz. 267	With LSSAH in Italy	73 738 Ausf K Bef (kz) Sd.kfz. 268	With LSSAH in Italy

LSSAH Pz IV 75mm L43 or L48 main gun (1 Bef Pz IV and 4 Pz IV remained with LSSAH)

	Fate		Fate		Fate		Fate
83 259 Ausf G L43	In DR inventory on 1.12.43	83 261 Ausf G L43		83 257 Ausf G L43		83 255 Ausf G L43	
83 298 Ausf G L43		83 304 Ausf G L43		83 302 Ausf G L43		**83 262 Ausf G L43**	In DR inventory on 1.12.43
83 256 Ausf G L43	TF 1-10.11.43	83 274 Ausf G L43		83 291 Ausf G L43	TF 10.7.43 Citadel	**83 296 Ausf G L43**	3a and sent to Reich for repair 1-10.1.44 (almost certainly 3a for a period before 20.10.43 as well)
83 260 Ausf G L43		83 990 Ausf G L43		**83 288 Ausf G 43**	In DR inventory on 1.12.43	83 175 Ausf G L43	In DR inventory on 1.12.43
83 238 Ausf G L43		83 279 Ausf G L43		**83 282 Ausf G L43**	In DR inventory on 1.12.43	**83 285 Ausf G L43**	In DR inventory on 31.10.43

~~83 293 Ausf G L43~~	TF 10.7.43 *Citadel*	83 471 Ausf G L43		83 299 Ausf G L43		83 474 Ausf G L43	TF 10–20.11.43
83 183 Ausf G L43		83 473 Ausf G L43		**82 717 Ausf G L43**	In DR inventory on 1.12.43	83 306 Ausf G L43	
83 460 Ausf G L43		**83 185 Ausf G L43**	3a and sent to Reich for repair 1–10.1.44	**83 472 Ausf G L43**	In DR inventory on 1.12.43	83 276 Ausf G L43	
~~83 481 Ausf G L43~~	TF 10.7.43 *Citadel*	**82 712 Ausf G L43**	TF (behind enemy lines) 11–20.1.44. Recovered 23.1.44 and returned to inventory. Handed over by DR to 19 Pz Div 29.2.44	82 721 Ausf G L43		82 716 Ausf G L43	
83 792 Ausf G L43		83 305 Ausf G L43		83 311 Ausf G L43			
82 600 Ausf F2 L43	In DR inventory on 1.12.43	83 264 Ausf G L43		84 062 Ausf G L48		82 714 Ausf G L43	
83 841 Ausf G L48	3a and sent to Reich for repair 10–20.11.43	83 830 Ausf G L48		~~84 088 Ausf G L48~~		84 093 Ausf G L48	
						84 076 Ausf G L48	TF 10.7.43 *Citadel*

84 096 Ausf G L48	84 079 Ausf G L48	**84 208 Ausf G L48** — In DR inventory on 1.12.43	**84 197 Ausf G L48** — 3a and sent to Reich for repair 1–10.1.44
83 824 Ausf G L48 — In DR inventory on 1.12.43	**84 903 Ausf H L48** — In DR inventory on 1.12.43	84 210 Ausf G L48 — In DR inventory on 1.12.43	84 219 Ausf G L48
84 087 Ausf G L48	83 856 Ausf G L48	83 870 Ausf G L48	83 854 Ausf G L48
83 863 Ausf G L48	84 241 Ausf G L48	84 280 Ausf G L48	84 229 Ausf G L48
84 228 Ausf G L48	84 244 Ausf G L48	**84 913 Ausf H L48** — In DR inventory on 1.12.43	***83 942 Ausf G L48*** — Received by 4.7.43. Embedded with other ex-LSSAH in DR reports. In DR inventory on 1.12.43
83 858 Ausf G L48 — Received by 4.7.43. Embedded with other ex-LSSAH in DR reports. In DR inventory on 1.12.43	***85 625 Ausf H L48*** — Received by 4.7.43. Embedded with other ex-LSSAH in DR reports. In DR inventory on 1.12.43	***85 001 Ausf H L48*** — Received by 4.7.43. Embedded with other ex-LSSAH in DR reports. In DR inventory on 1.12.43	***85 006 Ausf H L48*** — Received by 4.7.43. Embedded with other ex-LSSAH in DR reports. 3a and sent to Reich for repair 1–10.1.44 / TF 10–20.11.43
8x xxx — Received by 4.7.43	8x xxx — Received by 4.7.43	8x xxx — Received by 4.7.43	8x xxx — Received by 4.7.43
8x xxx — Received by 4.7.43	8x xxx — Received by 4.7.43	8x xxx — Received by 4.7.43	8x xxx — Received by 4.7.43
8x xxx — Received by 4.7.43	8x xxx — Received by 4.7.43	8x xxx — Received by 4.7.43	

LSSAH Pz VI (Tiger) 88mm L56 main gun

	Fate		Fate		Fate		Fate
250 066		**250 062**	In DR inventory on 1.12.43	**250 068**	In DR inventory on 1.12.43. Returned from 3a 1–10.1.44. TF in same period	**250 071**	TF 1–10.1.44
250 072		250 073		**250 075**	TF 1–10.1.44 (also listed as 3a and sent to Reich for repair – duplicated in error for unidentified Tiger?)	250 048	
250 223		**250 214**	TF 1–10.1.44	**250 210**	TF 1–10.1.44	**250 226**	TF 1–10.1.44
250 194	TF 10–20.11.43	**250 192**	Received 25.7.43. TF 10–20.11.43	*250 xxx*	Received 25.7.43 – joined SS-T 28.7.43	*250 xxx*	Received 25.7.43 – joined SS-T 28.7.43
250 xxx	Received 25.7.43 – joined SS-T 28.7.43	*250 xxx*	Received 25.7.43 – joined SS-T 28.7.43				

LSSAH StuG 75mm L43 or L48 main gun (remained with LSSAH)

	Fate		Fate		Fate		Fate
91 152 Ausf F L43		91 743 Ausf F/8 L48		91 736 Ausf F/8 L48		91 733 Ausf F/8 L48	
91 107 Ausf F L43		91 732 Ausf F/8 L48		~~91 143 Ausf F L43~~	TF 5.7.43 *Citadel*	91 749 Ausf F/8 L48	

Vehicle	Fate	Vehicle	Fate	Vehicle	Fate	Vehicle	Fate
91 097 Ausf F L43	TF 1–10.1.44	91 677 Ausf F/8 L48		91 686 Ausf F/8 L48		91 693 Ausf F/8 L48	TF 1–10.1.44
91 704 Ausf F/8 L48		91 147 Ausf F L43		91 729 Ausf F/8 L48		91 127 Ausf F L43	
91 141 Ausf F L43		91 135 Ausf F L43		91 708 Ausf F/8 L48		91 722 Ausf F/8 L48	
91 730 Ausf F/8 L48	TF 1–10.1.44	91 716 Ausf F/8 L48		92 150 Ausf G L48 *(struck)*	TF 10.7.43 *Citadel*	91 157 Ausf F L43	TF 1–10.1.44
92 141 Ausf G L48		92 161 Ausf G L48		92 162 Ausf G L48		92 127 Ausf G L48	
92 153 Ausf G L48		92 152 Ausf G L48		92 160 Ausf G L48		92 126 Ausf G L48	
92 315 Ausf G L48		92 239 Ausf G L48		92 318 Ausf G L48			

LSSAH Pz Jg 38t 75mm L46 main gun (remained with LSSAH)

Vehicle	Fate	Vehicle	Fate	Vehicle	Fate	Vehicle	Fate
1 820		1 821 *(struck)*	TF 5–10.7.43 *Citadel*	1 822	TF 1–10.1.44	1 856	
1 824	TF 1–10.1.44	1 825		1 860		1 829	
1 830		1 831		1 832		1 834	

Chassis No.	Fate	Chassis No.	Fate	Chassis No.	Fate	Chassis No.	Fate
1 835	TF 22.11–2.12.43	1 837	TF 5–10.7.43 *Citadel*	1 847		1 848	TF 22.11–2.12.43
1 850	TF 22.11–2.12.43	1 855	x xxx			1 858	x xxx
x xxx	Received after 10.7.43	x xxx	Received after 10.7.43	x xxx	Received after 10.7.43	x xxx	Received after 10.7.43
x xxx	Received after 10.7.43	x xxx	Received after 10.7.43	x xxx	Received after 10.7.43	x xxx	Received after 10.7.43

LSSAH Pz Jg II 76.2mm gun (remained with LSSAH)

Chassis No.	Fate
x xxx	

LSSAH s.F.H. 18 Sfl. (Hummel) 150mm heavy field howitzer (remained with LSSAH)

Chassis No.	Fate	Chassis No.	Fate	Chassis No.	Fate
320 033		320 035		320 037	
320 042		320 044		320 041	

LSSAH l.F.H. 18 Sfl. (Wespe) 105mm light field howitzer (remained with LSSAH)

Chassis No.	Fate	Chassis No.	Fate	Chassis No.	Fate	Chassis No.	Fate
31 075		31 068		31 070		31 072	
31 074		31 078		31 067		31 069	
31 071		31 073		31 076		31 077	

LSSAH Pz III Art. Beob. Wg. Armoured observation post (remained with LSSAH)

Chassis No.	Fate	Chassis No.	Fate	Chassis No.	Fate	Chassis No.	Fate
61 065		61 336		61 554		61 616	
65 118		65 233		65 373		65 734	
65 805							

LSSAH s.I.G. 33 Sfl. 38t (Grille) 150mm heavy infantry gun (remained with LSSAH)

	Fate		Fate		Fate		Fate
2 141		2 148		2 150		2 152	TF 21–30.12.43
2 143		2 149		2 151		2 153	
2 154	TF 21–30.12.43	2 155		2 156		2 157	

LSSAH Sd.-kfz. 221 – 28mm sPzB41 – light armoured car (remained with LSSAH)

	Fate		Fate		Fate		Fate
810 492		810 845		810 346		810 831	

LSSAH Sd.-kfz. 222 – 20mm cannon – light armoured car (remained with LSSAH)

	Fate		Fate		Fate		Fate
810 947		810 957		810 1308		810 1303	

LSSAH Sd.-kfz. 223 (FU) – MG34 – light armoured car – radio version (remained with LSSAH)

	Fate		Fate		Fate
810 1385		810 1396		810 1389	

LSSAH Sd.-kfz. 231 – 20mm cannon – heavy armoured car (remained with LSSAH)

	Fate
60 046	

LSSAH Sd. -kfz. 232 (FU) – 20mm cannon – heavy armoured car – radio version (remained with LSSAH)

Serial	Fate	Serial	Fate	Serial	Fate	Serial	Fate
59 953		79 496		79 497		79 498	

LSSAH Sd. -kfz. 261 – light armoured radio car – long-range radio (remained with LSSAH)

Serial	Fate	Serial	Fate	Serial	Fate	Serial	Fate
810 1391		810 0257		810 0060		810 1364	
810 1374		811 0249		810 1373		810 1403	
810 1411		811 0259		810 1381		811 0260	

LSSAH Sd. -kfz. 263 (FU) – MG13 – heavy armoured car – radio version (remained with LSSAH)

Serial	Fate
79 607	

LSSAH Sd. -kfz. 247 – heavy wheeled armoured personnel carrier (remained with LSSAH)

Serial	Fate	Serial	Fate
140 011		402 824	

DR Pz 1b Bef

Serial	Fate
15 036	In inventory 1.12.43

DR Pz II 20mm cannon

Serial	Fate
23 076	TF 20–31.10.43

DR Pz III Bef 50mm L42 main gun Sd.kfz. 267

	Fate
68 790 Ausf J	In inventory on 1.12.43

DR T-34 76.2mm main gun

	Fate		Fate		Fate		Fate
1		2		3		4	
5		6		7		8	
9		10		11		12	
13		14		~~15~~ (14)	TF 5–10.7.43 *Citadel*	16	
17		18		~~19~~ (17)	TF 5–10.7.43 *Citadel*	20	
21		22		23		24	

DR Pz III Bef 50mm L42 main gun

	Fate		Fate		Fate		Fate
70 159 Ausf H Bef Dummy gun	Does not appear in 31.10.43 inventory	73 751 Ausf K Bef (kz)	TF 1–10.1.44	73 760 Ausf K Bef (kz)	In inventory on 29.2.44	73 744 Ausf K Bef (kz)	In inventory on 1.12.43
73 722 Ausf K Bef (kz)	In inventory on 1.12.43	73 714 Ausf K Bef (kz)	In inventory on 1.12.43	73 695 Ausf K Bef (kz)	Does not appear in 31.10.43 inventory	73 679 Ausf K Bef (kz)	Does not appear in 31.10.43 inventory

DR Pz III 50mm L60 main gun

Entry	Fate	Entry	Fate	Entry	Fate	Entry	Fate
72 241 Ausf J	In inventory on 1.12.43	73 458 Ausf J	Does not appear in 31.10.43 inventory	72 266 Ausf J	TF 20–31.10.43	73 104 Ausf J	Does not appear in 31.10.43 inventory
74 601 Ausf L	In inventory on 1.12.43	74 140 Ausf L	Does not appear in 31.10.43 inventory	74 355 Ausf L	Does not appear in 31.10.43 inventory	73 455 Ausf J	Does not appear in 31.10.43 inventory
72 245 Ausf J	Does not appear in 31.10.43 inventory	~~72 267 Ausf J (992)~~	TF 5–10.7.43 *Citadel*	72 213 Ausf J	In inventory on 1.12.43	~~73 102 Ausf J (514)~~	TF 5–10.7.43 *Citadel*
74 353 Ausf L	Does not appear in 31.10.43 inventory	73 466 Ausf J	3a and sent to Reich for repair 1–10.12.43	74 149 Ausf L	Does not appear in 31.10.43 inventory	73 770 Ausf J	Does not appear in 31.10.43 inventory
72 284 Ausf J	In inventory on 1.12.43	72 724 Ausf J	Does not appear in 31.10.43 inventory	76 444 Ausf M	Does not appear in 31.10.43 inventory	75 035 Ausf L	Does not appear in 31.10.43 inventory
76 490 Ausf M	Does not appear in 31.10.43 inventory	76 494 Ausf M	Does not appear in 31.10.43 inventory	75 029 Ausf L	3a and sent to Reich for repair 10–20.11.43	75 391 Ausf L	In inventory on 1.12.43
75 027 Ausf L	Does not appear in 31.10.43 inventory	75 040 Ausf L	TF 1–10.11.43	77 560 Ausf M	3a and sent to Reich for repair 1–10.12.43	75 045 Ausf L	TF 10–20.11.43
76 503 Ausf M	In inventory on 1.12.43	76 516 Ausf M	TF 1–10.11.43	75 383 Ausf L	3.a and sent to Reich for repair 1–10.11.43	76 515 Ausf M	Does not appear in 31.10.43 inventory
75 020 Ausf L	TF 10–20.11.43	75 030 Ausf L	Does not appear in 31.10.43 inventory	75 354 Ausf L	Does not appear in 31.10.43 inventory	76 495 Ausf M	Does not appear in 31.10.43 inventory
76 510 Ausf M	Does not appear in 31.10.43 inventory	76 486 Ausf M	Does not appear in 31.10.43 inventory	75 483 Ausf L	In inventory on 1.12.43	74 579 Ausf L	Does not appear in 31.10.43 inventory
75 356 Ausf L	Does not appear in 31.10.43 inventory	75 366 Ausf L	3a and sent to Reich for repair 10–20.11.43	75 388 Ausf L	Does not appear in 31.10.43 inventory	75 380 Ausf L	3a and sent to Reich for repair 1–10.11.43

	Fate		Fate		Fate		Fate
75 084 Ausf L	Does not appear in 31.10.43 inventory	75 071 Ausf L	3a and sent to Reich for repair 1–10.11.43	75 089 Ausf L	3a and sent to Reich for repair 1–10.11.43	77 579 Ausf M	TF 10–20.11.43
74 597 Ausf L	Does not appear in 31.10.43 inventory	77 593 Ausf M	Does not appear in 31.10.43 inventory	77 601 Ausf M	Does not appear in 31.10.43 inventory	77 564 Ausf M	Does not appear in 31.10.43 inventory
77 600 Ausf M	Does not appear in 31.10.43 inventory	75 094 Ausf L	In inventory on 1.12.43	77 583 Ausf M	Does not appear in 31.10.43 inventory	61 417 Ausf F	Does not appear in 31.10.43 inventory
65 009 Ausf G	Does not appear in 31.10.43 inventory	65 119 Ausf G	Does not appear in 31.10.43 inventory	68 529 Ausf J	In inventory on 1.12.43	68 676 Ausf J	In inventory on 1.12.43
68 870 Ausf J	In inventory on 1.12.43	65 090 Ausf J	Does not appear in 31.10.43 inventory				

DR Pz IV 75mm L43 or L48 main gun

	Fate		Fate		Fate		Fate
82 843 Ausf G L43	In inventory on 1.12.43	82 752 Ausf G L43	In inventory on 1.12.43	82 755 Ausf G L43	In inventory on 1.12.43	82 760 Ausf G L43	Does not appear in 31.10.43 inventory
82 741 Ausf G L43	Does not appear in 31.10.43 inventory	83 013 Ausf G L43	Does not appear in 31.10.43 inventory	83 247 Ausf G L43	Does not appear in 31.10.43 inventory	83 263 Ausf G L43	Does not appear in 31.10.43 inventory
83 463 Ausf G L43	In inventory on 1.12.43	83 241 Ausf G L43	In inventory on 31.10.43. Returned from 3a 1–10.1.44. TF 11–20.1.44	83 243 Ausf G L43	Does not appear in 31.10.43 inventory	83 456 Ausf G L43	In inventory on 1.12.43
83 813 Ausf G L48	TF 10–20.11.43	83 848 Ausf G L48	Does not appear in 31.10.43 inventory	83 852 Ausf G L48	TF 20–31.10.43	84 077 Ausf G L48	In inventory on 1.12.43

84 091 Ausf G L48	Does not appear in 31.10.43 inventory
84 ̶2̶2̶3̶ Ausf G L48 (823)	Listed as TF 5–10.7.43 *Citadel* in a report dated 23.7.43. 10.7.43 ten-day status report lists only 1 Pz IV (i.e. 84 231). In DR inventory from 31.10.43. Listed as 3a and sent to Reich for repair 1–10.1.44
84 242 Ausf G L48	In inventory on 1.12.43. Returned from 3a 1–10.1.44. Handed over to 19 Pz Div 29.2.44
83 875 Ausf G L48	Does not appear in 31.10.43 inventory. Returned from 3a 1–10.11.43. In inventory on 1.12.43
84 072 Ausf G L48	Does not appear in 31.10.43 inventory
84 092 Ausf G L48	Does not appear in 31.10.43 inventory
84 225 Ausf G L48	TF 1–10.1.44
84 905 Ausf H L48	Does not appear in 31.10.43 inventory
84 226 Ausf G L48	TF 1–10.1.44
84 094 Ausf G L48	Does not appear in 31.10.43 inventory
84 ̶2̶3̶1̶ Ausf G L48 (832)	TF 5–10.7.43 *Citadel*
84 224 Ausf G L48	3a and sent to Reich for repair 1–10.1.44
84 904 Ausf H L48	TF 20–31.10.43
84 100 Ausf G L48	Does not appear in 31.10.43 inventory
84 236 Ausf G L48	In inventory on 31.10.43
83 849 Ausf G L48	In inventory on 1.12.43
83 866 Ausf G L48	Does not appear in 31.10.43 inventory

DR Pz VI (Tiger) 88mm L56 main gun

	Fate		Fate		Fate		Fate
250 077	TF 20–31.10.43	250 092	3a and sent to Reich for repair 11–20.12.43	250 088	Does not appear in 31.10.43 inventory (lost after *Citadel* but prior to 20.10.43)	250 084	In inventory on 1.12.43
250 076	In inventory on 1.12.43	250 086	In inventory on 1.12.43	250 087 (S24)	TF 5–10.7.43 *Citadel*	250 049	Long-term non-operational from 10–20.3.43 to at least 4 July – does not appear in 31.10.43 inventory (lost after *Citadel* but prior to 20.10.43)
250 225	In inventory on 1.12.43	250 220	TF 10–20.11.43	250 201	Does not appear in 31.10.43 inventory (lost after *Citadel* but prior to 20.10.43)	250 213	Does not appear in 31.10.43 inventory (lost after *Citadel* but prior to 20.10.43)
250 217	TF 11–20.12.43	250 219	2c Inst. Heimat and sent to Reich for repair (remains in inventory) 20–30.11.43				

DR StuG 75mm L48 main gun

	Fate		Fate		Fate		Fate
91 705 Ausf F/8 L48	TF 20–31.10.43	91 710 Ausf F/8 L48	In inventory on 1.12.43	91 712 Ausf F/8 L48	In inventory on 1.12.43	91 713 Ausf F/8 L48	TF 1–10.1.44

Vehicle	Status	Vehicle	Status	Vehicle	Status	Vehicle	Status
91 714 Ausf F/8 L48	In inventory on 1.12.43	91 717 Ausf F/8 L48	Does not appear in 31.10.43 inventory	91 719 Ausf F/8 L48	TF 1–10.1.44	91 721 Ausf F/8 L48	TF 1–10.1.44
91 723 Ausf F/8 L48	Does not appear in 31.10.43 inventory	91 724 Ausf F/8 L48	In inventory on 29.2.44	91 667 Ausf F/8 L48	In inventory on 1.12.43	91 671 Ausf F/8 L48	In inventory on 1.12.43
91 673 Ausf F/8 L48	In inventory on 29.2.44	91 674 Ausf F/8 L48	TF 1–10.1.44	91 681 Ausf F/8 L48	Does not appear in 31.10.43 inventory	91 687 Ausf F/8 L48	In inventory on 1.12.43
91 698 Ausf F/8 L48	Does not appear in 31.10.43 inventory	91 668 Ausf F/8 L48	In inventory on 29.2.44	91 679 Ausf F/8 L48	Does not appear in 31.10.43 inventory	91 684 Ausf F/8 L48	In inventory on 29.2.44 – listed in error as 91 864. Correctly listed in inventory on 1.12.43
95 177 Ausf G L48	Does not appear in 31.10.43 inventory	95 125 Ausf G L48	Does not appear in 31.10.43 inventory	92 297 Ausf G L48	Does not appear in 31.10.43 inventory	92 263 Ausf G L48	Does not appear in 31.10.43 inventory
92 266 Ausf G L48	In inventory on 1.12.43	92 311 Ausf G L48	In inventory on 29.2.44	92 287 Ausf G L48	In inventory on 29.2.44	92 306 Ausf G L48	In inventory on 1.12.43
95 172 Ausf G L48	In inventory on 29.2.44	76 203 Ausf G L48	Listed TF 10–20.11.43 yet in inventory on 1.12.43	95 170 Ausf G L48	In inventory on 29.2.44	95 178 Ausf G L48	Does not appear in 31.10.43 inventory
95 126 Ausf G L48	In inventory on 1.12.43	95 176 Ausf G L48	In inventory on 1.12.43				

DR Pz Jg 38t 76.2mm main gun

	Fate		Fate		Fate		Fate
1 556	Does not appear in 1.12.43 inventory	1 560	In inventory on 1.12.43	1 562	Does not appear in 1.12.43 inventory	1 563	In inventory on 1.12.43
1 564	In inventory on 1.12.43	1 565	In inventory on 1.12.43	1 567	In inventory on 1.12.43	1 568	In inventory on 1.12.43
1 708	In inventory on 1.12.43						

DR Pz Jg PzII 75mm L46 main gun

	Fate		Fate		Fate
28 998	In inventory on 1.12.43	29 999	Does not appear in 31.10.43 inventory	30 000	Does not appear in 31.10.43 inventory

DR s.F.H. 18 Sfl. (Hummel) 150mm heavy field howitzer

	Fate		Fate		Fate		Fate
320 083	In inventory on 1.12.43	320 076	In inventory on 1.12.43	320 046	In inventory on 1.12.43	320 051	In inventory on 1.12.43
320 087	In inventory on 1.12.43. Returned from 3a 11–20.2.44. In inventory on 29.2.44	320 084	In inventory on 1.12.43				

DR l.F.H. 18 Sfl. (Wespe) 105mm light field howitzer

	Fate		Fate		Fate		Fate
31 079	In inventory on 1.12.43	31 080	In inventory on 1.12.43	31 081	In inventory on 1.12.43	31 082	In inventory on 29.2.44

	Fate		Fate		Fate		Fate
31 083	In inventory on 1.12.43	31 084	In inventory on 29.2.44	31 085		31 086	In inventory on 1.12.43
31 087	In inventory on 1.12.43	31 088	In inventory on 1.12.43	31 089	In inventory on 1.12.43	31 090	In inventory on 1.12.43

DR Pz III Art. Beob. Wg. Armoured observation post

	Fate		Fate		Fate		Fate
60 464	In inventory on 1.12.43	61 601	In inventory on 1.12.43	65 113	In inventory on 1.12.43	65 122	In inventory on 1.12.43
65 178	TF 31.12.43	65 446	In inventory on 1.12.43	65 463	In inventory on 1.12.43	65 483	In inventory on 1.12.43
65 789	TF 30.12.43						

DR s.I.G. 33 Sfl. 38t (Grille) 150mm heavy infantry gun

	Fate		Fate		Fate		Fate
2 158	In inventory on 29.2.44 – listed in error as 2 168	2 159	In inventory on 1.12.43	2 160	In inventory on 1.12.43	2 161	In inventory on 1.12.43
2 162	In inventory on 1.12.43	2 163	In inventory on 1.12.43	2 164	In inventory on 1.12.43	2 165	In inventory on 1.12.43
2 176	In inventory on 1.12.43	2 177	In inventory on 29.2.44	2 178	In inventory on 1.12.43	2 179	In inventory on 1.12.43

DR Sd.-kfz. 221 – 28mm sPzB41 – light armoured car

	Fate		Fate		Fate		Fate
810 493	In inventory on 1.12.43	810 496	3a and sent to Reich for repair 10–20.1.44	810 573	Does not appear in 31.10.43 inventory	810 584	In inventory on 1.12.43

DR Sd.-kfz. 222 – 20mm cannon – light armoured car

	Fate		Fate		Fate		Fate
810 137	In inventory on 1.12.43	810 011	In inventory on 1.12.43. Returned from 3a 10–20.1.44. 3.a and sent to Reich for repair 1–10.2.44	810 946	In inventory on 1.12.43. Returned from 3a 10–20.1.44. 3a and sent to Reich for repair 1–10.2.44	810 754	In inventory on 1.12.43. Returned from 3a 10–20.1.44. 3a and sent to Reich for repair 1–10.2.44
810 909	Returned from 3a 10–20.1.44. In inventory on 29.2.44	810 689	3a and sent to Reich for repair 1–10.2.44	810 578	In inventory on 1.12.43	810 360	Does not appear in 31.10.43 inventory
811 1135	In inventory on 1.12.43	811 1159	Does not appear in 31.10.43 inventory	811 1097	Does not appear in 31.10.43 inventory		

DR Sd.-kfz. 223 (FU) – MG34 – light armoured car (radio version)

	Fate		Fate		Fate		Fate
811 0065	In inventory on 1.2.44	811 0066	In inventory on 1.12.43	811 0063	TF 1–10.1.44	810 781	In inventory on 1.12.43
810 979	TF 1–10.2.44	810 712	Does not appear in 31.10.43 inventory	8xx xxx	Does not appear in 31.10.43 inventory	8xx xxx	
8xx xxx							

DR Sd.-kfz. 231 – 20mm cannon – heavy armoured car

	Fate		Fate		Fate		Fate
59 975	3a and sent to Reich for repair 1–10.2.44	60 608	In inventory on 1.12.43	60 679	3a and sent to Reich for repair 1–10.2.44	79 540	TF 1–10.12.43

DR Sd.-kfz. 232 (FU) – 20mm cannon – heavy armoured car (radio version)

Serial	Fate	Serial	Fate	Serial	Fate
60 665	3a and sent to Reich for repair 1–10.2.44	60 667	TF 21–30.11.43	60 687	3a and sent to Reich for repair 1–10.2.44

DR Sd.-kfz. 260 – light armoured radio car (medium-range radio)

Serial	Fate	Serial	Fate	Serial	Fate
811 0088	In inventory on 1.12.43	811 0239	In inventory on 1.12.43	811 0248	In inventory on 1.12.43

DR Sd.-kfz. 261 – light armoured radio car (long-range radio)

Serial	Fate	Serial	Fate	Serial	Fate	Serial	Fate
811 0362	In inventory on 1.12.43	811 0348	In inventory on 1.12.43	811 0034	In inventory on 1.12.43	811 0037	In inventory on 1.12.43
811 0073	In inventory on 1.12.43	811 0107	TF 26.12.43				

DR Sd.-kfz. 263 (FU) – MG13 – heavy armoured car (radio version)

Serial	Fate	Serial	Fate	Serial	Fate
79 435	In inventory on 1.12.43	87 160	3a and sent to Reich for repair 20.1–1.2.44	87 163	In inventory on 29.2.44

DR Sd.-kfz. 247 – heavy wheeled armoured personnel carrier

Serial	Fate	Serial	Fate
140 048	Returned from 3a 10–20.1.44. In inventory on 29.2.44	140 025	In inventory on 1.12.43

December 1942–July 1943 issued LSSAH Tigers Pz VI (Tiger) 88mm L56 main gun

	Fate		Fate		Fate		Fate
250 053	TF 1–10.3.43 Kharkov counter-offensive	250 066		**250 067**	In DR inventory on 1.12.43	**250 068**	In DR inventory on 1.12.43. Returned from 3a 1–10.1.44. TF in same period
250 071	TF 1–10.1.44	250 072		250 073		**250 075**	TF 1–10.1.44 (also listed as 3a and sent to Reich for repair – duplicated in error for unidentified Tiger?)
250 048		250 223		**250 214**	TF 1–10.1.44	**250 210**	TF 1–10.1.44
250 226	TF 1–10.1.44	**250 194**	TF 10–20.11.43	**250 197**	Received 25.7.1943. TF 10–20.11.43	250 xxx	Received 25.7.1943 – joined SS-T 28.7.43
250 xxx	Received 25.7.1943 – joined SS-T 28.7.43	250 xxx	Received 25.7.1943 – joined SS-T 28.7.43	250 xxx	Received 25.7.1943 – joined SS-T 28.7.43		

December 1942–July 1943 issued DR Tigers Pz VI (Tiger) 88mm L56 main gun

	Fate		Fate		Fate		Fate
250 077	3a and sent to Reich for repair 11–20.12.43	250 092	3a and sent to Reich for repair 1–10.1.44	250 078	TF 20.2–2.3.43 Kharkov counteroffensive	250 088	Does not appear in 31.10.43 inventory (lost after *Citadel* but prior to 20.10.43)
250 084	In inventory on 1.12.43	250 076	In inventory on 1.12.43	250 086	TF 1–10.1.44	250 083	TF 10–20.3.43 Kharkov counteroffensive

	Fate		Fate		Fate		Fate
~~250 085 (S24)~~	TF 5–10.7.43 *Citadel*	250 049	Long-term non-operational from 10–20.3.43 to at least 4 July – does not appear in 31.10.43 inventory (lost after *Citadel* but prior to 20.10.43)	250 225	In inventory on 1.12.43	250 220	TF 10–20.11.43
250 201	Does not appear in 31.10.43 inventory (lost after *Citadel* but prior to 20.10.43)	250 213	Does not appear in 31.10.43 inventory (lost after *Citadel* but prior to 20.10.43)	250 217	TF 11–20.12.43	250 219	2c Inst. Heimat and sent to Reich for repair (remains in inventory) 20–30.11.43

January–July 1943 issued SS-T Tigers Pz VI (Tiger) 88mm L56 main gun

	Fate		Fate		Fate		Fate
250 079		250 080		250 089		250 094	
~~250 095~~	TF 5–10.7.43 *Citadel*	250 096		250 101		250 102	
250 103	At some point after 2.8.43. In 1944 converted to *Sturmmörser*	250 152		250 211		250 212	
250 216		250 224		250 230	At some point after 2.8.43 3a. In 1944 converted to *Sturmmörser*		

APPENDIX F.[6] German total losses of the Army 22.6.41–20.3.42					
Losses of personnel	KIA	WIA	MIA	Total	Sick
Army total	228,059	804,085	57,389	1,089,533	88,403
Of these in the East	225,559	796,516	50,991	1,073,066	78,479
Losses of horses	Dead	Sick or wounded			
Total	264,854	38,967			
Of these in the East	259,814	32,935			
Gains and losses of vehicles in the East	Losses	Gains	Shortfall		
Panzer I–IV	3,319	732	2,097		
Self-propelled guns	173	17	154		
Armoured artillery tractors	357	47	280		
Other armoured vehicles	945	193	637		
Artillery tractors	3,774	503	3,211		
Trucks	53,149	17,615	35,534		
Staff cars	35,572	4,578	31,194		
Motorbikes	50,165	4,391	44,087		
Losses of weapons in the East	Pieces				
Rifles	76,883				
Machine guns	30,374				
Anti-tank rifles	2,791				
Anti-tank guns (37–50mm)	5,249				
Mortars	7,263				
Flak (20–88mm)	334				
Tank cannons	357				
Field howitzers	2,403				
Other artillery	2,128				
Captured men and materiel					
Soviet POWs	3,461,338				
Rifles	238,037				
Machine guns	33,742				

Anti-tank rifles	259				
Mortars	5,754				
Sundry artillery	27,814				
Aircraft	1,042				
Tanks	15,004				
Fuel (cu.m.)	106,745				
Horses	160,959				
Flour (t.)	89,286				
Meat (t.)	6,585				

APPENDIX G.[7] Strength of the German Field Army (Heer only)				
	Men	Formations	Shortfall if 1941 OB is used	Shortfall if 1943 OB is used
1.7.41	4,025,000	202		
1.7.42	3,950,000	220		
1.7.43	4,480,000	245	620,000	257,000

APPENDIX H.[8] Changes in strength of the German Army on the Eastern Front 15.6.41–1.7.44	
15.6.41	3,300,000
1.11.41	3,100,000
1.1.42	3,000,000
1.4.42	2,900,000
1.5.42	2,850,000
1.6.42	2,800,000
1.7.42	2,750,000
1.9.42	2,800,000
1.10.42	2,900,000
1.1.43	2,900,000
1.3.43	2,800,000
1.4.43	2,700,000
1.6.43	2,900,000
1.7.43	3,138,000
1.8.43	2,985,000

1.9.43	2,676,000
1.10.43	2,568,000
1.11.43	2,579,000
1.12.43	2,619,000
1.1.44	2,528,000
1.2.44	2,366,000
1.3.44	2,340,000
1.4.44	2,245,000
1.5.44	2,235,000
1.6.44	2,215,000
1.7.44	2,200,000

APPENDIX I.[9] Comparative strength of the Wehrmacht and Red Army in 1943 (some figures estimated)

Section of Front	Unit	Wehrmacht			Red Army		
		1.4.43	20.7.43	14.10.43	1.4.43	20.7.43	14.10.43
Army Group A	Inf. Div	8	12	17	46	49	75
	Pz. Div	1	1	2	9	10	35
	Tanks	43	77	226	145	204	960
	Artillery	581	576	808	1,836	1,992	2,900
	Men	321,800	281,000	253,000	411,500	460,000	756,500
Army Group South	Inf. Div	26	29	44	140	148	163
	Pz. Div	13	13	16	94	104	101
	Tanks	887	1,161	1,338	1,420	2,872	3,290
	Artillery	928	1,601	2,263	5,614	5,981	6,380
	Men	548,000	822,000	719,000	1,532,500	1,713,500	1,759,500
Army Group Centre	Inf. Div	70.5	67	46	162	170	172
	Pz. Div	8	8	8	67	94	101
	Tanks	396	801	594	1,375	3,171	3,060
	Artillery	2,732	3,479	2,577	6,835	7,124	6,720
	Men	1,221,000	1,251,000	925,000	1,560,500	1,943,000	1,664,000
Army Group North	Inf. Div	42.5	43	44	120	103	94
	Pz. Div				52	34	25

	Tanks	10	49	146	900	1,052	650
	Artillery	2,119	2,407	2,389	4,943	4,593	3,680
	Men	642,000	710,000	601,000	1,217,500	1,225,000	959,000
Entire Eastern Front	Inf. Div	147	151	151	504	506	536
	Pz. Div	22	22	26	251	275	324
	Tanks	1,336	2,088	2,304	6,040	7,855	8,400
	Artillery	6,360	8,063	8,037	20,683	21,050	20,770
	Men	2,732,000	3,064,000	2,498,000	5,152,000	5,755,000	5,512,000

Appendix J. The wider 'Prokhorovka Axis': Divisional/Unit AFV strength of Operation *Citadel*'s 'southern pincer' (Heer only) – July 1943

XXXXVIII Panzer Korps:

3rd Panzer AFV strength during July 1943[10]

	Pz III	Pz IV	T-34	Pz VI	Bef	Total Pz	StuG	Sf Pak	Total AFV
Inventory 30.6.43	59	23			1	83	2	14	99
New AFV 1–10.7.43	5	1				6			6
TF 4–10.7.43	4					4			4
Inventory 10.7.43	60	24			1	85	2	14	101
New AFV 11–20.7.43	3				4	7	10		17
TF 11–20.7.43	3	1				4		1	5
Inventory 20.7.43	60	23			5	88	12	13	113
New AFV 21–31.7.43						0			0
TF 21–31.7.43	3	2				5	2 (10)		7 (17)
Inventory 1.8.43	57	21			5	83	0	13	96
July new AFV	8	1			4	13	10	0	23
July TF (not including 10 StuG transferred to 11th Panzer)	10	3				13	2 (10)	1	16 (26)
Operational 30.6.43	55	23			1	79	2	13	94
Operational 10.7.43	32	4			1	37	2	14	53
Operational 20.7.43	30	11			4	45	12	9	66
Operational 1.8.43	18	9			5	32	0	12	44

Grossdeutschland AFV strength during July 1943[11]									
	Pz III	Pz IV	Flame	Pz VI	Bef	Total Pz	StuG	Sf Pak	Total AFV
Inventory 30.6.43	23	68	14	15	8	128	35	20	183
New AFV 1–10.7.43		2				2			2
TF 4–10.7.43	5	6				11			11
Inventory 10.7.43	18	64	14	15	8	119	35	20	174
New AFV 11–20.7.43						0			0
TF 11–20.7.43	1	11	2			14	1		15
Inventory 20.7.43 estimate (AGS report)	17	53	12	15	8	105	34	20	159
New AFV 21–31.7.43		2				2		8	10
TF 21–31.7.43						0		2	2
Inventory 1.8.43	17	55	12	15	8	107	34	26	167
July new AFV		4				4		8	12
July TF	6	17	2	0	0	25	1	2	28
Operational 30.6.43	21	60	14	12	8	115	34	19	168
Operational 10.7.43	8	36	13	11	3	71	26	17	114
Operational 18.7.43 (1a)	13	29	10	8	2	62	25	c.17	104
Operational 1.8.43	8	27	7	5	6	53	21	c.20	94

Pz Rgt. v. Lauchert AFV strength during July 1943[12]									
	Pz III	Pz IV	Pz V	Pz VI	Bef	Total Pz	StuG	Sf Pak	Total AFV
Inventory 30.6.43			200			200			200
New AFV 1–10.7.43						0			0
TF 4–10.7.43			31			31			31
Inventory 10.7.43			169			169			169
New AFV 11–20.7.43						0			0
TF 11–20.7.43			27			27			27
Inventory 20.7.43			142			142			142
New AFV 21–31.7.43			12			12			12
TF (3a) 21–31.7.43			11 (15)			11 (15)			26

Inventory 31.7.43			128			128			128
July new AFV			12			12			12
July TF/3a			69 (15)			69 (15)			84
Operational 30.6.43			200			200			200
Operational 10.7.43			38			38			38
Operational 20.7.43			41			41			41
Operational 31.7.43			20			20			20

11th Panzer AFV strength during July 1943[13]

	Pz III	Pz IV	Flame	Pz VI	Bef	Total Pz	StuG/StuH Abt 911	Sf Pak	Total AFV
Inventory 30.6.43	62	26	13		4	105	22/0	13	140
New AFV 1–10.7.43						0	0/9		9
TF 4–10.7.43	1	2				3	1/0		4
Inventory 10.7.43	61	24	13		4	102	21/9	13	145
New AFV 11–20.7.43						0		3	3
TF 11–20.7.43	1	1				2	1/0	3	6
Inventory 20.7.43	60	23	13		4	100	20/9	13	142
New AFV 21–31.7.43		5				5	(10)/0		5 (15)
TF 21–31.7.43	3					3	2/0	2	7
Inventory 31.7.43	57	28	13		4	102	28/9	11	150
July new AFV 9 StuH, 3 Sf Pak, five Pz IV (not inc transfer of 10 StuG from 3rd Panzer)		5				5	0/9	3	17
July TF	5	3	0		0	8	4/0	5	17

Operational 30.6.43	49	21	5		4	79	22/0	12	113
Operational 10.7.43	24	8	6		1	39	16/7	8	70
Operational 20.7.43	39	16	4		4	63	15/8	9	95
Operational 31.7.43	29	18	5		4	56	19/6	6	87

III Panzer Korps:

6th Panzer AFV strength during July 1943[14]

	Pz III	Pz IV	Flame	Pz VI	Bef	Total Pz	StuG	Sf Pak	Total AFV
Inventory 30.6.43	52	32	14		6	104		14	118
New AFV 1–10.7.43						0			0
TF 4–10.7.43 (estimate)	5 est.	9 est.				14 est.			14 est.
Inventory 10.7.43 estimate (AGS report)	47	23	14		6	90		14	104
New AFV 11–20.7.43						0		7	7
TF 11–20.7.43	6 est.	2 est.	1 est.			9			9
Inventory 20.7.43	41	21	13		6	81		21	102
New AFV 21–31.7.43		5				5			5
TF 21–31.7.43	6	1			1	8		1	9
Inventory 31.7.43	35	25	13		5	78		20	98
July new AFV		5				5		7	12
July TF	17	12	1		1	31		1	32
Operational 30.6.43	48	29	13		5	95		13	108
Operational 11.7.43 (am – 1a)	11	6	? 5 est.		2	24 est.		? 5 est.	29 est.
Operational 21.7.43 (am – 1a)	8	4	? 2 est.		4	18 est.		? 8 est.	26 est.
Operational 31.7.43	13	10	0		4	27		14	41

19th Panzer AFV strength during July 1943[15]									
	Pz III	Pz IV	T-34	Pz VI	Bef	Total Pz	StuG	Sf Pak	Total AFV
Inventory 30.6.43	38	38			3	79		12	91
New AFV 1–10.7.43	2	2			2	6		2	8
TF 4–10.7.43		3				3			3
Inventory 10.7.43	40	37			5	82		14	96
New AFV 11–20.7.43						0			0
TF 11–20.7.43	6	10				16		1	17
Inventory 20.7.43	34	27			5	66		13	79
New AFV 21–31.7.43		10				10			10
TF 21–31.7.43	1	2				3			3
Inventory 31.7.43	33	35			5	73		13	86
July new AFV	2	12			2	16		2	18
July TF	7	15				22		1	23
Operational 30.6.43	38	38			3	79		12	91
Operational 11.7.43 (am –1a)	12	2			2	16		6 est.	22
Operational 20.7.43	17	11			5	33		8	41
Operational 30.7.43	21	18			5	44		11	55

7th Panzer AFV strength during July 1943[16]									
	Pz III	Pz IV	T-34	Pz VI	Bef	Total Pz	StuG	Sf Pak	Total AFV
Inventory 30.6.43	55	38			7	100		6	106
New AFV 1–10.7.43						0		6	6
TF 4–10.7.43	7	2			1	10			10
Inventory 10.7.43	48	36			6	90		12	102
New AFV 11–20.7.43						0		1	1
TF 11–20.7.43	7	3			1	11			11
Inventory 20.7.43	41	33			5	79		13	92
New AFV 21–31.7.43	2					2			2
TF 21–31.7.43	1					1			1
Inventory 31.7.43	42	33			5	80		13	93
July New AFV	2					2		7	9
July TF	15	5			2	22			22

Operational 30.6.43	51	36			4	91		6	97
Operational 10.7.43	24	26			6	56		9	65
Operational 20.7.43	24	22			4	50		10	60
Operational 31.7.43	42	28			5	75		10	85

503rd s.Pz.Abt strength during July 1943[17]									
	Pz III	Pz IV	T-34	Pz VI	Bef	Total Pz	StuG	Sf Pak	Total AFV
Inventory 30.6.43				45		45			45
New AFV 1–10.7.43						0			0
TF 4–10.7.43						0			0
Inventory 10.7.43				45		45			45
New AFV 11–20.7.43						0			0
TF 11–20.7.43						4			4
Inventory 20.7.43				41		41			41
New AFV 21–31.7.43						0			0
TF 21–31.7.43						3			3
Inventory 31.7.43				38		38			38
July new AFV						0			0
July TF				7		7			7
Operational 30.6.43				40		40			40
Operational 10.7.43				22		22			22
Operational 20.7.43				15		15			15
Operational 31.7.43				9		9			9

228th StuG Abt AFV strength during July 1943[18]									
	Pz III	Pz IV	Pz V	Pz VI	Bef	Total Pz	StuG	Sf Pak	Total AFV
Inventory 4.7.43							31		31
New AFV 1–10.7.43							0		0
TF 4–10.7.43							0		0
Inventory 10.7.43							31		31
New AFV 11–20.7.43							2		2
TF 11–20.7.43							1		1

	Pz III	Pz IV	Pz V	Pz VI	Bef	Total Pz	StuG/ StuH	Sf Pak	Total AFV
Inventory 20.7.43							32		32
New AFV 21–31.7.43							7		7
TF 21–31.7.43							0		0
Inventory 31.7.43							39		39
July new AFV							9		9
July TF							1		1
Operational 4.7.43							30		30
Operational 10.7.43							25		25
Operational 20.7.43							27		27
Operational 31.7.43							18		18

Korps Raus:									
905th StuG Abt AFV strength during July 1943[19]									
	Pz III	Pz IV	Pz V	Pz VI	Bef	Total Pz	StuG/ StuH	Sf Pak	Total AFV
Inventory 4.7.43							23/9		32
New AFV 1–10.7.43							0		0
TF 4–10.7.43							3		3
Inventory 10.7.43							20/9		29
New AFV 11–20.7.43							3		3
TF 11–20.7.43							1		1
Inventory 20.7.43							22/9		31
New AFV 21–31.7.43							0		0
TF 21–31.7.43							0		0
Inventory 31.7.43							22/9		31
July new AFV							3		3
July TF							4		4
Operational 4.7.43							23/9		32
Operational 10.7.43							20/9		29
Operational 20.7.43							22/8		30
Operational 31.7.43							16/7		23

393rd StuG Battery AFV strength during July 1943[20]									
	Pz III	Pz IV	Pz V	Pz VI	Bef	Total Pz	StuG	Sf Pak	Total AFV
Inventory 4.7.43							12		12
New AFV 1–10.7.43							0		0
TF 4–10.7.43							1		1
Inventory 10.7.43							11		11
New AFV 11–20.7.43							0		0
TF 11–20.7.43							1		1
Inventory 20.7.43							10		10
New AFV 21–31.7.43							0		0
TF 21–31.7.43							2		2
Inventory 31.7.43							8		8
July new AFV							0		0
July TF							4		4
Operational 4.7.43							10		10
Operational 10.7.43							8		8
Operational 20.7.43							7		7
Operational 31.7.43							6		6

APPENDIX K. The wider 'Prokhorovka Axis': AFV losses – TF and 3a – of the 'southern pincer' during Operation *Citadel* and its aftermath (July 1943)[21]

5–10.7.43	Pz III	Pz IV	T-34	Pz V	Pz VI	Bef (Flame)	StuG	Sf Pak	Total AFV
XXXXVIII Panzer Korps									
3rd Panzer Division	4								4
GD	5	6							11
Pz Rgt. v. Lauchert			31						31
11th Panzer Div and 911th StuG Abt	1	2					1		4
II SS Panzer Korps									

	Pz III	Pz IV	T-34	Pz V	Pz VI	Bef (Flame)	StuG	Sf Pak	Total AFV
LSSAH	1	4 (1)			(1)		2	2	11
DR	2	2	2		1				7
SS-T	2	4			1		1		8
III Panzer Korps									
6th Panzer Division	5 est.	9 est.							14
19th Panzer Division		3							3
7th Panzer Division	7	2			1				10
503rd s.Pz. Abt									0
228th StuG Abt									0
Korps Raus									
905th StuG Abt							3		3
393rd StuG Battery							1		1
5–10.7.43 total AFV Losses	27	32 (1)	2	31	2 (1)	1	8	2	107
11–20.7.43	**Pz III**	**Pz IV**	**T-34**	**Pz V**	**Pz VI**	**Bef (Flame)**	**StuG**	**Sf Pak**	**Total AFV**
XXXXVIII Panzer Korps									
3rd Panzer Division	3	1						1	5
GD	1	11				[2]	1		15
Pz Rgt. v. Lauchert				27					27
11th Panzer Div and 911th StuG Abt	1	1					1	3	6
II SS Panzer Korps									

	Pz III	Pz IV	T-34	Pz V	Pz VI	Bef (Flame)	StuG	Sf Pak	Total AFV
LSSAH		3 (1)			0 or 1?		1	(1)	6
DR		4	1				2		7
SS-T								2	2
III Panzer Korps									
6th Panzer Division	6 est.	2 est.			[1] est.				9
19th Panzer Division	6	10						1	17
7th Panzer Division	7	3			1				11
503rd s.Pz. Abt				4					4
228th StuG Abt							1		1
Korps Raus									
905th StuG Abt							1		1
393rd StuG Battery							1		1
11–20.7.43 total AFV losses	24	35 (1)	1	27	4	1 [3]	8	7 (1)	112
Total AFV losses of units involved in the 'southern pincer' of Operation *Citadel*	51	67 (2)	3	58	6 (1)	2 [3]	16	9 (1)	219
21–31.7.43 (post-*Citadel*)	**Pz III**	**Pz IV**	**T-34**	**Pz V**	**Pz VI**	**Bef (Flame)**	**StuG**	**Sf Pak**	**Total AFV**
XXXXVIII Panzer Korps									
3rd Panzer Div (left area)	3	2					2		7
GD (left area)								2	2

Pz Rgt. v. Lauchert				11 (15)					26
11th Panzer Div and 911th StuG Abt	3						2	2	7
II SS Panzer Korps									
LSSAH (left area)									0
DR (left area)	4	6							10
SS-T (left area)	4	11							15
III Panzer Korps									
6th Panzer Division	6	1				1		1	9
19th Panzer Division	1	2							3
7th Panzer Division	1								1
503rd s.Pz. Abt					3				3
228th StuG Abt									0
Korps Raus									
905th StuG Abt									0
393rd StuG Battery							2		2
21–31.7.43 total AFV losses (post-*Citadel*)	22	22	0	11 (15)	3	1	6	5	85
Total AFV losses in July of units involved in the 'southern pincer' of Operation *Citadel*	73	89 (2)	3	69 (15)	9 (1)	3 [3]	22	14 (1)	304

APPENDIX L.[22] The wider 'Prokhorovka Axis': Army Group South's faulty 5–10.7.43 and 5–17.7.43 AFV total loss reports (supplied to the General Inspector of Panzer Troops)

5–10.7.43	Pz III	Pz IV	T-34 – not listed	Pz V	Pz VI	Bef – not listed (Flame)	StuG	Sf Pak – not listed	Total AFV
XXXXVI-II Panzer Korps									
3rd Panzer Division	4	2							6
GD	3	6							9
Pz Rgt. v. Lauchert			28						28
11th Panzer Div and 911th StuG Abt	1	2					1		4
II SS Panzer Korps									
LSSAH	1	5			1.		1		8
DR		1					1		2
SS-T		8			1		1		10
III Panzer Korps									
6th Panzer Division	5	9							14
19th Panzer Division	4	14							18
7th Panzer Division	7	2							9
503rd s.Pz. Abt		2			2				4
228th StuG Abt									
Korps Raus									

	Pz III	Pz IV	T-34 – not listed	Pz V	Pz VI	Bef – not list-ed (Flame)	StuG	Sf Pak – not listed	
905th StuG Abt							3		3
393rd StuG Battery							I		I
5–10.7.43 total AFV losses	25	51		28	4		8		116
5–17.7.43	**Pz III**	**Pz IV**	**T-34 – not listed**	**Pz V**	**Pz VI**	**Bef – not list-ed (Flame)**	**StuG**	**Sf Pak – not listed**	
XXXXVI-II Panzer Korps									
3rd Panzer Division	6	3							9
GD	3	16					I		20
Pz Rgt. v. Lauchert				44					44
11th Panzer Div and 911th StuG Abt	2	3					3		8
II SS Pan-zer Korps									
LSSAH	I	9			I		I		12
DR	I	6			I		I		9
SS-T	2	8			I		I		12
III Panzer Korps									
6th Panzer Division	9	13				[3]			25
19th Panzer Division	8	19							27
7th Panzer Division	8	2							10
503rd s.Pz. Abt					3				3

228th StuG Abt								1		1
Korps Raus										
905th StuG Abt								6		6
393rd StuG Battery								5		5
5–17.7.43 total AFV losses	40	79			44	6	[3]		19		191

APPENDIX M. The wider 'Prokhorovka Axis': Korps AFV strength of Operation *Citadel*'s 'southern pincer' – July 1943

XXXXVIII Panzer Korps AFV strength during Operation *Citadel* July 1943[23]	Pz III	Pz IV	Pz V	Pz VI	Bef/ Flame	Total Pz	StuG/ StuH	Sf Pak	Total AFV
0100 1.7.43 inventory	144	117	200	15	13/27	516	59/0	47	622
0100 11.7.43 inventory	139	112	169	15	13/27	475	58/9	47	589
0100 21.7.43 inventory	137	99	142	15	17/25	435	66/9	46	556
0100 1.7.43 operational total	125	104	200	12	13/19	473	58/0	44	575
0100 11.7.43 operational total	64	48	38	11	5/19	185	44/7	39	275
0100 21.7.43 operational total	82	56	41	8	10/14	211	52/8	35	306

II SS Panzer Korps AFV strength during Operation *Citadel* 1943[24]	Pz III	Pz IV	T-34	Pz VI	Bef	Total Pz	StuG	Sf Pak	Total AFV
1.7.43 inventory (2.7.43 for LSSAH Pz IV figure)	138	168	24	42	27	399	104	44	547
0100 11.7.43 inventory	133	157	22	39–40	27	378–379	101	42	521–522

0100 21.7.43 inventory	133	149	21	39	27	369	98	43–45	510–512
1.7.43 operational total (2.7.43 Ia for LSSAH Pz IV figure)	115	143	15	33	25	331	95	42	468
0100 11.7.43 operational total	98	87	8	16	18	227	73	39	339
2300 18.7.43 (as had left area by 21.7.43) operational total (Ia)	73	107	17	25	22	244	76	29	349

III Panzer Korps AFV strength during Operation *Citadel* July 1943[25]

	Pz III	Pz IV	Flame	Pz VI	Bef	Total Pz	StuG	Sf Pak	Total AFV
0100 1.7.43 inventory	145	108	14	45	16	328	31	32	391
0100 11.7.43 inventory	135	96	14	45	17	307	31	40	378
0100 21.7.43 inventory	116	81	13	41	16	267	32	47	346
0100 1.7.43 operational total	137	103	13	40	12	305	30	31	366
0100 11.7.43 operational total	47	34	5	22	10	118	25	20	163
21.7.43 operational total	49	37	2	15	13	116	27	26	169

Korps Raus AFV strength during Operation *Citadel* July 1943[26]

	Pz III	Pz IV	Pz V	Pz VI	Bef/ Flame	Total Pz	StuG/ StuH	Sf Pak	Total AFV
0100hrs 1.7.43 inventory							35/9		44
0100 11.7.43 inventory							31/9		40
0100 21.7.43 inventory							32/9		41

0100 1.7.43 operational total							33/9		42
0100 11.7.43 operational total							28/9		37
0100 21.7.43 operational total							29/8		37

APPENDIX N. The wider 'Prokhorovka Axis': Total AFV strength of the 'southern pincer' during Operation *Citadel* and its aftermath, July 1943[27]

	Pz III	Pz IV	Pz V/T-34	Pz VI	Bef/ Flame	Total Pz	StuG/ StuH	Sf Pak	Total AFV
1.7.43 inventory	427	393	200/24	102	56/41	1,243	229/9	123	1,604
0100 11.7.43 inventory	407	365	169/22	99–100	57/41	1,160–1,161	221/18	129	1,528–1,529
0100 21.7.43 inventory	386	329	142/21	95	60/38	1,071	228/18	136–138	1,453–1,455
0100 17.43 operational total	377	350	200/15	85	50/32	1,109	216/9	117	1,451
0100 11.7.43 operational total	209	169	38/8	49	33/24	530	170/16	98	814
0100 21.7.43 operational total	204	200	41/17	48	45/16	571	184/16	90	861

APPENDIX O. AFV strength of units that remained with AGS in the '*Citadel*' area in late July 1943[28]

	Pz III	Pz IV	Pz V	Pz VI	Bef/ Flame	Total Pz	StuG/ StuH	Sf Pak	Total AFV
21.7.43 inventory	176	104	142	41	20/26	509	84/18	60	671
1.8.43 inventory	167	121	128	38	19/26	499	97/18	57	671
0100 21.7.43 operational total	88	53	41	15	17/6	220	71/16	35	342
0100 1.8.43 operational total	105	74	20	9	18/5	231	59/13	41	344

APPENDIX P. Daytime air sorties and losses
5–15.7.43[29]

| | Germany | | Soviet Union | |
| | Fliegerkorps VIII | | 2nd VA/17th VA | |
	Sorties	Losses	Sorties	Losses
5.7.43	2,387	19	1,744	114/73
6.7.43	1,686	7	1,285	51/28
7.7.43	1,829	10	1,478	45/42
8.7.43	1,686	5	1,185	47/14
9.7.43	1,621	11	845	37/9
10.7.43	682	3	534	25/0
11.7.43	1,039	14	596	19/0
12.7.43	654	11	903	28/3
13.7.43	656	5	778	27/1
14.7.43	1,452	9	1,029	24/6
15.7.43	706	5	363	11/0
Total	14,398	99	10,740	428/176

List of Figures

LIST OF FIGURES

List of Illustrations in Plate Section

1. The Leibstandarte lost three assault guns (StuG) during Operation *Citadel*; two of these losses occurred between 5 and 10 July (chassis numbers 92 150 and 91 143). Here we see one of these two early losses. The StuG had a powerful 75mm main gun which was similar to that used in the upgraded versions of Panzer IV medium tanks. (NARA, RG 242, Waffen-SS Photographer, Max Büschel)

2. The Marder tank destroyer also had a powerful 75mm main gun; however, weak armour meant the AFV was vulnerable to attack. For this reason the Marder was often deployed to ambush enemy armour. This picture was taken in the first phase of Operation *Citadel* (5–10 July). (NARA, RG 242, Waffen-SS Photographer, Max Büschel)

3. The Soviet SU-76 assault gun mounted the 76mm main gun on the T-70 light tank's chassis; typically this gun was seen on the medium T-34 tank. (Photo 160478338 © Ryzhov Sergey | Dreamstime.com)

4. The Soviet SU-122 assault gun mounted a 122mm howitzer on the T-34's chassis. The SU-76 and SU-122 were designed to play a supporting role and only appeared in small numbers during the battle of Prokhorovka. (Photo 160453775 © Ryzhov Sergey | Dreamstime.com)

5. In March 1943 Das Reich captured 24 new Soviet T-34s in Kharkov. After minor modifications the tanks were absorbed into the division's inventory and saw action throughout July 1943. By 1943 the T-34's main gun was inferior to that of the upgraded Panzer IV, which crucially often allowed the Germans to strike first. (NARA, RG 242, Waffen-SS Photographer, Max Büschel)

6. Das Reich's sole Tiger tank (Panzer VI) loss during Operation *Citadel* also occurred during the period 5–10 July. The tank had the chassis number 250 085 (the number S24 seen on the tank is the AFV's tactical number). The Tiger tank had an extremely powerful 88mm main gun and thick armour. (Author's collection)

7. Leibstandarte troops training with the powerful 75mm Pak 40 in May 1943. Categorized as a heavy anti-tank gun the Pak 40 had the same penetrating ability as the upgraded versions of the Panzer IV. The weapon greatly aided the German defence at Prokhorovka. (Bundesarchiv, Bild 101III-Weill-168-12, Fotograf(in): Weill)

Leibstandarte Tiger tank can be seen awaiting its next mission. (NARA, RG 242, Waffen-SS Photographer, Johan King, 10.7.43)

18. The order is soon given to leave the Teterevino–Prokhorovka road. The Leibstandarte Panzer Regiment's Aufklärung Zug leads the way. (NARA, RG 242, Waffen-SS Photographer, Johan King, 10.7.43)

19. The Leibstandarte's 'Wespe' 105mm self-propelled artillery supported the advance. (NARA, RG 242, Waffen-SS Photographer, Johan King, 10.7.43)

20. The threat of injury has returned with officers of Leibstandarte's panzer regiment taking cover behind one of the division's Bef (Command) tanks. (NARA, RG 242, Waffen-SS Photographer, Johan King, 10.7.43)

21. At 1300hrs the Leibstandarte Panzer Regiment resumed the advance, this time under combat conditions. The goal of the attack was to secure the Komsomolets state farm and the dominating heights of Hill 241.6. (NARA, RG 242, Waffen-SS Photographer, Johan King, 10.7.43)

22. Once again Panzer IVs of the Leibstandarte Panzer Regiment's Aufklärung Zug were in the vanguard of the advance. (NARA, RG 242, Waffen-SS Photographer, Johan King, 10.7.43)

23. By 1420hrs the Leibstandarte had occupied Komsomolets state farm and the heights of Hill 241.6. By the evening of 10 July 1943 s.F.H. 18 Sfl. (Hummel) 150mm heavy field howitzers of the Leibstandarte artillery regiment had been established at the Komsomolets state farm. (NARA, RG 242, Waffen-SS Photographer, Johan King, 10.7.43)

24. At Komsomolets state farm in order to support SS-T's operations the Leibstandarte Hummel were aimed across the River Psel. From these positions on 12 July the Leibstandarte artillery regiment would be forced to engage infiltrating Soviet tanks at point-blank range. (NARA, RG 242, Waffen-SS Photographer, Johan King, 10.7.43)

25. The farm at Komsomolets. (Google Earth)

26. On the evening of 10 July the Leibstandarte's panzer regiment began to prepare for the following day's assault on Prokhorovka. Panzer IV '529' of the Leibstandarte's 5th Panzer Company is seen undertaking this reorganization. (NARA, RG 242, Waffen-SS Photographer, Johan King, 10.7.43)

27. The majority of the Leibstandarte's SPWs were also repositioned for the coming drive on Prokhorovka. (NARA, RG 242, Waffen-SS Photographer, Johan King, 10.7.43)

28. At 0450hrs on 11 July the final drive on Prokhorovka began. Throughout the day the Leibstandarte defeated numerous armoured counter-attacks. One such encounter resulted in the destruction of several British-built Churchill tanks. (NARA, RG 242, Waffen-SS Photographer, Johan King, 11.7.43)

29. On 11 July the Leibstandarte Assault Gun Battalion and Tiger tanks, working in tandem with the 2nd SS Panzergrenadier Regiment, once again led the main attack. The right flank of the assault advanced along the Teterevino–Prokhorovka road which hugged the embankment of the Prokhorovka–Belgorod railway line. (NARA, RG 242, Waffen-SS Photographer, Johan King, 11.7.43)

52. At 0850hrs on 11 July the Leibstandarte occupied the anti-tank ditch. Surprisingly, the Leibstandarte was able to capture the road bridge over the obstacle intact. (NARA, RG 242, Waffen-SS Photographer, Johan King, 11.7.43)

53. The location of the road bridge over the anti-tank ditch. (Google Earth)

54. To consolidate its gains the Leibstandarte rapidly sent its armour across the anti-tank ditch and onto the slope of Hill 252.2 (the hill's north-eastern slope, visible in the picture, had already been secured). (NARA, RG 242, Waffen-SS Photographer, Johan King, 11.7.43)

55. As the photographer's vehicle crosses the anti-tank ditch, the pictures clearly show the men of the Leibstandarte's 2nd SS Panzergrenadier Regiment urgently working to improve the anti-tank ditch defences. Here we look left. (NARA, RG 242, Waffen-SS Photographer, Johan King, 11.7.43)

56. The view to the left of the bridge over the anti-tank ditch. (NARA, RG 242, Waffen-SS Photographer, Johan King, 11.7.43)

57. The view to the left from the location of the bridge over the anti-tank ditch. (Google Earth)

58. The view to the left of the bridge over the anti-tank ditch; the photographer is now looking along the length of the anti-tank ditch. (NARA, RG 242, Waffen-SS Photographer, Johan King, 11.7.43)

59. The view to the left at the location of the bridge over the anti-tank ditch, looking along the length of the former anti-tank ditch. (Google Earth)

60. The view to the right of the bridge over the anti-tank ditch, looking towards the railway embankment. (NARA, RG 242, Waffen-SS Photographer, Johan King, 11.7.43)

61. The view to the right at the location of the bridge over the anti-tank ditch, looking towards the railway embankment. (Google Earth)

62. The view to the right at the location of the bridge over the anti-tank ditch, looking towards the railway embankment. (Google Earth)

63. The view of the anti-tank ditch from the base of Hill 252.2. (Google Earth)

64. The right half of the anti-tank ditch. (NARA GX-3734-SK-61, 16.7.43)

65. The right half of the anti-tank ditch. (NARA GX-3942-SD-124, 7.8.43)

66. The right half of the anti-tank ditch. (Google Earth)

67. German field of fire towards Hill 252.2 from behind the anti-tank ditch. (Google Earth)

68. The crest of Hill 252.2 was defended resolutely; as a result Leibstandarte attempts to take the north-west part of the hill's summit (which began at 10:30) were initially rebuffed. One of the Leibstandarte's four Panzer IIs is seen in the foreground. The subsequent Johan King pictures were all taken on Hill 252.2 and once again follow in chronological order. (NARA, RG 242, Waffen-SS Photographer, Johan King, 11.7.43)

69. The majority of the 2nd SS Panzergrenadier Regiment took up defensive positions across the slope of Hill 252.2 or near the anti-tank ditch. Here infantry of the 2nd SS Panzergrenadier Regiment occupy part of the hill's

battalion's subsequent probing attack towards Hill 252.4 and the town of Prokhorovka, 2.5km away. (NARA, RG 242, Waffen-SS Photographer, Johan King, 11.7.43)

84. Beyond Hill 252.2 the Leibstandarte SPW battalion and attached Grille soon came under intense Soviet bombardment. As a result, the Germans only managed to advance a short distance beyond Hill 252.2. (NARA, RG 242, Waffen-SS Photographer, Johan King, 11.7.43)

85. The Leibstandarte SPW battalion and Grille were forced to seek cover in the undulating terrain. By 2015hrs the Germans had withdrawn back to Hill 252.2. The abortive nature of this attack confirmed to II SS Panzer Korps leadership that any frontal assault on Prokhorovka would be extremely costly given the Soviet's anti-tank and artillery strength. (NARA, RG 242, Waffen-SS Photographer, Johan King, 11.7.43)

86. The site of the initial armoured combat on 12 July. Two destroyed Panzer IVs can be identified beyond the crest of Hill 252.2 (bottom left quarter of picture). A third destroyed Panzer IV is located further back close to Hill 252.2's summit (top left quarter of picture). (NARA GX-3734-SK-61, 16.7.43)

87. The site of the initial armoured combat on 12 July. Two destroyed Panzer IVs can be identified beyond the crest of Hill 252.2 (bottom left quarter of picture). A third destroyed Panzer IV is located further back close to Hill 252.2's summit (top left quarter of picture). (NARA GX-3942-SD-124, 7.8.43)

88. The site of the initial armoured combat on 12 July. The location of three destroyed Panzer IVs has been highlighted. (Google Earth)

89. Enhanced view of the knocked-out Panzer IV (centre of picture) which is closest to the Prokhorovka–Belgorod railway. (NARA GX-3958-SD-10, 15.8.43)

90. Enhanced view of the knocked-out Panzer IV (left of picture) which was furthest forward of Hill 252.2. (NARA GX-3942-SD-123, 7.8.43)

91. The undulating ground beyond the crest of Hill 252.2 where two Panzer IVs were knocked out when the battle of Prokhorovka began on 12 July. (Google Earth)

92. A remarkable post-battle picture taken from a Soviet aircraft flying low over the Prokhorovka battlefield. A destroyed Panzer IV and T-34 can be seen close to Hill 252.2's summit. (Valeriy Zamulin)

93. The site of the destroyed Panzer IV close to Hill 252.2's summit. Today the track in front of the Panzer IV takes a slightly different route, as does the road on the other side of the railway embankment. (Google Earth)

94. The summit of Hill 252.2 (near the Victory 'Belfry') looking down towards the anti-tank ditch. The modern masts on the right of the picture help to indicate the location of the destroyed Panzer IV (compare with Plate 88). (Google Earth)

95. Another remarkable post-battle picture taken from the same low-flying Soviet aircraft over the Prokhorovka battlefield. The aircraft has travelled closer to the parallel road. A destroyed Leibstandarte SPW (one of eight lost by the Leibstandarte between 11 and 20 July) and a decapitated T-34 are the most prominent losses. (Valeriy Zamulin)

110. Battlefield of 181st Tank Brigade vs. Leibstandarte Tiger tank company. (NARA GX-2696-SK-52, 14.7.43)
111. The topography of the battlefield looking towards Andreyevka from Point 228.4. (Google Earth)
112. Detail of destruction caused by the four Leibstandarte Tiger tanks. (NARA GX-2696-SK-52, 14.7.43)
113. 181st Tank Brigade's view looking up to the Leibstandarte Tiger tanks' firing positions. (Google Earth)
114. The battlefield of the 25th Tank Brigade. (Google Earth)
115. The battlefield of the 25th Tank Brigade. (NARA GX-3734-SK-61, 16.7.43)
116. Line of advance of the 25th Tank Brigade towards Storozhevoye Woods. The railway embankment is on the right. (Google Earth)
117. The battlefield of the 25th Tank Brigade. (NARA GX-3942-SD-124, 7.8.43)
118. As the 25th Tank Brigade neared Storozhevoye Woods it was ambushed by Leibstandarte Marder tank destroyers located in Stalinsk state farm (shown ahead). (Google Earth)
119. The German Tiger tank holds a symbolic role in the battle of Prokhorovka. Outside the 'Third Battlefield of Russia' museum in Prokhorovka stands a mighty sculpture of two Tiger tanks being rammed and destroyed by Soviet T-34s. This image closely fits the Soviet narrative of the battle. However, on 12 July only five Tiger tanks were available to participate in the battle and a maximum of one was lost in combat. (Author's collection)
120. The spectacular 67m-long Cold War-era Belgorod diorama 'Tank battle near Prokhorovka' opened on 4 August 1987. The diorama perpetuates the Soviet myth of the battle being a mass armoured meeting engagement which cost the Germans between 300 (58 per cent) and 400 (77 per cent) of their AFVs. In reality, the Germans lost a maximum of 16 (3 per cent) of their AFVs during the battle of Prokhorovka. (Dmytro Tsykhmystro / Alamy Stock Photo)
121. Despite its appearance in the Belgorod diorama, the Panther tank did not enter combat with any SS division until 22 August – the penultimate day of the battle of Kursk. This picture depicts one of Das Reich's first actions with the Panther tank near Kharkov in late August 1943. (Bundesarchiv, Bild 101III-Merz-023-22, Fotograf(in): Merz, Willi)
122. In the first week of December 1943 a column of Das Reich Tiger tanks is seen negotiating woods west of Kiev. On 1 December Das Reich possessed 16 Tiger tanks, 15 of which had been present with the Leibstandarte or Das Reich on 11 July, i.e. they were of Prokhorovka vintage. On 1 December, four and a half months after the battle, 49 per cent of the Leibstandarte and Das Reich 11 July AFV inventory was still in service with SS units on the Eastern Front. (Bundesarchiv, Bild 101I-571-1721-29, Fotograf(in): Schnitzer)
123. Since the dissolution of the Soviet Union an extensive memorial complex (State Military Historical Museum-Reserve 'Prokhorovskoye Pole') has been established at Prokhorovka, one befitting the location of 'The Third Battlefield of Russia'. In 1995 the Church of the Holy Apostles Peter and Paul was

completed, the shrine being consecrated on 3 May 1995. Next to the church can be seen the 'Third Battlefield of Russia' museum which opened to the public on 2 May 2010. (Igor Golovnov / Alamy Stock Photo)

124. On 27 January 2017 the impressive Museum of Armoured Vehicles opened. The museum gives a complete picture of the development and history of tank building from the period of antiquity and the Middle Ages to the present day. Next to the museum is 'Tankodrome' (opened 16 May 2015) which has a 1.2-hectare AFV demonstration track with a seating capacity for over 1,300 spectators. The site also contains an outdoor AFV exhibition area. Outside the museum stands a sculpture depicting the iconic scene of Soviet troops joining battle from a T-34. (Photo 105086154 © Denis Ivanov | Dreamstime.com)

125. On 12 July 2020 the 'Battle for the Weapons of the Great Victory' museum opened. This remarkable museum, which contains around 2,000 exhibits, chronicles the role of the Soviet Home Front throughout the Second World War. The museum includes a close examination of the staggeringly successful large-scale evacuation of Soviet industry and workers from the path of the German invasion in 1941. (Photo 208735250 © Blossfeldia | Dreamstime.com)

126. The Victory Monument 'Belfry' on Hill 252.2 opened in 1995 (note the close proximity of Prokhorovka, 2.5km away). The 59m-high Belfry houses a 3.5-ton bell which strikes three times an hour to honour the memory of those who fought at the 'three battlefields of Russia': Kulikovo, Borodino and Prokhorovka. The Soviet soldiers who fought so courageously against Nazism at Prokhorovka deserve our deepest respect and gratitude for their victory. (Russian Look Ltd. / Alamy Stock Photo)

List of Maps

List of Tables

Acknowledgements

This book has its origins in the autumn of 2017. Three years after obtaining my doctorate I had still not secured an academic position. This changed when quite out of the blue I was asked by David Morgan-Owen if I would be interested in undertaking a short period of teaching for King's College London's (KCL) Defence Studies Department (DSD) at the Joint Services Command and Staff College (JSCSC) in Shrivenham. Amongst other things, the role involved constructing an Operational Studies module of my choice for the Advanced Command and Staff Course at the JSCSC. Having long held an interest in armoured warfare and the titanic battles around Kursk in the summer of 1943 the choice of subject was an easy one. The secondary research I undertook for the module enabled me to note many gaps in the level of understanding of the available documentary evidence concerning the battle of Prokhorovka. Given the dramatic narrative of the battle I asked myself were there really no detailed post-battle Luftwaffe reconnaissance images of the Prokhorovka battlefield (particularly the notorious anti-tank ditch and Hill 252.2) or post-battle German armoured inventories? Similarly, where was the SS war correspondents' photographic evidence? Given the documentary evidence that I had already seen, I refused to believe that such records did not exist. The rest as they say is history. As a result, I owe David a great deal of thanks for his opening act of kindness in recommending me for employment at KCL.

My initial research into the available Luftwaffe reconnaissance of the Prokhorovka battlefield was greatly aided by John Calvin. John kindly informed me precisely where he had located a series of reconnaissance images of the Eastern Front that he had made available on his website. This led me to making contact with Corbin Apkin at the US National Archives Records Administration (NARA). Corbin very kindly directed me to the relevant finding aids. The NARA cartographic grids are of such detail and accuracy that I knew I had located many original records (at least in terms of publication and detail) of the key areas of the Prokhorovka battlefield before I had even viewed the records. I then made the important decision to obtain only the best digital reproductions possible of these visual records. I asked the renowned cartographic researcher Susan Strange to undertake this task on my behalf. The results were spectacular. My thanks therefore are owed to John, Corbin and Susan. More recently, Eugene Matyukhin has kindly helped with the wider examination of these photographs.

From 2019 my research shifted to the more familiar territory of documentary records. For many years I had been aware that the Germans had documented the operations of their panzer units in staggering detail. I therefore wondered whether there would be sufficient surviving records to track the fate of the 'Prokhorovka panzers' into late 1943. It soon became clear that enough of 4th Panzer Army's records had survived for this task to be attempted. The fact that the records were available for digital download made this mammoth task at least theoretically possible. As somebody who grew up as a railway enthusiast, I was well equipped for the task of tracking individual panzers by chassis number. This no doubt accounts for why I found this task a remarkably enjoyable one. I understand this might not have been the case for every historian! My thanks again to John Calvin, Jeff Leach, Stephen Ballantyne and the operators of the Strumpanzer website for making the searching and downloading of thousands of NARA records possible. Later in 2020, as the Covid-19 pandemic took hold, this ability to view masses of records remotely became priceless.

When it became clear that the pandemic would force the closure of NARA, I quickly ordered a raft of digital scans which I knew would not be available for download elsewhere. I am indebted to the excellent staff at NARA for quickly providing digital copies of these records while it was still possible to do so. Karl-Heinz Frieser very kindly sent me some records from Germany which I did not manage to obtain from NARA. Karl-Heinz, without doubt the preeminent scholar of Germany's war on the Eastern Front, has over the last few years been a source of great support and encouragement. It is an honour that Karl-Heinz felt able to provide this book with a foreword. My thanks also go to Dieter Brand, Niklas Zetterling, Christopher Moran, Valeriy Zamulin, Christopher Lawrence, Lukas Friedli, Victoria Taylor and Robert Forczyk for providing assistance at various points in this book's construction.

At KCL I have been fortunate to have Marcus Faulkner as a scholarly confidant and ideas sounding board. His intellect and wisdom often helped guide my research and consequently this book. I am in your debt Marcus. Marcus is primarily a naval historian so I can only offer my apologies for distracting him from more seafaring matters. I am also grateful to Jonathan Fennell, another leading KCL scholar, for encouraging me to submit a proposal for publication. Equally, I must thank Marcus Cowper and Gemma Gardner at Osprey Publishing for first commissioning and then ensuring the safe passage of this book. Finally, thanks must be offered to Ian Farr and Cathie Carmichael at the UEA School of History for moulding me into the historian that I am today.

List of Frequently Used Abbreviations

Abt Abteilung: battalion, detachment

AFV Armoured Fighting Vehicle

AGC Army Group Centre

AGS Army Group South

BA-MA Bundesarchiv/Militärarchiv

DR Das Reich SS Panzergrenadier Division

KIA Killed in Action

LSSAH Leibstandarte SS Adolf Hitler Panzergrenadier Division

MGFA *Militärgeschichtliches Forschungsamt* (Military History Research Office)

MIA Missing in Action

MTO Motor Transport Officer

NARA US National Archives Records Administration

NSDAP Nationalsozialistische Deutsche Arbeiterpartei (Nazi Party)

OKH Oberkommando des Heeres (High Command of the Army)

OKW Oberkommando des Wehrmacht (High Command of the Armed Forces)

Pz Panzer (tank)

Rgt. Regiment

Sf Self-propelled

SPW Semi-tracked Armoured Personnel Carrier

SS Schutzstaffel (Protection Echelon)

SS-N Nordland SS Panzergrenadier Division

SS-T SS-Totenkopf Panzergrenadier Division

SS-W Wiking SS Panzergrenadier Division

TF *Totalausfälle* (total loss)

WIA Wounded in Action

1a Operations department

Notes

INTRODUCTION

1 Geomerid Online Travel Guide – Museum Third Battlefield of Russia: https://geomerid.com/en/place/third-battlefield-of-russia-belgorod-travel -guide/overview/, accessed on 12/11/2021; The Prokhorovka Memorial Complex: Bearing witness to sacrifice and faith https://www.rbth.com /special_projects/discovering_russia_1/2016/09/02/the-prokhorovka -memorial-complex-bearing-witness-to-sacrifice-and-faith_626611, accessed on 12/11/2021.

2 Frieser, Karl-Heinz, *The Battle of the Kursk Salient* in The Research Institute for Military History, Potsdam, Germany, *Germany and the Second World War Volume VIII – The Eastern Front 1943–1944* (Oxford: Clarendon Press 2017), 83–4. The breakdown of total write-offs of Soviet tanks and assault guns was 1,614 during the defensive phase (Operation *Citadel*), 2,586 during the Orel counteroffensive and 1,864 during the Belgorod-Kharkov counteroffensive.

3 Wegner, Bernd, *The War against the Soviet Union 1942–1943* in The Research Institute for Military History, Potsdam, Germany, *Germany and the Second World War Volume VI – The Global War* (Oxford: Clarendon Press 2001), 863–71; see also Kroener, Bernhard R., *Management of Human Resources, Deployment of the Population, and Manning the Armed Forces in the Second Half of the War (1942–1944)* in The Research Institute for Military History, Potsdam, Germany, *Germany and the Second World War Volume VIII – Organization and Mobilization in the German Sphere of Power: Wartime Administration, Economy, and Manpower Resources 1942–1944/5* (Oxford: Clarendon Press 2003), 1012–23.

4 Frieser, Karl-Heinz, *The Battle of the Kursk Salient* in The Research Institute for Military History, Potsdam, Germany, *Germany and the Second World War Volume VIII – The Eastern Front 1943–1944*, 200 and 200n. According to Russian sources, during the battle of Kursk the Soviets lost 863,303 men, of whom 254,470 were dead or missing. Of these personnel losses, 177,847 were incurred in the defensive phase, 429,890 during the Orel counteroffensive,

and 255,566 during the Belgorod-Kharkov counteroffensive. Boris V. Sokolov points out a number of contradictions in the official Soviet account and estimates the losses at 1,677,000 men. See Sokolov, Boris V., 'The Battle for Kursk, Orel and Charkov: Strategic Intentions and Results. A Critical View of Soviet Historiography', in *Gezeitenwechsel*, 69–88. German losses over this period (5.7–23.8.43) were approximately 170,000, of whom 46,500 were dead or missing: 54,182 (11,023 dead or missing) during Operation *Citadel*; Orel offensive 86,064 (25,515 dead or missing); Belgorod-Kharkov offensive just under 30,000 (10,000 dead or missing).

5 Frieser, Karl-Heinz, *The Battle of the Kursk Salient* in The Research Institute for Military History, Potsdam, Germany, *Germany and the Second World War Volume VIII – The Eastern Front 1943–1944*, 120–21, 128–34; see post from the Official Twitter account of the Ministry of Foreign Affairs of Russia on 12.7.2020: https://twitter.com/mfa_russia/status /1282197556626432000, accessed on 12.7.2020. See also post from the Russian Foreign Ministry's official Facebook account on 12.7.2022: http:// www.facebook.com/MIDRussia/posts/pfbid02Q3voBi6fezsQSuwTV41P m9PaodBP15Fu1MNnLVvf8AehprtwgmBNyH7sQ5tdKzccl, accessed on 12.7.2022. Both of these social media posts were accompanied by an image of the same section of the Belgorod diorama that can be found in Plate 120. Given the historiography of the battle of Prokhorovka, this is quite understandable.

6 Frieser, Karl-Heinz, *The Battle of the Kursk Salient* in The Research Institute for Military History, Potsdam, Germany, *Germany and the Second World War Volume VIII – The Eastern Front 1943–1944*, 120–21, 128–34; Zamulin, Valeriy, 'Soviet Troop Losses in the Battle of Prokhorovka, 10–16 July 1943', *Journal of Slavic Military Studies*, 32:1 (2019), 118–20.

7 Bundesarchiv/Militärarchiv, RH 10/64, General Inspector of Panzer Troops – AGS: 5–10.7.43 *Totalverluste*; 5–13.7.43 *Totalverluste*; 5–14.7.43 *Totalverluste*; 5–15.7.43 *Totalverluste*; 5–16.7.43 *Totalverluste*; 5–17.7.43 *Totalverluste*. See also Appendix L.

8 Frieser, Karl-Heinz, *The Battle of the Kursk Salient* in The Research Institute for Military History, Potsdam, Germany, *Germany and the Second World War Volume VIII – The Eastern Front 1943–1944*, 124–25, 128–29; see also Månsson, Martin, *Prokhorovka – Verdens største panserslag in Ostfronten* (2017); Restayn, Jean, *Operation Citadel, Volume 1: The South* (Wininpeg: J.J. Fedorowicz Publishing 2021), 60–69; Karl-Heinz kindly relayed the reaction to his 1993 presentation in Moscow to the author.

9 *Tank Archives* blog: http://www.tankarchives.ca/2019/08/burn-before-reading .html#more 'Burn Before Reading', accessed on 17.9.2021.

10 All archival documents in this book, unless otherwise stated, are located at the US National Archives and Records Administration, College Park, MD. AOK 6, 1a, KTB 9, *Zustandsberichte, Wochenmeldung über Panzer und Sturmgeschülzlage Stand* 1.8.43 (written 6.8.43), T312, R1483, F000441.

11   See Tables 18, 65, 66 and 67. The lack of a II SS Panzer Korps AFV inventory
      for 20.7.43 is alluded to in the transcript of a 2018 interview with the noted
      Kursk historian Valeriy Zamulin. This transcript can be found on the excellent
      Tank Archives blog: http://www.tankarchives.ca/2018/11/zamulin-on-losses
      .html, accessed on 15.12.2018.

12   AOK 6, 1a, KTB 9, *Zustandsberichte,* Wochenmeldung über Panzer und
      Sturmgeschülzlage Stand 1.8.43 (written 6.8.43), T312, R1483, F000441.

13   Lak, Martijn, 'The Death Ride of the Panzers? Recent Historiography on the
      Battle of Kursk', *Journal of Military History,* 82:3 (2018) 909–19.

14   BBC *Timewatch* documentary 'Mother of all Battles' first aired September
      1993. Available to view at 'Internet Archive'.

15   Lak, Martijn, 'The Death Ride of the Panzers? Recent Historiography on the
      Battle of Kursk', *Journal of Military History,* 82:3 (2018) 909–19.

16   Friedli, Lukas, Repairing the Panzers: German Tank Maintenance in World
      War 2 Vol 1 (Monroe: Panzerwrecks Publishing 2010), 162.

17   Frieser, Karl-Heinz, *The Battle of the Kursk Salient* in The Research Institute
      for Military History, Potsdam, Germany, *Germany and the Second World War
      Volume VIII – The Eastern Front 1943–1944,* 157–68.

18   PzAOK 4, O.Qu.V, LSSAH, DR and SS-T, Fahrgestell-Nr. Pz.kpf.Wg.
      1–2.7.43, T313, R390; PzAOK 4, O.Qu.V, LSSAH, DR and SS-T, Gep. Kfz.
      Bestandsmeldung, 1–2.7.43 and 10.7.43, T313, R390.

19   Frieser, Karl-Heinz, *The Battle of the Kursk Salient* in The Research Institute
      for Military History, Potsdam, Germany, *Germany and the Second World War
      Volume VIII – The Eastern Front 1943–1944,* 157–68.

20   Compare declining operational AFV numbers in Tables 43, 44, 47, 48 and
      Table 50.

21   The photographs used in this book are located at the US National Archives and
      Records Administration, College Park, MD (NARA) and can be found in the
      Series RG 373: German Flown Aerial Photography, 1939–1945. See specifically
      photographs relating to the battlefield of Prokhorovka: for 14.7.43 (tactical
      reconnaissance by a Bf 110 from NAG 6 2.(H)33) see GX-2696-SK-23, GX-
      2696-SK-24 and GX-2696-SK-52. For 16.7.43 (strategic reconnaissance by a Ju
      88 from 2.(F)11) see GX-3734-SK-61 (incorrectly dated as 15.7.43 by NARA).
      For 7.8.43 (strategic reconnaissance by a Ju 88 from 2.(F)100) see GX-3942-
      SK-69, GX-3942-SD-122, GX-3942-SD-123, GX-3942-SD-124. For 15.8.43
      (strategic reconnaissance by a Ju 88 from 2.(F)100) see GX-3958-SD-10 and
      GX-3958-SD-11. For 7.9.43 (strategic reconnaissance by a Ju 88 from 2.(F)11)
      see GX-4255-SD-16. For 6.10.43 (strategic reconnaissance by a Ju 88 from
      2.(F)100) see GX-3977-SD-45 and GX-3977-SD-48.

22   See Tables 19, 52 and 60.

23   II SS Panzer Korps, DR and SS-T Ia 667/43 and 668/43, 28.7.43, T354,
      R605, F000879-80.

24   Frieser, Karl-Heinz, *The Battle of the Kursk Salient* in The Research Institute
      for Military History, Potsdam, Germany, *Germany and the Second World*

War Volume VIII – The Eastern Front 1943–1944, 130. For an account of the research that led to this study see the author's article 'In Pursuit of Prokhorovka', in Defence in Depth (2019): https://defenceindepth.co/

25   Zamulin, Valeriy, *Demolishing the Myth: The Tank Battle at Prokhorovka, Kursk, July 1943: An Operational Narrative*; for 5th Guards Tank Army inventory on 11.7.43 see Table 18. Note the author has not included the 29th Tank Corps 1529 SU Regiment (which was equipped with the new powerful SU-152) as it was not present at the front or tanks under repair at corps level. Regarding the latter the data Zamulin supplies suggests all damaged tanks were already more accurately recorded at brigade level; Zamulin, Valeriy, 'Soviet Troop Losses in the Battle of Prokhorovka, 10–16 July 1943', *Journal of Slavic Military Studies*, 32:1 (2019). For 5th Guards Tank Army 17.7.43 inventory and Zamulin's views see 118–20.

26   NARA RG 373: German Flown Aerial Photography, 1939–1945. Compare 16.7.43 GX-3734-SK-61 (incorrectly dated as 15.7.43 by NARA) with 7.8.43 GX-3942-SK-69, GX-3942-SD-123, GX-3942-SD-124; see also 15.8.43 GX-3958-SD-10 and 6.10.43 GX-3977-SD-45.

27   Frieser, Karl-Heinz, *The Battle of the Kursk Salient* in The Research Institute for Military History, Potsdam, Germany, *Germany and the Second World War Volume VIII – The Eastern Front 1943–1944*, 130.

28   The LSSAH made a limited attack on 13.7.43 in an attempt to find a weak spot in the Soviet defences. The attack was aborted as soon as the panzers were met by anti-tank fire. In any event the advance was away and forward of the original battlefield of 12.7.43, i.e. from the anti-tank ditch, Hill 252.2 and the Oktiabrskiy state farm and, as a result, the battlefield around these sites was largely preserved until the Germans withdrew on 17.7.43 – which of course is visually significant in terms of the content of GX-3734-SK-61 which is dated 16.7.43. Frieser, Karl-Heinz, *The Battle of the Kursk Salient* in The Research Institute for Military History, Potsdam, Germany, *Germany and the Second World War Volume VIII – The Eastern Front 1943–1944*, 130 and 136n. For the direction of this German attack see Glantz, David, and House, Jonathan, *The Battle of Kursk* (London: Ian Allan 1999), 214–15; see also II SS Panzer Korps, Map of Korps actions, 13.7.43 (this map also crudely displays the Soviet 29th Tank Corps 12.7.43 operations), T354, R606, F000034.

29   Frieser, Karl-Heinz, *The Battle of the Kursk Salient* in The Research Institute for Military History, Potsdam, Germany, *Germany and the Second World War Volume VIII – The Eastern Front 1943–1944*, 129.

30   Ibid., 177.

31   Frieser, Karl-Heinz, *The Battle of the Kursk Salient* in The Research Institute for Military History, Potsdam, Germany, *Germany and the Second World War Volume VIII – The Eastern Front 1943–1944*, 162.

32   NARA RG 373: German Flown Aerial Photography, 1939–1945. GX-3734-SK-61 (16.7.43).

33 Frieser, Karl-Heinz, *The Battle of the Kursk Salient* in The Research Institute for Military History, Potsdam, Germany, *Germany and the Second World War Volume VIII – The Eastern Front 1943–1944*, 182.

CHAPTER 1

1 All archival documents are located at NARA unless otherwise stated. See PzAOK 4, O.Qu.V, LSSAH (available until July 1943), DR (available until July 1943 and from October 1943 until March 1944) and SS-T (available until July 1943), Fahrgestell-Nr. Pz.kpf.Wg. in T313, Rolls 364, 387, 390. Combined in DR Gep. Kfz. Bestandsmeldung in Rolls 391 and 408.

2 PzAOK 4, O.Qu.V, LSSAH, DR and SS-T, Fahrgestell-Nr. Pz.kpf.Wg. 1–2.7.43, T313, R390.

3 PzAOK 4, O.Qu.V, LSSAH, DR and SS-T, Gep. Kfz. Bestandsmeldung, 1–2.7.43, T313, R390.

4 See PzAOK 4, O.Qu.V, LSSAH (available until July 1943 and from October 1943 until January 1944), DR (available until July 1943 and from October 1943 until March 1944) and SS-T (available until July 1943), Gep. Kfz. Bestandsmeldung in T313, Rolls 364, 387, 390, 391 and 408.

5 AOK 6, 1a, KTB 9, *Zustandsberichte, Wochenmeldung über Panzer und Sturmgeschülzlage Stand* 1.8.43 (written 6.8.43), T312, R1483, F000441.

6 Frieser, Karl-Heinz, *The Swing of the Pendulum: The Withdrawal of the Eastern Front from Summer 1943 to Summer 1944* in The Research Institute for Military History, Potsdam, Germany, Germany and the Second World War Volume VIII – The Eastern Front 1943–1944 (Oxford: Clarendon Press 2017), 340–41.

7 For example as early as 29.6.43 the LSSAH daily AFV reports (produced by the 1a) seem to contradict the more detailed LSSAH 1.7.43 inventory and 1.7.43 and 10.7.43 ten-day AFV status reports by recording operational numbers above the 21 Sf Pak 75mm in the division's pre-*Citadel* inventory, seemingly indicating the presence of four new Sf Paks. However, it is likely the LSSAH daily AFV reports are including Sf Paks which, although already issued to the LSSAH (on 10.6.43), had not yet reached the troops on the front line – or even left Germany (they departed 6.7.43)! Neither the 1.7.43 nor the 10.7.43 ten-day status reports record any new Sf Paks arriving at the front (the latter does record 16 new Pz IVs arriving); instead an inventory of 21 and 19 Sf Paks is respectively recorded. See PzAOK 4, O.Qu.V, LSSAH, Fahrgestell-Nr. Pz.kpf.Wg. 1.7.43, T313, R390; PzAOK 4, O.Qu.V, LSSAH Gep. Kfz. Bestandsmeldung, 1.7.43 and 10.7.43, T313, R390 and II SS Panzer Korps, LSSAH daily AFV reports 29.6–10.7.43, T354, R605, F000401-636; further, when one studies the LSSAH, DR and SS-T daily AFV report for 4.7.43, T354, R605, F000470, we can see that one DR Pz III L/42 was reported as operational by the Korps 1a; however, this Panzer III L/42 was one of two (65831 and 65726) which were training with DR's Panther battalion at Mailly le Camp in France, PzAOK 4, O.Qu.V, DR Fahrgestell-Nr. Pz.kpf .Wg. 1.7.43, T313, R390. Throughout July 1943 DR's divisional engineer

made no mention of any Pz III L/42 being at the front, PzAOK 4, O.Qu.V, LSSAH, DR and SS-T, Gep. Kfz. Bestandsmeldung, 1–2.7.43 and 10.7.43, T313, R390. Full delivery reports for all panzer, assault gun and self-propelled gun types are available from the Sturmpanzer website. See also Lukas Friedli, *Repairing the Panzers: German Tank Maintenance in World War 2, Vol 2* (Monroe: Panzerwrecks Publishing 2011), 160.

8 See PzAOK 4, O.Qu.V, LSSAH, DR and SS-T, Betr.: Totalausfälle an Pz.Kpfwg. und gep. Kfz. in T313, Rolls 364, 387, 390, 391 and 408.

9 PzAOK 4, O.Qu.V, LSSAH, DR and SS-T, Betr.: Totalausfälle an Pz.Kpfwg. und gep. Kfz. 1–10.7.43 (LSSAH written 12.7.43, DR and SS-T Lageskizzen written 23.7.43) T313, R390.

10 See PzAOK 4, O.Qu.V, LSSAH and DR, Gep. Kfz. Bestandsmeldung in T313, Rolls 391 and 408.

11 GenInsp.d.Pz.Truppen, Stabsoffizier für AOK 8, 5.10.43, T78, R619, F000836. Full delivery reports for all panzer, assault gun and self-propelled gun types are available from the Sturmpanzer website. For Waffen-SS monthly divisional *Meldung* and OB charts see GenInsp.d.Pz.Truppen, T78, R719.

12 PzAOK 4, O.Qu.V, DR, Gep. Kfz. Bestandsmeldung, 10.6.43, T313, R387.

13 Lukas Friedli, *Repairing the Panzers: German Tank Maintenance in World War 2 Vol 1* (Monroe: Panzerwrecks Publishing 2010), 8, 16–17, 56, 126–28.

14 Ibid., 16.

15 Ibid., 8.

CHAPTER 2

1 Jentz, Thomas, (ed.) *Panzer Truppen II* (Atglen: Schiffer 1996), 37, 47, and 64; PzAOK 4, O.Qu.V, LSSAH, Gep. Kfz. Bestandsmeldung, 10.3.43, T313, R364; PzAOK 4, O.Qu.V, DR and SS-T, Gep. Kfz. Bestandsmeldung, 2–3.3.43, T313, R364.

2 Wegner, Bernd, *The War against the Soviet Union 1942–1943* in The Research Institute for Military History, Potsdam, Germany, *Germany and the Second World War Volume VI – The Global War*, 1187.

3 Jentz, Thomas, (ed.) *Panzer Truppen II*, 37; PzAOK 4, O.Qu.V, LSSAH, Gep. Kfz. Bestandsmeldung, 10.3.43, T313, R364; PzAOK 4, O.Qu.V, DR and SS-T, Gep. Kfz. Bestandsmeldung, 2–3.3.43, T313, R364.

4 Wegner, Bernd, *The War against the Soviet Union 1942–1943* in The Research Institute for Military History, Potsdam, Germany, *Germany and the Second World War Volume VI – The Global War*, 1195, 1199–200, 1204.

5 GenInsp.d.Pz.Truppen, Panzerkampfwagenlage, 28.3–1.4.43, T78, R619, F000689; PzAOK 4, O.Qu.V, LSSAH, Gep. Kfz. Bestandsmeldung, 20.3.43, T313, R387; PzAOK 4, O.Qu.V, DR and SS-T, Gep. Kfz. Bestandsmeldung, 28.3–1.4.43, T313, R387.

6 PzAOK 4, O.Qu.V, SS-T, Gep. Kfz. Bestandsmeldung, 10.3.43, T313, R364.

7 Schneider, Wolfgang, *Tigers in Combat II* (Winnipeg: J.J. Fedorowicz 1998), 219.

8   PzAOK 4, O.Qu.V, SS-T, Gep. Kfz. Bestandsmeldung, 1.4.43, T313, R387;
    see also PzAOK 4, O.Qu.V, SS-T, Gep. Kfz. Bestandsmeldung, 20.3.43, T313,
    R387.
9   PzAOK 4, O.Qu.V, SS-T, Gep. Kfz. Bestandsmeldung, 1.5.43, T313, R387;
    PzAOK 4, O.Qu.V, SS-T, Fahrgestell-Nr. Pz.kpf.Wg. 1.5.43, T313, R387.
10 PzAOK 4, O.Qu.V, SS-T, Gep. Kfz. Bestandsmeldung, 10.5.43, T313, R387.
11 GenInsp.d.Pz.Truppen, Panzerkampfwagenlage, see SS-T 1.4.43, T78, R619,
    F000689.
12 Compare PzAOK 4, O.Qu.V, SS-T, Gep. Kfz. Bestandsmeldung, 1.5.43 and
    10.5.43, T313, R387.
13 250 101 was the only Totenkopf Tiger tank to remain in the 2c category from
    1.5.43 (the earliest surviving SS-T inventory) through to at least 2.7.43 (the
    final divisional SS-T inventory to have survived). Compare PzAOK 4, O.Qu.V,
    SS-T, Fahrgestell-Nr. Pz.kpf.Wg. 1.5.43 and 1.6.43 in T313, R387 with
    PzAOK 4, O.Qu.V, SS-T, Fahrgestell-Nr. Pz.kpf.Wg. 2.7.43 in T313, R390.
14 Frieser, Karl-Heinz, *The Battle of the Kursk Salient* in The Research Institute
    for Military History, Potsdam, Germany, *Germany and the Second World War
    Volume VIII – The Eastern Front 1943–1944*, 66.
15 See following section.
16 Jentz, Thomas, (ed.) *Panzer Truppen II*, 52, 66.
17 Ibid., 52.
18 Guderian, Heinz, *Panzer Leader* (London: Penguin 2009), 295–98.
19 PzAOK 4, O.Qu.V, LSSAH, DR and SS-T, Gep. Kfz. Bestandsmeldung,
    20.5.43, T313, R387.
20 PzAOK 4, O.Qu.V, LSSAH, Gep. Kfz. Bestandsmeldung, 10.3.43, T313,
    R364; PzAOK 4, O.Qu.V, DR, Gep. Kfz. Bestandsmeldung, 25.2.43, T313,
    R364; PzAOK 4, O.Qu.V, DR, Gep. Kfz. Bestandsmeldung, 17.3.43, T313,
    R387.
21 PzAOK 4, O.Qu.V, LSSAH Gep. Kfz. Bestandsmeldung, 10.3.43, T313, R364.
22 Zetterling, Niklas, and Frankson, Anders, *Kursk 1943: A Statistical Analysis*
    (London: Frank Cass 2000), 46; PzAOK 4, O.Qu.V, LSSAH, Gep. Kfz.
    Bestandsmeldung, 1.7.43, T313, R390.
23 This tank (tactical number 055) would be one of the few retained by the
    LSSAH after the division transferred to Italy at the end of July 1943. Images
    of these tanks heading to Italy can be found on the following website: https://
    www.thirdreichmedals.com/article/WSS.html. See also Jentz, Thomas, (ed.)
    Panzer Truppen II, 136.
24 Friedli, Lukas, *Repairing the Panzers: German Tank Maintenance in World War 2
    Vol 1*, 180.
25 II SS Panzer Korps, Abschrift Fernschreiben, LSSAH Ia, 23.7.43, T354, R605,
    F000856.
26 Content of Table 3 kindly supplied by the researcher Stephen Ballantyne.
27 Zetterling, Niklas, and Frankson, Anders, *Kursk 1943: A Statistical Analysis*,
    236–37; see also 225 and 38.

94. The summit of Hill 252.2 (near the Victory 'Belfry') looking down towards the anti-tank ditch (compare with Plate 88.). (Google Earth)

95. The Soviet aircraft has travelled closer to the parallel road. A destroyed Leibstandarte SPW and a decapitated T-34 are the most prominent losses. (Valeriy Zamulin)

96. After the battle the Soviets had to drag many destroyed tanks off the battlefield; those with broken tracks left their mark on the terrain. The destroyed Panzer IV and T-34 close to Hill 252.2's summit were amongst those so treated, 6 October. (NARA)

97. The two destroyed Panzer IVs that were lost beyond the crest of Hill 252.2 in the initial armoured combat on 12 July were also dragged from the battlefield, 6 October. (NARA)

98. Following the battle large numbers of destroyed AFVs were brought to a railway spur on the outskirts of Prokhorovka, 7 August. (NARA)

99. Following the battle large numbers of destroyed AFVs were brought to a railway spur on the outskirts of Prokhorovka, 15 August. (NARA)

100. Following the battle large numbers of destroyed AFVs were brought to a railway spur on the outskirts of Prokhorovka, 7 September. (NARA)

101. Following the battle large numbers of destroyed AFVs were brought to a railway spur on the outskirts of Prokhorovka, 6 October. (NARA)

102. The railway spur was located directly behind the 29th Tank Corps line of advance. Since the war there has been a great deal of industrial development close to the site. (Google Earth)

103. The terminus of the original railway spur. (Google Earth)

104. The 18th Tank Corps Battlefield. (Google Earth)

105. The location of 170th Tank Brigade's breakthrough. Soviet tank wrecks in 'wedge' formation can be seen in upper centre of image, 16 July. (NARA)

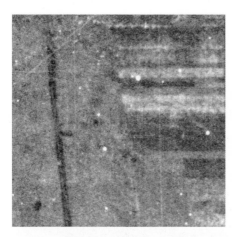

106. Confirmation of the Soviet 'wedge' group's appearance, 7 August. (NARA)

107. Leibstandarte Tiger tanks' direct view from Point 228.4 of 170th Tank Brigade's advance in wedge formation. (Google Earth)

108. 170th & 181st Tank Brigades advance on Point 228.4. Showing the wedge group (lower centre of image) and advance from the gully (on right of image), 16 July. (NARA)

109. View of the gully from the Leibstandarte Tiger tanks' perspective on Point 228.4. (Google Earth)

110. Battlefield of 181st Tank Brigade vs. Leibstandarte
Tiger tank company, 14 July. (NARA)

111. The topography of the battlefield looking towards Andreyevka from Point 228.4.
(Google Earth)

112. Detail of destruction caused by the four Leibstandarte Tiger tanks, 14 July. (NARA)

113. 181st Tank Brigade's view looking up to the Leibstandarte Tiger tanks' firing positions. (Google Earth)

114. The battlefield of the 25th Tank Brigade. (Google Earth)

115. The battlefield of the 25th Tank Brigade, 16 July. (NARA)

116. Line of advance of the 25th Tank Brigade towards Storozhevoye Woods. The railway embankment is on the right. (Google Earth)

117. The battlefield of the 25th Tank Brigade, 7 August. (NARA)

118. As the 25th Tank Brigade neared Storozhevoye Woods it was ambushed by Leibstandarte Marder tank destroyers located in Stalinsk state farm (shown ahead). (Google Earth)

119. The German Tiger tank holds a symbolic role in the battle of Prokhorovka. Outside the 'Third Battlefield of Russia' museum in Prokhorovka stands a mighty sculpture of two Tiger tanks being rammed and destroyed by Soviet T-34s. This image closely fits the Soviet narrative of the battle. However, on 12 July only five Tiger tanks were available to participate in the battle and a maximum of one was lost in combat. (Author's collection)

120. The spectacular 67m-long Cold War-era Belgorod diorama 'Tank battle near Prokhorovka' opened on 4 August 1987. The diorama perpetuates the Soviet myth of the battle being a mass armoured meeting engagement which cost the Germans between 300 (58%) and 400 (77%) of their AFVs. In reality, the Germans lost a maximum of 16 (3%) of their AFVs during the battle of Prokhorovka. (Alamy)

121. Despite its appearance in the Belgorod diorama, the Panther tank did not enter combat with any SS division until 22 August – the penultimate day of the battle of Kursk. This picture depicts one of Das Reich's first actions with the Panther tank near Kharkov in late August 1943. (Bundesarchiv)

122. In the first week of December 1943 a column of Das Reich Tiger tanks is seen negotiating woods west of Kiev. On 1 December Das Reich possessed 16 Tiger tanks, 15 of which had been present with the Leibstandarte or Das Reich on 11 July, i.e., they were of Prokhorovka vintage. On 1 December, 4.5 months after the battle, 49 per cent of the Leibstandarte and Das Reich 11 July AFV inventory was still in service with SS units on the Eastern Front. (Bundesarchiv)

123. Since the dissolution of the Soviet Union an extensive memorial complex (State Military Historical Museum-Reserve 'Prokhorovskoye Pole') has been established at Prokhorovka, one befitting the location of 'The Third Battlefield of Russia'. In 1995 the Church of the Holy Apostles Peter and Paul was completed, the shrine being consecrated on 3 May 1995. Next to the church can be seen the 'Third Battlefield of Russia' museum which opened to the public on 2 May 2010. (Alamy)

124. On 27 January 2017 the impressive Museum of Armoured Vehicles opened. The museum gives a complete picture of the development and history of tank building from the period of antiquity and the Middle Ages to the present day. Next to the museum is 'Tankodrome' (opened 16 May 2015) which has a 1.2-hectare AFV demonstration track with a seating capacity for over 1,300 spectators. The site also contains an outdoor AFV exhibition area. Outside the museum stands a sculpture depicting the iconic scene of Soviet troops joining battle from a T-34. (Dreamstime.com)

125. On 12 July 2020 the 'Battle for the Weapons of the Great Victory' museum opened. This remarkable museum, which contains around 2,000 exhibits, chronicles the role of the Soviet Home Front throughout the Second World War. The museum includes a close examination of the staggeringly successful large-scale evacuation of Soviet industry and workers from the path of the German invasion in 1941. (Dreamstime.com)

126. The Victory Monument 'Belfry' on Hill 252.2 opened in 1995 (note the close proximity of Prokhorovka, 2.5km away). The 59m-high Belfry houses a 3.5-ton bell which strikes three times an hour to honour the memory of those who fought at the 'three battlefields of Russia': Kulikovo, Borodino and Prokhorovka. The Soviet soldiers who fought so courageously against Nazism at Prokhorovka deserve our deepest respect and gratitude for their victory. (Alamy)

28 Niehorster, Leo, *German World War II Organization Series, Volume V/III* (Milton Keynes: The Military Press 2005), 31.

29 Ibid., 46–47.

30 Ibid., 32–33.

31 Ibid., 31.

32 Zetterling, Niklas, and Frankson, Anders, *Kursk 1943: A Statistical Analysis*, 30; see also Niehorster, Leo, *German World War II Organization Series, Volume V/III*, 31.

33 Kroener, Bernhard, *Management of Human Resources, Deployment of the Population, and Manning the Armed Forces in the Second Half of the War (1942–1944)* in The Research Institute for Military History, Potsdam, Germany, *Germany and the Second World War Volume V/III*, 1018–20. See also Frieser, Karl-Heinz, *The Battle of the Kursk Salient* in The Research Institute for Military History, Potsdam, Germany, *Germany and the Second World War Volume VIII – The Eastern Front 1943–1944*, 168–69.

34 Wegner, Bernd, *From Stalingrad to Kursk* in The Research Institute for Military History, Potsdam, Germany, *Germany and the Second World War Volume VIII – The Eastern Front 1943–1944* (Oxford: Clarendon Press 2001), 62.

35 Ibid., 69–72.

36 Forczyk, Robert, *Kursk 1943: The Southern Front* (Oxford: Osprey 2017), 30.

37 Frieser, Karl-Heinz, *The Battle of the Kursk Salient* in The Research Institute for Military History, Potsdam, Germany, *Germany and the Second World War Volume VIII – The Eastern Front 1943–1944*, 168–69.

38 Wegner, Bernd, *From Stalingrad to Kursk* in The Research Institute for Military History, Potsdam, Germany, *Germany and the Second World War Volume VIII – The Eastern Front 1943–1944*, 76.

39 Glantz, David, *Soviet Military Intelligence in War* (Oxon: Frank Cass 1990), 185–99.

40 For 9th Army: 185 Pz III, 314 Pz IV, 27 Pz VI, 33 Bef Pz, 199 StuG, 30 StuH, 83 Ferdinand, 201 Pak Sf, GenInsp.d.Pz.Truppen, Panzerkampfwagenlage, 30.6.43, T78, R619, F000643, GenInsp.d.Pz.Truppen, StuG-lage, 30.6.43, T78, R620, F000188; Spielberger, Walter, Doyle, Hilary, and Jentz, Tomas, *Heavy Jagdpanzer: Development, Production, Operations* (Atglen: Schiffer 2007), 85–86; Zetterling, Niklas, and Frankson, Anders, *Kursk 1943: A Statistical Analysis*, 26–27, 42; Niehorster, Leo, *German World War II Organization Series, Volume V/I* (Milton Keynes: The Military Press 2004), 74. For 4th Panzer Army and Army Detachment Kempf see Appendix N. For 2nd Panzer Army and 2nd Army see Frieser, Karl-Heinz, *The Battle of the Kursk Salient* in The Research Institute for Military History, Potsdam, Germany, *Germany and the Second World War Volume VIII – The Eastern Front 1943–1944*, 100.

41 Ibid.

42 Frieser, Karl-Heinz, *The Battle of the Kursk Salient* in The Research Institute for Military History, Potsdam, Germany, *Germany and the Second World War Volume VIII – The Eastern Front 1943–1944*, 106–12.

43 Ibid., 117.

44 See Appendix M – the supporting Korps Raus saw its meagre pool of 42 operational AFVs fall to 37 operational AFVs over the same period; see also Frieser, Karl-Heinz, *The Battle of the Kursk Salient* in The Research Institute for Military History, Potsdam, Germany, *Germany and the Second World War Volume VIII – The Eastern Front 1943–1944*, 113–14.

45 Ibid., 115.

46 See Appendix K and N; see also Frieser, Karl-Heinz, *The Battle of the Kursk Salient* in The Research Institute for Military History, Potsdam, Germany, *Germany and the Second World War Volume VIII – The Eastern Front 1943–1944*, 117.

47 PzAOK 4, O.Qu.V, LSSAH, DR and SS-T, Betr.: Totalausfälle an Pz.Kpfwg. und gep. Kfz. 1–10.7.43 (LSSAH written 12.7.43, DR and SS-T Lageskizzen written 23.7.43) T313, R390.

48 PzAOK 4, O.Qu.V, LSSAH, Gep. Kfz. Bestandsmeldung, 10.7.43, T313, R390.

49 PzAOK 4, O.Qu.V, LSSAH, DR and SS-T, Betr.: Totalausfälle an Pz.Kpfwg. und gep. Kfz. 1–10.7.43 (LSSAH written 12.7.43, DR and SS-T Lageskizzen written 23.7.43) T313, R390.

50 PzAOK 4, O.Qu.V, LSSAH, DR and SS-T, Betr.: Totalausfälle an Pz.Kpfwg. und gep. Kfz. 1–10.7.43 (LSSAH written 12.7.43, DR and SS-T Lageskizzen written 23.7.43) T313, R390; PzAOK 4, O.Qu.V, LSSAH, DR and SS-T, Gep. Kfz. Bestandsmeldung, 1–2.7.43 and 10.7.43, T313, R390; PzAOK 4, O.Qu.V, DR, Gep. Kfz. Bestandsmeldung, 31.10.43, T313, R391; PzAOK 4, O.Qu.V, LSSAH, Gep. Kfz. Bestandsmeldung, 1.11.43, T313, R391. PzAOK 4, O.Qu.V, DR, Gep. Kfz. Bestandsmeldung, 10.1.44, T313, R408; II SS Panzer Korps, LSSAH, Rgt.Bef.Std., 27.7.43, T354, R607, F000825; II SS Panzer Korps, DR and SS-T Ia 667/43 and 668/43, 28.7.43, T354, R605, F000879-80; Jentz, Thomas, (ed.) *Panzer Truppen II*, 136.

51 PzAOK 4, O.Qu.V, DR, Gep. Kfz. Bestandsmeldung, 20.1.44, 1.2.44 and 29.2.44, T313, R408.

52 PzAOK 4, O.Qu.V, DR, Gep. Kfz. Bestandsmeldung, 31.10.43 and 10.11.43, T313, R391.

CHAPTER 3

1 Bundesarchiv/Militärarchiv, RH 10/64, General Inspector of Panzer Troops – AGS, 5–17.7.43 *Totalverluste*; II SS Panzer Korps, Correspondence from II SS Panzer Korps 1a to Hitler's SS adjutant Fritz Darges at FHQ, Status of II SS Panzer Korps at midday 21.7.43 (sent 23.7.43), T354, R605, F000853; II SS Panzer Korps, Ingenieur, Betr.: Kinsatz Raum Belgorod. 5–18.7.43, updated to 22.7.43 (written 28.7.43), T354, R607, F000629-31. See also Appendix L.

2 II SS Panzer Korps, Ingenieur, Betr.: Kinsatz Raum Belgorod. 5–18.7.43, updated to 22.7.43 (written 28.7.43), T354, R607, F000629-31.

3   See Alexander Tomzov's chapter in *Tankovy udar. Sovetskie tanki v boyakh. 1942–1943* (Moscow: Eksmo 2007).

4   II SS Panzer Korps, Map of Korps actions, new and proposed front lines 14–18.7.43, T354, R606, F000035; II SS Panzer Korps, Ablauf der Marschbewegungen II SS Panzer Korps, 18–22.7.43, T354, R606, F000038; II SS Panzer Korps, Gliederung des II SS Panzer Korps am 22 und 23.7.43 bis zur Bereitstellung und Lage bei XXXX.A.K., T354, R606, F000039; II SS Panzer Korps, Bereitstellungs u. Angriffsplan für den Angriff am 24.7.43, T354, R606, F000040; II SS Panzer Korps, Ablauf der Marschbewegungen II SS Panzer Korps, 24–29.7.43, T354, R606, F000043; II SS Panzer Korps, Bereitstellung des II SS Panzer Korps am 29.7.3 und Verlauf des 30.7.43, T354, R606, F000050-51.

5   AOK 6, 1a, KTB 9, *Zustandsberichte, Wochenmeldung über Panzer und Sturmgeschülzlage Stand* 1.8.43 (written 6.8.43), T312, R1483, F000441.

6   II SS Panzer Korps, Ablauf der Marschbewegungen II SS Panzer Korps, 24–29.7.43, T354, R606, F000043.

7   AOK 6, 1a, KTB 9, *Zustandsberichte, Wochenmeldung über Panzer und Sturmgeschülzlage Stand* 1.8.43 (written 6.8.43), T312, R1483, F000441. For an unknown reason DR's sole Pz II was not included in *Wochenmeldung* even though there was a column for this type – the Pz II was not lost until the autumn of 1943 – see Appendix E. DR also had a Bef Pz I; however, Pz I were not recorded in the *Wochenmeldung*. SS-T had neither Pz I nor Pz II. The LSSAH also had begun Operation *Citadel* with three Pz Is (of which one was Bef) and four Pz IIs. The only light panzer lost by II SS Panzer Korps during Operation *Citadel* was a LSSAH Pz I Bef which was lost between 5 and 10.7.43, PzAOK 4, O.Qu.V, LSSAH Betr.: Totalausfälle an Pz.Kpfwg. und gep. Kfz. 1–10.7.43, written 12.7.43, T313, R390; for consistency the author has not recorded light tanks in the tables contained in this book.

8   AOK 6, 1a, KTB 9, *Zustandsberichte, Wochenmeldung über Panzer und Sturmgeschülzlage Stand* 1.8.43 (written 6.8.43), T312, R1483, F000441; III Pz Korps, 1a Anlage z, KTB Band 1 and 2, DR Tagesmeldung, 11.8.43, T314, R201; II SS Panzer Korps, SS-T Fehlbestäde an Waffen und Grossgerät, 3.8.43, T354, R605, F001001; PzAOK 4, O.Qu.V, LSSAH, DR and SS-T, Gep. Kfz. Bestandsmeldung, 1–2.7.43 and 10.7.43, T313, R390. In addition for the launch of Operation *Citadel* each of the three divisions of II SS Panzer Korps possessed the following fully tracked AFV: 12 l.F.H. 18 Sfl. (Wespe) 105mm light field howitzers, six s.F.H. 18 Sfl. (Hummel) 150mm heavy field howitzers and nine Pz III Art. Beob. Wg (artillery armoured observation post). While the LSSAH and DR each possessed 12 s.I.G. 33 Sfl. 38t (Grille) 150mm heavy infantry guns. No losses amongst these weapons were reported during Operation *Citadel*. See Appendix E.

9   AOK 6, 1a, KTB 9, Zustandsberichte, *Wochenmeldung über Panzer und Sturmgeschülzlage Stand* 1.8.43 (written 6.8.43), T312, R1483, F000441.

10 AOK 6, 1a, KTB 9, *Zustandsberichte, Wochenmeldung über Panzer und Sturmgeschülzlage Stand* 1.8.43 (written 6.8.43), T312, R1483, F000441; III Pz Korps, 1a Anlage z, KTB Band 1 and 2, DR Tagesmeldung, 11.8.43, T314, R201; II SS Panzer Korps, SS-T Fehlbestäde an Waffen und Grossgerät, 3.8.43, T354, R605, F001001; II SS Panzer Korps, Ingenieur, Betr.: Kinsatz Raum Belgorod. 5–18.7.43, updated to 22.7.43 (written 28.7.43), T354, R607, F000629-31; PzAOK 4, O.Qu.V, LSSAH, DR and SS-T, Gep. Kfz. Bestandsmeldung, 1–2.7.43 and 10.7.43, T313, R390.

11 PzAOK 4, O.Qu.V, LSSAH, DR and SS-T, Fahrgestell-Nr. Pz.kpf.Wg. 1–2.7.43, T313, R390; PzAOK 4, O.Qu.V, LSSAH, DR and SS-T, Gep. Kfz. Bestandsmeldung, 1–2.7.43 and 10.7.43, T313, R390; PzAOK 4, O.Qu.V, LSSAH, DR and SS-T, Betr.: Totalausfälle an Pz.Kpfwg. und gep. Kfz. 1–10.7.43 (LSSAH written 12.7.43, DR and SS-T Lageskizzen written 23.7.43) T313, R390; II SS Panzer Korps, Ingenieur, Betr.: Kinsatz Raum Belgorod. 5–18.7.43, updated to 22.7.43 (written 28.7.43), T354, R607, F000629-31; AOK 6, 1a, KTB 9, *Zustandsberichte, Wochenmeldung über Panzer und Sturmgeschülzlage Stand* 1.8.43 (written 6.8.43), T312, R1483, F000441; III Pz Korps, 1a Anlage z, KTB Band 1 and 2, DR Tagesmeldung, 11.8.43, T314, R201; II SS Panzer Korps, SS-T Fehlbestäde an Waffen und Grossgerät, 3.8.43, T354, R605, F001001. Full delivery reports for all panzer, assault gun and self-propelled gun types are available from the Sturmpanzer website.

12 PzAOK 4, O.Qu.V, LSSAH, DR and SS-T, Fahrgestell-Nr. Pz.kpf.Wg. 1–2.7.43, T313, R390; PzAOK 4, O.Qu.V, LSSAH, DR and SS-T, Gep. Kfz. Bestandsmeldung, 1–2.7.43 and 10.7.43, T313, R390. Full delivery reports for all panzer, assault gun and self-propelled gun types are available from the Sturmpanzer website.

13 LSSAH, DR and SS-T daily AFV report 4.7.43, T354, R605, F000470; for accurate Sf Pak numbers see Note 7 Chapter 1 and LSSAH, DR and SS-T, Gep. Kfz. Bestandsmeldung, 1–2.7.43 and 10.7.43, T313, R390. For the record the LSSAH, DR and SS-T daily AFV report 4.7.43, T354, R605, F000470 reports the following Sf Pak as being operational on 4.7.43: LSSAH 21, DR 10, SS-T 11 for the same total of 42 Sf Pak available to II SS Panzer Korps. In addition one Pz III L/42 was also reported as operational by the Korps 1a; however, this panzer III L/42 was one of two (65831 and 65726) which were training with DR's Panther battalion at Mailly le Camp in France, PzAOK 4, O.Qu.V, DR Fahrgestell-Nr. Pz.kpf.Wg. 1.7.43, T313, R390. Throughout July 1943 DR's divisional engineer made no mention of any Pz III L/42 being at the front, PzAOK 4, O.Qu.V, LSSAH, DR and SS-T, Gep. Kfz. Bestandsmeldung, 1–2.7.43 and 10.7.43, T313, R390. The SS divisional 1a compiled the daily operational AFV reports, whereas, the SS divisional engineers (who were best placed to know the true totals/location of AFV) compiled the ten-day status reports and chassis number inventories. See Lukas Friedli, *Repairing the Panzers: German Tank Maintenance in World War 2, Vol 2*, 160.

14 PzAOK 4, O.Qu.V, LSSAH, DR and SS-T, Fahrgestell-Nr. Pz.kpf.Wg.
1–2.7.43, T313, R390; PzAOK 4, O.Qu.V, LSSAH, DR and SS-T, Gep.
Kfz. Bestandsmeldung, 1–2.7.43 and 10.7.43, T313, R390; PzAOK 4,
O.Qu.V, LSSAH, DR and SS-T, Betr.: Totalausfälle an Pz.Kpfwg. und
gep. Kfz. 1–10.7.43 (LSSAH written 12.7.43, DR and SS-T Lageskizzen
written 23.7.43) T313, R390. Full delivery reports for all panzer, assault
gun and self-propelled gun types are available from the Sturmpanzer
website.

15 II SS Panzer Korps, LSSAH, DR and SS-T daily AFV reports 29.6–31.7.43,
T354, R605, F000401-949; PzAOK 4, O.Qu.V, LSSAH, DR and SS-T, Gep.
Kfz. Bestandsmeldung, 1–2.7.43 and 10.7.43, T313, R390.

16 PzAOK 4, O.Qu.V, LSSAH, DR and SS-T, Fahrgestell-Nr. Pz.kpf.Wg.
1–2.7.43, T313, R390; PzAOK 4, O.Qu.V, LSSAH, DR and SS-T, Gep.
Kfz. Bestandsmeldung, 1–2.7.43 and 10.7.43, T313, R390; PzAOK 4,
O.Qu.V, LSSAH, DR and SS-T, Betr.: Totalausfälle an Pz.Kpfwg. und
gep. Kfz. 1–10.7.43 (LSSAH written 12.7.43, DR and SS-T Lageskizzen
written 23.7.43) T313, R390; II SS Panzer Korps, Ingenieur, Betr.: Kinsatz
Raum Belgorod. 5–18.7.43, updated to 22.7.43 (written 28.7.43), T354,
R607, F000629-31; AOK 6, 1a, KTB 9, *Zustandsberichte, Wochenmeldung
über Panzer und Sturmgeschülzlage Stand* 1.8.43 (written 6.8.43),
T312, R1483, F000441; III Pz Korps, 1a Anlage z, KTB Band 1 and
2, DR Tagesmeldung, 11.8.43, T314, R201; II SS Panzer Korps, SS-T
Fehlbestäde an Waffen und Grossgerät, 3.8.43, T354, R605, F001001;
II SS Panzer Korps, LSSAH Ia, Tagesmeldung für den 24.7.43, T354,
R605, F000867; II SS Panzer Korps, DR and SS-T Ia 667/43 and 668/43,
28.7.43, T354, R605, F000879-80; GenInsp.d.Pz.Truppen, Waffen-SS
monthly divisional *Meldung* and OB charts, LSSAH, 1.9.43, T78, R719;
PzAOK 4, O.Qu.V, LSSAH, Gep. Kfz. Bestandsmeldung, 1.11.43, T313,
R391. Full delivery reports for all panzer, assault gun and self-propelled
gun types are available from the Sturmpanzer website.

17 II SS Panzer Korps, LSSAH, DR and SS-T daily AFV reports 29.6–31.7.43,
T354, R605, F000401-949; PzAOK 4, O.Qu.V, LSSAH, DR and SS-T,
Gep. Kfz. Bestandsmeldung, 1–2.7.43 and 10.7.43, T313, R390; XXXXVIII.
Pz-AK, XXXXVIII. Pz-AK daily reports for SS-T 18–20.7.43, T314, R1171,
F000388-482.

18 AOK 6, 1a, KTB 9, *Zustandsberichte, Wochenmeldung über Panzer und
Sturmgeschülzlage Stand* 1.8.43 (written 6.8.43), T312, R1483, F000441;
II SS Panzer Korps, III Pz Korps, 1a Anlage z, KTB Band 1 and 2, DR
Tagesmeldung, 11.8.43, T314, R201; II SS Panzer Korps, SS-T Fehlbestäde an
Waffen und Grossgerät, 3.8.43, T354, R605, F001001. Full delivery reports
for all panzer, assault gun and self-propelled gun types are available from the
Sturmpanzer website.

19 AOK 6, 1a, KTB 9, *Zustandsberichte, Wochenmeldung über Panzer und
Sturmgeschülzlage Stand* 1.8.43 (written 6.8.43), T312, R1483, F000441; II

SS Panzer Korps, daily reports for LSSAH, DR and SS-T 18.7–2.8.43, T354, R605, F000807-982.

20 II SS Panzer Korps, Bereitstellung des II SS Panzer Korps am 29.7.3 und Verlauf des 30.7.43, T354, R606, F000050-51.

21 Frieser, Karl-Heinz, *The Battle of the Kursk Salient* in The Research Institute for Military History, Potsdam, Germany, *Germany and the Second World War Volume VIII – The Eastern Front 1943–1944*, 143–44; see also Frieser, Karl-Heinz, *The Swing of the Pendulum: The Withdrawal of the Eastern Front from Summer 1943 to Summer 1944* in The Research Institute for Military History, Potsdam, Germany, *Germany and the Second World War Volume VIII – The Eastern Front 1943–1944* (Oxford: Clarendon Press 2017), 338–43.

22 AOK 6, 1a, KTB 9, *Zustandsberichte, Wochenmeldung über Panzer und Sturmgeschützlage Stand* 1.8.43 (written 6.8.43), T312, R1483, F000441.

23 Full delivery reports for all panzer, assault gun and self-propelled gun types are available from the Sturmpanzer website. Regarding the transfer of LSSAH Tigers see section: 'Tiger tank losses at Prokhorovka: Myth versus reality'. As early as 29.6.43 the LSSAH daily AFV reports seem to contradict the more detailed LSSAH 1.7.43 inventory and 1.7.43 and 10.7.43 ten-day AFV status reports by recording operational numbers above the 21 Sf Pak 75mm in the division's inventory, seemingly indicating the presence of four new Sf Pak. However, it is likely the LSSAH daily AFV reports are including Sf Pak which, although already issued to LSSAH (on 10.6.43), had not yet reached the troops on the front line – or even left Germany (they departed 6.7.43)! Neither the 1.7.43 nor 10.7.43 ten-day status reports record any new Sf Pak arriving at the front (the latter does include 16 new Pz IVs); instead an inventory of 21 and 19 Sf Paks is respectively recorded. See PzAOK 4, O.Qu.V, LSSAH, Fahrgestell-Nr. Pz.kpf.Wg. 1.7.43, T313, R390; PzAOK 4, O.Qu.V, LSSAH Gep. Kfz. Bestandsmeldung, 1.7.43 and 10.7.43, T313, R390 and II SS Panzer Korps, LSSAH daily AFV reports 29.6–10.7.43, T354, R605, F000401-636.

24 GenInsp.d.Pz.Truppen, Waffen-SS monthly divisional *Meldung* and OB charts, LSSAH, 1.9.43 and 1.10.43, T78, R719; PzAOK 4, O.Qu.V, LSSAH, Gep. Kfz. Bestandsmeldung, 1.11.43, T313, R391. Full delivery reports for all panzer, assault gun and self-propelled gun types are available from the Sturmpanzer website.

25 Full delivery reports for all panzer, assault gun and self-propelled gun types are available from the Sturmpanzer website; PzAOK 4, O.Qu.V, DR, Gep. Kfz. Bestandsmeldung, 31.10.43, T313, R391.

26 Full delivery reports for all panzer, assault gun and self-propelled gun types are available from the Sturmpanzer website; GenInsp.d.Pz.Truppen, Stabsoffizier für AOK 8, 5.10.43, T78, R619, F000836.

27 AOK 6, 1a, KTB 9, *Zustandsberichte, Wochenmeldung über Panzer und Sturmgeschützlage Stand* 1.8.43 (written 6.8.43), T312, R1483, F000441.

28 PzAOK 4, O.Qu.V, LSSAH, DR and SS-T, Betr.: Totalausfälle an Pz.Kpfwg.
und gep. Kfz. 1–10.7.43 (LSSAH written 12.7.43, DR and SS-T Lageskizzen
written 23.7.43) T313, R390; PzAOK 4, O.Qu.V, LSSAH, DR and SS-T,
Gep. Kfz. Bestandsmeldung, 10.7.43, T313, R390; II SS Panzer Korps,
Ingenieur, Betr.: Kinsatz Raum Belgorod. 5–18.7.43, updated to 22.7.43
(written 28.7.43), T354, R607, F000629-31; II SS Panzer Korps, LSSAH,
Rgt.Bef.Std., 27.7.43, T354, R607, F000825; II SS Panzer Korps, DR
and SS-T Ia 667/43 and 668/43, 28.7.43, T354, R605, F000879-80; II
SS Panzer Korps, LSSAH Ia, Tagesmeldung für den 24.7.43, T354, R605,
F000867. Images of the tanks retained by the LSSAH can be found on
the following website: https://www.thirdreichmedals.com/article/WSS
.html; Jentz, Thomas, (ed.) *Panzer Truppen II*, 136; GenInsp.d.Pz.Truppen,
Waffen-SS monthly divisional *Meldung* and OB charts, LSSAH, 1.9.43,
T78, R719. See June/July 1943 delivery reports for five LSSAH Tigers,
four LSSAH self-propelled guns and August delivery report for 53 LSSAH
Pz IVs on Sturmpanzer website; PzAOK 4, O.Qu.V, LSSAH, Gep. Kfz.
Bestandsmeldung, 1.11.43, T313, R391.

29 Delivery reports for all panzer, assault gun and self-propelled gun types are
available from the Sturmpanzer website.

30 AOK 6, 1a, KTB 9, *Zustandsberichte, Wochenmeldung über Panzer und
Sturmgeschülzlage Stand* 1.8.43 (written 6.8.43), T312, R1483, F000441.

31 AOK 6, 1a, KTB 9, *Zustandsberichte, Wochenmeldung über Panzer und
Sturmgeschülzlage Stand* 1.8.43 (written 6.8.43), T312, R1483, F000441;
III Pz Korps, 1a Anlage z, KTB Band 1 and 2, DR Tagesmeldung, 11.8.43,
T314, R201; II SS Panzer Korps, SS-T Fehlbestäde an Waffen und Grossgerät,
3.8.43, T354, R605, F001001; II SS Panzer Korps, Ingenieur, Betr.: Kinsatz
Raum Belgorod. 5–18.7.43, updated to 22.7.43 (written 28.7.43), T354,
R607, F000629-31; PzAOK 4, O.Qu.V, LSSAH, DR and SS-T, Gep. Kfz.
Bestandsmeldung, 1–2.7.43 and 10.7.43, T313, R390.

32 AOK 6, 1a, KTB 9, *Zustandsberichte, Wochenmeldung über Panzer und
Sturmgeschülzlage Stand* 1.8.43 (written 6.8.43), T312, R1483, F000441; II SS
Panzer Korps, War diary entries for 30.7–2.8.43, T354, R605, F000123-41.

33 AOK 6, 1a, KTB 9, *Zustandsberichte, Wochenmeldung über Panzer und
Sturmgeschülzlage Stand* 1.8.43 (written 6.8.43), T312, R1483, F000441;
II SS Panzer Korps, Ingenieur, Betr.: Kinsatz Raum Belgorod. 5–18.7.43,
updated to 22.7.43 (written 28.7.43), T354, R607, F000629-31; PzAOK
4, O.Qu.V, LSSAH, DR and SS-T, Gep. Kfz. Bestandsmeldung, 1–2.7.43
and 10.7.43, T313, R390; PzAOK 4, O.Qu.V, LSSAH, DR and SS-T,
Fahrgestell-Nr. Pz.kpf.Wg. 1–2.7.43, T313, R390; PzAOK 4, O.Qu.V,
LSSAH, DR and SS-T, Betr.: Totalausfälle an Pz.Kpfwg. und gep. Kfz.
1–10.7.43 (LSSAH written 12.7.43, DR and SS-T Lageskizzen written
23.7.43) T313, R390.

34 AOK 6, 1a, KTB 9, *Zustandsberichte, Wochenmeldung über Panzer und
Sturmgeschülzlage Stand* 1.8.43 (written 6.8.43), T312, R1483, F000441;

PzAOK 4, O.Qu.V, LSSAH, DR and SS-T, Betr.: Totalausfälle an Pz.Kpfwg. und gep. Kfz. 1–10.7.43 (LSSAH written 12.7.43, DR and SS-T Lageskizzen written 23.7.43) T313, R390; PzAOK 4, O.Qu.V, LSSAH, DR and SS-T, Gep. Kfz. Bestandsmeldung, 10.7.43, T313, R390; PzAOK 4, O.Qu.V, LSSAH, DR and SS-T, Fahrgestell-Nr. Pz.kpf.Wg. 1–2.7.43, T313, R390; II SS Panzer Korps, Ingenieur, Betr.: Kinsatz Raum Belgorod. 5–18.7.43, updated to 22.7.43 (written 28.7.43), T354, R607, F000629-31; II SS Panzer Korps, LSSAH, Rgt.Bef.Std., 27.7.43, T354, R607, F000825; II SS Panzer Korps, DR and SS-T Ia 667/43 and 668/43, 28.7.43, T354, R605, F000879-80; II SS Panzer Korps, LSSAH Ia, Tagesmeldung für den 24.7.43, T354, R605, F000867. Images of the tanks retained by the LSSAH can be found on the following website: https://www.thirdreichmedals.com/article /WSS.html; Jentz, Thomas, (ed.) *Panzer Truppen II*, p.136; GenInsp.d.Pz. Truppen, Waffen-SS monthly divisional *Meldung* and OB charts, LSSAH, 1.9.43, T78, R719. See June/July 1943 delivery reports for five LSSAH Tigers, four LSSAH self-propelled guns and August delivery report for 53 LSSAH Pz IVs on Sturmpanzer website; PzAOK 4, O.Qu.V, LSSAH, Gep. Kfz. Bestandsmeldung, 1.11.43, T313, R391.

35   For examples of AFV reclassifications see sections: 'Prokhorovka looms: The southern pincer of Operation *Citadel*, 5–11 July 1943' and 'Tiger tank losses at Prokhorovka: Myth versus reality'; see also Appendix E. The Heer's Pz Rgt. v.Lauchert (the only Panther tank unit involved in Operation *Citadel* – the Panther was making its operational debut) provides excellent examples of AFV reclassification between documents (and the dangers of reading documents in isolation). In July Pz Rgt. v.Lauchert (which fought alongside the Grossdeutschland division in XXXXVIII Panzer Korps' sector) provided three ten-day armoured status reports covering 5–10.7.43, 11–20.7.43 and 21–31.7.43. The 31.7.43 report stated that Panther 211 015 which had been listed as a total loss (3b) in the 20.7.43 ten-day-status report had in fact since been reclassified to 3a and sent to homeland maintenance in Germany. The 31.7.43 ten-day status report also stated that Panther 210 054 which had similarly been listed as a total loss in the 20.7.43 report had (after a change of turret) been reclassified to 2c and sent to AGS's *K-Werk* in Dnepropetrovsk. The 20.7.43 ten-day status report listed no Panthers in either the 2c or 3a categories. The 31.7.43 report states that of the 212 Panthers utilized by Pz Rgt. v.Lauchert during July, 69 became total losses and 15 were sent to homeland maintenance. The Panther, having been rushed into service, suffered numerous mechanical issues during Operation *Citadel* which meant many of the 69 losses stemmed from abandonment. PzAOK 4, O.Qu.V, Pz Rgt. v.Lauchert, Gep. Kfz. Bestandsmeldung, 11.7.43, 20.7.43 and 31.7.43, T313, R390.

36   PzAOK 4, O.Qu.V, LSSAH, DR and SS-T, Fahrgestell-Nr. Pz.kpf.Wg. 1–2.7.43, T313, R390; PzAOK 4, O.Qu.V, LSSAH, DR and SS-T, Gep. Kfz. Bestandsmeldung, 1–2.7.43 and 10.7.43, T313, R390; PzAOK 4, O.Qu.V,

LSSAH, DR and SS-T, Betr.: Totalausfälle an Pz.Kpfwg. und gep. Kfz. 1–
10.7.43 (LSSAH written 12.7.43, DR and SS-T Lageskizzen written 23.7.43)
T313, R390; II SS Panzer Korps, Ingenieur, Betr.: Kinsatz Raum Belgorod.
5–18.7.43, updated to 22.7.43 (written 28.7.43), T354, R607, F000629-
31; AOK 6, 1a, KTB 9, *Zustandsberichte, Wochenmeldung über Panzer und
Sturmgeschülzlage Stand* 1.8.43 (written 6.8.43), T312, R1483, F000441;
III Pz Korps, 1a Anlage z, KTB Band 1 and 2, DR Tagesmeldung, 11.8.43,
T314, R201; II SS Panzer Korps, SS-T Fehlbestäde an Waffen und Grossgerät,
3.8.43, T354, R605, F001001; II SS Panzer Korps, LSSAH Ia, Tagesmeldung
für den 24.7.43, T354, R605, F000867; II SS Panzer Korps, DR and SS-T
Ia 667/43 and 668/43, 28.7.43, T354, R605, F000879-80; GenInsp.d.Pz.
Truppen, Waffen-SS monthly divisional *Meldung* and OB charts, LSSAH,
1.9.43, T78, R719; PzAOK 4, O.Qu.V, LSSAH, Gep. Kfz. Bestandsmeldung,
1.11.43, T313, R391. Full delivery reports for all panzer, assault gun and self-
propelled gun types are available from the Sturmpanzer website.

37 Jentz, Thomas, (ed.) *Panzer Truppen II*, 136.
38 See June/July 1943 delivery reports for 71 LSSAH Panthers on Sturmpanzer
website; Jentz, Thomas, (ed.) *Panzer Truppen II*, 66–68.
39 See August delivery report for 53 LSSAH Pz IVs on Sturmpanzer website.
40 Heiber, Helmut, and Glantz, David, *Hitler and his Generals: Military
Conferences 1942–1945*, Midday Situation Report, 26.7.1943, 225–26, 233–34,
248–49. Meeting of the *Führer* with Field Marshal von Kluge, 26.7.43,
260–61, 263, 265.
41 PzAOK 4, O.Qu.V, LSSAH, Gep. Kfz. Bestandsmeldung, 1.11.43, T313,
R391.
42 GenInsp.d.Pz.Truppen, Waffen-SS monthly divisional *Meldung* and OB
charts, LSSAH, 1.9.43 and 1.10.43, T78, R719.
43 GenInsp.d.Pz.Truppen, Waffen-SS monthly divisional *Meldung* and OB
charts, LSSAH, 1.10.43, T78, R719.
44 Images of these tanks heading to Italy can be found on the following website:
https://www.thirdreichmedals.com/article/WSS.html.
45 GenInsp.d.Pz.Truppen, Waffen-SS monthly divisional *Meldung* and OB
charts, LSSAH, 1.10.43, T78, R719.
46 PzAOK 4, O.Qu.V, LSSAH, Gep. Kfz. Bestandsmeldung, 1.11.43, T313,
R391.
47 Jentz, Thomas, (ed.) *Panzer Truppen II*, 136; GenInsp.d.Pz.Truppen, Waffen-
SS monthly divisional *Meldung* and OB charts, LSSAH, 1.9.43 and 1.10.43,
T78, R719.
48 II SS Panzer Korps, LSSAH, Rgt.Bef.Std., 27.7.43, T354, R607, F000825; II
SS Panzer Korps, DR and SS-T Ia 667/43 and 668/43, 28.7.43, T354, R605.
49 GenInsp.d.Pz.Truppen, Waffen-SS monthly divisional *Meldung* and OB
charts, LSSAH, 1.9.43 and 1.10.43, T78, R719.
50 Images of these tanks heading to Italy can be found on the following website:
https://www.thirdreichmedals.com/article/WSS.html; Heiber, Helmut,

and Glantz, David, *Hitler and his Generals: Military Conferences 1942–1945*, Midday Situation Report, 26.7.1943, 225–26, 233–34, 248–49. Meeting of the *Führer* with Field Marshal von Kluge, 26.7.43, 260–61, 263, 265.

51 PzAOK 4, O.Qu.V, LSSAH, Gep. Kfz. Bestandsmeldung, 1.11.43, T313, R391.

52 Forczyk, Robert, *The Dnepr 1943: Hitler's Eastern Rampart Crumbles* (Oxford: Osprey Publishing 2016), 75–78.

53 PzAOK 4, O.Qu.V, DR, Gep. Kfz. Bestandsmeldung, 31.10.43, T313, R391; PzAOK 4, O.Qu.V, LSSAH and DR, Fahrgestell-Nr. Pz.kpf.Wg. 1.7.43, T313, R390; Zetterling, Niklas, and Frankson, Anders, *Kursk 1943: A Statistical Analysis*, 182.

54 Full delivery reports for all panzer, assault gun and self-propelled gun types are available from the Sturmpanzer website; PzAOK 4, O.Qu.V, DR, Gep. Kfz. Bestandsmeldung, 31.10.43 and 30.11.43, T313, R391; PzAOK 4, O.Qu.V, LSSAH and DR, Fahrgestell-Nr. Pz.kpf.Wg. 1.7.43, T313, R390; PzAOK 4, O.Qu.V, LSSAH and DR, Fahrgestell-Nr. Pz.kpf.Wg. 31.3.43, T313, R387; Schneider, Wolfgang, *Tigers in Combat II*, 416–18; Tigers 250 195 and 250 199 issued to Grossdeutschland in late June 1943 were both command tanks. By June 1943 new standard issue Tiger tank chassis numbers had already reached the 250 250–300 range. It seems highly likely that Tigers 250 195–199 were all command tanks which were held in reserve until such a Tiger was required by a unit. PzAOK 4, O.Qu.V, Grossdeutschland, Anlage zur gep. Kfz. Bestandsmeldung, 31.8.43, T313, R390.

55 GenInsp.d.Pz.Truppen, Waffen-SS monthly divisional *Meldung* and OB charts, LSSAH, 1.9.43, T78, R719; II SS Panzer Korps, Ingenieur, Betr.: Kinsatz Raum Belgorod. 5–18.7.43, updated to 22.7.43 (written 28.7.43), T354, R607, F000629-31; PzAOK 4, O.Qu.V, LSSAH, DR and SS-T, Fahrgestell-Nr. Pz.kpf.Wg. 1–2.7.43, T313, R390.

56 II SS Panzer Korps, LSSAH Ia, Tagesmeldung für den 24.7.43, T354, R605, F000867; see June 1943 delivery report for four LSSAH self-propelled guns on Sturmpanzer website; II SS Panzer Korps, Ingenieur, Betr.: Kinsatz Raum Belgorod. 5–18.7.43, updated to 22.7.43 (written 28.7.43), T354, R607, F000629-31; PzAOK 4, O.Qu.V, LSSAH, Betr.: Totalausfälle an Pz.Kpfwg. und gep. Kfz. 1–10.7.43 (written 12.7.43) T313, R390; PzAOK 4, O.Qu.V, LSSAH, Gep. Kfz. Bestandsmeldung, 10.7.43, T313, R390; PzAOK 4, O.Qu.V, LSSAH, Fahrgestell-Nr. Pz.kpf.Wg. 1.7.43, T313, R390. In relation to the arrival date of four new Sf Paks see Note 7 of Chapter 1 above. It can reasonably be expected that the four new Sf Paks which left Germany on 6.7.43 would have reached the LSSAH troops by 24.7.43.

57 GenInsp.d.Pz.Truppen, Waffen-SS monthly divisional *Meldung* and OB charts, LSSAH, 1.9.43, T78, R719.

58 AOK 6, 1a, KTB 9, *Zustandsberichte, Wochenmeldung über Panzer und Sturmgeschülzlage Stand* 1.8.43 (written 6.8.43), T312, R1483, F000441.

59 AOK 6, 1a, KTB 9, *Zustandsberichte, Wochenmeldung über Panzer und Sturmgeschülzlage Stand* 1.8.43 (written 6.8.43), T312, R1483, F000441; II SS

Panzer Korps, Ingenieur, Betr.: Kinsatz Raum Belgorod. 5–18.7.43, updated to
22.7.43 (written 28.7.43), T354, R607, F000629-31; PzAOK 4, O.Qu.V, DR
and SS-T, Betr.: Totalausfälle an Pz.Kpfwg. und gep. Kfz. 1–10.7.43 (DR and
SS-T Lageskizzen written 23.7.43) T313, R390; PzAOK 4, O.Qu.V, DR Gep.
Kfz. Bestandsmeldung, 1.7.43 and 10.7.43, T313, R390; PzAOK 4, O.Qu.V,
DR, Fahrgestell-Nr. Pz.kpf.Wg. 1.7.43, T313, R390.

60   Ibid.

61   II SS Panzer Korps, Ingenieur, Betr.: Kinsatz Raum Belgorod. 5–18.7.43,
updated to 22.7.43 (written 28.7.43), T354, R607, F000629-31; PzAOK
4, O.Qu.V, DR and SS-T, Betr.: Totalausfälle an Pz.Kpfwg. und gep. Kfz.
1–10.7.43 (DR and SS-T Lageskizzen written 23.7.43) T313, R390; PzAOK
4, O.Qu.V, DR Gep. Kfz. Bestandsmeldung, 1.7.43 and 10.7.43, T313, R390;
PzAOK 4, O.Qu.V, DR, Fahrgestell-Nr. Pz.kpf.Wg. 1.7.43, T313, R390; III
Pz Korps, 1a Anlage z, KTB Band 1 and 2, DR Tagesmeldung, 11.8.43, T314,
R201. Full delivery reports for all panzer, assault gun and self-propelled gun
types are available from the Sturmpanzer website.

62   AOK 6, 1a, KTB 9, *Zustandsberichte, Wochenmeldung über Panzer und
Sturmgeschülzlage Stand* 1.8.43 (written 6.8.43), T312, R1483, F000441; II SS
Panzer Korps, Ingenieur, Betr.: Kinsatz Raum Belgorod. 5–18.7.43, updated to
22.7.43 (written 28.7.43), T354, R607, F000629-31; PzAOK 4, O.Qu.V, DR
and SS-T, Betr.: Totalausfälle an Pz.Kpfwg. und gep. Kfz. 1–10.7.43 (DR and
SS-T Lageskizzen written 23.7.43) T313, R390; PzAOK 4, O.Qu.V, DR Gep.
Kfz. Bestandsmeldung, 1.7.43 and 10.7.43, T313, R390; II SS Panzer Korps,
see T-34 amongst DR vanguard units for Mius counteroffensive, 28.7.43,
T354, R605, F000888-89; Forczyk, Robert, *Panther vs. T-34: Ukraine 1943*
(Oxford: Osprey Publishing 2007), 24–25 and 61–63.

63   Chamberlain, Peter, and Doyle, Hilary, *Encyclopaedia of German Tanks of World
War Two* (London: Arms and Armour 2001), 238–39.

64   AOK 6, 1a, KTB 9, *Zustandsberichte, Wochenmeldung über Panzer und
Sturmgeschülzlage Stand* 1.8.43 (written 6.8.43), T312, R1483, F000441; II SS
Panzer Korps, Ingenieur, Betr.: Kinsatz Raum Belgorod. 5–18.7.43, updated
to 22.7.43 (written 28.7.43), T354, R607, F000629-31; PzAOK 4, O.Qu.V,
DR and SS-T, Betr.: Totalausfälle an Pz.Kpfwg. und gep. Kfz. 1–10.7.43 (DR
and SS-T Lageskizzen written 23.7.43) T313, R390; PzAOK 4, O.Qu.V, SS-T
Gep. Kfz. Bestandsmeldung, 1.7.43 and 10.7.43, T313, R390; PzAOK 4,
O.Qu.V, SS-T, Fahrgestell-Nr. Pz.kpf.Wg. 2.7.43, T313, R390.

65   Ibid.

66   Ibid.

67   AOK 6, 1a, KTB 9, *Zustandsberichte, Wochenmeldung über Panzer und
Sturmgeschülzlage Stand* 1.8.43 (written 6.8.43), T312, R1483, F000441.

68   II SS Panzer Korps, Meldung über Verluste, durchgegeben am 30.7, 2330 Uhr,
Fernmündl. An o 1 AOK.6, T354, R605, F000940.

69   AOK 6, 1a, KTB 9, *Zustandsberichte, Wochenmeldung über Panzer und
Sturmgeschülzlage Stand* 1.8.43 (written 6.8.43), T312, R1483, F000441; II

SS Panzer Korps, Meldung über Verluste, durchgegeben am 30.7, 23,30 Uhr, Fernmündl. An 0 1 AOK 6, T354, R605, F000940; II SS Panzer Korps, War diary entries for 18.7–2.8.43, T354, R605, F000104-41; II SS Panzer Korps, Bereitstellung des II SS Panzer Korps am 29.7.3 und Verlauf des 30.7.43, T354, R606, F000050-51; II SS Panzer Korps, Verlauf des 31.7.43, T354, R606, F000052-53; II SS Panzer Korps, Verlauf des 1.8.43, T354, R606, F000055-56; II SS Panzer Korps, Verlauf des 2.8.43, T354, R606, F000059.

70   AOK 6, 1a, KTB 9, *Zustandsberichte, Wochenmeldung über Panzer und Sturmgeschülzlage Stand* 1.8.43 (written 6.8.43), T312, R1483, F000441; II SS Panzer Korps, Ingenieur, Betr.: Kinsatz Raum Belgorod. 5–18.7.43, updated to 22.7.43 (written 28.7.43), T354, R607, F000629-31.

71   II SS Panzer Korps, War diary entries for 17.7–2.8.43, T354, R605, F000100-41; XXXXVIII.Pz-AK, XXXXVIII.Pz-AK daily reports relating to Totenkopf 18–20.7.43, T314, R1171, F000388-482; II SS Panzer Korps, Map of Korps actions, new and proposed front lines 14–18.7.43, T354, R606, F000035; II SS Panzer Korps, Ablauf der Marschbewegungen II SS Panzer Korps, 18–22.7.43, T354, R606, F000038; II SS Panzer Korps, Gliederung des II SS Panzer Korps am 22 und 23.7.43 bis zur Bereitstellung und Lage bei XXXX.A.K., T354, R606, F000039; II SS Panzer Korps, Bereitstellungs u. Angriffsplan für den Angriff am 24.7.43, T354, R606, F000040; II SS Panzer Korps, Ablauf der Marschbewegungen II SS Panzer Korps, 24–29.7.43, T354, R606, F000043; II SS Panzer Korps, Bereitstellung des II SS Panzer Korps am 29.7.43 und Verlauf des 30.7.43, T354, R606, F000050-51; AOK 6, 1a, KTB 9, *Zustandsberichte,* Wochenmeldung über Panzer und Sturmgeschülzlage Stand 1.8.43 (written 6.8.43), T312, R1483, F000441; II SS Panzer Korps, Ingenieur, Betr.: Kinsatz Raum Belgorod. 5–18.7.43, updated to 22.7.43 (written 28.7.43), T354, R607, F000629-31.

72   Ibid.

73   Frieser, Karl-Heinz, *The Swing of the Pendulum: The Withdrawal of the Eastern Front from Summer 1943 to Summer 1944* in The Research Institute for Military History, Potsdam, Germany, *Germany and the Second World War Volume VIII – The Eastern Front 1943–1944*, 339–41; II SS Panzer Korps, Bereitstellungs u. Angriffsplan für den Angriff am 24.7.43, T354, R606, F000040; II SS Panzer Korps, Ablauf der Marschbewegungen II SS Panzer Korps, 24–29.7.43, T354, R606, F000043.

74   II SS Panzer Korps, Ingenieur, Betr.: Kinsatz Raum Belgorod. 5–18.7.43, updated to 22.7.43 (written 28.7.43), T354, R607, F000629-31; AOK 6, 1a, KTB 9, *Zustandsberichte, Wochenmeldung über Panzer und Sturmgeschülzlage Stand* 1.8.43 (written 6.8.43), T312, R1483, F00044. For examples of AFV reclassifications see sections: 'The southern pincer of Operation *Citadel*' and 'Tiger tank losses at Prokhorovka: Myth versus reality'; see also Appendix E.

75   II SS Panzer Korps, Ingenieur, Betr.: Kinsatz Raum Belgorod. 5–18.7.43, updated to 22.7.43 (written 28.7.43), T354, R607, F000629-31; AOK 6, 1a,

KTB 9, *Zustandsberichte, Wochenmeldung über Panzer und Sturmgeschülzlage Stand* 1.8.43 (written 6.8.43), T312, R1483, F00044; PzAOK 4, O.Qu.V, LSSAH, DR and SS-T, Betr.: Totalausfälle an Pz.Kpfwg. und gep. Kfz. 1–10.7.43 (LSSAH written 12.7.43, DR and SS-T Lageskizzen written 23.7.43) T313, R390; PzAOK 4, O.Qu.V, LSSAH, DR and SS-T, Gep. Kfz. Bestandsmeldung, 10.7.43, T313, R390; PzAOK 4, O.Qu.V, LSSAH, DR and SS-T, Fahrgestell-Nr. Pz.kpf.Wg. 1–2.7.43, T313, R390; Bundesarchiv/ Militärarchiv, RH 10/64, General Inspector of Panzer Troops – AGS, 5–10.7.43 *Totalverluste;* see also 5–13.7.43, 5–14.7.43, 5–15.7.43, 5–16.7.43, 5–17.7.43 editions and Appendix L.

76   Ibid.

77   Ibid.

78   II SS Panzer Korps, War diary entries for 17–19.7.43, T354, R605, F000100-110; XXXXVIII.Pz-AK, XXXXVIII.Pz-AK daily reports relating to Totenkopf 18–20.7.43, T314, R1171, F000388-482.

79   Bundesarchiv/Militärarchiv, RH 10/64, General Inspector of Panzer Troops – AGS, 5–10.7.43 *Totalverluste,* see 5–13.7.43, 5–14.7.43, 5–15.7.43, 5–16.7.43 and 5–17.7.43 editions. See also Appendix L.

80   Friedli, Lukas, *Repairing the Panzers: German Tank Maintenance in World War 2, Vol 2*, 235.

81   See section: 'Tiger tank losses at Prokhorovka: Myth versus reality'.

82   AOK 6, 1a, KTB 9, *Zustandsberichte,* Wochenmeldung über Panzer und Sturmgeschülzlage Stand 1.8.43 (written 6.8.43), T312, R1483, F000441; III Pz Korps, 1a Anlage z, KTB Band 1 and 2, DR Tagesmeldung, 11.8.43, T314, R201; II SS Panzer Korps, SS-T Fehlbestäde an Waffen und Grossgerät, 3.8.43, T354, R605, F001001; II SS Panzer Korps, Ingenieur, Betr.: Kinsatz Raum Belgorod. 5–18.7.43, updated to 22.7.43 (written 28.7.43), T354, R607, F000629-31; PzAOK 4, O.Qu.V, SS-T, Gep. Kfz. Bestandsmeldung, 1–2.7.43 and 10.7.43, T313, R390; GenInsp.d.Pz.Truppen, Waffen-SS monthly divisional *Meldung* and OB charts, SS-T, 1.8.43, T78, R719; PzAOK 4, O.Qu.V, DR and SS-T, Betr.: Totalausfälle an Pz.Kpfwg. und gep. Kfz. 1–10.7.43, DR and SS-T Lageskizzen written 23.7.43, T313, R390; PzAOK 4, O.Qu.V, SS-T, Fahrgestell-Nr. Pz.kpf.Wg. 1–2.7.43, T313, R390.

83   AOK 6, 1a, KTB 9, *Zustandsberichte, Wochenmeldung über Panzer und Sturmgeschülzlage Stand* 1.8.43 (written 6.8.43), T312, R1483, F000441; Zetterling, Niklas, and Frankson, Anders, *Kursk 1943: A Statistical Analysis,* 218–19; II SS Panzer Korps, daily report for SS-T, 28.7.43, T354, R605, F000886; II SS Panzer Korps, daily report, 1.8.43, T354, R605, F000970-71.

84   PzAOK 4, O.Qu.V, LSSAH, DR and SS-T, Fahrgestell-Nr. Pz.kpf.Wg. 1–2.7.43, T313, R390; PzAOK 4, O.Qu.V, LSSAH, DR and SS-T, Gep. Kfz. Bestandsmeldung, 1–2.7.43 and 10.7.43, T313, R390; PzAOK 4, O.Qu.V, LSSAH, DR and SS-T, Betr.: Totalausfälle an Pz.Kpfwg. und gep. Kfz. 1–10.7.43 (LSSAH written 12.7.43, DR and SS-T Lageskizzen written 23.7.43) T313, R390; II SS Panzer Korps, Ingenieur, Betr.: Kinsatz Raum

Belgorod. 5–18.7.43, updated to 22.7.43 (written 28.7.43), T354, R607, Fooo629-31; AOK 6, 1a, KTB 9, *Zustandsberichte, Wochenmeldung über Panzer und Sturmgeschülzlage Stand* 1.8.43 (written 6.8.43), T312, R1483, Fooo441; III Pz Korps, 1a Anlage z, KTB Band 1 and 2, DR Tagesmeldung, 11.8.43, T314, R201; II SS Panzer Korps, SS-T Fehlbestäde an Waffen und Grossgerät, 3.8.43, T354, R605, Foo1001; II SS Panzer Korps, LSSAH Ia, Tagesmeldung für den 24.7.43, T354, R605, Fooo867; II SS Panzer Korps, DR and SS-T Ia 667/43 and 668/43, 28.7.43, T354, R605, Fooo879-80; GenInsp.d.Pz.Truppen, Waffen-SS monthly divisional *Meldung* and OB charts, LSSAH, 1.9.43, T78, R719; PzAOK 4, O.Qu.V, LSSAH, Gep. Kfz. Bestandsmeldung, 1.11.43, T313, R391. Full delivery reports for all panzer, assault gun and self-propelled gun types are available from the Sturmpanzer website.

85   PzAOK 4, O.Qu.V, LSSAH, DR and SS-T, Fahrgestell-Nr. Pz.kpf. Wg. 1–2.7.43, T313, R390; PzAOK 4, O.Qu.V, LSSAH, DR and SS-T, Gep. Kfz. Bestandsmeldung, 1–2.7.43 and 10.7.43, T313, R390; PzAOK 4, O.Qu.V, LSSAH, DR and SS-T, Betr.: Totalausfälle an Pz.Kpfwg. und gep. Kfz. 1–10.7.43 (LSSAH written 12.7.43, DR and SS-T Lageskizzen written 23.7.43) T313, R390; II SS Panzer Korps, Ingenieur, Betr.: Kinsatz Raum Belgorod. 5–18.7.43, updated to 22.7.43 (written 28.7.43), T354, R607, Fooo629-31; AOK 6, 1a, KTB 9, *Zustandsberichte, Wochenmeldung über Panzer und Sturmgeschülzlage Stand* 1.8.43 (written 6.8.43), T312, R1483, Fooo441; III Pz Korps, 1a Anlage z, KTB Band 1 and 2, DR Tagesmeldung, 11.8.43, T314, R201; II SS Panzer Korps, SS-T Fehlbestäde an Waffen und Grossgerät, 3.8.43, T354, R605, Foo1001; II SS Panzer Korps, LSSAH Ia, Tagesmeldung für den 24.7.43, T354, R605, Fooo867; II SS Panzer Korps, DR and SS-T Ia 667/43 and 668/43, 28.7.43, T354, R605, Fooo879-80; GenInsp.d.Pz.Truppen, Waffen-SS monthly divisional *Meldung* and OB charts, LSSAH, 1.9.43, T78, R719; PzAOK 4, O.Qu.V, LSSAH, Gep. Kfz. Bestandsmeldung, 1.11.43, T313, R391. Full delivery reports for all panzer, assault gun and self-propelled gun types are available from the Sturmpanzer website.

86   Frieser, Karl-Heinz, *The Battle of the Kursk Salient* in The Research Institute for Military History, Potsdam, Germany, *Germany and the Second World War Volume VIII – The Eastern Front 1943–1944*, 129, 127n, 136n; Bundesarchiv/Militärarchiv, RH 10/64, General Inspector of Panzer Troops – AGS, 5–10.7.43 *Totalverluste*, see 5–13.7.43, 5–14.7.43, 5–15.7.43, 5–16.7.43 and 5–17.7.43 editions; see also Appendix L; PzAOK 4, O.Qu.V, LSSAH, DR and SS-T, Fahrgestell-Nr. Pz.kpf.Wg. 1–2.7.43, T313, R390; PzAOK 4, O.Qu.V, LSSAH, DR and SS-T, Gep. Kfz. Bestandsmeldung, 1–2.7.43 and 10.7.43, T313, R390; PzAOK 4, O.Qu.V, LSSAH, DR and SS-T, Betr.: Totalausfälle an Pz.Kpfwg. und gep. Kfz. 1–10.7.43 (LSSAH written 12.7.43, DR and SS-T Lageskizzen

written 23.7.43) T313, R390; II SS Panzer Korps, Ingenieur, Betr.: Kinsatz
Raum Belgorod. 5–18.7.43, updated to 22.7.43 (written 28.7.43), T354,
R607, Fo00629-31; AOK 6, 1a, KTB 9, *Zustandsberichte, Wochenmeldung
über Panzer und Sturmgeschülzlage Stand* 1.8.43 (written 6.8.43), T312,
R1483, Fo00441; III Pz Korps, 1a Anlage z, KTB Band 1 and 2, DR
Tagesmeldung, 11.8.43, T314, R201; II SS Panzer Korps, SS-T Fehlbestäde
an Waffen und Grossgerät, 3.8.43, T354, R605, Fo01001; II SS Panzer
Korps, LSSAH Ia, Tagesmeldung für den 24.7.43, T354, R605, Fo00867;
II SS Panzer Korps, DR and SS-T Ia 667/43 and 668/43, 28.7.43, T354,
R605, Fo00879-80; GenInsp.d.Pz.Truppen, Waffen-SS monthly divisional
Meldung and OB charts, LSSAH, 1.9.43, T78, R719; PzAOK 4, O.Qu.V,
LSSAH, Gep. Kfz. Bestandsmeldung, 1.11.43, T313, R391; II SS Panzer
Korps, Map of Korps actions, new and proposed front lines 14–18.7.43,
T354, R606, Fo00035; II SS Panzer Korps, Correspondence from II SS
Panzer Korps 1a to Hitler's SS adjutant Fritz Darges at FHQ, Status of II
SS Panzer Korps at midday 21.7.43 (sent 23.7.43), T354, R605, Fo00853;
NARA Series RG 373: German Flown Aerial Photography, 1939–1945.
See specifically photographs relating to the battlefield of Prokhorovka:
for 14.7.43 see GX-2696-SK-23, GX-2696-SK-24 and GX-2696-SK-52.
For 16.7.43 see GX-3734-SK-61 (incorrectly dated as 15.7.43 by NARA).
For 7.8.43 see GX-3942-SK-69, GX-3942-SD-122, GX-3942-SD-123
and GX-3942-SD-124. For 15.8.43 see GX-3958-SD-10 and GX-3958-
SD-11. For 7.9.43 see GX-4255-SD-16. For 6.10.43 see GX-3977-SD-45
and GX-3977-SD-48. Full delivery reports for all panzer, assault gun and
self-propelled gun types are available from the Sturmpanzer website; Lukas
Friedli, *Repairing the Panzers: German Tank Maintenance in World War 2*,
180; Zetterling, Niklas, and Frankson, Anders, *Kursk 1943: A Statistical
Analysis*, 124–25, 207; Frieser, Karl-Heinz, *The Battle of the Kursk Salient* in
The Research Institute for Military History, Potsdam, Germany, *Germany
and the Second World War Volume VIII – The Eastern Front 1943–1944*, 182;
Zamulin, Valeriy, *The Battle of Kursk 1943: The View through the Camera Lens*
(Solihull: Helion 2015). Two remarkable post-battle pictures (177 and 178)
taken by a low-flying aircraft over the Prokhorovka battlefield can be found
in this book.

87 Ibid.

88 Ibid.; see also the concerns raised in Note 4 of the Bibliography.

89 II SS Panzer Korps, Correspondence from II SS Panzer Korps 1a to Hitler's SS
adjutant Fritz Darges at FHQ, Status of II SS Panzer Korps at midday 21.7.43
(sent 23.7.43), T354, R605, Fo00853; II SS Panzer Korps, Ingenieur, Betr.:
Kinsatz Raum Belgorod. 5–18.7.43, updated to 22.7.43 (written 28.7.43),
T354, R607, Fo00629-31.

90 Frieser, Karl-Heinz, *The Battle of the Kursk Salient* in The Research Institute
for Military History, Potsdam, Germany, *Germany and the Second World War
Volume VIII – The Eastern Front 1943–1944*, 182.

91 Zetterling, Niklas, and Frankson, Anders, *Kursk 1943: A Statistical Analysis*, 124–25.

92 Ibid.

93 Ibid. On 12.7.43 SS-T lost 69 men KIA, 231 WIA, 16 MIA. II SS Panzer Korps HQ saw four men WIA that day. In total II SS Panzer Korps suffered 842 casualties on 12.7.43.

94 PzAOK 4, O.Qu.V, LSSAH, DR and SS-T, Fahrgestell-Nr. Pz.kpf.Wg. 1–2.7.43, T313, R390; PzAOK 4, O.Qu.V, LSSAH, DR and SS-T, Gep. Kfz. Bestandsmeldung, 1–2.7.43 and 10.7.43, T313, R390; PzAOK 4, O.Qu.V, LSSAH, DR and SS-T, Betr.: Totalausfälle an Pz.Kpfwg. und gep. Kfz. 1–10.7.43 (LSSAH written 12.7.43, DR and SS-T Lageskizzen written 23.7.43) T313, R390; II SS Panzer Korps, Ingenieur, Betr.: Kinsatz Raum Belgorod. 5–18.7.43, updated to 22.7.43 (written 28.7.43), T354, R607, F000629-31; AOK 6, 1a, KTB 9, *Zustandsberichte, Wochenmeldung über Panzer und Sturmgeschülzlage Stand* 1.8.43 (written 6.8.43), T312, R1483, F000441; III Pz Korps, 1a Anlage z, KTB Band 1 and 2, DR Tagesmeldung, 11.8.43, T314, R201; II SS Panzer Korps, SS-T Fehlbestäde an Waffen und Grossgerät, 3.8.43, T354, R605, F001001; II SS Panzer Korps, LSSAH Ia, Tagesmeldung für den 24.7.43, T354, R605, F000867; II SS Panzer Korps, DR and SS-T Ia 667/43 and 668/43, 28.7.43, T354, R605, F000879-80; GenInsp.d.Pz.Truppen, Waffen-SS monthly divisional *Meldung* and OB charts, LSSAH, 1.9.43, T78, R719; PzAOK 4, O.Qu.V, LSSAH, Gep. Kfz. Bestandsmeldung, 1.11.43, T313, R391. Full delivery reports for all panzer, assault gun and self-propelled gun types are available from the Sturmpanzer website.

95 Zamulin, Valeriy, 'Soviet Troop Losses in the Battle of Prokhorovka, 10–16 July 1943', *Journal of Slavic Military Studies,* 32:1 (2019), 118–20.

96 Ibid.

97 II SS Panzer Korps, LSSAH Ia, Tagesmeldung for 13.7.43, T354, R605, F000698.

98 Zamulin, Valeriy, 'Soviet Troop Losses in the Battle of Prokhorovka, 10–16 July 1943', *Journal of Slavic Military Studies,* 32:1 (2019), 118–19.

99 Zamulin, Valeriy, *Demolishing the Myth: The Tank Battle at Prokhorovka, Kursk, July 1943: An Operational Narrative,* for 5th Guards Tank Army inventory on 11.7.43 see Table 18. Note the author has not included the 29th Tank Corps 1529 SU Regiment (which was equipped with the new powerful SU-152) as it was not present at the front or tanks under repair at corps level. Regarding the latter the data Zamulin supplies suggests all damaged tanks were already more accurately recorded at brigade level; Zamulin, Valeriy, 'Soviet Troop Losses in the Battle of Prokhorovka, 10–16 July 1943', *Journal of Slavic Military Studies,* 32:1 (2019), for 5th Guards Tank Army 17.7.43 inventory see 118–19.

100 Zamulin, Valeriy, *Demolishing the Myth: The Tank Battle at Prokhorovka, Kursk, July 1943: An Operational Narrative,* for 5th Guards Tank Army

inventory on 11.7.43 see Table 18. Note the author has not included the 29th Tank Corps 1529 SU Regiment (which was equipped with the new powerful SU-152) as it was not present at the front or tanks under repair at corps level. Regarding the latter the data Zamulin supplies suggests all damaged tanks were already more accurately recorded at brigade level.

101 Zamulin, Valeriy, 'Soviet Troop Losses in the Battle of Prokhorovka, 10–16 July 1943', *Journal of Slavic Military Studies,* 32:1 (2019), for 5th Guards Tank Army 17.7.43 inventory see 118–19.

102 Zamulin, Valeriy, *Demolishing the Myth: The Tank Battle at Prokhorovka, Kursk, July 1943: An Operational Narrative,* for 5th Guards Tank Army inventory on 11.7.43 see Table 18. Note the author has not included the 29th Tank Corps 1529 SU Regiment (which was equipped with the new powerful SU-152) as it was not present at the front or tanks under repair at corps level. Regarding the latter the data Zamulin supplies suggests all damaged tanks were already more accurately recorded at brigade level; Zamulin, Valeriy, 'Soviet Troop Losses in the Battle of Prokhorovka, 10–16 July 1943', *Journal of Slavic Military Studies,* 32:1 (2019), for 5th Guards Tank Army 17.7.43 inventory see 118–19.

103 Ibid.

104 Ibid.

105 Ibid.

106 Ibid. See also Table 18.

107 Zamulin, Valeriy, 'Soviet Troop Losses in the Battle of Prokhorovka, 10–16 July 1943', *Journal of Slavic Military Studies,* 32:1 (2019), 118–19.

108 Ibid.

109 Frieser, Karl-Heinz, *The Battle of the Kursk Salient* in The Research Institute for Military History, Potsdam, Germany, *Germany and the Second World War Volume VIII – The Eastern Front 1943–1944,* 132.

110 Zamulin, Valeriy, 'Soviet Troop Losses in the Battle of Prokhorovka, 10–16 July 1943', *Journal of Slavic Military Studies,* 32:1 (2019), 118–19.

CHAPTER 4

1 Zamulin, Valeriy, *Demolishing the Myth: The Tank Battle at Prokhorovka, Kursk, July 1943: An Operational Narrative;* for 5th Guards Tank Army inventory on 11.7.43 see Table 18. Note the author has not included the 29th Tank Corps 1529 SU Regiment (which was equipped with the new powerful SU-152) as it was not present at the front or tanks under repair at corps level. Regarding the latter the data Zamulin supplies suggests all damaged tanks were already more accurately recorded at brigade level.

2 AOK 4, O.Qu.V, LSSAH, DR and SS-T, Fahrgestell-Nr. Pz.kpf.Wg. 1–2.7.43, T313, R390; PzAOK 4, O.Qu.V, LSSAH, DR and SS-T, Gep. Kfz. Bestandsmeldung, 1–2.7.43 and 10.7.43, T313, R390; PzAOK 4, O.Qu.V, LSSAH, DR and SS-T, Betr.: Totalausfälle an Pz.Kpfwg. und gep. Kfz. 1–10.7.43 (LSSAH written 12.7.43, DR and SS-T Lageskizzen written 23.7.43)

T313, R390. Full delivery reports for all panzer, assault gun and self-propelled gun types are available from the Sturmpanzer website.

3   The XXXXVIII Panzer Korps and II SS Panzer Korps were to be attacked from four directions: from the west by 1st Tank Army, including 5th Guards Tank Corps and the newly arrived 10th Tank Corps, reinforced by infantry and artillery units; from the north-west by units of 6th Guards Army; from the north-east by 5th Guards Army, newly brought in from Steppe Front; from the east by 5th Guards Tank Army, also brought in from Steppe Front, reinforced by 2nd Tank Corps and 2nd Guards Tank Corps, plus a number of attached units. Further to the south-east 7th Guards Army had the task of breaking through the front on III Panzer Korps' right flank and advancing its rear towards Razumnoye (in the direction of Belgorod). Frieser, Karl-Heinz, *The Battle of the Kursk Salient* in The Research Institute for Military History, Potsdam, Germany, *Germany and the Second World War Volume VIII – The Eastern Front 1943– 1944*, 119–20; PzAOK 4, O.Qu.V, LSSAH, DR and SS-T, Fahrgestell-Nr. Pz.kpf.Wg. 1–2.7.43, T313, R390; PzAOK 4, O.Qu.V, LSSAH, DR and SS-T, Gep. Kfz. Bestandsmeldung, 1–2.7.43 and 10.7.43, T313, R390. Full delivery reports for all panzer, assault gun and self-propelled gun types are available from the Sturmpanzer website.

4   Frieser, Karl-Heinz, *The Battle of the Kursk Salient* in The Research Institute for Military History, Potsdam, Germany, *Germany and the Second World War Volume VIII – The Eastern Front 1943–1944* (Oxford: Clarendon Press 2017), 121–22; for LSSAH Sf Pak see LSSAH, Gep. Kfz. Bestandsmeldung, 10.7.43, T313, R390. As early as 29.6.43 the LSSAH daily 1a AFV reports seem to contradict the more detailed LSSAH 1.7.43 inventory and 1.7.43 and 10.7.43 ten-day AFV status reports by recording operational numbers above the 21 Sf Pak 75mm in the division's inventory, seemingly indicating the presence of four new Sf Pak. However, it is likely the LSSAH daily 1a AFV reports are including Sf Pak which, although already issued to LSSAH (on 10.6.43), had not yet reached the troops on the front line – or even left Germany (they departed 6.7.43)! Neither the 1.7.43 nor 10.7.43 ten-day status reports record any new Sf Pak arriving at the front (the latter does include the arrival of 16 new Pz IV), instead an inventory of 21 and 19 Sf Pak is respectively recorded. The discrepancy between the daily AFV reports of operational Sf Pak and their equivalent in the ten-day status reports is due to the fact that the SS divisional 1a compiled the daily AFV reports, whereas the SS divisional engineers (who were best placed to know the true totals) complied the ten-day status reports. This is yet another reason why the author favours ten-day status reports for accuracy; the daily reports' accuracy is questionable and should be used with caution. See Friedli, Lukas, *Repairing the Panzers: German Tank Maintenance in World War 2, Vol 2*, 160; PzAOK 4, O.Qu.V, LSSAH, Fahrgestell-Nr. Pz.kpf.Wg. 1.7.43, T313, R390; PzAOK 4, O.Qu.V, LSSAH Gep. Kfz. Bestandsmeldung, 1.7.43 and 10.7.43, T313, R390 and II SS Panzer Korps,

LSSAH daily AFV reports 29.6–10.7.43, T354, R605, F000401-636; for
SS-T Sf Pak see SS-T, Gep. Kfz. Bestandsmeldung, 10.7.43, T313, R390;
Bearing in mind the LSSAH and SS-T Sf Pak issue see LSSAH, DR and SS-T
daily AFV report for 11.7.43, T354, R605, F000653-54; see also Töppel,
Roman, 'Kursk – Mythen und Wirklichkeit einer Schlacht', in *Vierteljahrshefte
für Zeitgeschichte*, 57 (2009), 375. Töppel believes at least 20 LSSAH StuG
were operational on the morning of 12.7.43; however, this figure is based on
Töppel's post-war correspondence with veterans and this information therefore
also needs to be treated with caution.

5   LSSAH, DR and SS-T daily AFV report for 11.7.43, T354, R605, F000653-54.
6   Zamulin, Valeriy, *Demolishing the Myth: The Tank Battle at Prokhorovka, Kursk,
    July 1943: An Operational Narrative*, see Table 18. Note the author has not
    included the 29th Tank Corps 1529 SU Regiment (which was equipped with
    the new powerful SU-152) as it was not present at the front; LSSAH, DR and
    SS-T daily AFV report for 11.7.43, T354, R605, F000653-54; see Note 7 of
    Chapter 1 for details of true Sf Pak numbers.
7   Ibid.
8   Zamulin, Valeriy, *Demolishing the Myth: The Tank Battle at Prokhorovka, Kursk,
    July 1943: An Operational Narrative*, see Table 18. Note the author has not
    included the 29th Tank Corps 1529 SU Regiment (which was equipped with
    the new powerful SU-152) as it was not present at the front.
9   Frieser, Karl-Heinz, *The Battle of the Kursk Salient* in The Research Institute
    for Military History, Potsdam, Germany, *Germany and the Second World War
    Volume VIII – The Eastern Front 1943–1944* (Oxford: Clarendon Press 2017),
    123–24; NARA, RG 242, Photographs taken by Waffen-SS Photographer
    Johan King; Zamulin, Valeriy, *Demolishing the Myth: The Tank Battle at
    Prokhorovka, Kursk, July 1943: An Operational Narrative*; regarding the lack
    of artillery barrage see E-book locations 7313 and 7326. For timings of the
    German attack on the Prokhorovka area on 11.7.43 and the start of the Soviet
    attack on the morning of 12.7.43 see II SS Panzer Korps, LSSAH daily reports
    11–12.7.43, T354, R605, F000648 and F000671-72; RG 242, Photographs
    taken by Waffen-SS Photographer Johan King.
10 Ibid.
11 Glantz, David, and House, Jonathan, *The Battle of Kursk*, 182–85; see also
    Frieser, Karl-Heinz, *The Battle of the Kursk Salient* in The Research Institute
    for Military History, Potsdam, Germany, *Germany and the Second World
    War Volume VIII – The Eastern Front 1943–1944*, 124; Månsson, Martin,
    Prokhorovka – Verdens største panserslag in Ostfronten (2017); Restayn, Jean,
    Operation Citadel, Volume 1: The South, 60–69.
12 Frieser, Karl-Heinz, *The Battle of the Kursk Salient* in The Research Institute
    for Military History, Potsdam, Germany, *Germany and the Second World
    War Volume VIII – The Eastern Front 1943–1944*, 125–26; Zamulin, Valeriy,
    *Demolishing the Myth: The Tank Battle at Prokhorovka, Kursk, July 1943: An
    Operational Narrative*, for 5th Guards Tank Army inventory on 11.7.43 see

Table 18. Note the author has not included the 29th Tank Corps 1529 SU Regiment (which was equipped with the new powerful SU-152) as it was not present at the front or tanks under repair at corps level. Regarding the latter the data Zamulin supplies suggests all damaged tanks were already more accurately recorded at brigade level; Månsson, Martin, *Prokhorovka – Verdens største panserslag in Ostfronten* (2017); Restayn, Jean, *Operation Citadel, Volume 1: The South*, 60–69; RG 242, Photographs taken by Waffen-SS Photographer Johan King.

13   Ibid.

14   Ibid.

15   NARA RG 373: German Flown Aerial Photography, 1939–1945.

16   NARA RG 373: German Flown Aerial Photography, 1939–1945.

17   Frieser, Karl-Heinz, *The Battle of the Kursk Salient* in The Research Institute for Military History, Potsdam, Germany, *Germany and the Second World War Volume VIII – The Eastern Front 1943–1944*, 129n. Ribbentrop and Walter Schüle (Ribbentrop's driver) offer slightly conflicting testimony of the fate of the four disabled panzers, the interpretation of which is open to question. See Månsson, Martin, *Prokhorovka – Verdens største panserslag in Ostfronten* (2017); Restayn, Jean, *Operation Citadel, Volume 1: The South*, 60–69.

18   Ibid.

19   NARA RG 373: German Flown Aerial Photography, 1939 – 1945. Compare 16.7.43 GX-3734-SK-61 (incorrectly dated as 15.7.43 by NARA) with the following: 7.8.43 GX-3942-SK-69, GX-3942-SD-123, GX-3942-SD-124, 15.8.43 GX-3958-SD-10 and 6.10.43 GX-3977-SD-45.

20   Frieser, Karl-Heinz, *The Battle of the Kursk Salient* in The Research Institute for Military History, Potsdam, Germany, *Germany and the Second World War Volume VIII – The Eastern Front 1943–1944*, 124. See Månsson, Martin, *Prokhorovka – Verdens største panserslag in Ostfronten* (2017); Restayn, Jean, *Operation Citadel, Volume 1: The South*, 60–69.

21   See section 'Reappraising Prokhorovka' above.

22   NARA RG 373: German Flown Aerial Photography, 1939–1945. Compare 16.7.43 GX-3734-SK-61 (incorrectly dated as 15.7.43 by NARA) with 7.8.43 GX-3942-SK-69, GX-3942-SD-123, GX-3942-SD-124; 15.8.43 GX-3958-SD-10 and 6.10.43 GX-3977-SD-45.

23   Zamulin, Valeriy, *The Battle of Kursk 1943: The View through the Camera Lens*. Two remarkable post-battle pictures (177 and 178) taken by a low-flying Soviet aircraft over the Prokhorovka battlefield can be found in this book. Zamulin kindly provided the author with these images and the permission to use them.

24   NARA RG 373: German Flown Aerial Photography, 1939–1945. Compare 16.7.43 GX-3734-SK-61 (incorrectly dated as 15.7.43 by NARA) with 7.8.43 GX-3942-SK-69, GX-3942-SD-123, GX-3942-SD-124; 15.8.43 GX-3958-SD-10, 6.10.43 GX-3977-SD-45 and photographs 177 and 178 in Zamulin,

Valeriy, *The Battle of Kursk 1943: The View through the Camera Lens*; see also
Walter Schüle's testimony in Månsson, Martin, *Prokhorovka – Verdens største
panserslag in Ostfronten* (2017) and Restayn, Jean, *Operation Citadel, Volume 1:
The South*, 60–69.

25 Ibid.

26 NARA RG 373: German Flown Aerial Photography, 1939–1945. Compare
16.7.43 GX-3734-SK-61 (incorrectly dated as 15.7.43 by NARA) with 7.8.43
GX-3942-SD-124.

27 Ibid.

28 NARA RG 373: German Flown Aerial Photography, 1939–1945. Compare
7.8.43 GX-3942-SD-122 with 15.8.43 GX-3958-SD-11, 7.9.43 GX-4255-
SD-16 and 6.10.43 GX-3977-SD-48; see also 6.10.43 GX-3977-SD-45; note
the lack of AFV movement in 5.11.43 GX-4517-SK-65; Glantz, David, *From
the Don to the Dnepr* (London: Frank Cass 1991), 289.

29 In 1995 Richard Overy stated 'Over three hundred German tanks
were destroyed on the 12th alone'; Overy, Richard, *Why the Allies Won*
(Pimlico: London 1995), 95–96. For an excellent summary of the evolving
historiography of the battle of Kursk see Lak, Martijn, 'The Death Ride of the
Panzers? Recent Historiography on the Battle of Kursk', *Journal of Military
History*, 82:3 (2018), 909–19. See also Frieser, Karl-Heinz, *The Battle of
the Kursk Salient* in The Research Institute for Military History, Potsdam,
Germany, *Germany and the Second World War Volume VIII – The Eastern Front
1943–1944*, 132.

30 NARA RG 373: German Flown Aerial Photography, 1939–1945. For Pz IV on
Hill 252.2 compare 16.7.43 GX-3734-SK-61 (incorrectly dated as 15.7.43 by
NARA) with 7.8.43 GX-3942-SK-69, GX-3942-SD-123, GX-3942-SD-124;
15.8.43 GX-3958-SD-10; 6.10.43 GX-3977-SD-45; for site of destroyed/
damaged Soviet AFV compare 7.8.43 GX-3942-SD-122 with 15.8.43 GX-
3958-SD-11; 7.9.43 GX-4255-SD-16 and 6.10.43 GX-3977-SD-48; note
the lack of AFV movement in 5.11.43 GX-4517-SK-65; Zamulin, Valeriy,
The Battle of Kursk 1943: The View through the Camera Lens. Two remarkable
post-battle pictures (177 and 178) taken by a low-flying aircraft over the
Prokhorovka battlefield can be found in this book.

31 Frieser, Karl-Heinz, *The Battle of the Kursk Salient* in The Research Institute
for Military History, Potsdam, Germany, *Germany and the Second World War
Volume VIII – The Eastern Front 1943–1944*, 126.

32 Frieser, Karl-Heinz, *The Battle of the Kursk Salient* in The Research Institute
for Military History, Potsdam, Germany, *Germany and the Second World
War Volume VIII – The Eastern Front 1943–1944*, 126–27 and 127n. See also
Zamulin, Valeriy, 'Soviet Troop Losses in the Battle of Prokhorovka, 10–16
July 1943', *Journal of Slavic Military Studies*, 32:1 (2019), 118–19.

33 NARA Series RG 373: German Flown Aerial Photography, 1939–1945. See
specifically photographs relating to the battlefield of Prokhorovka: for 14.7.43
see GX-2696-SK-23, GX-2696-SK-24 and GX-2696-SK-52. For 16.7.43 see

GX-3734-SK-61 (incorrectly dated as 15.7.43 by NARA). For 7.8.43 see GX-3942-SK-69; see map in Schneider, Wolfgang, *Das Reich Tigers* (Winnipeg: J.J. Fedorowicz 2006), 110.

34   Zamulin, Valeriy, *Demolishing the Myth: The Tank Battle at Prokhorovka, Kursk, July 1943: An Operational Narrative*, E-book locations: 7804 and 7951.

35   NARA Series RG 373: German Flown Aerial Photography, 1939–1945. GX-3734-SK-61 (incorrectly dated as 15.7.43 by NARA). For 7.8.43 see GX-3942-SK-69.

36   Zamulin, Valeriy, *Demolishing the Myth: The Tank Battle at Prokhorovka, Kursk, July 1943: An Operational Narrative*, E-book location: 7804.

37   Forczyk, Robert, *Kursk 1943: The Southern Front*, 85. See also; Zamulin, Valeriy, *Demolishing the Myth: The Tank Battle at Prokhorovka, Kursk, July 1943: An Operational Narrative*, E-book location: 14637, see map of the battlefield (the author believes some elements of this map to be incorrect, for example in reference to 25th Tank Brigade; however, the 170th Tank Brigade's route is correct).

38   Forczyk, Robert, *Kursk 1943: The Southern Front*, 78. See also Zamulin, Valeriy, *Demolishing the Myth: The Tank Battle at Prokhorovka, Kursk, July 1943: An Operational Narrative*, E-book location: 7891.

39   Glantz, David and House, Jonathan, *The Battle of Kursk*, 185.

40   Frieser, Karl-Heinz, *The Battle of the Kursk Salient* in The Research Institute for Military History, Potsdam, Germany, *Germany and the Second World War Volume VIII – The Eastern Front 1943–1944*, 127.

41   NARA Series RG 373: German Flown Aerial Photography, 1939– 945. GX-3734-SK-61 (incorrectly dated as 15.7.43 by NARA). For 7.8.43 see GX-3942-SK-69.

42   Frieser, Karl-Heinz, *The Battle of the Kursk Salient* in The Research Institute for Military History, Potsdam, Germany, *Germany and the Second World War Volume VIII – The Eastern Front 1943–1944*, 160.

43   Zamulin, Valeriy, *Demolishing the Myth: The Tank Battle at Prokhorovka, Kursk, July 1943: An Operational Narrative*, E-book locations: 8035, 8041 and 8055. See also Forczyk, Robert, *Kursk 1943: The Southern Front*, 78.

44   Frieser, Karl-Heinz, *The Battle of the Kursk Salient* in The Research Institute for Military History, Potsdam, Germany, *Germany and the Second World War Volume VIII – The Eastern Front 1943–1944*, 127n.

45   Ibid., 182.

46   NARA Series RG 373: German Flown Aerial Photography, 1939–1945. See specifically photographs relating to the battlefield of Prokhorovka: for 14.7.43 images see GX-2696-SK-23, GX-2696-SK-24 and GX-2696-SK-52.

47   Frieser, Karl-Heinz, *The Battle of the Kursk Salient* in The Research Institute for Military History, Potsdam, Germany, *Germany and the Second World War Volume VIII – The Eastern Front 1943–1944*, 127 and 127n.

48   Zaloga, Steven, *Armoured Champion: The Top Tanks of World War II* (Mechanicsburg: Stackpole Books 2015), 3–4 and 221.

49 NARA Series RG 373: German Flown Aerial Photography, 1939–1945. See specifically photographs relating to the battlefield of Prokhorovka: for 14.7.43 images see GX-2696-SK-23, GX-2696-SK-24 and GX-2696-SK-52.

50 Frieser, Karl-Heinz, *The Battle of the Kursk Salient* in The Research Institute for Military History, Potsdam, Germany, *Germany and the Second World War Volume VIII – The Eastern Front 1943–1944* (Oxford: Clarendon Press 2017), 127.

51 NARA Series RG 373: German Flown Aerial Photography, 1939–1945. See specifically photographs relating to this area of the battlefield: for 16.7.43 see GX-3734-SK-61 (incorrectly dated as 15.7.43 by NARA). For 7.8.43 see GX-3942-SK-69, GX-3942-SD-124. For 6.10.43 see GX-3977-SD-45.

52 Glantz, David, and House, Jonathan, *The Battle of Kursk*, 185–87. See also Niehorster, Leo, *German World War II Organization Series, Volume V/III*, 31.

53 Töppel, Roman, *Kursk 1943: The Greatest Battle of the Second World War*, E-book locations: 3115, 3121 and 3126.

54 Compare GX-3734-SK-61 with GX-3942-SK-69, GX-3942-SD-124 and GX-3977-SD-45.

55 Frieser, Karl-Heinz, *The Battle of the Kursk Salient* in The Research Institute for Military History, Potsdam, Germany, *Germany and the Second World War Volume VIII – The Eastern Front 1943–1944*, 182.

56 Frieser, Karl-Heinz, *The Battle of the Kursk Salient* in The Research Institute for Military History, Potsdam, Germany, *Germany and the Second World War Volume VIII – The Eastern Front 1943–1944* (Oxford: Clarendon Press 2017), 127–28.

57 Elements of DR and SS-T wider operations on 12.7.43 are clearly visible on the periphery of a number of photographs used in this book's formation. For example images GX-2696-SK-23, GX-2696-SK-24 and GX-2696-SK-52 clearly show the route of advance of SS-T's Panzer Regiment on 12.7.43. While images GX-3734-SK-61 and GX-3942-SK-69 provide evidence of DR's operations on the division's left flank.

58 Frieser, Karl-Heinz, *The Battle of the Kursk Salient* in The Research Institute for Military History, Potsdam, Germany, *Germany and the Second World War Volume VIII – The Eastern Front 1943–1944*, 133. Interestingly, a wider anti-tank ditch had to be avoided by the tanks of the 29th Tank Corps before they even reached Hill 252.2. Perhaps this fact caused some confusion in the army? NARA RG 373: German Flown Aerial Photography, 1939–1945. See 7.8.43 GX-3942-SD-122, 15.8.43 GX-3958-SD-11, 7.9.43 GX-4255-SD-16 and 6.10.43 GX-3977-SD-48.

59 LSSAH, DR and SS-T daily AFV report for 16.7.43, T354, R605, F000764.

60 Zamulin, Valeriy, 'Soviet Troop Losses in the Battle of Prokhorovka, 10–16 July 1943', *Journal of Slavic Military Studies*, 32:1 (2019), 118–19.

61 II SS Panzer Korps, LSSAH daily reports 11.7.43, T354, R605, F000648.

62 Zamulin, Valeriy, 'Soviet Troop Losses in the Battle of Prokhorovka, 10–16 July 1943', *Journal of Slavic Military Studies*, 32:1 (2019), 118–21; Frieser,

Karl-Heinz, *The Battle of the Kursk Salient* in The Research Institute for Military History, Potsdam, Germany, *Germany and the Second World War Volume VIII – The Eastern Front 1943–1944,* 136n, 138–45; II SS Panzer Korps, LSSAH daily AFV report 13.7.43, T354, R605, F000698; see also II SS Panzer Korps, Map of Korps actions, 13.7.43 (this map also crudely displays the Soviet 29th Tank Corps' 12.7.43 operations), T354, R606, F000034.

63   Zetterling, Niklas, and Frankson, Anders, *Kursk 1943: A Statistical Analysis,* 121. See also Frieser, Karl-Heinz, *The Battle of the Kursk Salient* in The Research Institute for Military History, Potsdam, Germany, *Germany and the Second World War Volume VIII – The Eastern Front 1943–1944,* 175–76.

64   Frieser, Karl-Heinz, *The Battle of the Kursk Salient* in The Research Institute for Military History, Potsdam, Germany, *Germany and the Second World War Volume VIII – The Eastern Front 1943–1944,* 111, 186–87 (estimated German armoured losses due to the unreliable nature of the July AGC report to the General Inspector of Panzer Troops Office; however, there is no doubt that these figures are in the correct ballpark). During the Soviet Orel counteroffensive, the heavily armoured Ferdinand tank destroyer (the AFV was armed with the same high-velocity 88mm L71 main gun, arguably the best tank gun of the war, that would later be used in the Tiger II tank) proved itself to be a devastating weapon when used in its designed role as a heavily armoured long-range tank destroyer. Between 5.7 and 1.8.43 s.Pz.Jg.Rgt.656 (which was issued all 90 of the tank destroyers produced) lost 39 Ferdinands (19 of which occurred during Operation *Citadel*). During Operation *Citadel* the Ferdinand (making its operational debut) was often employed poorly in the vanguard of Model's offensive; this negated the Ferdinand's supreme firepower. It was also during the Orel battles that the lightly armoured but heavily armed Hornisse (later known as Nashorn) tank destroyer made its operational debut, with a single company (13 Hornissen) of s.Pz.Jg.Abt 655 (two were lost in July). The Hornisse was armed with the same devastating 88mm L71 main gun as the Ferdinand. Spielberger, Walter, Doyle, Hilary, and Jentz, Tomas, *Heavy Jagdpanzer: Development, Production, Operations* (Atglen: Schiffer 2007), 86.

65   Geomerid Online Travel Guide – Museum Third Battlefield of Russia: https:// geomerid.com/en/place/third-battlefield-of-russia-belgorod-travel-guide/ overview/, accessed on 12/11/2021; The Prokhorovka Memorial Complex: Bearing witness to sacrifice and faith: https://www.rbth.com/special_projects/ discovering_russia_1/2016/09/02/the-prokhorovka-memorial-complex-bearing -witness-to-sacrifice-and-faith_626611, accessed on 12/11/2021; Frieser, Karl-Heinz, *The Battle of the Kursk Salient* in The Research Institute for Military History, Potsdam, Germany, *Germany and the Second World War Volume VIII – The Eastern Front 1943–1944,* 120–21, 127n, 128–34; Zamulin, Valeriy, 'Soviet Troop Losses in the Battle of Prokhorovka, 10–16 July 1943', *Journal of Slavic Military Studies,* 32:1 (2019), 118–20.

66 The references over the following paragraphs are from: XXXXVIII.Pz-AK, XXXXVIII.Pz-AK daily report, Totenkopf reports Soviet attacks throughout the day in the area in question. 18.7.43, T314, R1171, F000388; XXXXVIII. Pz-AK, XXXXVIII Korps HQ planned orders for Totenkopf to begin to evacuate the area on the night of 18–19.7.43. 18.7.43, T314, R1171, F000394; II SS Panzer Korps, War diary entries for 17–19.7.43, T354, R605, F000100-10; II SS Panzer Korps, Map of Korps actions, new and proposed front lines 14–18.7.43, T354, R606, F000035; III Pz-AK, Map of Korps front line 17.7.43, T314, R198, F000323; III Pz-AK, Map of Attila line etc. 17–19.7.43, T314, R198, F000325; II SS Panzer Korps, Ingenieur, Betr.: Kinsatz Raum Belgorod. 5–18.7.43, updated to 22.7.43 (written 28.7.43), T354, R607, F000629-31.

67 Frieser, Karl-Heinz, *The Battle of the Kursk Salient* in The Research Institute for Military History, Potsdam, Germany, *Germany and the Second World War Volume VIII – The Eastern Front 1943–1944*, 127 and 127n.

68 See section titled 'The arrival of the SS Panzer Regiments and the origins of the battles of Kursk and Prokhorovka, February–4 July 1943'.

69 Friedli, Lukas, *Repairing the Panzers: German Tank Maintenance in World War 2*, 162.

70 PzAOK 4, O.Qu.V, DR, Gep. Kfz. Bestandsmeldung, 20.11.43, 30.11.43, 10.12.43, T313, R391.

71 PzAOK 4, O.Qu.V, DR, Gep. Kfz. Bestandsmeldung, 30.11.43, T313, R391.

72 II SS Panzer Korps, Ingenieur, Betr.: Kinsatz Raum Belgorod. 5–18.7.43, updated to 22.7.43 (written 28.7.43), T354, R607, F000629-31.

73 PzAOK 4, O.Qu.V, LSSAH, Betr.: Totalausfälle an Pz.Kpfwg. und gep. Kfz. 1–10.7.43 (LSSAH written 12.7.43) T313, R390; PzAOK 4, O.Qu.V, LSSAH, DR and SS-T, Gep. Kfz. Bestandsmeldung, 1–2.7.43 and 10.7.43, T313, R390; II SS Panzer Korps, LSSAH, Rgt.Bef.Std., 27.7.43, T354, R607, F000825; II SS Panzer Korps, DR and SS-T Ia 667/43 and 668/43, 28.7.43, T354, R605, F000879-80; AOK 6, 1a, KTB 9, *Zustandsberichte, Wochenmeldung über Panzer und Sturmgeschülzlage Stand* 1.8.43 (written 6.8.43), T312, R1483, F000441; see also Bundesarchiv/Militärarchiv, RH 10/64, General Inspector of Panzer Troops – AGS: 5–10.7.43 *Totalverluste*; 5–13.7.43 *Totalverluste*; 5–14.7.43 *Totalverluste*; 5–15.7.43 *Totalverluste*; 5–16.7.43 *Totalverluste*; 5–17.7.43 *Totalverluste*; see also Appendix L; Zetterling, Niklas, and Frankson, Anders, *Kursk 1943: A Statistical Analysis*, 182.

74 The historian Roman Töppel put this argument to the author via email correspondence in 2019.

75 See section titled 'The arrival of the SS Panzer Regiments and the origins of the battles of Kursk and Prokhorovka, February–4 July 1943'.

76 Schneider, Wolfgang, *Tigers in Combat II*, 105.

77 Friedli, Lukas, *Repairing the Panzers: German Tank Maintenance in World War 2*, 152–54, 162 and 166.

78   Friedli, Lukas, *Repairing the Panzers: German Tank Maintenance in World War 2, Vol 2*, 151–52. PzAOK 4, O.Qu.V, request from AGS to 4th Panzer Army MTO for a listing of the number of AFVs currently under short-term repair which had the spare parts available to be made ready for action in four days; 13.7.43 (01:30) T313, R390.

79   PzAOK 4, O.Qu.V, LSSAH, Betr.: Totalausfälle an Pz.Kpfwg. und gep. Kfz. 1–10.7.43 (LSSAH written 12.7.43) T313, R390.

80   Friedli, Lukas, *Repairing the Panzers: German Tank Maintenance in World War 2*, 16.

81   PzAOK 4, O.Qu.V, LSSAH, Betr.: Totalausfälle an Pz.Kpfwg. und gep. Kfz. 1–10.7.43 (LSSAH written 12.7.43) T313, R390; PzAOK 4, O.Qu.V, DR Gep. Kfz. Bestandsmeldung, 31.10.43, T313, R391.

82   Friedli, Lukas, *Repairing the Panzers: German Tank Maintenance in World War 2*, 8 and 180.

83   Frieser, Karl-Heinz, *The Swing of the Pendulum: The Withdrawal of the Eastern Front from Summer 1943 to Summer 1944* in The Research Institute for Military History, Potsdam, Germany, *Germany and the Second World War Volume VIII – The Eastern Front 1943–1944*, 341.

84   Zetterling, Niklas, and Frankson, Anders, *Kursk 1943: A Statistical Analysis*, 182; II SS Panzer Korps, LSSAH, Rgt.Bef.Std., 27.7.43, T354, R607, F000825; Jentz, Thomas, (ed.) *Panzer Truppen II*, 52.

85   XXXXVIII.Pz-AK, XXXXVIII.Pz-AK daily report, Totenkopf reports Soviet attacks throughout the day in the area in question. 18.7.43, T314, R1171, F000388; XXXXVIII.Pz-AK, XXXXVIII Korps HQ planned orders for Totenkopf to begin to evacuate the area on the night of 18–19.7,43. 18.7.43, T314, R1171, F000394; II SS Panzer Korps, War diary entries for 17–19.7.43, T354, R605, F000100-10; II SS Panzer Korps, Map of Korps actions, new and proposed front lines 14–18.7.43, T354, R606, F000035; III Pz-AK, Map of Korps front line 17.7.43, T314, R198, F000323; III Pz-AK, Map of Attila line etc. 17–19.7.43, T314, R198, F000325; II SS Panzer Korps, Ingenieur, Betr.: Kinsatz Raum Belgorod. 5–18.7.43, updated to 22.7.43 (written 28.7.43), T354, R607, F000629-31; II SS Panzer Korps, LSSAH, Rgt.Bef.Std., 27.7.43, T354, R607, F000825; II SS Panzer Korps, DR and SS-T Ia 667/43 and 668/43, 28.7.43, T354, R605, F000879-80.

86   Karl-Heinz, *The Battle of the Kursk Salient* in The Research Institute for Military History, Potsdam, Germany, *Germany and the Second World War Volume VIII – The Eastern Front 1943–1944*, 127n.

CHAPTER 5

1   Frieser, Karl-Heinz, *The Battle of the Kursk Salient* in The Research Institute for Military History, Potsdam, Germany, *Germany and the Second World War Volume VIII – The Eastern Front 1943–1944*, 144.

2   Ibid.

3 See Appendices K, M and N; see also Frieser, Karl-Heinz, *The Battle of the Kursk Salient* in The Research Institute for Military History, Potsdam, Germany, *Germany and the Second World War Volume VIII – The Eastern Front 1943–1944*, 117 and 152.

4 PzAOK 4, O.Qu.V, request from AGS to 4th Panzer Army MTO for a listing of the number of AFVs currently under short-term repair which had the spare parts available to be made ready for action in four days; 13.7.43 (01:30) T313, R390; Friedli, Lukas, *Repairing the Panzers: German Tank Maintenance in World War 2, Vol 2*, 151–52.

5 Frieser, Karl-Heinz, *The Battle of the Kursk Salient* in The Research Institute for Military History, Potsdam, Germany, *Germany and the Second World War Volume VIII – The Eastern Front 1943–1944*, 138–45.

6 PzAOK 4, O.Qu.V, request from AGS to 4th Panzer Army MTO for a listing of the number of AFVs currently under short-term repair which had the spare parts available to be made ready for action in four days; 13.7.43 (01:30) T313, R390.

7 Ibid.

8 Ibid.

9 Ibid.; II SS Panzer Korps, LSSAH, DR and SS-T daily AFV reports 29.6–31.7.43, T354, R605, F000401-949; XXXXVIII.Pz-AK, XXXXVIII. Pz-AK daily reports for SS-T 18–20.7.43, T314, R1171, F000388-482.

10 PzAOK 4, O.Qu.V, request from AGS to 4th Panzer Army MTO for a listing of the number of AFVs currently under short-term repair which had the spare parts available to be made ready for action in four days; 13.7.43 (01:30) T313, R390; II SS Panzer Korps, LSSAH, DR and SS-T daily AFV reports 29.6–31.7.43, T354, R605, F000401-949; XXXXVIII.Pz-AK, XXXXVIII. Pz-AK daily reports for SS-T 18–20.7.43 T314, R1171, F000388-482.

11 PzAOK 4, O.Qu.V, request from AGS to 4th Panzer Army MTO for a listing of the number of AFV currently under short-term repair which had the spare parts available to be made ready for action in four days; 13.7.43 (01:30) T313, R390; II SS Panzer Korps, DR and SS-T daily AFV reports 29.6–31.7.43, T354, R605, F000401-949; XXXXVIII.Pz-AK, XXXXVIII. Pz-AK daily reports for SS-T 18–20.7.43 T314, R1171, F000388-482.

12 PzAOK 4, O.Qu.V, request from AGS to 4th Panzer Army MTO for a listing of the number of AFV currently under short-term repair which had the spare parts available to be made ready for action in four days; 13.7.43 (01:30) T313, R390; II SS Panzer Korps, LSSAH, DR and SS-T daily AFV reports 29.6–31.7.43, T354, R605, F000401-949.

13 PzAOK 4, O.Qu.V, request from AGS to 4th Panzer Army MTO for a listing of the number of AFV currently under short-term repair which had the spare parts available to be made ready for action in four days; 13.7.43 (01:30) T313, R390; II SS Panzer Korps, LSSAH, DR and SS-T daily AFV reports 29.6–31.7.43, T354, R605, F000401-949; XXXXVIII.Pz-AK, XXXXVIII. Pz-AK daily reports for SS-T 18–20.7.43 T314, R1171, F000388-482.

14 PzAOK 4, O.Qu.V, request from AGS to 4th Panzer Army MTO for a listing
    of the number of AFV currently under short-term repair which had the spare
    parts available to be made ready for action in four days; 13.7.43 (01:30) T313,
    R390; II SS Panzer Korps, LSSAH, DR and SS-T daily AFV reports 29.6–
    31.7.43, T354, R605, F000401-949.

15 Frieser, Karl-Heinz, *The Battle of the Kursk Salient* in The Research Institute
    for Military History, Potsdam, Germany, *Germany and the Second World War
    Volume VIII – The Eastern Front 1943–1944*, 130 and 136n; see also II SS
    Panzer Korps, Map of Korps actions, 13.7.43 (this map also crudely displays
    the Soviet 29th Tank Corps 12.7.43 operations), T354, R606, F000034.
    PzAOK 4, O.Qu.V, request from AGS to 4th Panzer Army MTO for a listing
    of the number of AFVs currently under short-term repair which had the spare
    parts available to be made ready for action in four days; 13.7.43 (01:30) T313,
    R390; II SS Panzer Korps, LSSAH daily AFV reports 29.6–31.7.43, T354,
    R605, F000401-949.

16 II SS Panzer Korps, LSSAH, DR and SS-T daily AFV reports 29.6–31.7.43,
    T354, R605, F000401-949.

17 II SS Panzer Korps, LSSAH, DR and SS-T daily AFV reports 29.6–31.7.43,
    T354, R605, F000401-949.

18 II SS Panzer Korps, LSSAH, DR and SS-T daily AFV reports 29.6–31.7.43,
    T354, R605, F000401-949; XXXXVIII.Pz-AK, XXXXVIII. Pz-AK daily
    reports for SS-T 18–20.7.43 T314, R1171, F000388-482.

19 Frieser, Karl-Heinz, *The Battle of the Kursk Salient* in The Research
    Institute for Military History, Potsdam, Germany, *Germany and the Second
    World War Volume VIII – The Eastern Front 1943–1944*, 138–43. See also
    Zetterling, Niklas, and Frankson, Anders, *Kursk 1943: A Statistical Analysis*,
    137–39. For XXIV Panzer Korps: 73 Pz III, 74 Pz IV, 9 Bef Pz, 6 StuG,
    26 Sf Pak; GenInsp.d.Pz.Truppen, Panzerkampfwagenlage, 30.6.43, T78,
    R619, F000641; GenInsp.d.Pz.Truppen, StuG-lage, 30.6.43, T78, R620,
    F000187; Niehorster, Leo, *German World War II Organization Series, Volume
    VII*, 74.

20 XXXXVIII.Pz-AK, XXXXVIII.Pz-AK preparations for Operation *Roland*
    16.7.43, T314, R1171, F000361-63; II SS Panzer Korps, War diary entries
    regarding Operation *Roland* preparations 17–19.7.43, T354, R605, F000097-
    102; Frieser, Karl-Heinz, *The Battle of the Kursk Salient* in The Research
    Institute for Military History, Potsdam, Germany, *Germany and the Second
    World War Volume VIII – The Eastern Front 1943–1944*, 138–45.

21 PzAOK 4, O.Qu.V, LSSAH, DR and SS-T, Fahrgestell-Nr. Pz.kpf.Wg.
    1–2.7.43, T313, R390; PzAOK 4, O.Qu.V, LSSAH, DR and SS-T, Gep.
    Kfz. Bestandsmeldung, 1–2.7.43 and 10.7.43, T313, R390; PzAOK 4,
    O.Qu.V, LSSAH, DR and SS-T, Betr.: Totalausfälle an Pz.Kpfwg. und gep.
    Kfz. 1–10.7.43 (LSSAH written 12.7.43, DR and SS-T Lageskizzen written
    23.7.43) T313, R390; II SS Panzer Korps, Ingenieur, Betr.: Kinsatz Raum
    Belgorod. 5-18.7.43, updated to 22.7.43 (written 28.7.43), T354, R607,

F000629-31; AOK 6, 1a, KTB 9, *Zustandsberichte, Wochenmeldung über Panzer und Sturmgeschülzlage Stand* 1.8.43 (written 6.8.43), T312, R1483, F000441; III Pz Korps, 1a Anlage z, KTB Band 1 and 2, DR Tagesmeldung, 11.8.43, T314, R201; II SS Panzer Korps, SS-T Fehlbestäde an Waffen und Grossgerät, 3.8.43, T354, R605, F001001; II SS Panzer Korps, LSSAH Ia, Tagesmeldung für den 24.7.43, T354, R605, F000867; II SS Panzer Korps, DR and SS-T Ia 667/43 and 668/43, 28.7.43, T354, R605, F000879-80; GenInsp.d.Pz.Truppen, Waffen-SS monthly divisional *Meldung* and OB charts, LSSAH, 1.9.43, T78, R719; PzAOK 4, O.Qu.V, LSSAH, Gep. Kfz. Bestandsmeldung, 1.11.43, T313, R391. Full delivery reports for all panzer, assault gun and self-propelled gun types are available from the Sturmpanzer website.

22 II SS Panzer Korps, LSSAH, DR and SS-T daily AFV reports 29.6–31.7.43, T354, R605, F000401-949; PzAOK 4, O.Qu.V, LSSAH, DR and SS-T, Gep. Kfz. Bestandsmeldung, 1–2.7.43 and 10.7.43, T313, R390; XXXXVIII. Pz-AK, XXXXVIII. Pz-AK daily reports for SS-T 18–20.7.43, T314, R1171, F000388-482.

23 II SS Panzer Korps, daily reports for LSSAH, DR and SS-T 18.7–2.8.43, T354, R605, F000807-982; XXXXVIII.Pz-AK, XXXXVIII. Pz-AK daily reports for SS-T 18–20.7.43, T314, R1171, F000388-482.

24 PzAOK 4, O.Qu.V, LSSAH, DR and SS-T, Fahrgestell-Nr. Pz.kpf.Wg. 1–2.7.43, T313, R390; PzAOK 4, O.Qu.V, LSSAH, DR and SS-T, Gep. Kfz. Bestandsmeldung, 1–2.7.43 and 10.7.43, T313, R390; PzAOK 4, O.Qu.V, LSSAH, DR and SS-T, Betr.: Totalausfälle an Pz.Kpfwg. und gep. Kfz. 1–10.7.43 (LSSAH written 12.7.43, DR and SS-T Lageskizzen written 23.7.43) T313, R390; II SS Panzer Korps, Ingenieur, Betr.: Kinsatz Raum Belgorod. 5–18.7.43, updated to 22.7.43 (written 28.7.43), T354, R607, F000629-31; AOK 6, 1a, KTB 9, *Zustandsberichte, Wochenmeldung über Panzer und Sturmgeschülzlage Stand* 1.8.43 (written 6.8.43), T312, R1483, F000441; II SS Panzer Korps, III Pz Korps, 1a Anlage z, KTB Band 1 and 2, DR Tagesmeldung, 11.8.43, T314, R201; II SS Panzer Korps, SS-T Fehlbestäde an Waffen und Grossgerät, 3.8.43, T354, R605, F001001; II SS Panzer Korps, LSSAH Ia, Tagesmeldung für den 24.7.43, T354, R605, F000867; II SS Panzer Korps, DR and SS-T Ia 667/43 and 668/43, 28.7.43, T354, R605, F000879-80; GenInsp.d.Pz.Truppen, Waffen-SS monthly divisional *Meldung* and OB charts, LSSAH, 1.9.43, T78, R719; PzAOK 4, O.Qu.V, LSSAH, Gep. Kfz. Bestandsmeldung, 1.11.43, T313, R391. Full delivery reports for all panzer, assault gun and self-propelled gun types are available from the Sturmpanzer website.

25 II SS Panzer Korps, daily reports for LSSAH, DR and SS-T 18.7–2.8.43, T354, R605, F000807-982.

26 Frieser, Karl-Heinz, *The Battle of the Kursk Salient* in The Research Institute for Military History, Potsdam, Germany, *Germany and the Second World War Volume VIII – The Eastern Front 1943–1944*, 144.

27 Frieser, Karl-Heinz, *The Swing of the Pendulum: The Withdrawal of the Eastern Front from Summer 1943 to Summer 1944* in The Research Institute for Military History, Potsdam, Germany, *Germany and the Second World War Volume VIII – The Eastern Front 1943–1944*, 338–41; Rebentisch, Ernst, *The Combat History of the 23rd Panzer Division* (Mechanicsburg: Stackpole Books 2012), 280–85. The 6th Army *Wochenmeldung über Panzer und Sturmgeschülzlage Stand* for 20.7.43 and 1.8.43 shows that containing the 17–24.7.43 Soviet offensive cost the 16th Panzergrenadier Division 13 tanks and the 23rd Panzer Division 12 tanks. See AOK 6, 1a, KTB 9, *Zustandsberichte, Wochenmeldung über Panzer und Sturmgeschülzlage Stand* 20.7.43, T312, R1483, F000417 and 1.8.43, T312, R1483, F000441.

28 II SS Panzer Korps, War diary entries for 30.7–2.8.43, T354, R605, F000123-41; Manstein, Erich von, *Lost Victories* (Munich: Bernard and Graefe Verlag 1982), 452; AOK 6, 1a, KTB 9, *Zustandsberichte, Wochenmeldung über Panzer und Sturmgeschülzlage Stand* 1.8.43 (written 6.8.43), T312, R1483, F000441; II SS Panzer Korps, Map of Korps actions, new and proposed front lines 14–18.7.43, T354, R606, F000035; II SS Panzer Korps, Ablauf der Marschbewegungen II SS Panzer Korps, 18–22.7.43, T354, R606, F000038; II SS Panzer Korps, Gliederung des II SS Panzer Korps am 22 und 23.7.43 bis zur Bereitstellung und Lage bei XXXX.A.K., T354, R606, F000039; II SS Panzer Korps, Bereitstellungs u. Angriffsplan für den Angriff am 24.7.43, T354, R606, F000040; II SS Panzer Korps, Ablauf der Marschbewegungen II SS Panzer Korps, 24–29.7.43, T354, R606, F000043; II SS Panzer Korps, Bereitstellung des II SS Panzer Korps am 29.7.43 und Verlauf des 30.7.43, T354, R606, F000050-51; Zetterling, Niklas, and Frankson, Anders, *Kursk 1943: A Statistical Analysis*, 46 and 187–88; II SS Panzer Korps, daily reports for LSSAH, DR and SS-T 18.7–2.8.43, T354, R605, F000807-982; XXXXVIII.Pz-AK, XXXXVIII.Pz-AK daily reports for SS-T 18–20.7.43, T314, R1171, F000388-482; Friedli, Lukas, *Repairing the Panzers: German Tank Maintenance in World War 2 Vol 1* (Monroe: Panzerwrecks Publishing 2010), 152, 154 and 160.

29 AOK 6, 1a, KTB 9, *Zustandsberichte, Wochenmeldung über Panzer und Sturmgeschülzlage Stand* 1.8.43 (written 6.8.43), T312, R1483, F000441; II SS Panzer Korps, DR and SS-T Ia 667/43 and 668/43, 28.7.43, T354, R605, F000879-80; II SS Panzer Korps, LSSAH Ia, Tagesmeldung für den 24.7.43, T354, R605, F000867; Jentz, Thomas, (ed.) *Panzer Truppen II*, 136; GenInsp.d.Pz.Truppen, Waffen-SS monthly divisional *Meldung* and OB charts, LSSAH, 1.9.43, T78, R719; see June/July 1943 delivery reports for 71 LSSAH Panthers, five LSSAH Tigers, four LSSAH self-propelled guns and August delivery report for 53 LSSAH Pz IVs on Sturmpanzer website; PzAOK 4, O.Qu.V, LSSAH, Gep. Kfz. Bestandsmeldung, 1.11.43, T313, R391; Heiber, Helmut, and Glantz, David, *Hitler and his Generals: Military Conferences 1942–1945* (New York: Enigma Books 2004), Midday Situation Report, 26.7.43, 248–49; Forczyk, Robert, *Panther vs. T-34: Ukraine 1943*

(Oxford: Osprey Publishing 2007), 24–25 and 61–63. The reliability of the 71 LSSAH Panthers was so poor that, without seeing combat, between 20.10 and 1.11.43 they were exchanged for 96 new Panthers. The original faulty LSSAH Panthers were refitted in Germany and in December 1943 sent to Army Group North where they were used by Panzer Regiment 29 as semi-mobile pillboxes. In February 1944 Panzer Regiment 29 transferred its 13 surviving Panthers to SS Panzergrenadier Division Nordland (the original intended recipients), which operated them as conventional panzers. Two of these ex-LSSAH Panthers even participated with Nordland in the battle of Berlin in April 1945. As the LSSAH also received 24 new StuGs between 20.10 and 1.11.43, this allowed the LSSAH to transfer 14 ex-Prokhorovka StuGs to Nordland. PzAOK 4, O.Qu.V, LSSAH, Gep. Kfz. Bestandsmeldung, 1.11.43, T313, R391; Jentz, Thomas, (ed.) *Panzer Truppen II* (Atglen: Schiffer 1996), 257; MacDougall, Roddy, and Neely, Darren, *Nürnberg's Panzer Factory, A Photographic Study* (Monroe: Panzerwrecks Publishing 2013), 106–17; Archer, Lee, Kraska, Robert, and Lippert, Mario, *Panzers in Berlin 1945* (Old Heathfield: Panzerwrecks Publishing 2019), 12.

30 III Pz Korps, 1a Anlage z, KTB Band 1 and 2, DR Tagesmeldung, 9–21.8.43, T314, R201; III Pz Korps, 1a Anlage z, KTB Band 1 and 2, SS-T Tagesmeldung, 9–22.8.43, T314, R201.

31 II SS Panzer Korps, LSSAH Ia, Tagesmeldung für den 24.7.43, T354, R605, F000867; II SS Panzer Korps, LSSAH Ia, daily report for LSSAH, DR and SS-T, 28–29.7.43, T354, R605, F000885-921.

32 Even if one includes the operational AFVs of the III Panzer Korps' other armoured formations i.e. 503rd s.Pz.Abt (13 Pz VI) and SS-W (20 Pz III, 10 Pz IV, 1 Bef, 5 StuG and 6 Sf Pak) then the number of operational AFVs available to the III Panzer Korps on 12.8.43 is only raised by 55 AFVs to 210 AFVs. SS-W was organized as a conventional panzergrenadier division; therefore, it possessed just one panzer battalion and four organic infantry battalions; a fifth infantry battalion consisting of Estonian volunteers was attached. III Pz Korps, 1a Anlage z, KTB Band 1 and 2, 503rd s.Pz.Abt and SS-W Tagesmeldung, 11.8.43, T314, R201. On 1.7.43 SS-W possessed the following AFV inventory: 4 Pz IIs, 24 Pz IIIs, 17 Pz IVs, 1 Bef, 6 StuGs, 10 Sf Paks. On 1.9.43 following the battle of Kursk SS-W possessed 2 Pz IIs, 13 Pz IIIs, 16 Pz IVs, 1 Bef, 4 StuGs, 7 Sf Paks. GenInsp.d.Pz.Truppen, Waffen-SS monthly divisional *Meldung* and OB charts, SS-W, 1.7.43 and 1.9.43, T78, R719.

33 See Appendices N and O. See also Frieser, Karl-Heinz, *The Battle of the Kursk Salient* in The Research Institute for Military History, Potsdam, Germany, *Germany and the Second World War Volume VIII – The Eastern Front 1943–1944*, 189–90.

34 Zetterling, Niklas, and Frankson, Anders, *Kursk 1943: A Statistical Analysis*, 187–88; Friedli, Lukas, *Repairing the Panzers: German Tank Maintenance in World War 2 Vol 1* (Monroe: Panzerwrecks Publishing 2010), 152, 154 and 160.

35 PzAOK 4, O.Qu.V, LSSAH, DR and SS-T, Fahrgestell-Nr. Pz.kpf.Wg.
    1–2.7.43, T313, R390; PzAOK 4, O.Qu.V, LSSAH, DR and SS-T, Gep. Kfz.
    Bestandsmeldung, 1–2.7.43 and 10.7.43, T313, R390; PzAOK 4, O.Qu.V,
    LSSAH, DR and SS-T, Betr.: Totalausfälle an Pz.Kpfwg. und gep. Kfz. 1–
    10.7.43 (LSSAH written 12.7.43, DR and SS-T Lageskizzen written 23.7.43)
    T313, R390; II SS Panzer Korps, Ingenieur, Betr.: Kinsatz Raum Belgorod.
    5–18.7.43, updated to 22.7.43 (written 28.7.43), T354, R607, Fooo629-
    31; AOK 6, 1a, KTB 9, *Zustandsberichte, Wochenmeldung über Panzer und
    Sturmgeschülzlage Stand* 1.8.43 (written 6.8.43), T312, R1483, Fooo441;
    III Pz Korps, 1a Anlage z, KTB Band 1 and 2, DR Tagesmeldung, 11.8.43,
    T314, R201; II SS Panzer Korps, SS-T Fehlbestäde an Waffen und Grossgerät,
    3.8.43, T354, R605, Foo1oo1. Full delivery reports for all panzer, assault gun
    and self-propelled gun types are available from the Sturmpanzer website. See
    delivery of five Tigers and four Sf Paks in July plus June/July 1943 delivery
    reports for 71 LSSAH Panthers and 71 DR Panthers.

36 AOK 6, 1a, KTB 9, *Zustandsberichte, Wochenmeldung über Panzer und
    Sturmgeschülzlage Stand* 1.8.43 (written 6.8.43), T312, R1483, Fooo441;
    III Pz Korps, 1a Anlage z, KTB Band 1 and 2, DR Tagesmeldung, 9–
    21.8.43, T314, R201; III Pz Korps, 1a Anlage z, KTB Band 1 and 2, SS-T
    Tagesmeldung, 9–22.8.43, T314, R201; II SS Panzer Korps, SS-T Fehlbestäde
    an Waffen und Grossgerät, 3.8.43, T354, R605, Foo1oo1.

37 III Pz Korps, 1a Anlage z, KTB Band 1 and 2, DR Tagesmeldung, 9–
    21.8.43, T314, R201; III Pz Korps, 1a Anlage z, KTB Band 1 and 2, SS-T
    Tagesmeldung, 9–22.8.43, T314, R201.

38 II SS Panzer Korps, daily reports for LSSAH, DR and SS-T 18.7–2.8.43,
    T354, R605, Fooo807-982; XXXXVIII.Pz-AK, XXXXVIII.Pz-AK daily
    reports for SS-T 18–20.7.43 T314, R1171, Fooo388-482; Zetterling,
    Niklas and Frankson, Anders, *Kursk 1943: A Statistical Analysis*, 187–88;
    GenInsp.d.Pz.Truppen, Stabsoffizier für AOK 8, 5.10.43, T78, R619,
    Fooo836; XI Korps, 1a Anlagen z, KTB Band 13, SS-T Tagesmeldung,
    15–21.9.43 and 28–30.9.43, T314, R493; III Pz Korps, 1a Anlage z, KTB
    Band 1 and 2, SS-T Tagesmeldung, 9–22.8.43, T314, R201.

39 Frieser, Karl-Heinz, *The Battle of the Kursk Salient* in The Research Institute
    for Military History, Potsdam, Germany, *Germany and the Second World War
    Volume VIII – The Eastern Front 1943–1944*, 84, 143, 99–101, 171–72.

40 AOK 6, 1a, KTB 9, *Zustandsberichte, Wochenmeldung über Panzer und
    Sturmgeschülzlage Stand* 1.8.43 (written 6.8.43), T312, R1483, Fooo441;
    GenInsp.d.Pz.Truppen, Waffen-SS monthly divisional *Meldung* and OB
    charts, DR, 1.9.43, T78, R719; III Pz Korps, 1a Anlage z, KTB Band 1 and
    2, DR Tagesmeldung, 11.8.43, T314, R201. See August delivery report for 10
    DR Pz IVs on Sturmpanzer website; II SS Panzer Korps, Verlauf des 2.8.43,
    T354, R606, Fooo059.

41 III Pz Korps, 1a Anlage z, KTB Band 1 and 2, DR Tagesmeldung, 9–21.8.43,
    T314, R201.

42 III Pz Korps, 1a Anlage z, KTB Band 1 and 2, SS-T Tagesmeldung, 9–22.8.43, T314, R201.

43 III Pz Korps, 1a Anlage z, KTB Band 1 and 2, SS-W Tagesmeldung, 11–24.8.43, T314, R201.

44 AOK 6, 1a, KTB 9, *Zustandsberichte, Wochenmeldung über Panzer und Sturmgeschützlage Stand* 1.8.43 (written 6.8.43), T312, R1483, F00044; GenInsp.d.Pz.Truppen, Waffen-SS monthly divisional *Meldung* and OB charts, DR and SS-T, 1.9.43, T78, R719; GenInsp.d.Pz.Truppen, Stabsoffizier für AOK 8, 5.10.43, T78, R619, F000836. Full delivery reports for all panzer, assault gun and self-propelled gun types are available from the Sturmpanzer website.

45 GenInsp.d.Pz.Truppen, Waffen-SS monthly divisional *Meldung* and OB charts, DR and SS-T, 1.9.43, T78, R719.

46 XI Korps, 1a Anlagen z, KTB Band 13, SS-T Tagesmeldung, 15–21.9.43 and 28–30.9.43, T314, R493.

47 AOK 6, 1a, KTB 9, *Zustandsberichte, Wochenmeldung über Panzer und Sturmgeschützlage Stand* 1.8.43 (written 6.8.43), T312, R1483, F000441; GenInsp.d.Pz.Truppen, Stabsoffizier für AOK 8, 5.10.43, T78, R619, F000836; GenInsp.d.Pz.Truppen, Waffen-SS monthly divisional *Meldung* and OB charts, SS-T, 1.9.43, T78, R719; II SS Panzer Korps, SS-T Fehlbestäde an Waffen und Grossgerät, 3.8.43, T354, R605, F001001; III Pz Korps, 1a Anlage z, KTB Band 1 and 2, SS-T Tagesmeldung, 9–22.8.43, T314, R201. Full delivery reports for all panzer, assault gun and self-propelled gun types are available from the Sturmpanzer website.

48 Ibid.

49 Frieser, Karl-Heinz, *The Battle of the Kursk Salient* in The Research Institute for Military History, Potsdam, Germany, *Germany and the Second World War Volume VIII – The Eastern Front 1943–1944*, 188–99.

CHAPTER 6

1 Forczyk, Robert, *Panther vs T-34: Ukraine 1943* (Oxford: Osprey Publishing 2007), 24–25, 61–63; Zetterling, Niklas, and Frankson, Anders, *Kursk 1943: A Statistical Analysis*, 192; Friedli, Lukas, *Repairing the Panzers: German Tank Maintenance in World War 2*, 152–54, 160, 180.

2 GenInsp.d.Pz.Truppen, Waffen-SS monthly divisional *Meldung* and OB charts, LSSAH, DR and SS-T, 1.9.43, T78, R719. The report AOK 8, 1a Kriegstagebuch, übersicht über den Zustand der Divisionen und gep. Einheiten der 8. Armee. Stand 30.8.43, T312, R55 is not accurate; GenInsp.d.Pz.Truppen, Stabsoffizier für AOK 8, 5.10.43, T78, R619, F000836; PzAOK 4, O.Qu.V, LSSAH, DR and SS-T, Gep. Kfz. Bestandsmeldung, 1–2.7.43 and 10.7.43, T313, R390; PzAOK 4, O.Qu.V, DR, Gep. Kfz. Bestandsmeldung, 31.10.43, T313, R391; PzAOK 4, O.Qu.V, LSSAH, Gep. Kfz. Bestandsmeldung, 1.11.43, T313, R391; PzAOK 4, O.Qu.V, LSSAH, DR and SS-T, Betr.: Totalausfälle an Pz.Kpfwg. und gep.

Kfz. 1–10.7.43 (LSSAH written 12.7.43, DR and SS-T Lageskizzen written 23.7.43) T313, R390; II SS Panzer Korps, Ingenieur, Betr.: Kinsatz Raum Belgorod, 5–18.7.43, updated to 22.7.43 (written 28.7.43), T354, R607, F000629-31; II SS Panzer Korps, LSSAH, Rgt.Bef.Std., 27.7.43, T354, R607, F000825; II SS Panzer Korps, DR and SS-T Ia 667/43 and 668/43, 28.7.43, T354, R605, F000879-80; II SS Panzer Korps, LSSAH Ia, Tagesmeldung für den 24.7.43, T354, R605, F000867. Full delivery reports for all panzer, assault gun and self-propelled gun types are available from the Sturmpanzer website; Schneider, Wolfgang, *Tigers in Combat II*, 205–06.

3   GenInsp.d.Pz.Truppen, Waffen-SS monthly divisional *Meldung* and OB charts, DR and SS-T, 1.9.43, T78, R719.

4   Full delivery reports for all panzer, assault gun and self-propelled gun types are available from the Sturmpanzer website; PzAOK 4, O.Qu.V, DR, Gep. Kfz. Bestandsmeldung, 31.10.43 and 30.11.43, T313, R391; PzAOK 4, O.Qu.V, DR, Gep. Kfz. Bestandsmeldung, 10.1.44, 10.2.44, 20.2.44 and 29.2.44, T313, R408.

5   Frieser, Karl-Heinz, *The Swing of the Pendulum: The Withdrawal of the Eastern Front from Summer 1943 to Summer 1944* in The Research Institute for Military History, Potsdam, Germany, *Germany and the Second World War Volume VIII – The Eastern Front 1943–1944*, 356–58.

6   Ibid., 343.

7   Ibid., 351–53.

8   Jentz, Thomas, (ed.) *Panzer Truppen II*, 110.

9   Frieser, Karl-Heinz, *The Swing of the Pendulum: The Withdrawal of the Eastern Front from Summer 1943 to Summer 1944* in The Research Institute for Military History, Potsdam, Germany, *Germany and the Second World War Volume VIII – The Eastern Front 1943–1944*, 344; Forczyk, Robert, *The Dnepr 1943: Hitler's Eastern Rampart Crumbles*, 36.

10 Friedli, Lukas, *Repairing the Panzers: German Tank Maintenance in World War 2*, 174.

11 GenInsp.d.Pz.Truppen, Waffen-SS monthly divisional *Meldung* and OB charts, see in particular those for LSSAH, DR and SS-T from 1.9.43 to 15.4.44, T78, R719.

12 GenInsp.d.Pz.Truppen, Stabsoffizier für AOK 8, 5.10.43, T78, R619, F000836.

13 Full delivery reports for all panzer, assault gun and self-propelled gun types are available from the Sturmpanzer website; the report AOK 8, 1a Kriegstagebuch, übersicht über den Zustand der Divisionen und gep. Einheiten der 8. Armee. Stand 30.8.43, T312, R55 is not accurate; GenInsp.d.Pz.Truppen, Stabsoffizier für AOK 8, 5.10.43, T78, R619, F000836.

14 Frieser, Karl-Heinz, *The Swing of the Pendulum: The Withdrawal of the Eastern Front from Summer 1943 to Summer 1944* in The Research Institute for Military History, Potsdam, Germany, *Germany and the Second World War Volume VIII – The Eastern Front 1943–1944*, 361–62.

15 Forczyk, Robert, *The Dnepr 1943: Hitler's Eastern Rampart Crumbles*, 58–59, 63.

16 PzAOK 4, O.Qu.V, DR, Gep. Kfz. Bestandsmeldung, 31.10.43, T313, R391.

17 GenInsp.d.Pz.Truppen, Waffen-SS monthly divisional *Meldung* and OB charts, LSSAH, DR and SS-T, 1.10.43, T78, R719; GenInsp.d.Pz.Truppen, Stabsoffizier für AOK 8, 5.10.43, T78, R619, F000836; PzAOK 4, O.Qu.V, LSSAH, DR and SS-T, Gep. Kfz. Bestandsmeldung, 1–2.7.43 and 10.7.43, T313, R390; PzAOK 4, O.Qu.V, DR, Gep. Kfz. Bestandsmeldung, 31.10.43, T313, R391; PzAOK 4, O.Qu.V, LSSAH, Gep. Kfz. Bestandsmeldung, 1.11.43, T313, R391; PzAOK 4, O.Qu.V, LSSAH, DR and SS-T, Betr.: Totalausfälle an Pz.Kpfwg. und gep. Kfz. 1-10.7.43 (LSSAH written 12.7.43, DR and SS-T Lageskizzen written 23.7.43) T313, R390; II SS Panzer Korps, Ingenieur, Betr.: Kinsatz Raum Belgorod. 5–18.7.43, updated to 22.7.43 (written 28.7.43), T354, R607, F000629-31; II SS Panzer Korps, DR and SS-T Ia 667/43 and 668/43, 28.7.43, T354, R605, F000879-80. Full delivery reports for all panzer, assault gun and self-propelled gun types are available from the Sturmpanzer website; Totenkopf's five operational Tigers were all from a recently arrived new delivery. It should be noted that the '1.10.43' OB chart for DR which partners the accurate 1.10.43 DR *Meldung* in the archives is actually dated as giving the DR inventory for 5.9.43 (for example the OB chart states 38 Pz IIIs were on hand as opposed to 27). Further evidence that this is not a DR OB chart for 1.10.43 can be seen by the fact that the five other divisional inventories listed in the Stabsoffizier für AOK 8, 5.10.43 report (SS-T, 11 Pz, SS-W, three Pz and 19 Pz) all recorded near identical numbers of tanks on 5.10.43 and 1.10.43 in their respective *Meldung* or OB chart, see GenInsp.d.Pz.Truppen, Heer monthly divisional *Meldung* and OB charts, 1.10.43, T78, R616. On the other hand the DR inventory in the 5.10.43 AOK 8 report closely matches that found in its inventory in PzAOK 4, O.Qu.V, DR, Gep. Kfz. Bestandsmeldung for 20–31.10.43. There is also an error with the 5.9.43 DR OB chart data (as Appendix E indicates); DR inventory did not decline to the reported 17 Tigers in September or indeed October. In reality four DR Tigers were lost between 2.8.43 and 20.10.43 – three of which occurred prior to 5.10.43; there were no replacement Tigers of any kind (4a or 4b) received by DR between 2.8.43 and 20.10.43.

18 Frieser, Karl-Heinz, *The Swing of the Pendulum: The Withdrawal of the Eastern Front from Summer 1943 to Summer 1944* in The Research Institute for Military History, Potsdam, Germany, *Germany and the Second World War Volume VIII – The Eastern Front 1943–1944*, 377–79.

19 Ibid., 374.

20 Jentz, Thomas, (ed.) *Panzer Truppen II*, 55. SS-W was also so treated.

21 GenInsp.d.Pz.Truppen, Stabsoffizier für AOK 8, 5.10.43, T78, R619, F000836; PzAOK 4, O.Qu.V, LSSAH, DR and SS-T, Gep. Kfz. Bestandsmeldung, 1–2.7.43 and 10.7.43, T313, R390; PzAOK 4, O.Qu.V,

DR, Gep. Kfz. Bestandsmeldung, 31.10.43, T313, R391; PzAOK 4, O.Qu.V, LSSAH, Gep. Kfz. Bestandsmeldung, 1.11.43, T313, R391; PzAOK 4, O.Qu.V, LSSAH, DR and SS-T, Betr.: Totalausfälle an Pz.Kpfwg. und gep. Kfz. 1–10.7.43 (LSSAH written 12.7.43, DR and SS-T Lageskizzen written 23.7.43) T313, R390; II SS Panzer Korps, Ingenieur, Betr.: Kinsatz Raum Belgorod. 5–18.7.43, updated to 22.7.43 (written 28.7.43), T354, R607, F000629-31; II SS Panzer Korps, DR and SS-T Ia 667/43 and 668/43, 28.7.43, T354, R605, F000879-80. Full delivery reports for all panzer, assault gun and self-propelled gun types are available from the Sturmpanzer website.

22 GenInsp.d.Pz.Truppen, Stabsoffizier für AOK 8, 5.10.43, T78, R619, F000836; PzAOK 4, O.Qu.V, LSSAH, DR and SS-T, Gep. Kfz. Bestandsmeldung, 1–2.7.43 and 10.7.43, T313, R390; PzAOK 4, O.Qu.V, DR, Gep. Kfz. Bestandsmeldung, 31.10.43, T313, R391; PzAOK 4, O.Qu.V, LSSAH, Gep. Kfz. Bestandsmeldung, 1.11.43, T313, R391; PzAOK 4, O.Qu.V, LSSAH, DR and SS-T, Betr.: Totalausfälle an Pz.Kpfwg. und gep. Kfz. 1–10.7.43 (LSSAH written 12.7.43, DR and SS-T Lageskizzen written 23.7.43) T313, R390; II SS Panzer Korps, Ingenieur, Betr.: Kinsatz Raum Belgorod. 5–18.7.43, updated to 22.7.43 (written 28.7.43), T354, R607, F000629-31; II SS Panzer Korps, DR and SS-T Ia 667/43 and 668/43, 28.7.43, T354, R605, F000879-80. Full delivery reports for all panzer, assault gun and self-propelled gun types are available from the Sturmpanzer website.

23 Frieser, Karl-Heinz, *The Swing of the Pendulum: The Withdrawal of the Eastern Front from Summer 1943 to Summer 1944* in The Research Institute for Military History, Potsdam, Germany, *Germany and the Second World War Volume VIII – The Eastern Front 1943–1944*, 365–69, 346; Forczyk, Robert, *The Dnepr 1943: Hitler's Eastern Rampart Crumbles*, 73–75.

24 PzAOK 4, O.Qu.V, LSSAH, DR and SS-T, Gep. Kfz. Bestandsmeldung, 1–2.7.43 and 10.7.43, T313, R390; PzAOK 4, O.Qu.V, DR, Gep. Kfz. Bestandsmeldung, 10.11.43, T313, R391; PzAOK 4, O.Qu.V, LSSAH, Gep. Kfz. Bestandsmeldung, 1.11.43 and 21.11.43, T313, R391; PzAOK 4, O.Qu.V, LSSAH, DR and SS-T, Betr.: Totalausfälle an Pz.Kpfwg. und gep. Kfz. 1–10.7.43 (LSSAH written 12.7.43, DR and SS-T Lageskizzen written 23.7.43) T313, R390; II SS Panzer Korps, Ingenieur, Betr.: Kinsatz Raum Belgorod. 5–18.7.43, updated to 22.7.43 (written 28.7.43), T354, R607, F000629-31; II SS Panzer Korps, DR and SS-T Ia 667/43 and 668/43, 28.7.43, T354, R605, F000879-80. Full delivery reports for all panzer, assault gun and self-propelled gun types are available from the Sturmpanzer website.

25 Frieser, Karl-Heinz, *The Swing of the Pendulum: The Withdrawal of the Eastern Front from Summer 1943 to Summer 1944* in The Research Institute for Military History, Potsdam, Germany, *Germany and the Second World War Volume VIII – The Eastern Front 1943–1944*, 369–70, 346; Forczyk, Robert, *The Dnepr 1943: Hitler's Eastern Rampart Crumbles*, 77–78; Friedli, Lukas, *Repairing the Panzers: German Tank Maintenance in World War 2*, 138–40, 176; Lower, Wendy, *Nazi Empire-Building and the Holocaust in Ukraine* (Chapel Hill: The University of

North Carolina Press 2005), 174. Between October 1943 and early January 1944 the FHQ in Vinnitsa was used by Manstein as Army Group South's HQ.

26 PzAOK 4, O.Qu.V, LSSAH, DR and SS-T, Gep. Kfz. Bestandsmeldung, 1–2.7.43 and 10.7.43, T313, R390; PzAOK 4, O.Qu.V, DR, Gep. Kfz. Bestandsmeldung, 20.11.43, T313, R391; PzAOK 4, O.Qu.V, LSSAH, Gep. Kfz. Bestandsmeldung, 21.11.43, T313, R391; PzAOK 4, O.Qu.V, LSSAH, DR and SS-T, Betr.: Totalausfälle an Pz.Kpfwg. und gep. Kfz. 1–10.7.43 (LSSAH written 12.7.43, DR and SS-T Lageskizzen written 23.7.43) T313, R390; II SS Panzer Korps, Ingenieur, Betr.: Kinsatz Raum Belgorod. 5–18.7.43, updated to 22.7.43 (written 28.7.43), T354, R607, F000629-31; II SS Panzer Korps, DR and SS-T Ia 667/43 and 668/43, 28.7.43, T354, R605, F000879-80. Full delivery reports for all panzer, assault gun and self-propelled gun types are available from the Sturmpanzer website.

27 PzAOK 4, O.Qu.V, LSSAH, Betr.: Totalausfälle gep. Kfz. 20.11.43, Losses cover at least 19–28.11.43 (written 5.12.43) T313, R391; Frieser, Karl-Heinz, *The Swing of the Pendulum: The Withdrawal of the Eastern Front from Summer 1943 to Summer 1944* in The Research Institute for Military History, Potsdam, Germany, *Germany and the Second World War Volume VIII – The Eastern Front 1943–1944*, 371–72.

28 II SS Panzer Korps, Ingenieur, Betr.: Kinsatz Raum Belgorod. 5–18.7.43, updated to 22.7.43 (written 28.7.43), T354, R607, F000629-31.

29 Zetterling, Niklas, and Frankson, Anders, *Kursk 1943: A Statistical Analysis*, 187.

30 PzAOK 4, O.Qu.V, LSSAH, Gep. Kfz. Bestandsmeldung, 2.12.43, T313, R391.

31 Zetterling, Niklas, and Frankson, Anders, *Kursk 1943: A Statistical Analysis*, 46; PzAOK 4, O.Qu.V, LSSAH, Gep. Kfz. Bestandsmeldung, 21.11.43 and 2.12.43, T313, R391.

32 PzAOK 4, O.Qu.V, DR, Gep. Kfz. Bestandsmeldung, 20.11.43 and 30.11.43, T313, R391.

33 Frieser, Karl-Heinz, *The Swing of the Pendulum: The Withdrawal of the Eastern Front from Summer 1943 to Summer 1944* in The Research Institute for Military History, Potsdam, Germany, *Germany and the Second World War Volume VIII – The Eastern Front 1943–1944*, 370.

34 Forczyk, Robert, *The Dnepr 1943: Hitler's Eastern Rampart Crumbles*, 78, 83–85; Frieser, Karl-Heinz, *The Battle of the Kursk Salient* in The Research Institute for Military History, Potsdam, Germany, *Germany and the Second World War Volume VIII – The Eastern Front 1943–1944*, 162.

35 GenInsp.d.Pz.Truppen, Waffen-SS monthly divisional *Meldung* and OB charts, DR and SS-T, 1.12.43, T78, R719; PzAOK 4, O.Qu.V, LSSAH, DR and SS-T, Gep. Kfz. Bestandsmeldung, 1–2.7.43 and 10.7.43, T313, R390; PzAOK 4, O.Qu.V, DR, Gep. Kfz. Bestandsmeldung, 30.11.43, T313, R391; PzAOK 4, O.Qu.V, LSSAH, Gep. Kfz. Bestandsmeldung, 2.12.43, T313, R391; PzAOK 4, O.Qu.V, LSSAH, DR and SS-T, Betr.: Totalausfälle an

Pz.Kpfwg. und gep. Kfz. 1–10.7.43 (LSSAH written 12.7.43, DR and SS-T Lageskizzen written 23.7.43) T313, R390; II SS Panzer Korps, Ingenieur, Betr.: Kinsatz Raum Belgorod. 5–18.7.43, updated to 22.7.43 (written 28.7.43), T354, R607, F000629-31; II SS Panzer Korps, DR and SS-T Ia 667/43 and 668/43, 28.7.43, T354, R605, F000879-80. Full delivery reports for all panzer, assault gun and self-propelled gun types are available from the Sturmpanzer website.

36 GenInsp.d.Pz.Truppen, Stabsoffizier für AOK 8, 5.10.43, T78, R619, F000836; PzAOK 4, O.Qu.V, LSSAH, DR and SS-T, Gep. Kfz. Bestandsmeldung, 1–2.7.43 and 10.7.43, T313, R390; PzAOK 4, O.Qu.V, DR, Gep. Kfz. Bestandsmeldung, 30.11.43, T313, R391; PzAOK 4, O.Qu.V, LSSAH, Gep. Kfz. Bestandsmeldung, 2.12.43, T313, R391; PzAOK 4, O.Qu.V, LSSAH, DR and SS-T, Betr.: Totalausfälle an Pz.Kpfwg. und gep. Kfz. 1–10.7.43 (LSSAH written 12.7.43, DR and SS-T Lageskizzen written 23.7.43) T313, R390; II SS Panzer Korps, Ingenieur, Betr.: Kinsatz Raum Belgorod. 5–18.7.43, updated to 22.7.43 (written 28.7.43), T354, R607, F000629-31; II SS Panzer Korps, DR and SS-T Ia 667/43 and 668/43, 28.7.43, T354, R605, F000879-80. Full delivery reports for all panzer, assault gun and self-propelled gun types are available from the Sturmpanzer website.

37 Frieser, Karl-Heinz, *The Swing of the Pendulum: The Withdrawal of the Eastern Front from Summer 1943 to Summer 1944* in The Research Institute for Military History, Potsdam, Germany, *Germany and the Second World War Volume VIII – The Eastern Front 1943–1944*, 370–71, 346.

38 PzAOK 4, O.Qu.V, LSSAH, DR and SS-T, Gep. Kfz. Bestandsmeldung, 1–2.7.43 and 10.7.43, T313, R390; PzAOK 4, O.Qu.V, DR, Gep. Kfz. Bestandsmeldung, 10.12.43, T313, R391; PzAOK 4, O.Qu.V, LSSAH, Gep. Kfz. Bestandsmeldung, 10.12.43, T313, R391; PzAOK 4, O.Qu.V, LSSAH, DR and SS-T, Betr.: Totalausfälle an Pz.Kpfwg. und gep. Kfz. 1–10.7.43 (LSSAH written 12.7.43, DR and SS-T Lageskizzen written 23.7.43) T313, R390; II SS Panzer Korps, Ingenieur, Betr.: Kinsatz Raum Belgorod. 5–18.7.43, updated to 22.7.43 (written 28.7.43), T354, R607, F000629-31; II SS Panzer Korps, DR and SS-T Ia 667/43 and 668/43, 28.7.43, T354, R605, F000879-80. Full delivery reports for all panzer, assault gun and self-propelled gun types are available from the Sturmpanzer website.

39 Ibid.

40 PzAOK 4, O.Qu.V, LSSAH, DR and SS-T, Gep. Kfz. Bestandsmeldung, 1–2.7.43 and 10.7.43, T313, R390; PzAOK 4, O.Qu.V, Kampfgruppe DR, Gep. Kfz. Bestandsmeldung, 20.12.43, T313, R391; PzAOK 4, O.Qu.V, Kampfgruppe DR, Gep. Kfz. Bestandsmeldung, 10.1.44, 20.1.44 and 1.2.44, T313, R408; PzAOK 4, O.Qu.V, LSSAH, Gep. Kfz. Bestandsmeldung, 20.12.43, T313, R391; PzAOK 4, O.Qu.V, LSSAH, DR and SS-T, Betr.: Totalausfälle an Pz.Kpfwg. und gep. Kfz. 1–10.7.43 (LSSAH written 12.7.43, DR and SS-T Lageskizzen written 23.7.43) T313, R390; II SS Panzer Korps, Ingenieur, Betr.: Kinsatz Raum Belgorod. 5–18.7.43, updated to 22.7.43

(written 28.7.43), T354, R607, Fooo629-31; II SS Panzer Korps, DR and
SS-T Ia 667/43 and 668/43, 28.7.43, T354, R605, Fooo879-80. Full delivery
reports for all panzer, assault gun and self-propelled gun types are available
from the Sturmpanzer website.

41 Frieser, Karl-Heinz, *The Swing of the Pendulum: The Withdrawal of the Eastern
Front from Summer 1943 to Summer 1944* in The Research Institute for Military
History, Potsdam, Germany, *Germany and the Second World War Volume VIII –
The Eastern Front 1943–1944*, 379–80.

42 Lukas Friedli, *Repairing the Panzers: German Tank Maintenance in World War 2,
Vol 2* (Monroe: Panzerwrecks Publishing 2011), 235–37.

43 Ibid., 156.

44 Ibid., 238.

45 Ibid.

46 Ibid., 170.

47 Frieser, Karl-Heinz, *The Swing of the Pendulum: The Withdrawal of the Eastern
Front from Summer 1943 to Summer 1944* in The Research Institute for Military
History, Potsdam, Germany, *Germany and the Second World War Volume VIII –
The Eastern Front 1943–1944*, 381. See also 347 and 349.

48 Forczyk, Robert, *The Dnepr 1943: Hitler's Eastern Rampart Crumbles*, 86 and
91; Frieser, Karl-Heinz, *The Swing of the Pendulum: The Withdrawal of the
Eastern Front from Summer 1943 to Summer 1944* in The Research Institute
for Military History, Potsdam, Germany, *Germany and the Second World War
Volume VIII – The Eastern Front 1943–1944*, 347.

49 GenInsp.d.Pz.Truppen, Waffen-SS monthly divisional *Meldung* and OB
charts, LSSAH and SS-T, 1.1.44 (LSSAH 31.12.43), T78, R719; PzAOK
4, O.Qu.V, LSSAH, DR and SS-T, Gep. Kfz. Bestandsmeldung, 1–2.7.43
and 10.7.43, T313, R390; PzAOK 4, O.Qu.V, Kampfgruppe DR, Gep. Kfz.
Bestandsmeldung, 20.12.43, T313, R391; PzAOK 4, O.Qu.V, Kampfgruppe
DR, Gep. Kfz. Bestandsmeldung, 10.1.44, 20.1.44 and 1.2.44, T313, R408;
PzAOK 4, O.Qu.V, LSSAH, Gep. Kfz. Bestandsmeldung, 1.1.44, T313,
R408; PzAOK 4, O.Qu.V, LSSAH, DR and SS-T, Betr.: Totalausfälle an
Pz.Kpfwg. und gep. Kfz. 1–10.7.43 (LSSAH written 12.7.43, DR and SS-T
Lageskizzen written 23.7.43) T313, R390; II SS Panzer Korps, Ingenieur, Betr.:
Kinsatz Raum Belgorod. 5–18.7.43, updated to 22.7.43 (written 28.7.43),
T354, R607, Fooo629-31; II SS Panzer Korps, DR and SS-T Ia 667/43 and
668/43, 28.7.43, T354, R605, Fooo879-80. Full delivery reports for all panzer,
assault gun and self-propelled gun types are available from the Sturmpanzer
website.

50 GenInsp.d.Pz.Truppen, Stabsoffizier für AOK 8, 5.10.43, T78, R619,
Fooo836; PzAOK 4, O.Qu.V, LSSAH, DR and SS-T, Gep. Kfz.
Bestandsmeldung, 1–2.7.43 and 10.7.43, T313, R390; PzAOK 4, O.Qu.V,
Kampfgruppe DR, Gep. Kfz. Bestandsmeldung, 20.12.43, T313, R391;
PzAOK 4, O.Qu.V, Kampfgruppe DR, Gep. Kfz. Bestandsmeldung, 10.1.44,
20.1.44 and 1.2.44, T313, R408; PzAOK 4, O.Qu.V, LSSAH, Gep. Kfz.

Bestandsmeldung, 1.1.44, T313, R408; PzAOK 4, O.Qu.V, LSSAH, DR and SS-T, Betr.: Totalausfälle an Pz.Kpfwg. und gep. Kfz. 1–10.7.43 (LSSAH written 12.7.43, DR and SS-T Lageskizzen written 23.7.43) T313, R390; II SS Panzer Korps, Ingenieur, Betr.: Kinsatz Raum Belgorod. 5–18.7.43, updated to 22.7.43 (written 28.7.43), T354, R607, F000629-31; II SS Panzer Korps, DR and SS-T Ia 667/43 and 668/43, 28.7.43, T354, R605, F000879-80. Full delivery reports for all panzer, assault gun and self-propelled gun types are available from the Sturmpanzer website.

51 Frieser, Karl-Heinz, *The Swing of the Pendulum: The Withdrawal of the Eastern Front from Summer 1943 to Summer 1944* in The Research Institute for Military History, Potsdam, Germany, *Germany and the Second World War Volume VIII – The Eastern Front 1943–1944*, 347; Schneider, Wolfgang, *Tigers in Combat II*, 109–10.

52 PzAOK 4, O.Qu.V, LSSAH, Betr.: Totalausfälle gep. Kfz. 30.12.43, losses cover 21–30.12.43 (written 30.12.43) T313, R408; PzAOK 4, O.Qu.V, LSSAH, Betr.: Totalausfälle gep. Kfz. 10.1.44, losses cover 1–10.1.44 (written 13.1.44) T313, R408; PzAOK 4, O.Qu.V, LSSAH, Betr.: Totalausfälle gep. Kfz. 15.1.44, losses extend to 15.1.44 (written 18.1.44) T313, R408.

53 PzAOK 4, O.Qu.V, LSSAH, Betr.: Totalausfälle gep. Kfz. 30.12.43, losses cover 21–30.12.43 (written 30.12.43) T313, R408.

54 PzAOK 4, O.Qu.V, LSSAH, Betr.: Totalausfälle gep. Kfz. 10.1.44, losses cover 1.1.44–10.1.44 (written 13.1.44) T313, R408.

55 PzAOK 4, O.Qu.V, LSSAH, Betr.: Totalausfälle gep. Kfz. 15.1.44, losses extend to 15.1.44 (written 18.1.44) T313, R408.

56 PzAOK 4, O.Qu.V, LSSAH, Gep. Kfz. Bestandsmeldung, 1.1.44 and 10.1.44, T313, R408.

57 II SS Panzer Korps, Ingenieur, Betr.: Kinsatz Raum Belgorod. 5–18.7.43, updated to 22.7.43 (written 28.7.43), T354, R607, F000629-31.

58 Frieser, Karl-Heinz, *The Swing of the Pendulum: The Withdrawal of the Eastern Front from Summer 1943 to Summer 1944* in The Research Institute for Military History, Potsdam, Germany, *Germany and the Second World War Volume VIII – The Eastern Front 1943–1944*, 347.

59 PzAOK 4, O.Qu.V, LSSAH, Betr.: Totalausfälle gep. Kfz. 30.12.43, losses cover 21–30.12.43 (written 30.12.43) T313, R408; PzAOK 4, O.Qu.V, LSSAH, Betr.: Totalausfälle gep. Kfz. 10.1.44, losses cover 1.1.44–10.1.44 (written 13.1.44) T313, R408; PzAOK 4, O.Qu.V, LSSAH, Betr.: Totalausfälle gep. Kfz. 15.1.44, losses extend to 15.1.44 (written 18.1.44) T313, R408.

60 II SS Panzer Korps, Ingenieur, Betr.: Kinsatz Raum Belgorod. 5–18.7.43, updated to 22.7.43 (written 28.7.43), T354, R607, F000629-31.

61 PzAOK 4, O.Qu.V, LSSAH, Betr.: Totalausfälle gep. Kfz. 10.1.44, losses cover 1.1.44–10.1.44 (written 13.1.44) T313, R408.

62 The 16 Tiger losses on the Eastern Front in July 1943 were distributed as follows: s.Pz.Abt 502: 1, s.Pz.Abt 503: 7, s.Pz.Abt 505: 5, Pz.Rgt. Grossdeutschland: 0, LSSAH: 1, DR: 1, SS-T: 1. See Zetterling, Niklas, and Frankson, Anders, *Kursk*

1943: A Statistical Analysis, 121–22; PzAOK 4, O.Qu.V, Grossdeutschland, Gep. Kfz. Bestandsmeldung, 10.8.43, T313, R390; Schneider, Wolfgang, *Tigers in Combat I* (Winnipeg: J.J. Fedorowicz 2000), 86, 156–57; Schneider, Wolfgang, *Tigers in Combat II*, 206; see Appendices J and N.

63 PzAOK 4, O.Qu.V, Kampfgruppe DR, Gep. Kfz. Bestandsmeldung, 20.12.43, T313, R391.

64 PzAOK 4, O.Qu.V, DR, Gep. Kfz. Bestandsmeldung, 10.12.43, T313, R391; PzAOK 4, O.Qu.V, Kampfgruppe DR, Gep. Kfz. Bestandsmeldung, 20.12.43, T313, R391. Interestingly on 12.2.44 Pz. AOK 4, Abt V. reported that eight damaged Pz VIs had been, due to track changing problems, waiting on train flats at Zloczow station since 30.12.43. It is possible, perhaps even probable, that the majority of these Tiger tanks belonged to DR *1st* totals prior to its downsizing to a *Kampfgruppe*. The Zloczow Tigers' onward journey to Germany finally recommenced on 23.2.44. Friedli, Lukas, *Repairing the Panzers: German Tank Maintenance in World War 2, Vol 2*, 162–65.

65 PzAOK 4, O.Qu.V, Kampfgruppe DR, Gep. Kfz. Bestandsmeldung, 10.1.44, T313, R408. See Appendix E.

66 Forczyk, Robert, *The Dnepr 1943: Hitler's Eastern Rampart Crumbles*, 85; Schneider, Wolfgang, *Tigers in Combat II*, 146.

67 PzAOK 4, O.Qu.V, Kampfgruppe DR, Gep. Kfz. Bestandsmeldung, 10.1.44, T313, R408. This report lists 250 075 twice (TF and 3a) unless this was meant to read 250 147 in one instance then all nine of these Tigers were of Prokhorovka vintage. 250 068 had just returned to DR to make up the nine.

68 See Appendices J and N.

69 Frieser, Karl-Heinz, *The Swing of the Pendulum: The Withdrawal of the Eastern Front from Summer 1943 to Summer 1944* in The Research Institute for Military History, Potsdam, Germany, *Germany and the Second World War Volume VIII – The Eastern Front 1943–1944*, 387–88.

70 PzAOK 4, O.Qu.V, LSSAH, DR and SS-T, Gep. Kfz. Bestandsmeldung, 1–2.7.43 and 10.7.43, T313, R390; PzAOK 4, O.Qu.V, Kampfgruppe DR, Gep. Kfz. Bestandsmeldung, 20.12.43, T313, R391; PzAOK 4, O.Qu.V, Kampfgruppe DR, Gep. Kfz. Bestandsmeldung, 10.1.44, 20.1.44 and 1.2.44, T313, R408; PzAOK 4, O.Qu.V, LSSAH, Gep. Kfz. Bestandsmeldung, 10.1.44, T313, R408; PzAOK 4, O.Qu.V, LSSAH, DR and SS-T, Betr.: Totalausfälle an Pz.Kpfwg. und gep. Kfz. 1–10.7.43 (LSSAH written 12.7.43, DR and SS-T Lageskizzen written 23.7.43) T313, R390; II SS Panzer Korps, Ingenieur, Betr.: Kinsatz Raum Belgorod. 5–18.7.43, updated to 22.7.43 (written 28.7.43), T354, R607, F000629-31; II SS Panzer Korps, DR and SS-T Ia 667/43 and 668/43, 28.7.43, T354, R605, F000879-80. Full delivery reports for all panzer, assault gun and self-propelled gun types are available from the Sturmpanzer website.

71 Frieser, Karl-Heinz, *The Swing of the Pendulum: The Withdrawal of the Eastern Front from Summer 1943 to Summer 1944* in The Research Institute for Military History, Potsdam, Germany, *Germany and the Second World War Volume VIII*

– *The Eastern Front 1943–1944*, 385–87, 390, 347; and Schneider, Wolfgang, *Tigers in Combat II*, 110.

72 Schneider, Wolfgang, *Tigers in Combat II*, 110; Frieser, Karl-Heinz, *The Swing of the Pendulum: The Withdrawal of the Eastern Front from Summer 1943 to Summer 1944* in The Research Institute for Military History, Potsdam, Germany, *Germany and the Second World War Volume VIII – The Eastern Front 1943–1944*, 395–96, 409.

73 GenInsp.d.Pz.Truppen, Stabsoffizier für AOK 8, 5.10.43, T78, R619, F000836; PzAOK 4, O.Qu.V, LSSAH, DR and SS-T, Gep. Kfz. Bestandsmeldung, 1–2.7.43 and 10.7.43, T313, R390; PzAOK 4, O.Qu.V, Kampfgruppe DR, Gep. Kfz. Bestandsmeldung, 20.12.43, T313, R391; PzAOK 4, O.Qu.V, Kampfgruppe DR, Gep. Kfz. Bestandsmeldung, 10.1.44, 20.1.44 and 1.2.44, T313, R408; PzAOK 4, O.Qu.V, LSSAH, Gep. Kfz. Bestandsmeldung, 10.1.44, T313, R408; PzAOK 4, O.Qu.V, LSSAH, DR and SS-T, Betr.: Totalausfälle an Pz.Kpfwg. und gep. Kfz. 1–10.7.43 (LSSAH written 12.7.43, DR and SS-T Lageskizzen written 23.7.43) T313, R390; II SS Panzer Korps, Ingenieur, Betr.: Kinsatz Raum Belgorod. 5–18.7.43, updated to 22.7.43 (written 28.7.43), T354, R607, F000629-31; II SS Panzer Korps, DR and SS-T Ia 667/43 and 668/43, 28.7.43, T354, R605, F000879-80. Full delivery reports for all panzer, assault gun and self-propelled gun types are available from the Sturmpanzer website.

74 GenInsp.d.Pz.Truppen, Waffen-SS monthly divisional *Meldung* and OB charts, LSSAH, DR and SS-T, 1.2.44 (LSSAH 31.1.44), T78, R719; PzAOK 4, O.Qu.V, LSSAH, DR and SS-T, Gep. Kfz. Bestandsmeldung, 1–2.7.43 and 10.7.43, T313, R390; PzAOK 4, O.Qu.V, Kampfgruppe DR, Gep. Kfz. Bestandsmeldung, 1.2.44, T313, R408; PzAOK 4, O.Qu.V, LSSAH, DR and SS-T, Betr.: Totalausfälle an Pz.Kpfwg. und gep. Kfz. 1–10.7.43 (LSSAH written 12.7.43, DR and SS-T Lageskizzen written 23.7.43) T313, R390; II SS Panzer Korps, Ingenieur, Betr.: Kinsatz Raum Belgorod. 5–18.7.43, updated to 22.7.43 (written 28.7.43), T354, R607, F000629-31; II SS Panzer Korps, DR and SS-T Ia 667/43 and 668/43, 28.7.43, T354, R605, F000879-80. Full delivery reports for all panzer, assault gun and self-propelled gun types are available from the Sturmpanzer website.

75 Schneider, Wolfgang, *Tigers in Combat II*, 111–12; Jentz, Thomas, (ed.) *Panzer Truppen II*, 153; GenInsp.d.Pz.Truppen, Waffen-SS monthly divisional *Meldung* and OB charts, LSSAH, 1.3.44, T78, R719.

76 Frieser, Karl-Heinz, *The Swing of the Pendulum: The Withdrawal of the Eastern Front from Summer 1943 to Summer 1944* in The Research Institute for Military History, Potsdam, Germany, *Germany and the Second World War Volume VIII – The Eastern Front 1943–1944*, 349, 417.

77 Jentz, Thomas, (ed.) *Panzer Truppen II*, 153; Schneider, Wolfgang, *Tigers in Combat II*, 147–48.

78 GenInsp.d.Pz.Truppen, Waffen-SS monthly divisional *Meldung* and OB charts, LSSAH and SS-T, 1.3.44, T78, R719; PzAOK 4, O.Qu.V, LSSAH, DR

and SS-T, Gep. Kfz. Bestandsmeldung, 1–2.7.43 and 10.7.43, T313, R390;
PzAOK 4, O.Qu.V, Kampfgruppe DR, Gep. Kfz. Bestandsmeldung, 29.2.44,
T313, R408; PzAOK 4, O.Qu.V, LSSAH, DR and SS-T, Betr.: Totalausfälle
an Pz.Kpfwg. und gep. Kfz. 1–10.7.43 (LSSAH written 12.7.43, DR and SS-T
Lageskizzen written 23.7.43) T313, R390; II SS Panzer Korps, Ingenieur, Betr.:
Kinsatz Raum Belgorod. 5–18.7.43, updated to 22.7.43 (written 28.7.43),
T354, R607, F000629-31; II SS Panzer Korps, DR and SS-T Ia 667/43 and
668/43, 28.7.43, T354, R605, F000879-80. Full delivery reports for all panzer,
assault gun and self-propelled gun types are available from the Sturmpanzer
website.

79 Frieser, Karl-Heinz, *The Swing of the Pendulum: The Withdrawal of the Eastern
Front from Summer 1943 to Summer 1944* in The Research Institute for Military
History, Potsdam, Germany, *Germany and the Second World War Volume VIII –
The Eastern Front 1943–1944*, 349.

80 GenInsp.d.Pz.Truppen, Waffen-SS monthly divisional *Meldung* and OB
charts, SS-T, 1.3.44, T78, R719.

81 GenInsp.d.Pz.Truppen, Waffen-SS monthly divisional *Meldung* and OB
charts, SS-T, 15.4.44, T78, R719.

82 Frieser, Karl-Heinz, *The Swing of the Pendulum: The Withdrawal of the Eastern
Front from Summer 1943 to Summer 1944* in The Research Institute for Military
History, Potsdam, Germany, *Germany and the Second World War Volume VIII –
The Eastern Front 1943–1944*, 441–42.

CONCLUSION

1 PzAOK 4, O.Qu.V, LSSAH, DR and SS-T, Fahrgestell-Nr. Pz.kpf.Wg.
1–2.7.43, T313, R390; PzAOK 4, O.Qu.V, LSSAH, DR and SS-T, Gep.
Kfz. Bestandsmeldung, 1–2.7.43 and 10.7.43, T313, R390; PzAOK 4,
O.Qu.V, LSSAH, DR and SS-T, Betr.: Totalausfälle an Pz.Kpfwg. und
gep. Kfz. 1–10.7.43 (LSSAH written 12.7.43, DR and SS-T Lageskizzen
written 23.7.43) T313, R390; II SS Panzer Korps, Ingenieur, Betr.: Kinsatz
Raum Belgorod. 5–18.7.43, updated to 22.7.43 (written 28.7.43), T354,
R607, F000629-31; AOK 6, 1a, KTB 9, *Zustandsberichte,* Wochenmeldung
über Panzer und Sturmgeschülzlage Stand 1.8.43 (written 6.8.43),
T312, R1483, F000441; III Pz Korps, 1a Anlage z, KTB Band 1 and
2, DR Tagesmeldung, 11.8.43, T314, R201; II SS Panzer Korps, SS-T
Fehlbestäde an Waffen und Grossgerät, 3.8.43, T354, R605, F001001;
II SS Panzer Korps, LSSAH Ia, Tagesmeldung für den 24.7.43, T354,
R605, F000867; II SS Panzer Korps, DR and SS-T Ia 667/43 and 668/43,
28.7.43, T354, R605, F000879-80; GenInsp.d.Pz.Truppen, Waffen-SS
monthly divisional *Meldung* and OB charts, LSSAH, 1.9.43, T78, R719;
PzAOK 4, O.Qu.V, LSSAH, Gep. Kfz. Bestandsmeldung, 1.11.43, T313,
R391. Full delivery reports for all panzer, assault gun and self-propelled
gun types are available from the Sturmpanzer website.

2 PzAOK 4, O.Qu.V, LSSAH, DR and SS-T, Fahrgestell-Nr. Pz.kpf.Wg.
1–2.7.43, T313, R390; PzAOK 4, O.Qu.V, LSSAH, DR and SS-T, Gep. Kfz.
Bestandsmeldung, 1–2.7.43 and 10.7.43, T313, R390; PzAOK 4, O.Qu.V,
LSSAH, DR and SS-T, Betr.: Totalausfälle an Pz.Kpfwg. und gep. Kfz. 1–
10.7.43 (LSSAH written 12.7.43, DR and SS-T Lageskizzen written 23.7.43)
T313, R390; II SS Panzer Korps, Ingenieur, Betr.: Kinsatz Raum Belgorod.
5–18.7.43, updated to 22.7.43 (written 28.7.43), T354, R607, F000629-
31; AOK 6, 1a, KTB 9, *Zustandsberichte, Wochenmeldung über Panzer und
Sturmgeschülzlage Stand* 1.8.43 (written 6.8.43), T312, R1483, F000441;
III Pz Korps, 1a Anlage z, KTB Band 1 and 2, DR Tagesmeldung, 11.8.43,
T314, R201; II SS Panzer Korps, SS-T Fehlbestäde an Waffen und Grossgerät,
3.8.43, T354, R605, F001001; II SS Panzer Korps, LSSAH Ia, Tagesmeldung
für den 24.7.43, T354, R605, F000867; II SS Panzer Korps, DR and SS-T
Ia 667/43 and 668/43, 28.7.43, T354, R605, F000879-80; GenInsp.d.Pz.
Truppen, Waffen-SS monthly divisional *Meldung* and OB charts, LSSAH,
1.9.43, T78, R719; PzAOK 4, O.Qu.V, LSSAH, Gep. Kfz. Bestandsmeldung,
1.11.43, T313, R391. Full delivery reports for all panzer, assault gun and self-
propelled gun types are available from the Sturmpanzer website.

3 Ibid.

4 Frieser, Karl-Heinz, *The Battle of the Kursk Salient* in The Research Institute
for Military History, Potsdam, Germany, *Germany and the Second World War
Volume VIII – The Eastern Front 1943–1944*, 120–21, 128–34; see also post
from the Russian Foreign Ministry's official Facebook account on 12.7.2022:
http://www.facebook.com/MIDRussia/posts/pfbid02Q3voBi6fezsQSuwT
V41Pm9PaodBP15Fu1MNnLVvf8AehprtwgmBNyH7sQ5tdKzccl, accessed
on 12.7.2022.

5 PzAOK 4, O.Qu.V, LSSAH, DR and SS-T, Fahrgestell-Nr. Pz.kpf.Wg.
1–2.7.43, T313, R390; PzAOK 4, O.Qu.V, LSSAH, DR and SS-T, Gep.
Kfz. Bestandsmeldung, 1–2.7.43 and 10.7.43, T313, R390; PzAOK 4,
O.Qu.V, LSSAH, DR and SS-T, Betr.: Totalausfälle an Pz.Kpfwg. und
gep. Kfz. 1–10.7.43 (LSSAH written 12.7.43, DR and SS-T Lageskizzen
written 23.7.43) T313, R390; II SS Panzer Korps, Ingenieur, Betr.: Kinsatz
Raum Belgorod. 5–18.7.43, updated to 22.7.43 (written 28.7.43), T354,
R607, F000629-31; AOK 6, 1a, KTB 9, *Zustandsberichte, Wochenmeldung
über Panzer und Sturmgeschülzlage Stand* 1.8.43 (written 6.8.43),
T312, R1483, F000441; III Pz Korps, 1a Anlage z, KTB Band 1 and
2, DR Tagesmeldung, 11.8.43, T314, R201; II SS Panzer Korps, SS-T
Fehlbestäde an Waffen und Grossgerät, 3.8.43, T354, R605, F001001;
II SS Panzer Korps, LSSAH Ia, Tagesmeldung für den 24.7.43, T354,
R605, F000867; II SS Panzer Korps, DR and SS-T Ia 667/43 and 668/43,
28.7.43, T354, R605, F000879-80; GenInsp.d.Pz.Truppen, Waffen-SS
monthly divisional *Meldung* and OB charts, LSSAH, 1.9.43, T78, R719;
PzAOK 4, O.Qu.V, LSSAH, Gep. Kfz. Bestandsmeldung, 1.11.43, T313,

R391. Full delivery reports for all panzer, assault gun and self-propelled gun types are available from the Sturmpanzer website.

6 II SS Panzer Korps, LSSAH, DR and SS-T daily AFV reports 29.6–31.7.43, T354, R605, F000401-949 PzAOK 4, O.Qu.V, LSSAH, DR and SS-T, Gep. Kfz. Bestandsmeldung, 10.7.43, T313, R390; XXXXVIII.Pz-AK, XXXXVIII. Pz-AK daily reports for SS-T 18–20.7.43 T314, R1171, F000388-482; III Pz Korps, 1a Anlage z, KTB Band 1 and 2, DR Tagesmeldung, 9–21.8.43, T314, R201; III Pz Korps, 1a Anlage z, KTB Band 1 and 2, SS-T Tagesmeldung, 9–22.8.43, T314, R201.

7 II SS Panzer Korps, LSSAH, DR and SS-T daily AFV reports 29.6–31.7.43, T354, R605, F000401-949 PzAOK 4, O.Qu.V, LSSAH, DR and SS-T, Gep. Kfz. Bestandsmeldung, 10.7.43, T313, R390; XXXXVIII.Pz-AK, XXXXVIII. Pz-AK daily reports for SS-T 18–20.7.43 T314, R1171, F000388-482; III Pz Korps, 1a Anlage z, KTB Band 1 and 2, DR Tagesmeldung, 9–21.8.43, T314, R201; III Pz Korps, 1a Anlage z, KTB Band 1 and 2, SS-T Tagesmeldung, 9–22.8.43, T314, R201.

8 PzAOK 4, O.Qu.V, LSSAH, DR and SS-T, Fahrgestell-Nr. Pz.kpf.Wg. 1–2.7.43, T313, R390; PzAOK 4, O.Qu.V, LSSAH, DR and SS-T, Gep. Kfz. Bestandsmeldung, 1–2.7.43 and 10.7.43, T313, R390; AOK 6, 1a, KTB 9, *Zustandsberichte, Wochenmeldung über Panzer und Sturmgeschülzlage Stand* 1.8.43 (written 6.8.43), T312, R1483, F000441.

9 AOK 6, 1a, KTB 9, *Zustandsberichte, Wochenmeldung über Panzer und Sturmgeschülzlage Stand* 1.8.43 (written 6.8.43), T312, R1483, F000441; II SS Panzer Korps, Ingenieur, Betr.: Kinsatz Raum Belgorod. 5–18.7.43, updated to 22.7.43 (written 28.7.43), T354, R607, F000629-31; II SS Panzer Korps, LSSAH, Rgt.Bef.Std., 27.7.43, T354, R607, F000825; II SS Panzer Korps, DR and SS-T Ia 667/43 and 668/43, 28.7.43, T354, R605, F000879-80; II SS Panzer Korps, LSSAH Ia, Tagesmeldung für den 24.7.43, T354, R605, F000867; images of the tanks retained by the LSSAH can be found on the following website: https://www.thirdreichmedals.com/article /WSS.html; Jentz, Thomas, (ed.) *Panzer Truppen II*, 136; GenInsp.d.Pz. Truppen, Waffen-SS monthly divisional *Meldung* and OB charts, LSSAH, 1.9.43, T78, R719; see June/July 1943 delivery reports for five LSSAH Tigers, four LSSAH self-propelled guns and August delivery report for 53 LSSAH Pz IVs on Sturmpanzer website; PzAOK 4, O.Qu.V, LSSAH, Gep. Kfz. Bestandsmeldung, 1.11.43, T313, R391.

10 PzAOK 4, O.Qu.V, LSSAH, DR and SS-T, Fahrgestell-Nr. Pz.kpf.Wg. 1–2.7.43, T313, R390; PzAOK 4, O.Qu.V, LSSAH, DR and SS-T, Gep. Kfz. Bestandsmeldung, 1–2.7.43 and 10.7.43, T313, R390; AOK 6, 1a, KTB 9, *Zustandsberichte, Wochenmeldung über Panzer und Sturmgeschülzlage Stand* 1.8.43 (written 6.8.43), T312, R1483, F000441.

11 AOK 4, O.Qu.V, LSSAH, DR and SS-T, Fahrgestell-Nr. Pz.kpf.Wg. 1–2.7.43, T313, R390; PzAOK 4, O.Qu.V, LSSAH, DR and SS-T, Gep. Kfz. Bestandsmeldung, 1–2.7.43 and 10.7.43, T313, R390; PzAOK 4, O.Qu.V,

LSSAH, DR and SS-T, Betr.: Totalausfälle an Pz.Kpfwg. und gep. Kfz. 1–
10.7.43 (LSSAH written 12.7.43, DR and SS-T Lageskizzen written 23.7.43)
T313, R390; II SS Panzer Korps, Ingenieur, Betr.: Kinsatz Raum Belgorod.
5–18.7.43, updated to 22.7.43 (written 28.7.43), T354, R607, Fo00629-
31; AOK 6, 1a, KTB 9, *Zustandsberichte, Wochenmeldung über Panzer und
Sturmgeschülzlage Stand* 1.8.43 (written 6.8.43), T312, R1483, Fo00441;
III Pz Korps, 1a Anlage z, KTB Band 1 and 2, DR Tagesmeldung, 11.8.43,
T314, R201; II SS Panzer Korps, SS-T Fehlbestäde an Waffen und Grossgerät,
3.8.43, T354, R605, Fo01001; II SS Panzer Korps, LSSAH Ia, Tagesmeldung
für den 24.7.43, T354, R605, Fo00867; II SS Panzer Korps, DR and SS-T
Ia 667/43 and 668/43, 28.7.43, T354, R605, Fo00879-80; GenInsp.d.Pz.
Truppen, Waffen-SS monthly divisional *Meldung* and OB charts, LSSAH,
1.9.43, T78, R719; PzAOK 4, O.Qu.V, LSSAH, Gep. Kfz. Bestandsmeldung,
1.11.43, T313, R391. Full delivery reports for all panzer, assault gun and
self-propelled gun types are available from the Sturmpanzer website; Zamulin,
Valeriy, *Demolishing the Myth: The Tank Battle at Prokhorovka, Kursk, July 1943:
An Operational Narrative*, for 5th Guards Tank Army inventory on 11.7.43
see Table 18. Note the author has not included the 29th Tank Corps 1529
SU Regiment (which was equipped with the new powerful SU-152) as it was
not present at the front or tanks under repair at corps level. Regarding the
latter the data Zamulin supplies suggests all damaged tanks were already more
accurately recorded at brigade level; Zamulin, Valeriy, 'Soviet Troop Losses in
the Battle of Prokhorovka, 10–16 July 1943', *Journal of Slavic Military Studies*,
32:1 (2019). For 5th Guards Tank Army 17.7.43 inventory see 118–19.

12 Ibid.

13 II SS Panzer Korps, daily reports for LSSAH, DR and SS-T 18.7–2.8.43,
T354, R605, Fo00807-982; XXXXVIII.Pz-AK, XXXXVIII.Pz-AK daily
reports for SS-T 18–20.7.43 T314, R1171, Fo00388-482; Zetterling, Niklas,
and Frankson, Anders, *Kursk 1943: A Statistical Analysis*, 30–31, 46, 187–88;
Friedli, Lukas, *Repairing the Panzers: German Tank Maintenance in World War
2, Vol 1*, 152, 154 and 160; III Pz Korps, 1a Anlage z, KTB Band 1 and 2, DR
Tagesmeldung, 9–21.8.43, T314, R201; III Pz Korps, 1a Anlage z, KTB Band
1 and 2, SS-T Tagesmeldung, 9–22.8.43, T314, R201; XI Korps, 1a Anlagen
z, KTB Band 13, SS-T Tagesmeldung, 15–21.9.43 and 28–30.9.43, T314,
R493; GenInsp.d.Pz.Truppen, Waffen-SS monthly divisional *Meldung* and
OB charts, LSSAH, DR and SS-T, 1.9.43, T78, R719; GenInsp.d.Pz.Truppen,
Stabsoffizier für AOK 8, 5.10.43, T78, R619, Fo00836; Friedli, Lukas,
Repairing the Panzers: German Tank Maintenance in World War 2, Vol 2, 156;
see also Appendix M.

14 AOK 6, 1a, KTB 9, *Zustandsberichte, Wochenmeldung über Panzer und
Sturmgeschülzlage Stand* 1.8.43 (written 6.8.43), T312, R1483, Fo00441;
GenInsp.d.Pz.Truppen, Waffen-SS monthly divisional *Meldung* and OB
charts, DR, 1.9.43, T78, R719; III Pz Korps, 1a Anlage z, KTB Band 1 and
2, DR Tagesmeldung, 11.8.43, T314, R201; See August delivery report for 10

DR Pz IV on Sturmpanzer website; II SS Panzer Korps, Verlauf des 2.8.43,
T354, R606, F000059; II SS Panzer Korps, daily reports for LSSAH, DR
and SS-T 18.7–2.8.43, T354, R605, F000807-982; Zetterling, Niklas, and
Frankson, Anders, *Kursk 1943: A Statistical Analysis*, 187–88; III Pz Korps, 1a
Anlage z, KTB Band 1 and 2, DR Tagesmeldung, 9–21.8.43, T314, R201.

15 AOK 6, 1a, KTB 9, *Zustandsberichte, Wochenmeldung über Panzer und
Sturmgeschülzlage Stand 1.8.43* (written 6.8.43), T312, R1483, F000441; Gen.
Insp.d.Pz.Truppen, Stabsoffizier für AOK 8, 5.10.43, T78, R619, F000836;
GenInsp.d.Pz.Truppen, Waffen-SS monthly divisional *Meldung* and OB
charts, SS-T, 1.9.43, T78, R719; II SS Panzer Korps, SS-T Fehlbestäde an
Waffen und Grossgerät, 3.8.43, T354, R605, F001001; III Pz Korps, 1a
Anlage z, KTB Band 1 and 2, SS-T Tagesmeldung, 9–22.8.43, T314, R201.
Full delivery reports for all panzer, assault gun and self-propelled gun types are
available from the Sturmpanzer website.

16 Zetterling, Niklas, and Frankson, Anders, *Kursk 1943: A Statistical Analysis*,
135.

17 Forczyk, Robert, *The Dnepr 1943: Hitler's Eastern Rampart Crumbles*, 19–20,
22–23, 78, 83–85; Frieser, Karl-Heinz, *The Battle of the Kursk Salient* in The
Research Institute for Military History, Potsdam, Germany, *Germany and the
Second World War Volume VIII – The Eastern Front 1943–1944*, 162.

18 Zetterling, Niklas, and Frankson, Anders, *Kursk 1943: A Statistical Analysis*,
135.

19 PzAOK 4, O.Qu.V, LSSAH, Betr.: Totalausfälle gep. Kfz. 30.12.43, losses
cover 21–30.12.43 (written 30.12.43) T313, R408; PzAOK 4, O.Qu.V,
LSSAH, Betr.: Totalausfälle gep. Kfz. 10.1.44, losses cover 1.1.44–10.1.44
(written 13.1.44) T313, R408; PzAOK 4, O.Qu.V, LSSAH, Betr.: Totalausfälle
gep. Kfz. 15.1.44, losses extend to 15.1.44 (written 18.1.44) T313, R408.

20 II SS Panzer Korps, Ingenieur, Betr.: Kinsatz Raum Belgorod. 5–18.7.43,
updated to 22.7.43 (written 28.7.43), T354, R607, F000629-31.

21 See Appendix A and Tables 52, 56, 60 and 62. Early in 1944 an additional
14 ex-Prokhorovka LSSAH StuGs returned to the Eastern Front with the SS
Nordland Division.

22 See Appendix B.

23 See Table 52.

24 See Table 56.

25 PzAOK 4, O.Qu.V, Kampfgruppe DR, Gep. Kfz. Bestandsmeldung,
20.12.43, T313, R391; PzAOK 4, O.Qu.V, Kampfgruppe DR, Gep. Kfz.
Bestandsmeldung, 10.1.44, T313, R408.

26 See Table 62.

27 Compare GenInsp.d.Pz.Truppen, LSSAH Waffen-SS monthly divisional
Meldung and OB charts, for 1.3.44 with 1.6.44; Compare also GenInsp.d.Pz.
Truppen, DR Waffen-SS monthly divisional *Meldung* and OB charts for
1.2.44 with 1.3.44, 1.4.44, 15.4.44 and 1.6.44, T78, R719 (the reader should
be aware the DR monthly *Meldung* for this period are often inaccurate); see

also PzAOK 4, O.Qu.V, Kampfgruppe DR, Gep. Kfz. Bestandsmeldung, 29.2.44, T313, R408; There is a possibility that four ex-Prokhorovka DR StuG travelled back to the West.

28   See Appendix C and Tables 16, 49, 50, 51 and 52. See also GenInsp.d.Pz. Truppen, Waffen-SS monthly divisional *Meldung* and OB charts, SS-T, 15.4.44, T78, R719.

29   Frieser, Karl-Heinz, *The Swing of the Pendulum: The Withdrawal of the Eastern Front from Summer 1943 to Summer 1944* in The Research Institute for Military History, Potsdam, Germany, *Germany and the Second World War Volume VIII – The Eastern Front 1943–1944*, 280–90; PzAOK 4, O.Qu.V, LSSAH, Gep. Kfz. Bestandsmeldung, 1.11.43, T313, R391; GenInsp.d.Pz.Truppen, Waffen-SS monthly divisional *Meldung* and OB charts, Nordland, 1.1.44 and 1.2.44, T78, R719.

30   Frieser, Karl-Heinz, *The Swing of the Pendulum: The Withdrawal of the Eastern Front from Summer 1943 to Summer 1944* in The Research Institute for Military History, Potsdam, Germany, *Germany and the Second World War Volume VIII – The Eastern Front 1943–1944*, 419, 439–42, 681–83.

31   See Tables 7, 19 and 52.

32   See Table 56.

33   See Tables 49, 50, 51, 55, 59, 63 and 64.

34   See Table 62.

35   NARA RG 373: German Flown Aerial Photography, 1939–1945. For Pz IV on Hill 252.2 compare 16.7.43 GX-3734-SK-61 (incorrectly dated as 15.7.43 by NARA) with 7.8.43 GX-3942-SK-69, GX-3942-SD-123, GX-3942-SD-124; 15.8.43 GX-3958-SD-10; 6.10.43 GX-3977-SD-45. For site of destroyed/ damaged Soviet AFV compare 7.8.43 GX-3942-SD-122 with 15.8.43 GX-3958-SD-11; 7.9.43 GX-4255-SD-16 and 6.10.43 GX-3977-SD-48; Zamulin, Valeriy, *The Battle of Kursk 1943: The View through the Camera Lens*. Two remarkable post-battle pictures (177 and 178) taken by a low-flying aircraft over the Prokhorovka battlefield can be found in this book.

36   Zamulin, Valeriy, 'Soviet Troop Losses in the Battle of Prokhorovka, 10–16 July 1943', *Journal of Slavic Military Studies,* 32:1 (2019), 118–21; Frieser, Karl-Heinz, *The Battle of the Kursk Salient* in The Research Institute for Military History, Potsdam, Germany, *Germany and the Second World War Volume VIII – The Eastern Front 1943–1944,* 136n, 138–45; II SS Panzer Korps, LSSAH daily AFV report 13.7.43, T354, R605, F000698; see also II SS Panzer Korps, Map of Korps actions, 13.7.43 (this map also crudely displays the Soviet 29th Tank Corps 12.7.43 operations), T354, R606, F000034; II SS Panzer Korps, LSSAH daily reports 11.7.43, T354, R605, F000648.

37   Frieser, Karl-Heinz, *The Battle of the Kursk Salient* in The Research Institute for Military History, Potsdam, Germany, *Germany and the Second World War Volume VIII – The Eastern Front 1943–1944,* 118–23 and 133; interestingly, a wider anti-tank ditch had to be avoided by the tanks of the 29th Tank Corps before they even reached Hill 252.2. Perhaps this fact caused some confusion

in the army? NARA RG 373: German Flown Aerial Photography, 1939–1945. See 7.8.43 GX-3942-SD-122, 15.8.43 GX-3958-SD-11, 7.9.43 GX-4255-SD-16 and 6.10.43 GX-3977-SD-48.

38 Ibid., 115.

39 Frieser, Karl-Heinz, *The Battle of the Kursk Salient* in The Research Institute for Military History, Potsdam, Germany, *Germany and the Second World War Volume VIII – The Eastern Front 1943–1944*, Map II.IV.6, The Tank Battle at Prokhorovka on 12.7.43.

40 BBC News, 'Kursk WW2, Why Russia is still fighting world's biggest tank battle', 12.7.2019.

BIBLIOGRAPHY

1 Zamulin, Valeriy, *Demolishing the Myth: The Tank Battle at Prokhorovka, Kursk, July 1943: An Operational Narrative* (Solihull: Helion 2011), for 5th Guards Tank Army inventory on 11.7.43 see Table 18. Note the author has not included the 29th Tank Corps 1529 SU Regiment (which was equipped with the new powerful SU-152) as it was not present at the front or tanks under repair at corps level. Regarding the latter the data Zamulin supplies suggests all damaged tanks were already more accurately recorded at brigade level; Zamulin, Valeriy, 'Soviet Troop Losses in the Battle of Prokhorovka, 10–16 July 1943', *Journal of Slavic Military Studies*, 32:1 (2019). For 5th Guards Tank Army 17.7.43 inventory see 118–19; Bundesarchiv/Militärarchiv, RH 10/64, General Inspector of Panzer Troops – AGS: 5–10.7.43 *Totalverluste*; 5–13.7.43 *Totalverluste*; 5–14.7.43 *Totalverluste*; 5–15.7.43 *Totalverluste*; 5–16.7.43 *Totalverluste*; 5–17.7.43 *Totalverluste*. See also Appendix L.

2 II SS Panzer Korps, Ingenieur, Betr.: Kinsatz Raum Belgorod. 5–18.7.43, updated to 22.7.43 (written 28.7.43), T354, R607, F000629-31; II SS Panzer Korps, Correspondence from II SS Panzer Korps 1a to Hitler's SS adjutant Fritz Darges at FHQ, Status of II SS Panzer Korps at midday 21.7.43 (sent 23.7.43), T354, R605, F000853.

3 PzAOK 4, O.Qu.V, LSSAH, DR and SS-T, Betr.: Totalausfälle an Pz.Kpfwg. und gep. Kfz. 1–10.7.43 (LSSAH written 12.7.43, DR and SS-T Lageskizzen written 23.7.43) T313, R390; PzAOK 4, O.Qu.V, LSSAH, DR and SS-T, Gep. Kfz. Bestandsmeldung, 10.7.43, T313, R390; II SS Panzer Korps, Ingenieur, Betr.: Kinsatz Raum Belgorod. 5–18.7.43, updated to 22.7.43 (written 28.7.43), T354, R607, F000629-31. See Figures 2, 15 and 16 and compare the number of LSSAH Pz IVs declared *Totalausfälle* (4) and those declared needing homeland maintenance (1) between 5 and 10.7.43 with those LSSAH Pz IVs declared by II SS Korps' engineer as being *Totalausfälle* (7) and needing homeland maintenance (2) between 5 and 18.7.43. Clearly then between 11 and 18.7.43 the LSSAH suffered a maximum of three Pz IVs *Totalausfälle* and one Pz IV homeland maintenance in the Prokhorovka area.

4   For example in 'Die Panzerschlacht bei Prochorowka, Fakten gegen Fabeln', *Arbeitskreis Militärgeschichte e.V.* (2020) which was reprinted in English as 'The Battle of Prokhorovka: Facts Against Fables', *Journal of Slavic Military Studies*, 34:2 (2021) Roman Töppel makes a number of claims regarding German armoured losses during the battle of Prokhorovka which highlight Töppel's lack of knowledge of the available sources and his overreliance on unsubstantiated German testimony. To highlight one example, Töppel categorically states that during the battle of Prokhorovka four Pz IVs were lost as 'total losses' by the LSSAH, yet it appears that Töppel is relying on the faulty 5–17.7.43 AGS loss report and German testimony ('Schüle knew what happened to them…') as his sources. Töppel argued: 'All four tanks were Pz IV. Two of them appear in the loss summary of the panzer officer at the Chief of the Army General Staff on 13.7.43 [5–17.7.43 AGS loss report – ed.]; the other two which the troops initially wanted to salvage, were entered as total losses on 14.7.43'. However, the AGS loss report does not distinguish between 3a losses (homeland maintenance – i.e. salvaged tanks) and total losses. For example, two LSSAH 3a losses (homeland maintenance – 1 Pz VI and 1 Pz IV) are included in the AGS loss report for 5–10.7.43 in the same way as any other loss; importantly neither were reported as TF in the LSSAH's own total loss report for the same period. The fact that the AGS loss report records four LSSAH Pz IV losses between 13 and 14.7.43 offers no evidence to support the claim that none of these four Pz IVs were salvaged from the Prokhorovka battlefield for homeland maintenance. See also Figures 2, 15 and 16 and compare the number of LSSAH Pz IVs declared *Totalausfälle* (4) and those declared needing homeland maintenance (1) between 5 and 10.7.43 with those LSSAH Pz IV declared by II SS Korps' engineer as being *Totalausfälle* (7) and needing homeland maintenance (2) between 5 and 18.7.43. Clearly then between 11 and 18.7.43 the LSSAH suffered a maximum of three Pz IVs *Totalausfälle* and one Pz IV homeland maintenance in the Prokhorovka area. In addition, it is unclear why Töppel cites Schüle's testimony to support his argument. Schüle in fact declared that 'four of these seven Panzer IVs were knocked out at the beginning of the battle, two of which go up in smoke (2 TF), one is *damaged* and can no longer be used (1 homeland maintenance). The tank on the far left, under the command of … *SS Obersturmführer* Walter Malchow, is also hit by several hits in the engine compartment. When the entire crew has left the tank and come a few meters away, it explodes and the rest burns up (1 TF)'. Therefore according to Schüle three Pz IVs were written off, while the 'damaged' Pz IV would have required homeland maintenance – see Schüle's testimony in Månsson, Martin, *Prokhorovka – Verdens største panserslag in Ostfronten* (2017); Restayn, Jean, *Operation Citadel, Volume 1: The South*, 60–69; see also PzAOK 4, O.Qu.V, LSSAH, DR and SS-T, Betr.: Totalausfälle an Pz.Kpfwg. und gep. Kfz. 1–10.7.43 (LSSAH written 12.7.43, DR and SS-T Lageskizzen written 23.7.43)

T313, R390; PzAOK 4, O.Qu.V, LSSAH, DR and SS-T, Gep. Kfz. Bestandsmeldung, 10.7.43, T313, R390; II SS Panzer Korps, Ingenieur, Betr.: Kinsatz Raum Belgorod. 5–18.7.43, updated to 22.7.43 (written 28.7.43), T354, R607, F000629-31.

5   NARA, RG 242, photographs taken by Waffen-SS Photographer Johan King. In addition, these publications did not manage to establish the correct chronological order of the mislabelled NARA King images. The author manged to do so by comparing the NARA King images with copies located in the *Bundesarchiv/Militärarchiv*: 10.7.43 Bild 101III-King-049 = NARA King 6; 10.7.43 Bild 101III-King-050 = NARA King 7; 11.7.43 Bild 101III-King-051 = NARA King 8; 11.7.43 Bild 101III-King-052 = NARA King 9 (crossing the anti-tank ditch); 11.7.43 Bild 101III-King-053 = NARA King 15 (fighting for Hill 252.2); 11.7.43 Bild 101III-King-054 = NARA King 10 (continuation of fighting for Hill 252.2); 11.7.43 Bild 101III-King-055 = NARA King 11 (abortive LSSAH probing attack on Prokhorovka).

APPENDICES

1   PzAOK 4, O.Qu.V, LSSAH, Fahrgestell-Nr. Pz.kpf.Wg. 1–2.7.43, T313, R390; PzAOK 4, O.Qu.V, LSSAH, Gep. Kfz. Bestandsmeldung, 1.7.43 and 10.7.43, T313, R390; PzAOK 4, O.Qu.V, LSSAH, Betr.: Totalausfälle an Pz.Kpfwg. und gep. Kfz. 1–10.7.43, written 12.7.43, T313, R390; II SS Panzer Korps, Ingenieur, Betr.: Kinsatz Raum Belgorod. 5–18.7.43, updated to 22.7.43 (written 28.7.43), T354, R607, F000629-31; AOK 6, 1a, KTB 9, *Zustandsberichte, Wochenmeldung über Panzer und Sturmgeschülzlage Stand 1.8.43* (written 6.8.43), T312, R1483, F000441; II SS Panzer Korps, LSSAH Ia, Tagesmeldung für den 24.7.43, T354, R605, F000867; II SS Panzer Korps, DR and SS-T Ia 667/43 and 668/43, 28.7.43, T354, R605, F000879-80; GenInsp.d.Pz.Truppen, Waffen-SS monthly divisional *Meldung* and OB charts, LSSAH, 1.9.43, T78, R719; PzAOK 4, O.Qu.V, LSSAH, Gep. Kfz. Bestandsmeldung, 1.11.43, T313, R391. Full delivery reports for all panzer, assault gun and self-propelled gun types are available from the Sturmpanzer website; II SS Panzer Korps, daily AFV reports for LSSAH 29.6–2.8.43, T354, R605, F000401-982;

2   PzAOK 4, O.Qu.V, DR, Fahrgestell-Nr. Pz.kpf.Wg. 1.7.43, T313, R390; PzAOK 4, O.Qu.V, DR, Gep. Kfz. Bestandsmeldung, 1.7.43 and 10.7.43, T313, R390; PzAOK 4, O.Qu.V, DR and SS-T, Betr.: Totalausfälle an Pz.Kpfwg. und gep. Kfz. 1–10.7.43, DR and SS-T Lageskizzen written 23.7.43, T313, R390; II SS Panzer Korps, Ingenieur, Betr.: Kinsatz Raum Belgorod. 5–18.7.43, updated to 22.7.43 (written 28.7.43), T354, R607, F000629-31; AOK 6, 1a, KTB 9, *Zustandsberichte,* Wochenmeldung über Panzer und Sturmgeschülzlage Stand 1.8.43 (written 6.8.43), T312, R1483, F000441; II SS Panzer Korps, DR and SS-T Ia 667/43 and 668/43, 28.7.43, T354, R605, F000879-80. Full delivery reports for all panzer, assault gun and

self-propelled gun types are available from the Sturmpanzer website; II SS Panzer Korps, Daily AFV reports for DR 29.6–2.8.43, T354, R605, F000401-982; III Pz Korps, 1a Anlage z, KTB Band 1 and 2, DR Tagesmeldung, 9–21.8.43, T314, R201

3   PzAOK 4, O.Qu.V, SS-T, Fahrgestell-Nr. Pz.kpf.Wg. 2.7.43, T313, R390; PzAOK 4, O.Qu.V, LSSAH, DR and SS-T, Gep. Kfz. Bestandsmeldung, 2.7.43 and 10.7.43, T313, R390; PzAOK 4, O.Qu.V, SS-T, Betr.: Totalausfälle an Pz.Kpfwg. und gep. Kfz. 1–10.7.43, SS-T Lageskizzen written 23.7.43, T313, R390; II SS Panzer Korps, Ingenieur, Betr.: Kinsatz Raum Belgorod. 5–18.7.43, updated to 22.7.43 (written 28.7.43), T354, R607, F000629-31; AOK 6, 1a, KTB 9, *Zustandsberichte, Wochenmeldung über Panzer und Sturmgeschülzlage Stand* 1.8.43 (written 6.8.43), T312, R1483, F000441; II SS Panzer Korps, SS-T Fehlbestäde an Waffen und Grossgerät, 3.8.43, T354, R605, F001001; II SS Panzer Korps, DR and SS-T Ia 667/43 and 668/43, 28.7.43, T354, R605, F000879-80. Full delivery reports for all panzer, assault gun and self-propelled gun types are available from the Sturmpanzer website; II SS Panzer Korps, Daily AFV reports for SS-T 29.6–2.8.43, T354, R605, F000401-982; XXXXVIII. Pz-AK, XXXXVIII.Pz-AK, Daily AFV reports for SS-T 18–20.7.43, T314, R1171, F000388-482; III Pz Korps, 1a Anlage z, KTB Band 1 and 2, SS-T Tagesmeldung, 9–22.8.43, T314, R201.

4   II SS Panzer Korps, DR and SS-T Ia 667/43 and 668/43, 28.7.43, T354, R605, F000879-80; GenInsp.d.Pz.Truppen, Waffen-SS monthly divisional *Meldung* and OB charts, LSSAH, 1.9.43, T78, R719; PzAOK 4, O.Qu.V, LSSAH, Gep. Kfz. Bestandsmeldung, 1.11.43, T313, R391.

5   PzAOK 4, O.Qu.V, LSSAH, DR and SS-T, Gep. Kfz. Bestandsmeldung and Betr.: Totalausfälle an Pz.Kpfwg. und gep. Kfz, 1943–44, T313, R364, R387, R390, R391, R408.

6   Wegner, Bernd, *The War against the Soviet Union 1942–1943* in The Research Institute for Military History, Potsdam, Germany, *Germany and the Second World War Volume VI – The Global War*, 863–71.

7   Kroener, Bernhard R., *Management of Human Resources, Deployment of the Population, and Manning the Armed Forces in the Second Half of the War (1942–1944)* in The Research Institute for Military History, Potsdam, Germany, *Germany and the Second World War Volume VIII – Organization and Mobilization in the German Sphere of Power: Wartime Administration, Economy, and Manpower Resources 1942–1944/5*, 1012–23.

8   Ibid.

9   Ibid.

10   PzAOK 4, O.Qu.V, 3rd Panzer Division, Gep. Kfz. Bestandsmeldung, 30.6.43, 10.7.43 and 20.7.43 (attached 3rd Panzer Division Totalausfälle an Pz.Kpfwg. und gep. Kfz. 1–20.7.43), T313, R390; PzAOK 4, O.Qu.V, 3rd Panzer Division, Fahrgestell-Nr. Pz.kpf.Wg. 30.6.43, T313, R390; AOK 6, 1a, KTB 9, *Zustandsberichte, Wochenmeldung über Panzer und Sturmgeschülzlage*

Stand 1.8.43 (written 6.8.43), T312, R1483, F000441; GenInsp.d.Pz.Truppen, divisional *Meldung* and OB charts, 3rd Panzer Division, 1.8.43, T78, R616.

11 PzAOK 4, O.Qu.V, Grossdeutschland, Gep. Kfz. Bestandsmeldung, 30.6.43, 10.7.43 and 10.8.43, T313, R390; PzAOK 4, O.Qu.V, Grossdeutschland, Fahrgestell-Nr. Pz.kpf.Wg. 30.6.43, T313, R390; Bundesarchiv/Militärarchiv, RH 10/64, General Inspector of Panzer Troops – AGS: 5–10.7.43 *Totalverluste*; 5–17.7.43 *Totalverluste*; Zetterling, Niklas, and Frankson, Anders, *Kursk 1943: A Statistical Analysis*, 218.

12 PzAOK 4, O.Qu.V, Pz Rgt. v.Lauchert, Gep. Kfz. Bestandsmeldung, 11.7.43, 20.7.43 and 31.7.43, T313, R390; GenInsp.d.Pz.Truppen, Panzerkampfwagenlage, 30.6.43, T78, R619, F000641.

13 PzAOK 4, O.Qu.V, 11th Panzer Division, Gep. Kfz. Bestandsmeldung, 1.7.43, 10.7.43, 20.7.43 and 1.8.43, T313, R390; PzAOK 4, O.Qu.V, 11th Panzer Division, Fahrgestell-Nr. Pz.kpf.Wg. 30.6.43 and 31.7.43, T313, R390; PzAOK 4, O.Qu.V, StuG Abt 911, Gep. Kfz. Bestandsmeldung, 1.7.43, 10.7.43, 20.7.43 and 1.8.43, T313, R390; PzAOK 4, O.Qu.V, StuG Abt 911, Fahrgestell-Nr. StuG. 1.7.43 and 31.7.43, T313, R390.

14 GenInsp.d.Pz.Truppen, Panzerkampfwagenlage, 30.6.43, T78, R619, F000641; GenInsp.d.Pz.Truppen, divisional *Meldung* and OB charts, 6th Panzer Division, 1.7.43, T78, R616; PzAOK 4, O.Qu.V, 6th Panzer Division, Gep. Kfz. Bestandsmeldung, 31.7.43, T313, R390; PzAOK 4, O.Qu.V, 6th Panzer Division, Fahrgestell-Nr. Pz.kpf.Wg. 31.7.43, T313, R390; PzAOK 4, O.Qu.V, 6th Panzer Division Totalausfälle an Pz.Kpfwg. und gep. Kfz. 21–29.7.43, T313, R390; Bundesarchiv/Militärarchiv, RH 10/64, General Inspector of Panzer Troops – AGS: 5–10.7.43 *Totalverluste*; Zetterling, Niklas, and Frankson, Anders, *Kursk 1943: A Statistical Analysis*, 188.

15 GenInsp.d.Pz.Truppen, Panzerkampfwagenlage, 30.6.43, T78, R619, F000642; GenInsp.d.Pz.Truppen, divisional *Meldung* and OB charts, 19th Panzer Division, 1.7.43, T78, R616; PzAOK 4, O.Qu.V, 19th Panzer Division, Gep. Kfz. Bestandsmeldung, 20.7.43 and 31.7.43, T313, R390; PzAOK 4, O.Qu.V, 19th Panzer Division, Fahrgestell-Nr. Pz.kpf.Wg. 31.7.43, T313, R390; PzAOK 4, O.Qu.V, 19th Panzer Division Totalausfälle an Pz.Kpfwg. und gep. Kfz. 21–31.7.43, T313, R390; Zetterling, Niklas and Frankson, Anders, *Kursk 1943: A Statistical Analysis*, 189.

16 GenInsp.d.Pz.Truppen, Panzerkampfwagenlage, 30.6.43, T78, R619, F000641; GenInsp.d.Pz.Truppen, divisional *Meldung* and OB charts, 7th Panzer Division, 1.7.43, T78, R616; PzAOK 4, O.Qu.V, 7th Panzer Division, Gep. Kfz. Bestandsmeldung, 10.7.43, 20.7.43 and 31.7.43, T313, R390; PzAOK 4, O.Qu.V, 7th Panzer Division, Fahrgestell-Nr. Pz.kpf.Wg. 31.7.43, T313, R390.

17 Jentz, Thomas, (ed.) *Panzer Truppen II*, 93.

18 GenInsp.d.Pz.Truppen, StuG-lage, 30.6.43, 10.7.43, 20.7.43, 31.7.43, T78, R620, F000175-187; Zetterling, Niklas, and Frankson, Anders, *Kursk 1943: A Statistical Analysis*, 221.

19 GenInsp.d.Pz.Truppen, StuG-lage, 30.6.43, 10.7.43, 20.7.43, 31.7.43, T78, R620, F000175-187; Zetterling, Niklas, and Frankson, Anders, *Kursk 1943: A Statistical Analysis*, 31, 221.

20 GenInsp.d.Pz.Truppen, StuG-lage, 30.6.43, 10.7.43, 20.7.43, 31.7.43, T78, R620, F000175-187; Zetterling, Niklas, and Frankson, Anders, *Kursk 1943: A Statistical Analysis*, 31, 190; Bundesarchiv/Militärarchiv, RH 10/64, General Inspector of Panzer Troops – AGS: 5–10.7.43 *Totalverluste*; 5–17.7.43 *Totalverluste*.

21 See Appendices A, B, C and J.

22 Bundesarchiv/Militärarchiv, RH 10/64, General Inspector of Panzer Troops – AGS: 5–10.7.43 *Totalverluste*; 5–17.7.43 *Totalverluste*. See also 5–13.7.43 *Totalverluste*; 5–14.7.43 *Totalverluste*; 5–15.7.43 *Totalverluste*; 5–16.7.43 *Totalverluste*.

23 Consisting of 3rd and 11th Panzer Divisions, Grossdeutschland Division, Pz Rgt. v. Lauchert and 911th StuG Abt. See Appendix J.

24 Consisting of LSSAH, DR and SS-T. See Appendices A, B and C.

25 Consisting of 6th, 7th and 19th Panzer Divisions, 503rd s.Pz.Abt and 228th StuG Abt. See Appendix J.

26 Consisting of 905th StuG Abt and 393rd StuG Bty; see Appendix J.

27 Consisting of XXXXVIII Panzer Korps, II SS Panzer Korps, III Panzer Korps and Korps Raus; see Appendix M.

28 Consisting of 6th, 7th, 11th and 19th Panzer Divisions, Pz Rgt. v. Lauchert, 503rd s.Pz.Abt, 228th, 905th and 911th StuG Abt and 393rd StuG Bty; see Appendix J.

29 Forczyk, Robert, *Kursk 1943: The Southern Front*, 58.

Index

References to images are in **bold**.